FREEDOM AND THE COURT

Civil Rights and Liberties in the United States

Freedom and the Court

CIVIL RIGHTS AND LIBERTIES IN THE UNITED STATES

HENRY J. ABRAHAM

Professor of Political Science
University of Pennsylvania

New York

OXFORD UNIVERSITY PRESS

London 1967 *Toronto*

Copyright © 1967 by Oxford University Press, Inc.

Library of Congress Catalogue Card Number: 67-17862

PRINTED IN THE UNITED STATES OF AMERICA

TO

MY MOTHER

AND

THE MEMORY OF MY FATHER

Preface

THIS IS essentially a study of the lines that must be drawn by a democratic society as it attempts to reconcile individual freedom with the rights of the community. No single book could cope with the entire field of civil rights and liberties, and no attempt is made to do so here. Rather, it has been my aim to analyze and evaluate the basic problem of drawing lines between individual rights and community rights and to venture some conclusions or suggestions in those spheres that constitute the basic rights and liberties: freedom of religion and the attendant problem of separation of Church and State; freedom of expression; due process of law, particularly procedural safeguards in criminal law; and political and racial equality. The three introductory chapters—the third comprising a thorough analysis of the problem of Amendment Fourteen and "incorporation"—are designed to focus the study and to stress my belief that it is essential to recognize and comprehend the significant role the judicial branch of the United States Government, with the Supreme Court as its apex, has played in defining and strengthening the basic rights and liberties that accrue to us from the principle of a government under constitutionalism, a government that is limited in its impact upon individual freedom.

As usual, I am indebted to many colleagues for the essential stimulation, criticism, and encouragement. I am particularly grateful to Professor Alpheus T. Mason of Princeton who read the entire manuscript; to Professors David Fellman of Wisconsin and Rocco J. Tresolini of Lehigh who were generous discussants; and to my departmental colleague, Charles Jasper Cooper, who proved a valued "sounding board" down the hall. My research assistant, Judy F. Lang, was a delightful and industrious aid. Dr. Joan I. Gotwals of the Van Pelt Library kindly provided me with a "secret annex" in which I could work in quiet seclusion. Mrs. Dorothy E. Carpenter typed the manuscript cheerfully and conscientiously. Byron S. Hollinshead, Jr.,

Helen M. Richardson, and Mary Ollmann of Oxford University Press provided indispensable professional assistance. And my wife Mildred and our sons Philip and Peter, to each of whom earlier books were happily dedicated, made it all worthwhile.

Wynnewood, Pennsylvania   H. J. A.
January 1967

Contents

FREEDOM AND THE COURT

Civil Rights and Liberties in the United States

Introduction

ALTHOUGH, as David Fellman points out, the American people, both in political theory and in public law, have been committed for more than two hundred years to the "primacy of civil liberties in the constellation of human interests," [1] these civil liberties do not exist in a vacuum or even in anarchy but in a state of society. It is inevitable that the individual's civil rights and those of the community of which he is a part come into conflict and need adjudication.[2]

It is easy to state the need for a line between individual rights and the rights of the community, but how, where, and when it is to be drawn are questions that will never be resolved to the satisfaction of the entire community. Liberty and order are difficult to reconcile, particularly in a democratic society such as ours. We must have *both*, but a happy balance is not easy to maintain. Yet as a constitutional democracy, based upon a government of limited powers under a written constitution, and a majoritarianism duly checked by carefully guarded minority rights, we must be generous to the dissenter. In John Stuart Mill's exhortation, "all mankind has no right to silence one dissenter ... [for] all silencing of discussion is an assumption of infallibility." Even near-unanimity under our system does not give

[1] *The Limits of Freedom* (Brunswick, N.J.: Rutgers University Press, 1959), from the Foreword (unpaginated).

[2] Although some would object, the terms "rights" and "liberties" are used interchangeably in this book. They are to be distinguished from all the other rights and freedoms individuals may enjoy under law because they are especially protected, in one manner or another, against violations *by governments*. (In Canada, the term "civil *rights*" refers exclusively to *private* law—the legal relationship between person and person in private life.) See J. A. Corry and Henry J. Abraham, *Elements of Democratic Government*, 4th ed. (New York: Oxford University Press, 1964), pp. 234-9.

society the right to deprive the individual of his constitutional rights. That the plaintiff in a civil liberties case may not be a flower of society is beside the point. "The worst citizen no less than the best," once wrote Mr. Justice Hugo L. Black, dissenting from a Supreme Court reversal of some trespassing convictions, "is entitled to equal protection of the laws of his state and of his nation" [1]—and the citizen of whom he spoke was a defiant racist. In the *West Virginia Flag Salute* case,[2] in which the Supreme Court struck down as violating the freedom of religion guarantees of the First and Fourteenth Amendments a compulsory flag salute resolution adopted by the West Virginia State Board of Education, Mr. Justice Robert H. Jackson wrote that those "who begin coercive elimination of dissent soon find themselves eliminating dissenters. Compulsory unification of opinion achieves only the unanimity of the graveyard." He further elaborated in characteristically beautiful prose:

> If there is any fixed star in our constitutional constellation, it is that no official, high or petty, can prescribe what shall be orthodox in politics, nationalism, religion, or other matters of opinion or force citizens to confess by word or act their faith therein. . . . The very purpose of a Bill of Rights was to withdraw certain subjects from the vicissitudes of political controversy, to place them beyond the reach of majorities and officials and to establish them as legal principles to be applied by the courts. One's right to life, liberty, and property, to free speech, a free press, freedom of worship and assembly, and other fundamental rights may not be submitted to vote; *they depend on the outcome of no elections.*[3]

While these words raise as many questions as they state valid principles, they nevertheless point out the irreducible basis for our thinking about civil rights.

Role of the Judiciary. The framers of our Constitution chose a limited majority rule, but majority rule nonetheless; while tyranny by the majority is barred so also is tyranny by a minority. And the law must be obeyed—until such time as it is validly altered by legislative, judicial, or executive action or by constitutional amendment. Notwithstanding the numerous philosophical arguments to the contrary, disobedience of the law of the land, no matter by which valid agency

[1] *Bell v. Maryland*, 378 U.S. 226 (1964), at 328.
[2] *West Virginia State Board of Education v. Barnette*, 319 U.S. 624 (1943).
[3] *Ibid.*, at 642, 638. (Italics supplied.)

it may have been pronounced or by what margin it may have been enacted, is barred. *It must be barred.* Thus, under our system of government some agency must serve as the arbiter of what is and what is not legal or constitutional.

The Founding Fathers did recognize and call for the creation of an arbiter, not only between the states and the national government but also between any level of government and the individual. There was no unanimity, of course, on who might arbitrate; and the records of the debates now available to us demonstrate that nearly every segment of the incipient governmental framework received at least some consideration: the states themselves, Congress, the executive, the judiciary, and several combinations of these. But it was fairly clear that the role would fall to the judiciary and that it should include the power of *judicial review,* which authorizes the Supreme Court to hold unconstitutional and hence unenforceable any law, any official action based upon a law, and any other action by a public official that it deems—upon careful reflection and in line with the taught tradition of the law and judicial restraint—to be in conflict with the Constitution.[1]

Scholars continue to argue the authenticity of the power of judicial review. That so many doubts and challenges are raised is due preeminently to the failure of the American Founding Fathers to spell it out in the Constitution *in so many words.* Yet the records of the Philadelphia Constitutional Convention of 1787 indicate that the idea or principle of judicial review was a matter of distinct concern to the framers who, after all, had little use for unrestrained popular majoritarian government; that judicial review was indeed *known* to the colonists because the British Privy Council had established it over acts passed by colonial legislatures; that at least eight [2] of the ratifying state conventions had expressly discussed *and* accepted the judicial power to pronounce legislative acts void; and that prior to 1789 some eight instances of *state* court judicial review against state legislatures had taken place. The language of both Article III and the famed "supremacy clause" of Article VI clearly imply the necessary

[1] See the author's *The Judicial Process: An Introductory Analysis of the Courts of the United States, England, and France* (New York: Oxford University Press, 1962), Ch. 7.

[2] Virginia, Rhode Island, New York, Connecticut, Massachusetts, New Jersey, North Carolina, and South Carolina.

but controversial weapon. Research by constitutional historians such as Charles A. Beard, Edward S. Corwin, and Alpheus T. Mason indicates that between 25 and 32 of the 40 delegates at Philadelphia generally favored the adoption of judicial review.[1] And although it remained for Mr. Chief Justice John Marshall to spell it out in 1803 in *Marbury* v. *Madison*,[2] the issue has been decisively settled by history, and the debate over the legitimacy of judicial review should cease except as an academic exercise.

The Supreme Court has, since the enactment of the Judges Bill in 1925, been complete master of its docket. This bill gave to the Court absolute discretionary power to choose the cases it would hear on a writ of *certiorari*, a discretionary writ granted only if four justices agree to do so. In theory, certain classes of cases do reach the Court as a matter of "right," those known to come to it on writs of *appeal*, but even here review is not automatic since the tribunal itself must decide whether the question presented is of a "substantial federal nature." Its original jurisdiction docket is so small as to be dismissed for the purposes of this discussion.[3]

Since 1937 the overwhelming majority of judicial vetoes imposed upon the several states and *all* of those against the national government have been invoked because they infringed personal liberties, other than "property," safeguarded under the Constitution. This preoccupation with the "basic human freedoms"[4] is amply illustrated by the statistics of the docket of the Supreme Court and the application of its power of judicial review. Upwards of 45 per cent of all cases decided by the Court now fall into this category of "basic human freedoms"; whereas in the 1935-36 term only two of 160 written decisions had done so, in the 1965-66 term the ratio had increased to 54 out of 120. But this majoritarian philosophy is barely thirty years old, and a glance into its historical development should help to focus our study.

[1] See particularly Beard's "The Supreme Court—Usurper or Grantee?," 27 *Political Science Quarterly* 1 (1912).

[2] 1 Cranch 137.

[3] See Abraham, *op. cit.*, Ch. 5.

[4] See the Preface and Ch. II. As seen in these pages, they comprise the five enumerated by the First Amendment; the guarantees of procedural due process in the pursuit of criminal justice; and racial and political equality. (They are also known as the "cultural freedoms.")

II

The "Double Standard"

THE EVOLUTION OF THE DOUBLE STANDARD

THE EARLIEST LINES, drawn by the Marshall Court (1801-35), defined and strengthened the young nation, guarding the federal government against the state governments, and furthering its growth and ability to function. They were also drawn to protect the property interests of individuals. From 1836-64 Mr. Chief Justice Roger B. Taney's Court sought in part and in a variety of ways to redress the balance, as it saw it, in favor of the states, while continuing to defend the ownership of land and slaves. The disastrous *Dred Scott*[1] decision bears lasting witness to their posture. The decisions of the next two rather undistinguished eras of Chief Justices Salmon P. Chase (1864-74) and Morrison R. Waite (1874-88) were predominantly concerned with confirming state authority over individuals and federal authority over interstate commerce. In general they heralded the broadly proprietarian notions of the next five decades of Chief Justices Melvin W. Fuller (1888-1910), Edward D. White (1910-21), and William Howard Taft (1921-30).[2] The chief concern of this long era was to guard the sanctity of property. Economic experimentation by the legislatures, such as minimum-wage, maximum-hour, and child-labor regulations, was regarded with almost unshakeable disapproval by a majority of the Court. Again and again the justices struck down, as unconstitutional violations of substantive due process of law, legislation that majorities on both the national and state levels deemed

[1] *Dred Scott v. Sandford*, 19 Howard 393 (1857).
[2] He was the only person ever to hold the offices of *both* President and Chief Justice of the United States.

wise and necessary. Their grounds were that, because of the *substance* of the legislation involved, such statutory experimentations deprived "persons" (i.e. property owners, chiefly businessmen) of their liberty and property without due process of law. The deprivation of substantive due process was then judicially regarded as proscribed by the wording and command of Amendments Five and Fourteen of the Constitution. Admittedly, an occasional enactment would survive— such as maximum hours in hazardous occupations (an 8-hour Utah law for copper miners in 1896); [1] for women in most industrial establishments (an Oregon 10-hour law in 1908); [2] and even one for both men and women (another Oregon 10-hour factory statute, this one in 1917). [3] But until the advent of the "Roosevelt Court" in 1937, the Supreme Court under Mr. Chief Justice Charles Evans Hughes (1930-40) continued the substantive due process veto and struck down between 1934 and 1936 a total of sixteen New Deal laws that had been enacted chiefly under the taxing and interstate commerce powers of Congress. [4] Although President Roosevelt lost his battle to "pack" the Court in February of 1937, he was able, within a matter of three months, to win two favorable decisions by the Hughes Court, a victory often regarded as "the switch in time that saved nine."

Here the Chief Justice and Associate Justice Owen J. Roberts joined their colleagues Louis D. Brandeis, Benjamin N. Cardozo, and Harlan F. Stone in upholding a Washington State *minimum-wage law* for women and children—the first time that such a statute was upheld by the Court. [5] (It would be another four years before the Court would have the opportunity to uphold, [6] again for the first time, a *federal child-labor law*, the Fair Labor Standards Act of 1938, which also provided for minimum wages and maximum hours for all workers in interstate commerce. It had been declared beyond the power of Congress by a lower federal court.) In the other great "switch-in-time" case the new 5:4 majority upheld the National Labor Relations Act of 1935 against the challenge that it, too, exceeded the powers of

[1] *Holden v. Hardy*, 169 U.S. 366.
[2] *Muller v. Oregon*, 208 U.S. 412.
[3] *Bunting v. Oregon*, 243 U.S. 426.
[4] For two explanatory and statistical tables see the author's *The Judicial Process: An Introductory Analysis of the Courts of the United States, England, and France* (New York: Oxford University Press, 1962), pp. 254-9.
[5] *West Coast Hotel Co. v. Parrish*, 300 U.S. 379 (1937).
[6] *United States v. Darby Lumber Co.*, 312 U.S. 100 (1941).

Congress.[1] When Mr. Justice Willis van Devanter retired later in 1937 after 26 years on the Court, and Senator Black of Alabama replaced him, the day of declaring unconstitutionality through economic "substantive due process" was gone beyond recall.

Gradually the Court embarked upon a policy of paying close attention to any legislative and executive attempt to curb basic rights and liberties in the "non-economic" sphere. During the remaining years of the Hughes Court and continuing through the Stone (1941-46) and Vinson (1946-53) and into the Warren (1953-) Courts, the chief concern was, and still is today, to find a balance between the basic civil rights and liberties of the individual and those of the community of which he is a part. This change in judicial attitude reflects a conviction that certain fundamental freedoms *ipso facto* require closer judicial scrutiny lest they be irretrievably lost. A properly lodged complaint at the bar of the Court that legislative or executive action, be it state or national, had violated the complainant's due process of law, be it substantive or procedural, would at least be assured of judicial interest and probably of close judicial scrutiny. Whether this new concern has not in effect created a double standard of judicial scrutiny, whereby governmental economic experimentation is accorded all but carte blanche by the courts but alleged violations of individual civil rights are given meticulous judicial attention, is a question which we will carefully examine.

Historically, the judicial postures of certain justices have aided in the evolution of the double standard. Despite his close adherence to a philosophy of judicial self-restraint, Mr. Justice Oliver Wendell Holmes, Jr. spent much of his thirty-year career on the highest bench in its substantive due process era in dissent from judicial vetoes of economic legislation. He did so not because he particularly liked the legislation, but because he was convinced that democracy meant that people had the right to be foolish and unwise. In his own words, he was willing to go so far as "to help my country go to hell if that's what it wants." Yet he nevertheless drew the line when it came to the basic "non-economic" rights. Prior to Holmes and for ten years by his side, Mr. Justice John Marshall Harlan was the sole consistent dissenter in the substantive due process era. Harlan, who served from 1877 until his death in 1911, was a one-time Kentucky slave-holder

[1] *National Labor Relations Board v. Jones and Laughlin Steel Corporation,* 301 U.S. 1 (1937).

and grandfather of President Eisenhower's appointee by the same name. More than anyone else, he deserves the title of "the great dissenter";[1] he believed in a full measure of judicial self-restraint regarding legislative economic enactments. This stance was dramatically illustrated by his solitary dissent in the 1895 case of *United States v. E. C. Knight Co.*[2] when his eight colleagues on the Court virtually wiped out the hoped-for weapons of the fledgling Sherman Antitrust Act of 1890 by ruling that "commerce succeeds to manufacture and is not a part of it."[3] On the other hand, Harlan's resolute attachment to the role of the Court as the guardian of both the letter and the spirit of the basic constitutional guarantees of civil liberties is well demonstrated in his solitary dissenting opinion in *Plessy v. Ferguson.*[4] In this 1896 decision, the Court, with Mr. Justice Henry B. Brown— a Michigan Brahmin, born in Massachusetts and educated at Harvard and Yale—delivering the majority opinion of seven, upheld the "separate but equal doctrine" in racial segregation:

> We consider the underlying fallacy of the plaintiff's [Homer Plessy, a Louisianan, seven-eighths white, who had refused to give up his seat in a railroad car reserved for white passengers under an 1890 Louisiana statute] argument to consist in the assumption that the enforced separation of the two races stamps the colored race with a badge of inferiority. If this be so, it is not by reason of anything found in the act, but *solely because the colored race chooses to put that construction on it.*[5]

Thundered Harlan, the sole Southerner then on the Court,

> *Our Constitution is color-blind, and neither knows nor tolerates classes among citizens.* In respect of civil rights, all citizens are equal before the law. The humblest is the peer of the most powerful. The law regards man as man and takes no account of his surroundings or of his color when his civil rights as guaranteed by the supreme law of the land are involved.[6]

[1] See the author's "John Marshall Harlan: A Justice Neglected," *Virginia Law Review*, November 1955.

[2] 156 U.S. 1.

[3] *Ibid.*, majority opinion by Mr. Chief Justice Fuller, at 9. (Its impact was not effectively reversed until the Court's 1937 decision in *National Labor Relations Board v. Jones and Laughlin Steel Corporation*, 301 U.S. 1.)

[4] 163 U.S. 537.

[5] *Ibid.*, at 551. (Italics supplied.) Mr. Justice David Brewer did not participate in the case.

[6] *Ibid.*, at 559. (Italics supplied.)

As we shall see below, Harlan was the first Supreme Court jurist to advocate, unsuccessfully during his time of service, the total applicability of the federal Bill of Rights to the several states.[1] That he and Holmes were not particularly close personally did not alter their jurisprudential kinship (Holmes reserved some of his craftiest witticisms for Harlan).

However, in this respect Harlan was even closer to Louis Dembitz Brandeis, Woodrow Wilson's close ideological ally whom the President nominated to the highest bench in 1916, five years after Harlan's death and fifteen years after Holmes's accession to the Court. A pioneering lawyer and crusading supporter of social welfare legislation, a bitter opponent of trusts and monopolies, and the first Jew to be nominated to the Court, Brandeis won a furious and bitter four-month confirmation battle which was the longest in history. He was finally confirmed by a vote of 47:22, all but one [2] of the negative votes being cast by the Boston attorney's fellow Republicans! [3] Although the fervent opponent of what he regarded "the curse of bigness" and one who never wrote an opinion in favor of the government in an antitrust case, Mr. Justice Brandeis disappointed neither his nominator nor his "public." [4] He and Holmes, while of widely divergent backgrounds and temperaments, not only became warm friends but were usually on the same side of the Court's decisions, particularly in the interpretation of substantive due process and the double standard. That their reasons for agreement were often quite different affected neither the basic fact of agreement nor the close relationship be-

---

[1] E.g. *Hurtado v. California*, 110 U.S. 516 (1884); *Maxwell v. Dow*, 176 U.S. 581 (1900); and *Twining v. New Jersey*, 211 U.S. 78 (1908), to name but three cases.

[2] Democrat Francis G. Newlands of Nevada.

[3] Quite a number either did not vote or were paired, however. See A. L. Todd, *Justice on Trial: The Case of Louis D. Brandeis* (New York: McGraw-Hill Book Co., 1964), for a fascinating account of the confirmation battle. Brandeis was a registered Republican, but he probably voted the Democratic ticket more frequently.

[4] He did disappoint his colleague Mr. Justice John H. Clarke, however, who in a letter to President Wilson—on the President's inquiry regarding the reasons for Clarke's resignation from the Court in 1922—wrote that "Judge Brandeis and I were agreeing less and less frequently in the decision of cases involving what we call, for want of a better designation, liberal principles." As quoted by Alpheus T. Mason in *William Howard Taft: Chief Justice* (New York: Simon and Schuster, 1965), p. 166.

tween the great skeptic and the great crusader.[1] Holmes did not live
to see his position vindicated; he died at 93 in 1935, three years after
retiring from his beloved bench. He knew, however, that his successor,
Cardozo, would follow in his footsteps, and there were ample signs
that if the jurisprudential era begun by the Fuller Court had not yet
run its course, it was becoming increasingly beleaguered. Brandeis did
see the new era dawn. After twenty-three years on the Court, he retired in 1939 at the age of 83, secure in the knowledge that his philosophy would be followed by the post-1937 Court. He was succeeded
by William O. Douglas.

The Expression and Justification of the Double Standard

What the post-1937 judiciary did was to *assume* as constitutional
all legislation in the realm of property *unless* proved to the contrary
by a complainant, but to regard with a suspicious eye legislative and
executive experimentation with other basic human freedoms generally regarded as the "cultural freedoms" guaranteed by the Bill of
Rights—among them speech, press, worship, assembly, petition, due
process of law in criminal justice, a fair trial. In short, without denying its ultimate parental responsibility, the Court has come to regard
the legislative child of age in the economic realm, but keeps a very
close parental watch over that child in activities described as "basic"
or "cultural." What we have then is a judicially recognized area of
"preferred freedoms." Any quest for an obvious, clear line between
"property rights" and "basic human rights" is, of course, doomed
to fail, because by definition and implication *both are guaranteed
freedoms* under our national and state constitutions. Property, too,
is a "human right" and, because of this, the distinguished jurist
Learned Hand never failed to reject and challenge any advocacy of
the double standard. A policy urging that the courts, "when concerned with interests other than property . . . should have a wider
latitude for enforcing their own predilections than when they were
concerned with property itself," [2] was to him a dereliction of the judi-

[1] See the fine analysis of the jurisprudence of the two men in Samuel J.
Konefsky's *The Legacy of Holmes and Brandeis: A Study in the Influence of
Ideas* (New York: The Macmillan Company, 1956). Also available in a later
paperback edition.
[2] "Chief Justice Stone's Conception of the Judicial Function," 46 *Columbia
Law Review* 698 (1946).

cial function if not of the oath of the Constitution. And as Paul Freund, the famed scholar of constitutional law and Hand's admirer, has reminded us, it is indeed difficult to "compare the ultimate values of property with those of [for example] free inquiry and expression, or to compare the legislative compromises in the two realms; for laws dealing with libel or sedition or sound trucks or nonpolitical civil service are as truly adjustments and accommodations as are laws fixing prices or making grants of monopolies." [1] However, the values of property are *not* ignored by the judiciary when, in fact, the hand of the legislature falls upon it illegally. For example, in 1952 the Supreme Court, by an 8:1 vote, declared as a violation of substantive due process a provision of the Pure Food and Drug Act which had provided for federal powers of factory inspection. Almost unanimously the Court adjudged this provision to be unconstitutionally vague, a deprivation of liberty and property safeguarded by the Fifth Amendment.[2]

Of Preferred Freedoms. The term "preferred freedoms" is credited to a footnote appended to an opinion for the Court by the then Associate Justice Stone in the 1938 case of *United States v. Carolene Products Company*.[3] Stone's Footnote Four probably evolved from the celebrated Cardozo opinion delivered a few months earlier in *Palko v. Connecticut*.[4] In his last personally delivered opinion prior to his fatal illness in 1938, Mr. Justice Cardozo had established two major categories of rights: those that are and those that are not "implicit in the concept of ordered liberty." This distinction, subsequently referred to as the "Honor Roll of Superior Rights," Cardozo justified by explaining that "... we reach a different plane of social and moral values when we pass to ... freedom of thought and speech ... [which] is the matrix, the indispensable condition, of nearly every other form of freedom." [5] When Stone subsequently wrote his opinion in the *Carolene* case, he was very much aware of the Cardozo distinction. And, in a sense, he took it one step further: he explicitly enunciated the doctrine of the "double standard." *Carolene* dealt with a more or

---

[1] *The Supreme Court of the United States* (Cleveland: The World Publishing Co., 1961), p. 35.
[2] *United States v. Cardiff*, 344 U.S. 174.
[3] 304 U.S. 144.
[4] 302 U.S. 319 (1937). (The case will be discussed more fully in Chapter III, *infra*.)
[5] *Ibid.*, at 326-7.

less pedestrian federal commerce statute, the regulation of adulterated milk, and it would normally have passed into the annals of what the new Court regarded as routine exercise of valid congressional legislative power over interstate commerce. However, addressing himself to the inherent regulatory power, Stone commented in the body of the opinion that:

> Regulatory legislation affecting ordinary commercial transactions is not to be pronounced unconstitutional unless in the light of the facts made known or generally assumed, it is of such a character as to preclude the assumption that it rests upon some rational basis within the knowledge and experience of legislators.[1]

This expression of the double standard, from the pen of a jurist who had come to the nation's capital from one of the largest New York corporate law offices, is a reminder, as was the example of Brandeis in his posture toward monopolies and trusts described earlier, that Marxian forecasts and interpretations of the attitude of justices on the highest bench are not always viable gauges of their actual stance!

Having said what he did, Stone then appended his now famous Footnote Four from which we will examine the following three paragraphs:

(1) There may be narrower scope for operation of the presumption of constitutionality when legislation appears on its face to be within a specific prohibition of the Constitution, such as those of the first ten amendments, which are deemed equally specific when held to be embraced within the Fourteenth.

(2) It is unnecessary to consider now whether legislation which restricts *those political processes* which can ordinarily be expected to bring about repeal of undesirable legislation, is to be subjected to more exacting judicial scrutiny under the general prohibitions of the Fourteenth Amendment than are most other types of legislation....

(3) Nor need we enquire whether similar considerations enter into review of statutes directed at particular religious ... or national ... or racial minorities may be a special condition, which tends seriously to curtail the operation of *those political processes* ordinarily to be relied upon to protect minorities, and which may call for a correspondingly more searching judicial inquiry.

[1] 304 U.S. 144, at 152.

In paragraph one Stone would appear to be proposing that the judicially-taught-tradition-of-the-law assumption of the constitutionality of legislation must be at least limited and probably eschewed altogether if a statute *on its face* seems to abridge the constitutional guarantees of the Bill of Rights. However, it became evident soon thereafter that Stone really meant the five guarantees of the First Amendment (religion, speech, press, assembly, and petition) rather than the *whole* Bill of Rights. His colleagues Black, Douglas, Murphy, and Rutledge [1] interpreted the admonition as being all inclusive, and their opinion frequently prevailed during their joint tenure on the Court between 1943 and 1949—sometimes gaining Jackson's vote, occasionally even Frankfurter's or Reed's. Thus at least five votes to carry the day were frequently available, and a series of memorable decisions was made in behalf of the new concept.[2] And, contrary to some reporting, justices did in fact use the term "preferred position" in majority and minority opinions.[3] However, when Justices Murphy and Rutledge both died in the summer of 1949, their replacements, Justices Tom C. Clark and Sherman Minton, together with Mr. Chief Justice Fred M. Vinson (Stone had died on the bench in 1946), consigned the "preferred freedom" doctrine to relative limbo. It remained there until Mr. Chief Justice Warren succeeded Vinson on his death in 1953 and the Court renewed the emphasis on civil rights—whatever the announced or unannounced doctrine.

Paragraph two calls for a special judicial scrutiny of assaults on

[1] Actually it was not Stone but Wiley B. Rutledge who stated the "preferred freedom" doctrine most clearly, most expressly, and most extremely, in what was the heyday of the avowed utilization of the doctrine, in the 5:4 *Union Organization* case of 1945—in which Stone dissented (*Thomas v. Collins,* 323 U.S. 516, at 529-30 and 540). Rutledge carried Black, Douglas, and Murphy, and Jackson concurred to make the majority of five. In dissent, together with the now Chief Justice Stone, were Roberts, Reed, and Frankfurter.

[2] E.g. *Hague v. C.I.O.,* 307 U.S. 496 (1939); *Bridges v. California,* 314 U.S. 252 (1941); *Jones v. Opelika,* 319 U.S. 103 (1943); *West Virginia State Board of Education v. Barnette,* 319 U.S. 624 (1943); *Thomas v. Collins,* 323 U.S. 516 (1945); *Saia v. New York,* 334 U.S. 558 (1948); and *Terminiello v. Chicago,* 337 U.S. 1 (1949).

[3] E.g. Stone in *Jones v. Opelika,* 316 U.S. 584 (1942), at 608; Douglas in *Murdock v. Pennsylvania,* 319 U.S. 105 (1943), at 115; and Rutledge in *Thomas v. Collins, loc. cit.,* fn. 2, at 530. See also *Prince v. Massachusetts,* 321 U.S. 158 (1944); *Follett v. McCormick,* 321 U.S. 573 (1944); *Marsh v. Alabama,* 326 U.S. 501 (1946), at 509; and *Saia v. New York, loc. cit.,* fn. 2, at 562.

"those political processes" which in a very real sense make all other rights in our democratic society possible: equal access to the voting booth, for both nomination and election, and the ability to seek redress of political grievances, either by striving for public office or by "getting at the rascals" in office. It was this basic requirement of a representative democracy that precipitated the momentous Supreme Court decisions in the *Suffrage Cases* of 1941 and 1944. In the first, *United States v. Classic*,[1] the Court overruled precedent[2] and held that the language of the Constitution equated "primaries" with "elections" in races for federal office, and that the former would henceforth be subject to congressional regulation to the same extent and in the same manner as the latter. The second case, *Smith v. Allwright*,[3] logically resulted from the first. Here, the Court, again overruling precedent,[4] outlawed, as an unconstitutional violation of the Fifteenth Amendment, the so-called White Primary, a device to bar Negroes from the effective exercise of the ballot in several states of the deep South. Rejecting the contention that the Democratic Party of Texas was "a voluntary association" and thus free to discriminate in its membership, the 8:1 majority held that the Party acted as an agent of the State of Texas because of the character of its duties—such as providing election machinery and candidates. Of equal, if not greater, importance in the judicial assault on legislation restricting basic political processes is the matter of equitable representation. In March 1962 the Supreme Court finally found sufficient votes to declare that the age-old practice of deliberate mal-, mis-, or non-apportionment of representative legislative districts in the several states was a controversy which it had the power, the right, and the duty to adjudicate. This decision in the case of *Baker v. Carr*[5] sharply departed from the erstwhile Court practice of regarding this kind of controversy as a "political question"[6] to be "handled" by the political rather than the judiciary branches. *Baker* broke with that precedent. Mr. Justice Frankfurter, joined by Harlan, wrote an impassioned 68-page dissenting opinion reiterating his life-long judicial philosophy that the courts

---

[1] 313 U.S. 299 (1941).
[2] *Newberry v. United States*, 256 U.S. 232 (1921).
[3] 321 U.S. 649 (1944). (Mr. Justice Roberts was the sole dissenter here.)
[4] *Grovey v. Townsend*, 295 U.S. 45 (1935).
[5] 369 U.S. 186 (1962).
[6] E.g. *Colegrove v. Green*, 328 U.S. 549 (1946) and *South v. Peters*, 339 U.S. 276 (1950).

must stay out of what he termed the "political thicket." Warning that the Court would find itself immersed in a "mathematical quagmire," he admonished the majority of six that

> There is not under our Constitution a judicial remedy for every political mischief. In a democratic society like ours, relief must come through an aroused popular conscience that sears the conscience of the people's representatives.[1]

But the majority had seen one attempt to "sear the conscience" after another frustrated for generations. Indeed, in many of the transgressing states the very imbalance of representative districts rendered "an aroused public conscience" impossible. The Court, prodded by a swelling chorus of citizens who were discriminated against, notably the urban masses, had had enough, and the commands of Article One and Amendment Fourteen provided the necessary interpretative authority to bring about the "more exacting judicial scrutiny" called for in the second paragraph of Stone's Footnote Four.

The decision in *Baker v. Carr* [2] that the federal courts do have jurisdiction in cases involving state legislative apportionment became a vehicle for logical substantive extensions. In 1963, in the *Georgia County Unit* case,[3] the Court, agreeing with the lower federal district court that the notorious "county unit" scheme [4] violated the equal protection of the laws clause of the Fourteenth Amendment, enunciated the principle of "one person, one vote," [5] of the equality of every voter with every other voter in the state when he casts his vote in a state-wide election. One year later, the Court extended the principle to *congressional* districts.[6] Then, perhaps most dramatically, in a group of six cases in June of 1964, it required that representation for *both* houses of state legislatures must be apportioned to reflect "approximate equality." Wrote Mr. Chief Justice Warren for a majority of six: "Legislatures represent people, not trees or acres. Legislators are

[1] 369 U.S. 186, dissenting opinion, at 270.
[2] The vote was 6:2. Mr. Justice Charles E. Whittaker did not participate.
[3] *Gray v. Sanders*, 372 U.S. 368.
[4] Under it each of Georgia's counties received a minimum of two and a maximum of six electoral votes (for the eight most populous counties), with each county's vote going to the candidate receiving the largest popular vote therein—resulting in rank discrimination that saw the small counties receiving from eleven to 120 times as much representative weight as the largest.
[5] Mr. Justice Douglas spoke for the 8:1 Court here.
[6] *Wesberry v. Sanders*, 376 U.S. 1 (1964).

elected by voters, not farms or cities or economic interests. . . . To the extent that a citizen's right to vote is debased, he is that much less a citizen. The weight of a citizen's right to vote cannot be made to depend on where he lives." [1] Stone would have been pleased.

In paragraph three Stone so explicitly spells out the double standard as to be credited with its parenthood. It is self-evident that the special judicial protection he suggests for frequently unpopular minorities and other small groups is pre-eminently designed for and directed to their political-cultural activities. Underlying his call for special scrutiny is the fact that it is these groups who because of their unpopularity need particular protection if they are to attain their full measure of constitutionally guaranteed citizenship. The current struggle of political, religious, and particularly racial minority groups bears witness to the need for the "preferred freedom" doctrine suggested by Stone on that Opinion Monday in 1938.

But is the "double standard" justifiable at all? Does the Supreme Court of the United States have a constitutional *cum* moral mandate to apply such a standard, to guard against what has been called the "mistaken self-abnegation" that would allow the basic freedoms to be "eroded to the point where their restoration becomes impossible?" [2]

A QUARTET OF JUSTIFICATION FOR THE DOUBLE STANDARD

Of the numerous reasons which may be advanced in support of the double standard, four commend themselves strongly for consideration:

1. *The Crucial Nature of Basic Freedoms.* As Justices Holmes, Brandeis, Cardozo, and Stone have demonstrated, those freedoms which can be considered basic are those upon which all other freedoms in democratic society rest. For example, when the principles of freedom of speech and press are contingent upon prior censorship, they become a mockery. When the right to worship depends upon majoritarian whims or police ordinances, it becomes meaningless. When the rights to register and vote are dependent upon the race of the applicant or the amount of his property, they become travesties

---

[1] *Reynolds v. Sims,* 377 U.S. 533, at 562. Five other cases were decided simultaneously, all based on the same general principle, with the votes ranging from 8:1 to 6:3. (See *ibid.,* pp. 633-713.)

[2] Loren P. Beth, "The Case for Judicial Protection of Civil Liberties," 17 *The Journal of Politics* 112 (February 1955).

of the democratic political process. To paraphrase Mr. Justice Jackson in the *West Virginia Flag Salute* case,[1] the very purpose of the Bill of Rights was to withdraw those freedoms which can be considered basic from the "vicissitudes" of political controversy, from the grasps of majorities and public officials, and to hold them aloft as legal principles to be applied by the judiciary. As Justice Stone put it in a memorable dissenting opinion less than three years following his Footnote Four in *Carolene*:

> The very fact that we have constitutional guarantees of civil liberties and the specificity of their command where freedom of speech and religion are concerned require some accommodation of the powers which government normally exercises, when no question of civil liberty is involved, to the constitutional demand that these liberties be protected against the action of government itself. . . . The Constitution expresses more than the conviction of the people that democratic processes must be preserved at all costs. It also is an expression of faith and a command that freedom of mind and spirit must be preserved, which government must obey, if it is to adhere to that justice and moderation without which no free government can exist.[2]

Thus it has fallen to the Court to recognize and attempt to preserve those freedoms which are basic or crucial to the democratic process. And to do this, it has fallen to the Court to apply the double standard to them when the other branches of government have either consciously or unconsciously failed to heed or comprehend the essence of Stone's admonition.

2. *The Explicit Language of the Bill of Rights.* A good case can be made for the viability of the double standard from the language of the Bill of Rights (much of which, as we shall see below, has been made applicable to the several states by way of the "due process of law" clause of the Fourteenth Amendment). The economic-proprietarian safeguards of the Bill are couched in the most general of terms: the command of the Fifth and Fourteenth Amendments that no person "be deprived of life, liberty, or *property, without due process of law,*" raises more questions than it settles. Certainly the Founding Fathers did not spell out "property" except that one should not be "deprived" of it without "due process of law." As we have already

---

[1] *West Virginia State Board of Education v. Barnette,* 319 U.S. 624 (1943).
[2] *Minersville School District v. Gobitis,* 310 U.S. 586 (1940), at 602-3, 606-7.

noted, during the fifty years prior to 1937 the Court interpreted the clause so stringently that legislative efforts in the proprietarian-economic sphere were all but futile. To do so the Court had to read into the language of the "due process" clauses concepts that *may* have been implicit but were certainly not explicit. On the other hand, the language governing what we commonly regard as our basic human freedoms is explicit indeed. Madison's terminology for the First Amendment is precise: "Congress shall make no law respecting an establishment of religion, or prohibiting the free exercise thereof; or abridging the freedom of speech, or of the press; or the right of the people peaceably to assemble, and to petition the government for redress of grievances." Succeeding amendments in the Bill refer specifically to a host of other basic rights as well, be they substantive or procedural. That their interpretation has proved difficult and troublesome over the years does not, however, invalidate their explicitness, and it is their explicitness which makes a strong case for invocation of the double standard. This is not necessarily tantamount to accepting the contention of such an advanced advocate of the double standard as Mr. Justice Black, however appealing it may be in theory. His firm contention, reiterated throughout his long career on the high bench, is that when the First Amendment says "Congress *shall make no law . . . abridging* the freedom of speech, or of the press . . . ," [1] it means just that: NO LAW! It most emphatically does not mean, for example, "no law except such as may be necessary to prevent exhortation to riot"; or "no law except what may be needed to curb seditious utterances"; or "no law except one to punish libel and slander." As he put it in a famous article:

> Some people regard the prohibitions of the Constitution, even its most unequivocal commands, as mere admonitions which Congress [and by implication, the states] need not always observe . . . formulations [which] rest, at least in part, on the premise that there are no "absolute" prohibitions in the Constitution, and that all constitutional problems are questions of reasonableness, proximity, and degree. . . .
>
> I cannot accept this approach to the Bill of Rights. It is my belief that there *are* "absolutes" in our Bill of Rights, and they were put there on purpose by men who knew what words meant, and meant

[1] Hugo L. Black, "The Bill of Rights," 35 *New York University Law Review* 866 (April 1960).

their prohibitions to be "absolutes".... I am primarily discussing here whether liberties *admittedly* covered by the Bill of Rights can nevertheless be abridged on the ground that a superior public interest justifies the abridgement. I think the Bill of Rights made its safeguards superior.[1]

And later, discussing the First Amendment, which was to him the greatest amendment of all, Black wrote:

The phrase "Congress shall make no law" is composed of plain words, easily understood.... Neither as offered nor as adopted is the language of this Amendment anything less than absolute....[2]

Whether or not one agrees with Black's thesis—and this writer, for one, does not—it nonetheless lends strong support to the argument for the existence of a hierarchy of values and the priority within that hierarchy of those liberties specifically listed in the Bill of Rights. Even Mr. Justice Frankfurter, no friend of absolutism or formulae such as the double standard, declared in a significant opinion that matters like press censorship and separation of church and state are different from economic policy matters because "history, through the Constitution, speaks so decisively as to forbid legislative experimentation" with them.[3]

3. *The Appropriate Expertise of the Judiciary.* If we accept the first two reasons in support of the double standard, a third follows quite logically: that no other agency or institution of the United States government has proved itself either so capable of performing, or so willing to undertake, the necessary role of guardian of our basic rights as the judicial branch. Since the legislative and executive branches have, for reasons inherent in our system, failed to fulfill this role, it has fallen to the judiciary whose members are eminently qualified for it by tradition, experience, and instinct. As Robert H. Jackson, who had come to the Supreme Court from service in the executive branch, observed:

The people have seemed to feel that the Supreme Court, whatever its defects, is still the most detached, dispassionate, and trustworthy cus-

---

[1] *Ibid.*, pp. 866-7.
[2] *Ibid.*, p. 874.
[3] *American Federation of Labor v. American Sash and Door Co.*, 335 U.S. 538 (1949), at 550.

todian that our system affords for the translation of abstract into concrete constitutional commands.[1]

Yet, if the Supreme Court is indeed the appropriate governmental agency to buttress and safeguard our fundamental rights, few would seriously contend that its province is also economic legislation and administration. Because of its insufficient expertise and its crowded docket the Court is not prepared to make the kind of economic judgments that would veto legislative actions and intent. It is the people's representatives who are best qualified to give expression to the requirements of economic life, to the experimentation and resolution that go into public planning. "Whether the legislature," as Mr. Justice Black once noted, "takes for its textbook Adam Smith, Herbert Spencer, Lord Keynes, or some other is no concern of ours." [2] Here, then, judicial self-restraint and the assumption of legislative know-how and representativeness are in philosophical accord—and it is here that the double standard thus finds its clearest justification. Few have stated this distinction as well as Mr. Justice Oliver Wendell Holmes, Jr., who was no personal friend, indeed, of legislative "fooling around" with "economic do-gooding." But he was a jurist who believed resolutely, although he was often alone and practically never carried the Court with him, that the people in a democratic government have every right to experiment with their economic fate—even if he personally were to consider their action "stupid, asinine, silly, and ignorant." As he said to his 60-year-old colleague Stone, after more than a half-century on the Supreme Courts of Massachusetts and the United States and at the age of 90:

> Young man, about seventy-five years ago I learned that I was not God. And so, when the people want to do something [in the realm of economic legislation] I can't find anything in the Constitution expressly forbidding them to do, I say, whether I like it or not, "Goddamit, let 'em do it." [3]

[1] *The Supreme Court in the American System of Government* (Cambridge: Harvard University Press, 1955), p. 23. Designed as the Godkin Lectures at Harvard University, the book was edited and published with the aid of Jackson's son after his father's death of a heart attack shortly before he was to deliver the lectures.

[2] *Ferguson v. Skrupa*, 372 U.S. 726 (1963), at 732.

[3] As quoted by Charles P. Curtis in *Lions Under the Throne* (Boston: Houghton Mifflin Co., 1947), p. 281.

Holmes expressed the same judicial posture more specifically to John W. Davis, the unsuccessful Democratic nominee for the Presidency in 1924, sometime U.S. Solicitor-General, and famed criminal law attorney: "Of course, I know, and every other sensible man knows, that the Sherman Law [Anti-Trust Act of 1890] is damned nonsense, but if my country wants to go to hell, I am here to help it." [1] Yet, for the First Amendment liberties, Holmes rejected this "pure democracy" approach. He was convinced that the Constitution neither provided nor intended the luxury of such risk in that sphere. Whereas property, to him, was "social" in origin, civil liberties were "human." In full concord with such post-1916 allies as Justices John H. Clarke, Brandeis, Stone, and, on occasion, Hughes,[2] he simply did not consider the average American citizen "very enlightened"—to employ Mr. Justice Jackson's phrase—on the subject of civil rights and liberties.

4. *Discrepancy in Access to the Political Processes.* The usual economic-proprietarian pressure or interest group has infinitely more opportunities of ready access to the legislative and administrative process to obtain redress of public policy grievances than does the racial, political, or religious minority group or individual. And it is this latter group or individual which accounts for the overwhelming majority of the litigation involving civil liberties. Being minorities, and more often than not unpopular ones, their hope of access to litigation, let alone successful redress of grievances, has been scant indeed. The problem is twofold: first, minority groups normally fail to carry sufficient weight or influence with legislators; second, minority groups or individuals, by the very nature of their quest and purpose, are more often than not "unpopular" or "trouble-makers." As Mr. Justice Fankfurter once commented wistfully, the ordinary litigant in civil liberties cases "is not a very nice person." He was referring particularly to the average accused in criminal law violations where celebrated civil-liberty decisions have frequently favored nether elements of society, often felons of the most dangerous sort. The fact that their

---

[1] As told by Francis Biddle in *Justice Holmes, Natural Law, and the Supreme Court* (New York: The Macmillan Co., 1961), p. 9.

[2] Holmes served on the Court from 1902 to 1932; Clarke, 1916-22; Brandeis, 1916-39; Stone, 1925-46 (the last five years as Chief Justice); and Hughes, 1910-16 (Associate Justice) and again 1930-41 (as Chief Justice).

cases serve as vehicles for the interpretation and indeed strengthening of constitutional guarantees and safeguards does not inevitably endear the jurists to the citizenry, let alone to the public lawmakers and law enforcers. It is axiomatic that not only the procedurally wronged felon but also the actually or allegedly wronged member of religious and political minority groups, e.g. Jehovah's Witnesses, left-wing or right-wing extremists, will find little solace or hope in any attempt to "get to" the legislative or administrative levels. Hence, their appeal to the judicial branch is their sole hope for the attainment of justice under law. On the other hand, the aggrieved or dissatisfied economic-proprietarian interest or pressure group rarely, if ever, faces the stigmas and obstacles that come with the "not very nice" label. More often than not they are both "respectable" and influential, and seldom do they have any great difficulty in gaining access to the legislative and especially the administrative branches of government. An excellent example is the involved history of the federal government's efforts to cause the E. I. du Pont de Nemours & Company to divest itself of its ownership of 23 per cent of the stock of the General Motors Corporation. A long, expensive, and complex legal battle followed the initial complaint filed by the Antitrust Division of the U.S. Department of Justice in 1949—a battle that was not resolved by the courts until the Supreme Court's last decision in the matter on May 22, 1961, when the government finally "won" its suit. The Court held 4:3 that there must be complete divestiture of du Pont's 63,000,000 shares of General Motors stock.[1] Prior thereto, and in no small measure due to du Pont's superb (and well-paid) legal counsel, the government had seen itself alternately lose, win, lose, win, and lose at the sundry levels of the federal judicial process.[2]

When du Pont realized in the spring of 1961 that there was no further prospect of success at the judicial level, the giant and powerful firm set out to do what it had a perfect right to do: to set into motion its constitutional right to "petition the government for a redress of grievances." [3] It did this with the aid of Delaware's two United States senators and its congressman-at-large. As early as September 9, 1961, the House Ways and Means Committee submitted a favorable

[1] *United States v. E. I. du Pont de Nemours & Co.*, 366 U.S. 316.
[2] See the excellent compendium of May 31, 1962, issued by the Public Relations Department of du Pont and widely distributed.
[3] Constitution of the United States, Amendment I, Cl. 3.

report on a bill, which had been initially introduced by Senator J. Allen Frear, Jr. (D.-Del.) in 1958 and which was designed to permit du Pont to divest its General Motors stock without drastic economic consequences. The House approved the bill by voice vote exactly ten days later; the Senate Finance Committee submitted a favorable report two days thereafter; the Senate itself approved the bill on January 23, 1962, also by voice vote; and President Kennedy signed it into law exactly nine days later. In December 1964 du Pont broke its final ties with General Motors under the combined judicial and legislative terms outlined here. But in February 1965 du Pont, availing itself of its privilege to contest *administrative* adjudication as well, obtained an official Internal Revenue Service ruling that, reversing its own earlier *adverse* ruling in 1963, would save members of the du Pont family between $56 million and $100 million in taxes. The new ruling was stoutly defended before Congress by Secretary of the Treasury Douglas Dillon.[1]

Now there was nothing "illegal" or even "unethical" about du Pont's lengthy, expensive, and generally—although not wholly, of course—successful activities, and assuredly there was nothing "unconstitutional" about them. Numerous other illustrations could also be readily cited to substantiate the point at issue: the infinitely superior ability of the average economic-proprietarian interest to gain ready access to a generally sympathetic legislative and administrative ear as compared with that of the average civil libertarian interest.

The quartet of justification, considered separately and also as a unit, demonstrates a strong case, indeed, for the invocation of the judicial "double standard." Viewed in purely academic terms, the latter may be convincing neither morally nor logically—yet its existence and its application require that we recognize it as a pragmatic and necessary fact of life of government and politics under law in the American system of government.[2]

[1] See the special report by Eileen Shanahan, "Dillon Defends Tax Ruling in du Pont Divestiture," *The New York Times*, March 18, 1965.

[2] For a critical, if wistful, analysis of this conclusion, see Robert G. McCloskey, "Economic Due Process and the Supreme Court: An Exhumation and Reburial," in Philip B. Kurland, ed., *The Supreme Court Review* (Chicago: University of Chicago Press, 1962), pp. 34-62.

III

The Bill of Rights
and Its Applicability to the States

THE APPLICABILITY of the Bill of Rights to the several states is an intriguing question with some fascinating constitutional history attached to it. In so far as history is any guide at all, the clear intent of Madison and his supporters in composing and in submitting the Bill of Rights to Congress in April, 1789, and in seeing it approved and ratified by the necessary eleven states as the first eight amendments [1] on December 15, 1791, was that it be applicable to the *national* (federal) government. Since the states had their own bills of rights, the overriding reason for their authorship and sponsorship of the federal Bill of Rights was to place demonstrably far-reaching restraints on the fledgling central government.[2] Indeed, the very first phrase of Article I of the approximately twenty-five assorted rights to be found in the Bill of Rights, which has so aptly been termed "our 462-word pillar of life," is that "*Congress* shall make no law...." The word "Congress" does not, however, reappear in the remainder of the eight articles of amendment and since much of their language is more general than that of the First, the extent of their reach was bound to be litigated sooner or later.

HISTORICAL BACKGROUND

The question of the applicability of the Bill of Rights to the states was raised theoretically rather quickly by elements of the propertied

---

[1] Or ten, depending upon one's point of view. At least in common parlance, articles Nine and Ten are viewed as part of the Bill—and they were, indeed, adopted at the same time as the other eight. But their nature and language militate against their inclusion for present purposes.

[2] See the vivid study by Robert A. Rutland, *The Birth of the Bill of Rights,* 1776-1791 (New York: Collier Books, 1962).

community. But, appropriately, it remained for Mr. Chief Justice Marshall to be the first to adjudicate the question when, in 1833, at the end of a distinguished and influential career,[1] he decided the case of *Barron v. Baltimore*[2] for a unanimous Court. It has never been overruled *per se.*

Mr. Chief Justice Marshall and Barron's Wharf. The basis for the litigation in *Barron v. Baltimore* was laid when the City of Baltimore, Maryland, began to pave some of its streets. In so doing its engineers had found it necessary to divert several streams from their natural courses; this resulted in deposits near one Barron's Wharf of much gravel and sand which filled up the channel and prevented the approach of vessels. Barron's fine wharf, previously the one with the deepest water in the harbor, was thus turned into little more than a useless inlet. Not amused, Mr. Barron obtained eminent legal counsel and went to court. He alleged that Baltimore's actions had, in fact and deed, violated that clause of the Fifth Amendment of the United States Constitution which expressly proscribes the taking of private property "for public use without just compensation." Although Barron won his argument at the level of the trial court, his joy was short-lived. Baltimore appealed the verdict to the Maryland State Court of Appeals which reversed the decision below. The unhappy Barron then appealed his case to the United States Supreme Court on a writ of error.[3]

With his typical aplomb the fourth Chief Justice announced that "the question thus presented is, we think, of great importance, but not of much difficulty."[4] And in the space of but a handful of pages in Court Reporter Peters' notebook, Marshall demolished Barron's fundamental contention that whatever is forbidden by the terms of the Fifth Amendment to the national government is also forbidden to the states and that the Court therefore has an obligation to construe the Fifth's "guarantee in behalf of individual liberty" as a restraint upon *both* state and national governments. The Chief Justice's response was phrased in historical and constitutional terms:

[1] For the best biography of Marshall as Chief Justice see Albert J. Beveridge, *The Life of John Marshall,* 4 vols. (Boston: Houghton Mifflin Co., 1919).
[2] 7 Peters 243 (1833).
[3] A discontinued writ. It brought the entire record of a case proceeding in a lower court before the Supreme Court for its consideration for alleged "errors of law" committed below.
[4] *Barron v. Baltimore,* 7 Peters 243 (1833).

The Constitution was ordained and established by the people of the United States for themselves, for their own government, and not for the government of the individual States. Each State established a Constitution for itself, and, in that Constitution, provided such limitations and restrictions on the powers of its particular government as its judgment indicated. The people of the United States framed such a government for the United States as they supposed best adapted to their situation, and best calculated to promote their interests. The powers they conferred on the government were to be exercised by itself; and the limitations on power, if expressed in general terms, are naturally, and, we think, necessarily applicable to the government created by the instrument. They are limitations of power granted in the instrument itself; not of distinct governments, framed by different persons and for different purposes.

If these propositions be correct, the fifth amendment must be understood as restraining the power of the general government, not as applicable to the States. In their several constitutions they have imposed such restrictions on their respective governments as their own wisdom suggested, such as they deemed most proper for themselves. It is a subject on which they judge exclusively, and with which others interfere no further than they are supposed to have a common interest.

... These amendments [the Bill of Rights] contain no expression indicating an intention to apply them to the state governments. This court cannot so apply them.

... This court ... has no jurisdiction of the cause; and it is dismissed.[1]

Marshall had spoken, Barron had lost, and the Court's opinion that there was "no repugnancy between the several acts of the general assembly of Maryland ... and the Constitution of the United States," [2] became the law of the land. Citizens like Barron were destined to have no further recourse until the ratification in 1868 of the Fourteenth Amendment, probably the most controversial and certainly the most litigated, of all amendments adopted since the birth of the Republic.

THE FOURTEENTH AMENDMENT

The Fourteenth Amendment did not in and of itself overturn the *Barron* precedent: men continue to disagree over the purpose of the framers of the Amendment and the extent of its application to the states.

[1] *Ibid.*, at 247-8, 250, 251.
[2] *Ibid.*, at 251.

Some Historical Facts. The facts surrounding the proposal and passage of the Fourteenth Amendment in the 39th Congress (1865-67) —led by the Radical Republicans and their Committee of Fifteen [1]— are fewer than the resultant conjectures and analyses. We do know that: (a) the 52 United States Senators (42 Republicans and 10 Democrats) and 191 Representatives (145 Republicans and 46 Democrats) wanted to do something to ameliorate the lot of the Negro; (b) at least to some extent, they were concerned with civil rights, generally; and (c) they were interested in extending increased protection to property as well as to human rights.[2] We also know that (d) the Amendment was intended to remedy the lack of a "citizenship" clause in the original Constitution—and the initial sentence of the first of its five sections makes this clear: "All persons born or naturalized in the United States, and subject to the jurisdiction thereof, are citizens of the United States and of the State wherein they reside." This, of course, would include Negroes. We further know from the language of the last section, Number Five, that there was some intention to provide Congress with the necessary power, if not the tools, to enforce the provisions of the Amendment: "The Congress shall have power to enforce, by appropriate legislation, the provisions of this article." [3] And finally, we know that both the heart and the great-

[1] Composed of twelve Republicans and three Democrats, it consisted of nine U.S. Representatives and six U.S. Senators, under the Chairmanship of Republican Senator William Fessenden of Maine. It was essentially the congressional "policy committee," whose real leaders were Radical Republicans: Representatives Thaddeus Stevens of Pennsylvania and John A. Bingham of Ohio and Senators Jacob Howard of Michigan and Lyman Trumbull of Illinois.

[2] Historians now generally agree that the word "person" instead of "citizen" was adopted by the Drafting Committee in the "due process" and "equal protection" clauses to extend protection to corporations as well as human beings. The Supreme Court officially adopted this point of view in 1886 in *Santa Clara County v. Southern Pacific Railroad*, 118 U.S. 394.

[3] In part thanks to this provision and, by implication, to the almost identically worded one of Amendment Fifteen, Congress found authority to enact certain sections of the Civil Rights Act of 1964. One of its most significant sections, that dealing with discrimination in public accommodations, was passed under the congressional power over interstate commerce, and was specifically upheld by the U.S. Supreme Court in December 1964. (See *Heart of Atlanta Motel v. United States*, 379 U.S. 241 and *Katzenbach v. McClung*, 379 U.S. 294.)

Congress also utilized that section to enact portions of the Voting Rights Act of 1965, which met and withstood two constitutional challenges in 1966 on the strength of the section's wording and intent. (See *South Carolina v. Kazenbach*, 383 U.S. 301 and *Katzenbach v. Morgan*, 384 U.S. 641.)

est source of confusion and controversy of the famed Amendment
has been the now so well-known and debated phrasing of the second,
lengthy sentence of Section 1, which was chiefly composed by Republican Representative John A. Bingham of Ohio:

> No State shall make or enforce any law which shall abridge the privi-
> leges or immunities of citizens of the United States; *nor shall any
> State deprive any person of life, liberty, or property, without due process
> of law;* nor deny to any person within its jurisdiction the equal protec-
> tion of the laws.[1]

There is no disagreement that the italicized portion, which was lifted
verbatim from the language of the Fifth Amendment, thus provides
guarantees again *state* as well as federal infringement. What does
cause major disagreement, however, can be illustrated by two questions: first, did the framers of the Amendment intend to "incorporate"
or "nationalize" or "carry over" the entire Bill of Rights through the
wording of its "due process of law" clause, thereby making it applicable to the several states,[2] and second, regardless of their intention,
should the Bill of Rights be applied to the states, given the nature
of the rights involved and the demands of the democratic society in
which we live?

[1] Italics supplied.

[2] The author realizes that to use the terms "incorporation," "nationalization," "application," "carrying-over," and "absorption," more or less synony-
mously and interchangeably is heresy to a good many members of the legal and
academic community, if indeed it is not regarded as simply wrong. With all
due respect and deference to the scholars and jurists who do distinguish between
these terms both literally and substantively (see, for example, Mr. Justice
Frankfurter's important "Memorandum" described on pages 32 and 33, *infra*),
the basic issue involved clearly comes down to the answer to the following
crucial question: Is a certain provision in the federal Constitution, is a specific
right enumerated in the federal Bill of Rights, *applicable to the states* via the
"due process" clause of the Fourteenth Amendment or is it *not* applicable?
If it is held to be so applicable by the judiciary, then it is "incorporated,"
"nationalized," "carried over," "applied," or "absorbed." To the affected
litigants it does not matter what the process is called—what matters is whether
or not it signifies state acquiescence with federal standards. This is not to say,
of course, that the author does not recognize basic historical and linguistic
distinctions between the concepts of "incorporation" and "absorption," for example, and he has been fascinated and intrigued by the long-standing controversies that have engulfed them. But, given the judicio-legal developments
of the past decade, e.g. the 1965 decision in the *Connecticut Birth Control*
case (*Griswold v. Connecticut*, 381 U.S. 479, discussed at length, p. 69), the
distinctions are so blurred as to become academic. What matters constitutionally, to repeat, is whether a federal provision or standard does or does not apply
to the states.

The Intention of the Framers. The Fourteenth Amendment was passed by Congress on June 16, 1866, ratified by the required three-fourths of the states—ten of these then being Southern Reconstruction governments under duress [1]—and was proclaimed in effect on July 28, 1868. The Amendment had significant political overtones, for it was the key plank of the first Reconstruction platform drafted by the Radical Republicans, led by Thaddeus Stevens of Pennsylvania, Roscoe Conkling of New York, and George Boutwell of Massachusetts. Indeed, the Amendment's passage by Congress in June 1866 provided the Radical Republicans with a welcome, ready-made campaign issue for the November 1866 election campaigns. Attention directed to the Amendment was almost wholly to the political implications of bestowing full citizenship upon the Negro. But there is no record, whatsoever, of any campaign discussion or analysis of the matter of the application of the Bill of Rights to the states via its "due process of law" clause. There was much talk of the Amendment giving teeth to the Thirteenth Amendment and securing the "fundamental rights and fundamental freedoms of all men." [2]

In the face of the many disagreements on the "intent" of the framers, some argue that their intent really no longer matters, for the "felt necessities of the times" (Mr. Justice Holmes's celebrated and felicitous phrase) and the inevitable growth of the Constitution, may well dictate the application of the Bill of Rights to the several states regardless of the framers' intention. However, since it is preferable to have historical data to back one's contentions, both the proponents and opponents of total or even partial incorporation continue to refer

[1] By March 1, 1867, there were 37 states in the Union including those of the Old Confederacy. This meant that 28 would have to ratify the Amendment to bring it into effect. But by that time only 20 states had ratified, among them Tennessee as the sole Southern state. Consequently, the congressional Radicals passed a law which in fact put the Southern states on notice that they would not be readmitted to the Union "officially," unless they: (1) ratified the Fourteenth Amendment, and (2) extended the vote to adult males "of whatever race, color, or previous condition." This resulted in action by enough Southern states, where federal troops still attested to the Reconstruction Era. President Johnson vetoed the act, but Congress passed it over his veto. The law accomplished its purpose: between April and July 1868 the legislatures of Arkansas, Florida, North Carolina, Louisiana, South Carolina, Alabama, and Georgia acquiesced and the necessary figure 28 had been attained. (Actually, in the interim New Jersey and Ohio had withdrawn their earlier ratifications, but Massachusetts, Nebraska, and Iowa had come aboard.)

[2] The quotation is from a speech by Representative Lyman Trumbull of Pennsylvania.

to history. A great deal of published research on historical justification is available, yet there is, in fact, no conclusive answer, for such evidence as exists is not genuinely persuasive. Originally, those opposing the incorporation interpretation enjoyed a slight edge. Simply, they contended that had the framers of the Fourteenth Amendment intended to "incorporate" or "carry over" or "nationalize" the Bill of Rights to the states, they would have *said so specifically* rather than merely use the very general language of the "due process of law" clause. The proponents, on the other hand, continue to argue that the famous clause was adopted as "shorthand" for the Bill of Rights, and that the framers utilized it both to broaden and to strengthen fundamental guarantees of rights and liberties. It is still possible to emerge with opposite conclusions, particularly in the light of the lengthy and heated congressional debates on the subject. History is, in fact, not a reliable guide here, and historical analysis of the uncertain, while interesting, is not necessarily conclusive. Determining the intention of the framers may well now be academic. Since the Supreme Court first "incorporated" aspects of the Bill of Rights in 1925, the process has been sporadic, but continuous, and in all likelihood has not run its course—regardless of whether the rights thus made applicable to the states be regarded as "incorporated" or "absorbed."

Some Protagonists. The earliest spokesman for total incorporation of the Bill of Rights was Mr. Justice John Marshall Harlan (1877-1911), but his was a lonely voice. In his 34-year career on the highest bench—he served longer than any other except Mr. Justice Stephen J. Field (1863-97) and Mr. Chief Justice Marshall (1801-35)—time and again he unsuccessfully championed that interpretation.[1] He was not even partially vindicated until 1925 when Mr. Justice Edward T. Sanford delivered his dictum in *Gitlow v. New York*.[2] And as late as 1947 in the famous *Adamson* case,[3] Mr. Justice Frankfurter rejected the concept of incorporation as one manufactured out of whole cloth. (The concept and term "incorporation" were always anathema to

[1] See, for example, his solo dissenting opinions in *Hurtado v. California*, 110 U.S. 516 (1884); *Maxwell v. Dow*, 176 U.S. 581 (1900); and *Twining v. New Jersey*, 211 U.S. 78 (1908). There were several others—he was a consistent advocate. See Henry J. Abraham, "John Marshall Harlan: The Justice and the Man," *Kentucky Law Journal*, Spring 1958, especially pp. 469-70.
[2] 268 U.S. 652. Gitlow lost, but the carry-over principle was given its first public judicial notice. See pp. 50ff. *infra*.
[3] *Adamson v. California*, 332 U.S. 46.

him. His last publication before his death in retirement in 1965 was another attack on "incorporation" and a defense of "absorption." [1])

> Of all these [43] judges [of the Supreme Court who passed on the question of incorporating the Bill of Rights via the "due process of law" clause of Amendment Fourteen] only one, *who may respectfully be called an eccentric exception,* ever indicated the belief that the Fourteenth Amendment was a shorthand summary of the first eight Amendments, theretofore limiting only the Federal Government, and that due process incorporated those eight Amendments as restrictions upon the powers of the States.[2]

The "eccentric exception" was, of course, Harlan, whose grandson by the very same name became a Frankfurter ally in his posture on the incorporation question when he joined the Court as President Eisenhower's second appointee in 1954.[3]

It was Mr. Justice Black who became the leading protagonist for incorporation—and he seized upon the aforementioned case of *Adamson v. California* [4] to expound his views in what has become one of the most widely known dissenting opinions in the annals of the Court. At issue, briefly, was a provision of California law that permitted court and counsel to comment upon the failure of a defendant to explain or deny evidence against him, thus allowing the court and the jury to consider it in reaching a verdict. Admiral Dewey Adamson, under sentence of death for murder and with past convictions for burglary, larceny, and robbery, chose not to take the stand during his trial, a decision on which both the trial judge and the prosecuting attorney adversely commented. In his appeal, Adamson argued with considerable logic that the California law put him into an impossible situation: if he testified, the previous convictions would thus be revealed to the jury; and if he did not, comments by the judge and prosecutor would, in effect, convert his silence into a confession of guilt. (Only a few other states permitted the California procedure at the time.) In short, he claimed that the adverse comments by the two officials violated his constitutional privilege against compulsory

[1] See his "Memorandum on 'Incorporation' of the Bill of Rights into the Due Process Clause of the Fourteenth Amendment," 78 *Harvard Law Review* 746-83 (1965).

[2] *Adamson v. California, loc. cit.,* at 62. (Italics supplied.)

[3] Eisenhower's first appointee was Earl Warren to succeed the deceased Mr. Chief Justice Fred M. Vinson in 1953.

[4] *Loc. cit.*

self-incrimination under the Fifth Amendment of the federal Constitution, which he deemed incorporated and hence applicable to the states under the "due process of law" clause of the Fourteenth. He lost. The Supreme Court held 5:4, in an opinion written by Mr. Justice Stanley F. Reed for himself, Mr. Chief Justice Vinson, and Associate Justices Robert H. Jackson and Harold H. Burton, that the self-incrimination clause of the Fifth was *not* incorporated or applicable and that the State of California "may control such a situation in accordance with its own ideas of the most efficient administration of criminal justice." [1] Mr. Justice Frankfurter wrote a long concurring opinion in which, as noted above, he took specific issue with the heart of Mr. Justice Black's dissenting opinion.

In his dissent, supported by a 33-page appendix, Black was joined wholly by Mr. Justice Douglas and, in part, by Justices Murphy and Rutledge (who, as we shall see later, wanted to go even beyond the Black position on incorporation). Black's extensive opinion remains the most celebrated analysis of the intention of the framers of the pertinent sentence of Section 1. Elaborately researched, it insisted that one of the chief objects to be accomplished by the first section of the Fourteenth Amendment, "separately, and as a whole," was to apply the *entire* Bill of Rights to the states. In his own words:

> My study of the historical events that culminated in the Fourteenth Amendment, and the expressions of those who opposed its submission and passage, persuades me that one of the chief objects that the provisions of the Amendment's first section, separately, and as a whole, were intended to accomplish was to make the Bill of Rights applicable to the states. With full knowledge of the *Barron* decision, the framers and backers of the Fourteenth Amendment proclaimed its purpose to be to overturn the constitutional rule that case had announced. This historical purpose has never received full consideration or expression in any opinion of this Court interpreting the Amendment. . . .[2]

Responding to Mr. Justice Frankfurter's contrary views and call for more demonstrable proof (where Frankfurter believed none existed) Black made a famous observation:

> I cannot consider the Bill of Rights to be an outworn Eighteenth Century "straight jacket". . . .[3]

[1] *Adamson v. California*, 332 U.S. 46, at 57. (But see pp. 63-5, *infra*, for its overruling in 1964.)
[2] *Ibid.*, at 71-2.
[3] *Ibid.*, at 89.

and concluded:

> I believe [that] the original purpose of the Fourteenth Amendment [was] to extend to all the people of the nation the complete protection of the Bill of Rights. To hold that this Court can determine what, if any, provisions of the Bill of Rights will be enforced, and if so to what degree, is to frustrate the great design of a written Constitution.[1]

Mr. Justice Black, after three decades on the Supreme Court has never wavered from these basic convictions. His stanchest historical-constitutional ally has been Professor Horace Flack. In 1908, after a careful study of the debates of the Thirty-ninth Congress, their newspaper coverage, and the election speeches of members of Congress in the fall of 1866, Flack concluded that Congress

> had the following objects and motives in view for submitting the First Section of the Fourteenth to the states for ratification. First, to make the National Bill of Rights applicable to the states; secondly, to give constitutional validity to the Civil Rights Act; and thirdly, to declare who were the citizens of the United States.[2]

Black's strongest support on the matter of intent of the Founding Fathers in the Constitutional Convention, incidentally—he has had a great deal of support, of course, on the larger modern question of wisdom and advisability of incorporation—has come from a very controversial source: Professor W. W. Crosskey of the University of Chicago, whose over-all thesis of the intent of the Founding Fathers in his mammoth work, *Politics and the Constitution in the History of the United States*,[3] represents a drastic departure from generally accepted constitutional history and law.[4]

Black's opinion was soon challenged in almost every detail by Professor Charles Fairman of the Harvard Law School, a leading expert on constitutionalism, in an article in the *Stanford Law Review*.[5] Fairman accused Black of deliberate distortion of the verities of the debates in

[1] *Ibid*.
[2] Horace Flack, *The Adoption of the Fourteenth Amendment* (Baltimore: The Johns Hopkins University Press, 1908), p. 94.
[3] (Chicago: University of Chicago Press, 1953), Vol. II, Ch. 31.
[4] Crosskey, among his many controversial re-interpretations of the Constitution, suggested *inter alia*, that I-8-3 (the congressional power over interstate commerce) was intended to eschew any and all distinctions between *inter*- and *intra*-state trade.
[5] "Does the Fourteenth Amendment Incorporate the Bill of Rights? The Original Understanding," 2 *Stanford Law Review* (December 1949).

the Thirty-ninth Congress to prove his point. In a companion article in the same issue,[1] Professor Stanley Morrison, of the Stanford University School of Law, seconded Fairman's rejection of Black's thesis. But Morrison did so with considerably less vehemence, and not so much on the basis of what was said during the congressional debates as on the strength of the judicial history of the clause following the Amendment's adoption. Noting only that the elder Harlan had consistently supported Black's incorporation interpretation, Morrison sided with Frankfurter's analysis and statistics in his concurring opinion in the *Adamson* case.[2] He refers to the refusal of such "libertarian activist" justices as Holmes, Brandeis, Stone, Hughes [sic], and Cardozo to incorporate the Bill of Rights and *seems* to score a telling point by recalling that Black himself did not dissent from Cardozo's famous majority opinion in the 1937 *Palko* case [3] (see pp. 54ff. *infra*). Cardozo's opinion established a hierarchy of basic human rights which would henceforth be considered applicable to the states via Amendment Fourteen—those "implicit in the concept of ordered liberty"—while at the same time establishing a *non-applicable* group.[4]

It is only fair to note at once here in Black's defense, however, that (a) he had just joined the Court a few weeks earlier; (b) thus he might well have believed that it would be ungracious as well as foolhardy to proclaim a new jurisprudential posture; (c) the Cardozo majority opinion did, after all, announce the incorporation of the most precious of all basic human freedoms, notably First Amendment rights; and (d) as Black himself explained anew in a footnote to his dissent in *Griswold v. Connecticut* twenty-eight years after *Palko*, he "agreed to follow" the Palko rule as a second-best method to "make [at least some of the] Bill of Rights safeguards applicable to the States." [5] Although less dramatically critical than Fairman, Morrison does suggest that Black clearly had an ulterior motive in his interpretation of the events surrounding the framing of the Fourteenth Amendment: the establishing of a rule of law for civil rights and liberties that would be both drastic and simple and that would guar-

---

[1] "Does the Fourteenth Amendment Incorporate the Bill of Rights? The Judicial Interpretation," *ibid.*, p. 140
[2] *Adamson v. California, loc. cit.*
[3] *Palko v. Connecticut,* 302 U.S. 319.
[4] Among the latter were the Fifth Amendment's safeguards against double jeopardy (at issue in *Palko*) and compulsory self-incrimination (at issue in *Adamson*).
[5] 381 U.S. 479, at 526, n. 21.

antee certainty for all future litigation, the carrying-over in *toto* of the Bill of Rights via Amendment Fourteen, through either its "due process" or its "privileges and immunities" clause.

A fifth protagonist, Professor J. B. James of Georgia Wesleyan College, in his 1956 book *The Framing of the Fourteenth Amendment*,[1] agrees with Fairman and Morrison that Black's facile and sweeping interpretation of the congressional debates of 1866 is erroneous—but only *because* it is so sweeping and facile! With some reservations, James does share Black's and Flack's conclusion that, on balance, the Amendment's framers did intend to incorporate the Bill of Rights. Although such a thought may have been entirely foreign to the collective majority who supported its passage, James, as did Flack, presents strong evidence that the Amendment's floor managers indeed intended its incorporation.[2] This is particularly true of Representative Bingham, the author of the pertinent provisions of Section 1, whom Black called "the Madison of [that section] of the Fourteenth Amendment." Contrary to James's and other earlier belief, we now know that, significantly, Bingham *was* fully aware of the Supreme Court's decision in *Barron v. Baltimore* [3] when he led the debates on Amendment Fourteen in Congress.[4] As a matter of fact, it was this ruling, he said, which made necessary "the adopting of [the Fourteenth] Amendment." [5] Certain in his belief that the Bill of Rights was designed to be *national* in scope, Bingham argued on the floor that had the Thirty-

---

[1] (Urbana: University of Illinois). He had already explained this in considerable detail in *Adamson*, where he wrote: "If the choice must be between the selective process of the Palko decision applying some of the Bill of Rights to the states, or the Twining rule applying none of them, I would choose the Palko selective process. But rather than accept either of these choices I would follow what I believe was the original purpose of the Fourteenth Amendment —to extend to all of the people of the nation the complete protection of the Bill of Rights." (332 U.S. 46, at 89.)

[2] E.g. James, *op. cit.*, pp. 85, 130, *et seq.*

[3] 7 Peters 243 (1833).

[4] See *Congressional Globe*, 39th Congress, 1st Session (Washington, D.C.: Blair and Rives, 1866), pp. 1088-90.

[5] *Ibid.*, p. 1089. In 1871, during a debate on the now ratified Amendment, Bingham observed that in 1865-66 he had closely "reexamined" Marshall's decision in *Barron*, wherein the Chief Justice had stated that "had the framers of these Amendments [I-VIII] intended them to be limitations on the power of state governments, they would have imitated the framers of the Original Constitution and have expressed their intention." Bingham then significantly added, "acting upon this suggestion I did imitate the framers of the Original Constitution." (*The Globe*, 42nd Congress, 1st Session, 1871, Appendix, p. 150.)

ninth Congress meant the Bill of Rights to be solely applicable to the
federal government, the wording of the Amendment's Section 1 would
have so stated. James demonstrates quite convincingly that when
Bingham and Republican Senator Jacob M. Howard of Michigan, the
Amendment's floor manager in the upper house, spoke of the "fundamental rights of free men," they specifically meant the Bill of Rights.
They wanted the proposed Amendment to overrule *Barron v. Baltimore!*

Senator Howard, as a matter of fact, clearly and demonstrably insisted that the national Bill of Rights *in its entirety* was incorporated
into Section 1, a section which in his judgment embodied not only
the "privileges and immunities" of Article IV, Paragraph 2, of the
Constitution, but also all those rights guaranteed by the first eight
amendments to the Constitution. Thus, in explaining the contents of
the Amendment, he stated:

> To these privileges and immunities [Art. IV, ¶ 2], whatever they may
> be for they are not and cannot be fully defined . . . to these should
> be added the personal rights guaranteed and secured by the first eight
> amendments to the Constitution.[1]

Enumerating these, he then continued:

> [T]hese are secured to citizens solely as citizens of the United States,
> . . . they do not operate in the slightest degree as restraints or pro-
> hibitions upon state legislation. . . . The great object of the first section
> of this amendment is, therefore, to restrain the power of the states and
> compel them at all times to respect these fundamental guarantees.[2]

Nonetheless, Professor Fairman, with some support from Professor
Morrison, still insists that the use of the phrases "fundamental rights"
or "fundamental guarantees" specifically intended to *exclude* the
Bill of Rights. Fairman does admit that Senator Howard expressly
stated that the "privileges and immunities" clause of Section 1 should
be construed as embracing what Howard termed "the personal rights"
of the first eight amendments of the Bill of Rights. But Fairman insists that Bingham merely "talked around the point." The historians
Kelly and Harbison, on the other hand, side with James's and Flack's
historical (and, incidentally, Black's constitutional) interpretation
and state flatly that Bingham and Howard not only agreed that the

---

[1] *The Globe, op. cit.,* 39th Congress, p. 2765.
[2] *Ibid.*

"privileges and immunities" clause "incorporated the entire federal Bill of Rights as a limitation upon the states," but that the "due process" clause was lifted from the Fifth Amendment and thus "became a guarantee against state action." [1]

A Verdict? Regardless of personal intellectual and emotional commitments on the basic question of incorporation, the various positions indicate how speculative history can be and may become. To psychoanalyze the actors on the historical stage is good fun, and indeed welcome in the behavioristic developments of the social sciences, but to derive authentic answers, particularly as to the actor's intent, is a delicate and difficult task. The famed German historian Leopold von Ranke's exhortation that it is essential to determine "*wie es eigentlich gewesen*" [2] is noble and human, but at times futile. However, such evidence as the history of the debates provides, together with informed, if not always entirely objective, analysis of those who have supported incorporation, seems to substantiate Professor James's basic point that we need not accept Mr. Justice Black's expansive evaluation of the events of the Thirty-ninth Congress to side with his basic conclusion. There seems relatively little doubt that the Amendment's principal framers and managers, Representative Bingham and Senator Howard, if not every member of the majority in the two houses of Congress, did indeed believe the Bill of Rights to be made generally applicable to the several states via one or more segments of Section 1. And *no* member of that Congress, before he voted on the Amendment, contradicted Bingham's and Howard's final statements to that extent.[3]

[1] Alfred H. Kelly and Winfred A. Harbison, *The American Constitution: Its Origin and Development*, 3d ed. (New York: W. W. Norton & Co., 1963), p. 461.

[2] "How it actually was." (Ranke lived from 1795 to 1886.)

[3] Flack, *op. cit.*, pp. 81, 87. On the entire controversy, see also Ch. 3, "The Nationalization of the Bill of Rights," of Arthur A. North, S.J., *The Supreme Court: Judicial Process and Judicial Politics* (New York: Appleton-Century-Crofts, 1966). For its specific relevance to the desegregation-segregation issues of the 1950's and 1960's, see the lengthy and learned essay, "The Original Understanding and the Segregation Decision," by Alexander M. Bickel in his *Politics and the Warren Court* (New York: Harper & Row, 1965), pp. 211-61. Bickel's conclusion is that the authors of the Fourteenth Amendment ultimately chose language which would be capable of growth. It follows that "the record of history, properly understood, left the way open to, in fact invited, a decision based on the moral and material state of the Union in 1954, not 1866" (p. 261).

This conclusion does not, however, necessitate concurrence with the matter of the *wisdom* of such an incorporation, nor with the judicial formulae devised therefore.[1] Nor does it gainsay the fact that when Senator Howard's "privilege and immunities" clause (and his and Representative Bingham's incorporation contentions for it) had its first judicial test in the *Slaughterhouse Cases* [2] a mere five years after the adoption of the Fourteenth Amendment, it sustained a crushing defeat from which it has never recovered.

The Slaughterhouse Cases of 1873. These remarkable cases, also referred to as the "Dual Citizenship" cases, delivered the second of the one-two knockout punches to the theory of a national applicability of the Bill of Rights, the first punch being *Barron v. Baltimore* [3] 42 years earlier. It will be recalled that in *Barron* the unanimous Court ruled that the Bill was *not* applicable to the several states, either by expressed or by implied language. The *Slaughterhouse Cases* not only reconfirmed the *Barron* holding but went considerably further by ruling that the "privileges and immunities" clause of the Fourteenth Amendment did not, and was not intended to, protect the rights of *federal* citizenship, but solely those of *state* citizenship. In the words of this never overruled decision written for the narrow 5:4 majority [4] by Mr. Justice Samuel F. Miller of Kentucky:

> It is quite clear, then, that *there is a citizenship of the United States, and a citizenship of a state, which are distinct from each other,* and which depend upon different characteristics or circumstances in the individual.[5]

The cases had arisen as a result of a statute regulating the livestock slaughtering business, which had been enacted by the Louisiana Reconstruction government in 1867. In the law, its "carpetbag" [6] legislature (unquestionably under corrupt influence) had conferred upon a single firm what, to all intents and purposes, constituted a monopoly

---

[1] See pp. 46ff., *infra.*
[2] *The Butchers' Benevolent Association of New Orleans v. Crescent City Live-Stock Landing and Slaughter-House Co.,* 16 Wallace 36 (1873).
[3] 7 Peters 243 (1833).
[4] With Miller were Associate Justices Nathan Clifford (Maine), David Davis (Illinois), William Strong (Pennsylvania), and Ward Hunt (New York).
[5] *Loc. cit.,* at 74.
[6] "Carpetbagger" denotes a Northerner who went South after the Civil War to obtain office or employment by morally questionable and often corrupt methods.

of the New Orleans slaughterhouse business, preventing some one thousand firms and persons already established in the city from continuing in that activity. A number of the adversely affected parties filed suit in the courts of Louisiana, largely basing their complaint on alleged violation of their rights under the Fourteenth Amendment. Losing in the lower courts, they ultimately reached the State Supreme Court, which was equally unsympathetic to their claim and held that the contested Louisiana law was a valid and legal exercise of the state police power.[1] The aggrieved litigants then appealed to the United States Supreme Court.

Although four main constitutional issues were raised by the opponents of the Louisiana monopoly statute, the chief concern of the Court in its majority opinion was with the appellants' crucial contention that the law constituted a *prima facie* violation of that portion of Section 1 of Amendment Fourteen which states that "No State shall make or enforce any law which shall abridge the privileges of citizens of the United States. . . ."[2] In other words, the basic claim of the aggrieved businessmen was that the quoted clause clearly implied, indeed commanded, the protection of all civil rights and liberties *by the federal government* and that the several states could not, on pain of violating the Fourteenth Amendment, deny or abridge any rights accruing to citizens of the United States residing within their borders.

But the majority of five justices rejected this contention out of hand. They would have no part of this, or any related, notions of incorporating, of "carrying over," the prerogatives of the Bill of Rights so as to make them applicable to the states. Moreover, the Miller decision absolved the federal government from any obligation to protect "privileges and immunities" against state violation, a logical induction from his basic premise that the *states* had the obligation to protect not only the rights guaranteed by their own bills of rights but the entire body of rights and liberties under the common law.

---

[1] Accruing to the states under Article X of the Bill of Rights, the "police power" is generally regarded as embracing and extending to these concepts of state authority: (1) health; (2) welfare; (3) morals; (4) safety; (5) regulation of business (and labor and agricultural) activities.

[2] The other three were that the statute (1) created an "involuntary servitude" forbidden by Amendment Thirteen; (2) denied the appellants the "equal protection of the laws" under Amendment Fourteen; and (3) deprived them of their property "without due process of law," also safeguarded by Fourteen.

In short, the majority's decision meant that the "privileges and immunities" clause of the newly enacted Amendment really *meant nothing at all* insofar as the states were concerned. As has been well pointed out by one close student of the *Slaughterhouse Cases*, the Court's distinction between state and national citizenship made of the "P and I Clause," as it is commonly called, a mere tautology since the rights of "citizens in the several states" could never have been *constitutionally* abridged by any state, anyway. Thus, "the labors of the framers of the Fourteenth Amendment were nullified by a few strokes of Mr. Justice Miller's pen." [1] But *why?* The question is a natural one, given the history of the adoption of the Amendment (no matter which version) and the general acquaintance of all the justices with the activities and debates in the Thirty-ninth Congress. In the opinion of most competent observers, the Court majority was simply unwilling to permit such a far-reaching alteration in the ante-bellum federal system—the relation of state and federal governments—by an "ambiguous" amendment to the Constitution.[2] Consequently, the majority of five expounded the at least quite plausible conception of dual citizenship, by which practically all common private rights were removed from the federal sphere of control.[3] The majority also believed (and this idea was widely held at the time, as we have noted) that the overriding, if not the sole, purpose of Amendment Fourteen was the protection of the Negro.

But what, then, about existing "privileges and immunities" of *national* citizenship, which, by its own admission and by its creation of a "dual citizenship" the majority held to be protected against action by state governments? The Miller opinion avoided precise definitions and limits, but it suggested the appropriateness of the following "rights" of the national citizen:

> to come to the seat of government to assert any claim he may have upon that government, to transact any business he may have with it, to seek its protection, to share its offices, to engage in administering its functions . . . of free access to its seaports . . . to the subtreasuries, land offices, and courts of justice in the several states . . . to demand

---

[1] Loren P. Beth, "The Slaughterhouse Cases—Revisited," 23 *Louisiana Law Review* 487 (April 1963), at 492.
[2] *Ibid.*, p. 493.
[3] Kelly and Harbison, *op. cit.*, pp. 502-6.

the care and protection of the Federal government over his life, liberty, and property when on the high seas or within the jurisdiction of a foreign government . . . the writ of habeas corpus . . . to use the navigable waters of the United States, however they may penetrate the territory of the several States. . . .[1]

Also on his list, significantly re-emphasized as "rights of the citizen guaranteed by the *Federal* Constitution" were the "right[s] to peaceable assembly and petition for redress of grievances. . . ." [2] This represents, of course, a line of reasoning typical of the non-incorporation argument, then and today: that the Fourteenth Amendment extended no "rights" to citizens of the United States; that most of their rights remained in more or less the same status as before, existing under *state* protection rather than national protection; that the "citizens" presumably protected by the "P and I Clause" are "citizens" only in the sense that they are "citizens" of the United States—emphatically not in their capacity as *state* citizens.[3] As pointed out before, this kind of reasoning renders the Fourteenth Amendment useless as a legal tool, for no state could ever constitutionally abridge or deny the rights of "citizens in the several states." Thus, all that remained of the Amendment, given the majority's reasoning in the *Slaughterhouse Cases*, was a vague, generally accepted, understanding that it was intended to bring about citizenship for the Negro.

Of the three dissenting opinions by Associate Justices Noah H. Swayne, Stephen J. Field, and Joseph P. Bradley the most important was Field's, in which Mr. Chief Justice Salmon P. Chase concurred.[4] Although Field did begin his long judicial career [5] with a general inclination in favor of individual rights, this bias ultimately resolved

[1] The *Slaughterhouse Cases*, 16 Wallace 36 (1873), at 73-5.
[2] *Ibid.*
[3] The controversy recalls that James Wilson, one of Pennsylvania's delegates to the Constitutional Convention of 1787, had made a point of calling the attention of his fellow delegates to the fact that the Constitution, if ratified, would create a dual citizenship—but the significance of this was both overlooked and misunderstood.
[4] Field, whose longevity in service on the Court—almost 35 years—still constitutes a record, will be remembered in the annals of constitutional law and development primarily as the "spokesman of rugged American individualism and laissez faire." (Rocco J. Tresolini, *American Constitutional Law*, 2d. ed. [New York: The Macmillan Co., 1965], p. 742.)
[5] He served on the California Supreme Court for six and a half years before his elevation by President Lincoln in 1863.

itself into a "special emphasis on the sanctity of economic freedom." [1] Field's *Slaughterhouse* dissent is therefore deceptive in its over-all implications, for it does argue angrily for an interpretation of the Fourteenth Amendment and its "P and I Clause" that would insist upon man's "fundamental rights, privileges, and immunities which belong to him as a free man and a free citizen." [2] To Field, the citizenship clause made state citizenship both subordinate to and derivative of national citizenship. As a result of Section 1 of Amendment Fourteen, he argued, "a citizen of a state is now only a citizen of the United States *residing* in that state." [3] But as those familiar with the denouement of Field's jurisprudence know, his cardinal argument against the majority decision was based not so much on the cause of basic human freedoms as it was on the doctrine of vested property rights—a cause he was to espouse throughout his long tenure with consistency, self-assurance, and emotion. For Field, *the* "privilege" and/or "immunity" that was at issue here was the absolute right to engage in the business of butchering. Louisiana's statutory interference with that right was to Field the crime *par excellence* of a governmental roadblock in the path of Darwinian-Spencerian economics.[4] For him, as McCloskey observed, "the property right is the transcendent value; political ambition ranks next when it is relevant; and the cause of human or civil rights is subordinate to these higher considerations." [5] Field's dissenting opinion was thus of but limited comfort to those who looked toward a "nationalization" of basic human rights and liberties. When he spoke of the "equality of right" to labor freely, he looked toward that period of half a century when the Supreme Court would strike hard at any legislative (and administrative) action it deemed violated the sanctity of property, of the "freedom of contract" concept it was soon to read into the "due process of law" clause of both the Fifth and the Fourteenth Amend-

---

[1] Robert G. McCloskey, *American Conservatism in the Age of Enterprise* (Cambridge: Harvard University Press, 1951), pp. 122-3.

[2] The *Slaughterhouse Cases, loc. cit.,* at 95.

[3] *Ibid.* (Italics supplied.)

[4] Oversimply, perhaps, but quite appropriately, this was Field's philosophy of the survival of the fittest in terms of classical nineteenth-century capitalism.

[5] McCloskey, *op. cit.,* pp. 122-3. A considerably more charitable view of Field's stance is taken by Arthur A. North, S.J., in *The Supreme Court: Judicial Process and Judicial Politics* (New York: Appleton-Century-Crofts, 1966), pp. 91-6. He flatly states that not only Harlan but Field and Brewer "accepted the theory" of incorporation (*ibid.,* p. 96).

ments.[1] Except for a handful of instances,[2] and particularly when they involved a charge against a state for cruel and unusual punishment, Field found no such justification for protection of the basic freedoms of the Bill of Rights, however—and he was disdainful of his long-time colleague John Marshall Harlan's advocacy of total incorporation.

Nonetheless, the Field dissent served to dramatize both the interest in the meaning of the most important of the Civil War Amendments and its possible role as a catalyst in a "nationalization" of basic rights and liberties. The *Slaughterhouse* holding of a "dual citizenship" has never been overruled, and the "P and I Clause" of Amendment Fourteen has been more or less outflanked ever since.[3] Not so the "due process of law" and the "equal protection of the laws" clauses, however. To the former and the incorporation problem we can now return, noting en route the stinging criticism of *Slaughterhouse* by one of the earliest American formal political scientists, John W. Burgess, who pronounced the decision "entirely erroneous" from whatever view he regarded it, be that "historical, political, or juristic."[4] As he wrote in 1890 in his classic two-volume work, *Political Science and Comparative Constitutional Law:*

[1] To Field's great satisfaction, the word "person" in the latter clause was extended to corporations in 1886 in the *Santa Clara County v. Southern Pacific Railroad Co.*, 118 U.S. 394.

[2] *Neal v. Delaware*, 103 U.S. 379 (1880); *Bush v. Connecticut*, 107 U.S. 110 (1882); *In re Kemmler*, 136 U.S. 436 (1890); *McElvaine v. Brush*, 142 U.S. 155 (1891); and *O'Neil v. Vermont*, 144 U.S. 323 (1892). In the last-named case he did, however, note the following in his dissent:

> While, therefore, the ten Amendments, as limitations on power, and, so far as they accomplish their purpose and find their fruition in such limitations, are applicable to the Federal Government and not to the States, yet, so far as they declare or recognize the rights of persons, they are rights belonging to them as citizens of the United States under the Constitution; and the Fourteenth Amendment, as to all such rights, places a limit upon state power by ordaining that no State shall make or enforce any law which shall abridge them. If I am right in this view, then every citizen of the United States is protected from punishments which are cruel and unusual. (*Ibid.*, at 363.)

[3] After the Reconstruction government was turned out of office in Louisiana, the *Slaughterhouse* statute was promptly repealed. Then the *monopoly* went to court, claiming violation of its due process of law under Amendment Fourteen. But, with Mr. Justice Miller again writing the opinion, the due process claim lost 9:0 (*Butcher's Union Slaughter-House v. Crescent City Live-Stock Landing Co.*, 111 U.S. 746, in 1884.)

[4] *Political Science and Comparative Constitutional Law* (Boston: Ginn & Co., 1890), I, 226.

I say that if history has taught us anything in political science, it is that *civil liberty is national in its origin, content and sanction.* ... if there is but a single lesson to be learned from the history of the United States, it is this: Seventy years of debate and four years of terrible war turn substantially upon this issue, in some part or other; and when the Nation triumphed in the great appeal to arms, and addressed itself to the work of readjusting the forms of law to the now undoubted condition of fact, it gave its first attention to the nationalization in constitutional law of the domain of civil liberty. *There is no doubt that those who framed the thirteenth and fourteenth amendments intended to occupy the whole ground and thought that they had done so.* The opposition charged that these amendments would nationalize the whole sphere of civil liberty; the majority accepted the view; and the legislation of Congress for their elaboration and enforcement proceeded upon that view. In the face of all these well known facts it was hardly to be doubted that ... [the Supreme Court] *would unanimously declare the whole domain of civil liberty to be under its protection against both the general government and the commonwealths.* Great, therefore, was the surprise ... when the decision in the *Slaughterhouse Cases* was announced. . . ." [1]

Whatever one's conclusions regarding the intent of the framers of the Fourteenth Amendment and its role as a vehicle for the applicability of the Bill of Rights to the several states, we know that *there has been* piecemeal "incorporation" or "nationalization" or "absorption" of the Bill of Rights, by judicial interpretation and, as we shall see later, it has come about at an increasing rate since Mr. Justice Sanford's limited initial acceptance of the concept in 1925. Therefore, we now turn to the historical evolution of the incorporation issue, followed by a consideration of the various judicial "positions" on, and the wisdom of, incorporation.

The Evolution of "Incorporation"

Pre-1937 Developments

The 1833 *Barron v. Baltimore* [2] decision firmly shut the judicial *cum* constitutional door on any notions of incorporation until the passage of the Fourteenth Amendment in 1868; the *Slaughterhouse*

---

[1] *Ibid.,* pp. 225-6. (Italics supplied.)
[2] 7 Peters 243.

Cases [1] locked it in 1873; and matters seemed to be settled, *res adjudicata*.[2]

Mr. Justice Harlan. Only Harlan, the one-time Kentucky slaveholder,[3] continued to raise the incorporation problem with both conviction and consistency. The outspoken Hayes appointee would never fail in appropriate cases—of which there really were not very many—to write impassioned opinions in dissent, urging his associates to accept the principle of the nationalization of the Bill of Rights.

Harlan's solitary dissenting opinions in three well-known cases demonstrated his unshakeable belief that the Fourteenth Amendment was intended to incorporate the *entire* Bill of Rights. The first of these, *Hurtado v. California* (1884),[4] turned on the question of whether California's substitution of the practice of "information" [5] for indictment by a grand jury constituted a violation of the "due process" guarantees of the Fourteenth Amendment because of the requirements of the Fifth Amendment. Hurtado was tried on the basis of "information," convicted of murder, and sentenced to be hanged. His appeal to the United States Supreme Court accordingly alleged deficient procedural due process. But the Court, in a 7:1 decision, delivered by Mr. Justice Stanley Matthews, rejected that contention, ruling that the substitution of "information" for a grand jury indictment did not violate due process of law because it was merely a "preliminary proceeding" and thus not essential to due process. Harlan's scholarly and exhaustive dissenting opinion not only disagreed with the majority's analysis, but argued powerfully his belief that the Bill of Rights *is* incorporated via that clause of Amendment Fourteen: "There are principles of liberty and justice lying at the foundation of our civil and political institutions which no state can

[1] 16 Wallace 36.

[2] *Res adjudicata* (or *res judicata*) connotes authoritative settled law. In other words, it represents *the* essential law involved.

[3] See the Harlan symposium in the Spring 1958 issue of the *Kentucky Law Journal*. Also, Henry J. Abraham, "John Marshall Harlan: A Justice Neglected," 41 *Virginia Law Review* 871 (November 1955).

[4] 110 U.S. 516.

[5] "Information" is a common law practice whereby the prosecuting officer merely submits his charges in the form of an affidavit of evidence, supported by sworn statements, to a trial court. It is still used widely by the states and, to a much lesser degree, by the federal government, in civil and non-capital criminal cases at the district court level.

violate consistently with that due process of law required by the 14th Amendment in proceedings involving life, liberty or property." [1] The second case, *Maxwell v. Dow*,[2] came sixteen years later. Not only was the matter of the substitution of "information" for a grand jury indictment again present—this time by Utah—but an important collateral issue was at stake: Maxwell's trial by a jury of eight instead of twelve. Convicted of the crime of robbery, Maxwell claimed that he had been deprived of both "due process of law" and his "privileges and immunities" as a United States citizen, that the Bill of Rights' Fifth and Sixth Amendments, guaranteeing grand jury indictment and trial by jury, respectively, were incorporated via Amendment Fourteen. "No, not at all," said the Supreme Court, with Mr. Justice Rufus W. Peckham speaking for the 8:1 majority. Not only was there no violation of due process by the procedures employed by Utah, wrote Peckham, but neither the "due process" nor the "P and I Clause" comprehended the rights listed in the federal Bill of Rights. In short, any thoughts of incorporation were to be rejected out of hand:

> . . . when the Fourteenth Amendment prohibits abridgment by the states of those privileges and immunities which [the individual] enjoys as such citizen, it is not correct or reasonable to say that it covers and extends to certain rights which he does not enjoy by reason of his citizenship, but simply because those rights exist in favor of all individuals as against Federal government powers.[3]

Harlan, of course, was not impressed by this reasoning; scoffing at what he regarded as deliberate blindness and verbal gymnastics, he reiterated his *Hurtado* view that, indeed, the Fourteenth Amendment intended to incorporate the entire Bill of Rights. "No judicial tribunal," he warned, "has authority to say that some of [the Bill of Rights] may be abridged by the States while others may not be abridged." [4] The last example of Harlan's lone stand on the issue was the 1908 case of *Twining v. New Jersey*,[5] which involved the controversial constitutional guarantee against compulsory self-incrimination. Twining and an associate, Cornell, had been indicted by a New Jersey grand jury for having deliberately and knowingly displayed a false paper to

[1] *Hurtado v. California, loc. cit.,* at 546.
[2] 176 U.S. 581 (1900).
[3] *Ibid.,* at 595-6.
[4] *Ibid.,* at 616.
[5] 211 U.S. 78.

a bank examiner with full intent to deceive him as to the actual condition of their firm. At the trial the two defendants neither called witnesses nor took the stand in their own defense. Very much in the fashion of the trial judge in *Adamson v. California*,[1] the *Twining* trial judge commented from the bench on the defendants' failure to do so. His charge to the jury contained the following significant statements:

> Because a man does not go upon the stand you are not necessarily justified in drawing an inference of guilt. But you have a right to consider the fact that he does not go upon the stand where a direct accusation is made against him.

The jury returned a verdict of guilty as charged against both defendants. They ultimately appealed to the United States Supreme Court, contending first, that the exemption from self-incrimination is one of the privileges and immunities of citizens of the United States which the Fourteenth Amendment forbids the states to abridge, and second, that the alleged compulsory self-incrimination constituted a denial of due process of law. This time Mr. Justice William H. Moody spoke for another 8:1 majority that again rejected not only the specific contentions but the larger issue of the Bill of Rights' incorporation. "Is the right so fundamental in due process," asked Moody rhetorically, "that its refusal is a denial of due process?" "By no means," he responded, "it is nothing more than a just and useful principle of law." Again Harlan repeated his plea for incorporation, based on what he continued to regard as the commands of the Constitution. Until he died in 1911, he endeavored, with utter lack of success, to convince at least a bare majority of his colleagues of the correctness of his position. But he was not to see the victory that was to come from future judicial interpretations by the mid-1960's. Well might one of his biographers write that Harlan had always

> maintained an unswerving faith in the role of the Supreme Court as defender of the citizen's liberties and guardian of American constitutional ideals. . . .[2]

So he had indeed, and not only in the realm of incorporation as we shall have occasion to see later.[3]

[1] 332 U.S. 46 (1947).
[2] Alan F. Westin, "John Marshall Harlan and the Constitutional Rights of Negroes: The Transformation of a Southerner," 66 *Yale Law Journal* 710 (1957).
[3] See, for example, his most famous of all dissents, in *Plessy v. Ferguson*, 163 U.S. 537 (1896).

The Gitlow Case. Despite the rising concern expressed for civil rights and liberties by Justices Holmes and Brandeis, who joined the Court in 1902 and 1916, respectively, incorporation of the Bill of Rights lay unattended until 1925 when it received its first official judicial recognition on a *partial* basis in the famous case of *Gitlow v. New York.*[1]

Benjamin Gitlow, an active exponent of extreme left-wing causes and a member of the most radical wing of the Socialist Party, had run afoul of New York State's Criminal Anarchy Act of 1902. He was tried and convicted for having "advocated, advised, and taught the duty, necessity, and propriety of overthrowing and overturning organized government by force, violence, and unlawful means by certain writings" (the "Left Wing Manifesto" and "The Revolutionary Age"). He appealed his conviction through the appropriate New York State courts to the United States Supreme Court, alleging that the New York statute violated both the Fourteenth Amendment's due process clause and the freedom of speech guarantees of the First. Gitlow lost on his basic claims, for the Court ruled 7:2 that the statute neither violated due process in general nor free speech in particular. However, while clearing Mr. Gitlow's path to a New York jail, the author of the Supreme Court's majority opinion, Mr. Justice Sanford, made judicial history by announcing the first incorporation of two aspects of the Bill of Rights, speech and press:

> For present purposes we may and do assume that freedom of speech and of the press—which are now protected by the First Amendment from abridgement by Congress—*are among the fundamental personal rights and "liberties" protected by the due process clause of the Fourteenth Amendment from impairment by the States....*[2]

Sanford had indeed made judicial-constitutional history. His renowned *dictum,*[3] as quoted, was fully subscribed to by all of his colleagues, including, of course, Justices Holmes and Brandeis. That the two dissented was not because of the incorporation announcement, but, as we shall have occasion to assess in connection with freedom of expression in Chapter V, because they simply did not believe that Gitlow's

[1] 268 U.S. 652.
[2] *Ibid.,* at 666. (Italics supplied.)
[3] Properly known as *obiter dictum,* it is a statement of opinion by a judge that is not necessary to the conclusion on the merits of the case.

action presented any "clear and present" danger [1] to the State of New York. Drawing the kind of line that we discussed in Chapter I, Mr. Justice Holmes pointed out that "every idea is an incitement," that "eloquence may set fire to reason...." But regardless of Mr. Benjamin Gitlow's defeat—in later days he became an informant for the government in subversive activities matters [2]—the "carry-over" doctrine concerning the Fourteenth Amendment had been officially enunciated.

The Doctrine Confirmed and Expanded. That the Gitlow incorporation development was neither a fluke nor a passing pronouncement in *dictum* soon became apparent. Only two years later, the Supreme Court, again speaking through Mr. Justice Sanford, confirmed unanimously the nationalization of *freedom of speech* in the case of *Fiske v. Kansas*.[3] Here, for the first time, it upheld a personal liberty claim under the Fourteenth Amendment, ruling specifically that a Kansas criminal syndicalism statute—very similar to the New York one in *Gitlow*—did indeed violate the due process clause of the Fourteenth Amendment, as applied to Mr. Fiske, because of the free speech strictures of the First Amendment. Incorporation of *freedom of the press* followed not long thereafter in the well-known 1931 prior-censorship case of *Near v. Minnesota*.[4] In *Near*, speaking for a majority of five, Mr. Chief Justice Hughes declared unconstitutional, as "an infringement of the liberty of the press guaranteed by the Fourteenth Amendment," the so-called Minnesota Gag Law, which permitted prior restraint from publishing under certain circumstances.

Less than a year later, the incorporation doctrine moved out of the realm of the First Amendment and, for the first time, into the area of the guarantee of a fair trial, in general, and *counsel in capital criminal cases*, in particular. The vehicle was the first of the notorious "Scottsboro Cases," [5] *Powell v. Alabama*,[6] which was destined to become a *cause célèbre* in the records of applications of due process of law to Negro defendants. Writing for a majority of seven, Mr. Justice

---

[1] That famous doctrine, first enunciated in *Schenck v. United States*, 249 U.S. 47 (1919), by Holmes and Brandeis, will be fully discussed there.

[2] Especially in the 1940's and 1950's (usually at fifty dollars a day). He had served three years of a 5-10 year sentence, being pardoned by Governor Al Smith.

[3] 274 U.S. 380 (1927).

[4] 283 U.S. 697, at 723.

[5] So termed because the accused were all apprehended near the Alabama town of Scottsboro.

[6] 287 U.S. 45 (1932).

George Sutherland overturned the conviction in the Alabama courts of seven indigent, ignorant, minor Negroes, who had been falsely charged with the rape of two white girls, and convicted in a one-day trial in a mob-dominated atmosphere without the benefit of proper defense counsel. Reversing and remanding their conviction to the trial court with a stern call for a fair trial, the Court noted:

> ... the right to counsel ... provided in the Sixth Amendment [as applied to this case] is of such a character that it cannot be denied without violating those "fundamental principles of liberty and justice which lie at the base of all our civil and political institutions".... [It] is obviously one of those compelling considerations which must prevail in determining *whether it is embraced within the due process clause of the Fourteenth Amendment, although it is specifically dealt with in another part of the federal Constitution.* ... the necessity of counsel was so vital and imperative that the failure of the trial court to make an effective appointment of counsel was likewise a denial of due process of law within the meaning of the Fourteenth Amendment....[1]

Sutherland hinted of the applicability of the new role of law to *noncapital* criminal cases as well, but chose to state that it was not necessary to determine that question "now."[2] In any event, new ground had been broken. Justices Pierce Butler and James C. McReynolds dissented from the incorporation phase of the case.

The fourth aspect of the Bill of Rights to be thus nationalized was the First Amendment's guarantee of *freedom of religion* in 1934. This was determined in the interesting and important case of *Hamilton v. Regents of the University of California*.[3] All students at the University of California, a public state institution, were required to take military drill on pain of expulsion. One Albert Hamilton, however, having religious convictions that militated against bearing of arms, refused to participate in the program and was consequently expelled. He went to court contending that his religious beliefs entitled him to exemption by virtue of both Amendments One and Fourteen. When his case reached the United States Supreme Court, Mr. Justice

---

[1] *Ibid.*, at 71.
[2] The Court's ruling in *Betts v. Brady*, 316 U.S. 455 (1942), restricted its application to capital criminal cases, but *Gideon v. Wainwright*, 372 U.S. 335 (1963) extended it to all criminal cases.
[3] 293 U.S. 245.

Butler, speaking for the unanimous Court, ruled that Hamilton's religious convictions were indeed safeguarded by the Bill of Rights, and that freedom of religion was henceforth to be regarded as incorporated via the "due process of law" clause of Amendment Fourteen.[1] However, the Court went on to hold that, notwithstanding the incorporation ruling, Hamilton was *not* entitled to an exemption from the state requirement of military training since, after all, he was not *compelled to attend* the University of California. Because he chose to attend that institution of his own free will, his due process of law was in no sense being violated by a requirement to comply with the University's, i.e. California's, rules and regulations while in attendance.

In 1937, a few months earlier than the landmark-incorporation case of *Palko v. Connecticut* [2] the First Amendment's *freedom of assembly* and, by implication, its freedom "to *petition* the Government for a redress of grievances," became the fifth and sixth segments of the Bill of Rights to be "carried over." *De Jonge v. Oregon* [3] again involved a state criminal syndicalism law. Dirk De Jonge had been indicted in Oregon's Multnomah County under that statute, which made it a criminal offense to advocate "crime, physical violence, sabotage, or any unlawful acts or methods as a means of accomplishing industrial change or political revolution." There was no record that De Jonge had advocated what the statute proscribed, nor was he charged specifically with having done so. The sole charge against him was that he had participated in an advertised political meeting of the Communist Party, of which he was an admitted member. The meeting, concededly peaceful, had been held by the Portland section of the Party to protest alleged brutality and unlawful activity by the Portland police. Speaking for his unanimous Court, Mr. Chief Justice Hughes pointed out that "peaceable assembly for lawful discussion, "however unpopular the sponsorship, cannot be made a crime," and that "the holding of meetings for peaceable political action cannot be proscribed." Further declaring that the right of peaceable assembly "is a right cognate to those of free speech and free press and is

---

[1] Some observers, including North, *op. cit.*, regard this statement as well as a similar one made in the case by Mr. Justice Cardozo's concurring opinion (*ibid.*, at 265) as *dicta*. They prefer to point to *Cantwell v. Connecticut*, decided six years later, as the "incorporator" of the free exercise clause (310 U.S. 296, at 303).

[2] 302 U.S. 319.

[3] 299 U.S. 353 (1937).

equally fundamental," [1] he proceeded to hold that assembly, too, is thus one of "those fundamental principles of liberty and justice" that are made applicable to the states via the due process clause of the Fourteenth Amendment.[2]

Hence, when the *Palko* case appeared on the Court's calendar for decision, the entire First Amendment and counsel of the Sixth at least in capital criminal cases had been firmly incorporated. But what was needed was a more thorough discussion that would deal with the theoretical as well as the practical issues involved in "nationalizing" the Bill of Rights. Appropriately, it fell to the jurist whose pen was probably the most eloquent on the Supreme Court to perform that task: Mr. Justice Benjamin N. Cardozo. His all-too-brief six-year tenure on the Court culminated in *Palko v. Connecticut*.[3]

The Doctrine Spelled-Out: Cardozo and Palko

Frank Palko, not precisely a pillar of the community, had been indicted by the State of Connecticut for murder in the *first* degree for the fatal shooting of two policemen. The trial jury—as juries have been known to do with predictable unpredictability—found him guilty of *second* degree murder, however, and the trial judge accordingly sentenced him to life imprisonment. Pursuant to a statute of 1866, and with the permission of the trial judge in the case, the State of Connecticut then appealed the conviction on the lesser count to the highest state court, the Court of Errors. In its petition Connecticut charged that the action in the trial court constituted "error of law to the prejudice of the state"; the Court of Errors agreed, reversing the judgment below, and ordered a new trial. Although Palko objected that the second trial would place him twice in jeopardy for the same offense or action, forbidden by the terms of the Fifth Amendment and consequently also by those of the due process clause of the Fourteenth, his re-trial took place soon thereafter.

This time the trial jury returned a verdict of murder in the *first* degree, and the trial judge sentenced Palko to death. Having exhausted his judicial remedies at the state level, Palko then appealed to the United States Supreme Court, contending again that "whatever is forbidden by the Fifth Amendment is forbidden by the Fourteenth

[1] *Ibid.*, at 364.
[2] *Ibid.*
[3] 302 U.S. 319 (1937).

also."[1] For reasons to be outlined presently, the Supreme Court, speaking through Mr. Justice Cardozo, ruled against Palko's claims on all counts; Mr. Justice Butler dissented without opinion (an intriguing but not very helpful practice).[2] Frank Palko was subsequently executed. Macabre though it may be, a cynic could comment that, given the importance of his case for the future of civil rights and liberties, he did not die in vain.

The "Honor Roll" of Superior Rights. Mr. Justice Cardozo's opinion was at once recognized as a judicial landmark for several reasons: (1) It established a yardstick by which to measure the incorporation problem, and thus govern judicial action. (2) It provided official judicial recognition for the heretofore unpredictable claim that, under certain conditions, and in certain areas, the several states are beholden to the commands of the federal Bill of Rights via the Fourteenth Amendment. (3) It laid the groundwork for the support of both the theory and the practice of a judicial double standard in the interpretation of basic human rights.[3] Practically speaking, what the Cardozo opinion accomplished was to deny or reject any *general* rule of overall incorporation, while acknowledging that there are, and indeed must be, some rights in the Bill that are fundamental enough to require "incorporation" or "absorption."

Mr. Justice Cardozo's *Palko* opinion thus established the "Honor Roll of Superior Rights," to which his life-long admirer and ultimate successor on the Supreme Court, Felix Frankfurter, so irreverently referred as the "slot machine theory ... some are in and some are out." Although he refused to regard the "due process of law" clause of the Fourteenth Amendment as "shorthand" for the Bill of Rights, Cardozo nonetheless set himself the task of distinguishing those basic rights that he and his supporters viewed as "of the very essence of a scheme of ordered liberty" from those without which "justice would not perish" and which were not therefore "implicit in the concept of

---

[1] *Ibid.*, at 322.

[2] Robert Lewis Shayon told the author in November 1966 that he had discussed the *Palko* case in considerable detail with Frank Palko's court-appointed attorney, David Goldstein, a distinguished Bridgeport, Conn., lawyer. According to Goldstein, Butler's reason for dissenting—even without opinion—was based on his conviction that the State of Connecticut had in effect denied Palko's due process of law. During oral argument, Butler was "very tough" on the state's attorney, at one point shouting, "What do you want? Blood?"

[3] See the discussion in Chapter 2, *supra*.

ordered liberty." Explaining his rationale further, he wrote movingly of "those fundamental principles of liberty and justice which lie at the base of all our civil and political institutions," and of principles of justice "so rooted in the traditions and conscience of our people as to be ranked as fundamental." [1] (It is significant to note the recurrent use of the concept of "fundamental" rights in juxtaposition to what, as we shall see below, are termed "formal" rights on the scale of basic rights and liberties.) [2] Recognizing the difficulties of evaluation and interpretation inherent in his dichotomy, and anticipating both the criticism and some of the problems that would follow, Cardozo resorted to the "freedom of thought and speech" as his cardinal illustration:

> Of that freedom one may say that it is the matrix, the indispensable condition, of nearly every other form of freedom. With rare aberrations, a pervasive recognition of that truth can be traced in our history, political and legal. . . .[3]

For the other group, these "formal" rights in the Bill without which "justice would not perish," Cardozo cited the right to trial by jury and the immunity from prosecution except as a result of an indictment, explaining that, indeed, they may have "value and importance," but

> Even so, they are not of the essence of a scheme of ordered liberty. To abolish them is not to violate a "principle of justice so rooted in the traditions and conscience of our people as to be ranked as fundamental." . . . Few would be so narrow as to maintain that a fair and enlightened system of justice would be impossible without them. . . .[4]

Then, turning specifically to another right, the immunity from compulsory self-incrimination, he noted that "[T]his too might be lost, and justice still be done. . . . Justice . . . would not perish if the accused were subject to a duty to respond to orderly inquiry." [5] Cardozo thus

---

[1] *Ibid.*, at 325.

[2] The Court had established a dichotomy between "formal" and "fundamental" rights at the turn of the century in answering the question how many, and which, of the rights in the Constitution were to be applicable automatically to possessions and territories. The "fundamental" ones only, held the Court in the series of *Insular* cases from 1901 to 1905. See especially *Hawaii v. Mankichi*, 190 U.S. 197 (1903), and *Rasmussen v. United States*, 197 U.S. 516 (1905).

[3] *Palko v. Connecticut, loc. cit.*, at 327.

[4] *Ibid.*, at 325.

[5] *Ibid.*, at 326.

insisted that in the realm of chiefly *procedural* rights, in general, and the protection against double jeopardy at issue in the *Palko* ruling, the question to be posed by the appellate tribunal must be as Mr. Justice Harlan had phrased it: "Does it violate those 'fundamental principles of liberty and justice which lie at the base of all our civil and political institutions?'" "The answer," judged Cardozo, "surely must be 'no.'"

> [Connecticut] is not attempting to wear the accused out by a multitude of cases with accumulated trials. It asks no more than this, that the case against him shall go on until there shall be a trial free from the corrosion of substantial legal error.[1]

And he concluded on a note of assurance: "There is here no seismic innovation. The edifice of justice stands, in its symmetry, to many, greater than before."[2]

A Caveat. It is essential to recognize at once that, despite the *Palko* dichotomy between the components of the Bill of Rights that are and those that are not "implicit in the concept of ordered liberty," Mr. Justice Cardozo made it resolutely clear that the several states would still, of course, be subject to the judicial test of whether or not a duly challenged law or action constituted a violation of the "due process of law" concept of the Fourteenth Amendment *per se*. In other words, simply because only some of the rights are *ipso facto* applicable to the states via the Fourteenth Amendment, it does not mean that the states are free to violate the basic concepts of due process of law to which all persons in their jurisdictions are entitled. In such claims the judicial test then becomes the one so faithfully and ardently embraced by Mr. Justice Frankfurter during his career on the Supreme Court: does the alleged state violation constitute conduct that "shocks the conscience" or, in the somewhat less inhibited language of Mr. Justice Holmes, "does it make you vomit?" Given the divergent status of people's, even jurists', consciences, and the different physiological responses to shock, it is obvious that the answer in individual cases is difficult and often unpredictable! We shall have occasion to return to this particular problem of drawing lines when we consider the various choices or "positions" on the incorporation question offered by justices of the Supreme Court and other knowledgeable participants in the search for justice.

[1] *Ibid.*, at 328.
[2] *Ibid.*, at 328.

Post-Palko Developments

The test devised by Mr. Justice Cardozo in *Palko* permitted, if it did not indeed invite, alteration of the two sides of the newly created incorporation "line." That line, *as of the famous Opinion Monday in 1937*, is shown in this table:

Amendment (or Concept)	"Incorporated"	NOT "Incorporated"
I	Speech.* Press.* Free Exercise of Religion.* Peaceable Assembly.* Right of Petition.	Separation of Church and State.
II		Keep and Bear Arms.
III		No Quartering of Soldiers.
IV		Evidence Admitted as Result of Unreasonable Search and Seizure.*
V	Due Process of Law (as per XIV). Eminent Domain Safeguards.	Grand Jury Indictment.* Double Jeopardy.* Self-Incrimination.*
VI	Counsel in Criminal Cases* (later judicially abridged to read "in Capital" Criminal Cases only—but then reinterpreted to read "All Criminal Cases"). Fair Trial.	Jury Trial in Criminal Cases.* Nature and Cause of Accusation. Compulsory Process for Appearance of Witness. Confrontation of Accusers.
VII	Fair Trial.	Jury Trial in Civil Cases.*
VIII		Excessive Bail and Fines. Cruel and Unusual Punishment.

* Specifically mentioned in the *Palko* opinion by Mr. Justice Cardozo.

As the starred items in the table indicate, Cardozo did not cover each and every aspect of the Bill of Rights. But his language made quite clear that the underlying principles of our federal governmental structure demand that the states be permitted to follow their own practices and discretion in the realm of procedural due process as long as they provide a full measure of "due process of law" in each and every instance.

A 1947 Addition. The Cardozo "Honor Roll" stood for almost a quarter of a century. During that period it was extended only once to include the concept of *separation of Church and State* in the already incorporated exercise of freedom of religion. The vehicle was the 1947 *New Jersey Bus* case,[1] which we shall have occasion to discuss in considerable detail in Chapter VI. Pertinent here is the entire Court's acknowledgement (despite its 5:4 split on the specific merits of the case) that a *bona fide* violation of the principle of the separation of Church and State is constitutionally proscribed by *both* the terms of the First and the "due process of law" clause of the Fourteenth Amendment.

1961: *The Cleveland Search and Seizure Case.* The year 1961 heralded a new burst of judicial activity (some would say "activism"). It was the Fourth Amendment's guarantee against *unreasonable searches and seizures* that was next to be incorporated. The fruit of such seizures had long before ceased to be admissible as evidence in federal court.[2] But although states, too, had been judicially forbidden to engage in *unreasonable* searches and seizures, the traditions of common law nonetheless permitted their results as admissible evidence in court proceedings.[3] Because of her 1961 case, Miss Dolree Mapp, a Cleveland woman of somewhat questionable reputation, has now been enshrined in legal history as the catalyst that carried the federal principle over to the states. Acting on alleged information that Miss Mapp, and possibly her daughter by a former marriage, were hiding (a) a fugitive and (b) "a large amount of policy paraphernalia" in the top floor of their two-story family dwelling, police forced their way into the house without a warrant of any kind and found, after an

---

[1] *Everson v. Board of Education of Ewing Township*, 330 U.S. 1.

[2] *Weeks v. United States*, 232 U.S. 383 (1914).

[3] *Wolf v. Colorado*, 338 U.S. 25 (1949). Here, the Court announced the "incorporation" of the Fourth Amendment's pertinent guarantees, but at once neutralized or negated it by continuing to sanction admissibility of evidence so obtained.

unedifying struggle and a widespread search, some "obscene materials." On the strength of these, Miss Mapp was convicted of illegal possession of obscene materials in violation of an Ohio statute. The Ohio judiciary upheld her conviction, but the Supreme Court, on appeal, reversed it in *Mapp v. Ohio*.[1] Speaking for the 6:3 majority, Mr. Justice Tom C. Clark overruled the long-standing precedents and incorporated the Fourth Amendment's applicable guarantee, ruling that "all evidence obtained by searches and seizures in violation of the Constitution is, by that same authority [Amendment Four], inadmissible in a state court . . ."; and:

> Since the Fourth Amendment's right of privacy has been declared enforceable against the States through the Due Process Clause of the Fourteenth, it is enforceable against them by the same sanction of exclusion as is used against the Federal Government.[2]

The next incorporation came scarcely a year later in a case at the other end of the country.

1962: The California Narcotics Addiction Proof Case. California, a source of considerable litigation on constitutional questions, provided the issue that would bring about the nationalization of the Eighth Amendment's guarantees against the *infliction of "cruel and unusual punishments"* (for which Mr. Justice Field had called seventy years earlier).[3] There exists some doubt as to whether or not the Supreme Court actually intended to incorporate that provision, but the general assumption now is that Mr. Justice Stewart's language did, in effect, apply to the states these basic strictures of the last article of amendment in the Bill of Rights.[4] His allies in that interpretation were the Chief Justice and Justices Black, Douglas, and Brennan; Mr. Justice Harlan concurred, but predictably on a narrower ground: violation of due process of law. Mr. Justice Byron R. White wrote his first dissenting opinion in the case, joined by Mr. Justice Clark. At issue was a California statute making it a crime "to be under the influence of, or be addicted to narcotics, or to make unprescribed use of them," which was punishable by a mandatory 90-day jail sentence.

[1] 367 U.S. 643 (1961).
[2] *Ibid.*, at 655. Federal standards of "reasonableness" were specifically confirmed as applicable to the conduct of state police officers in *Ker v. California*, 374 U.S. 23 (1963).
[3] See pp. 44ff., *supra*.
[4] *Robinson v. California*, 370 U.S. 660 (1962).

One Lawrence Robinson was arrested on a Los Angeles street by police whom he told that he used narcotics; his arms bore what appeared to be hypodermic needle marks. (It is to be noted that the case had nothing to do with the *sale* of narcotics.) He was charged with violation of the statute and sentenced to jail. On appeal, Robinson's counsel successfully raised the "cruel and unusual punishment" issue on the grounds that the law did not require *proof* of purchase or use of the drugs. Accepting this argument for the Court majority, Mr. Justice Stewart declared the statute unconstitutional as a violation of the Eighth and Fourteenth Amendments. As he viewed it, the statute fell into the same category as one purporting to make it a criminal offense "for a person to be mentally ill, or a leper, or to be afflicted with venereal disease." Carrying over the pertinent provision of Amendment Eight, he held:

> ...a state which imprisons a person thus afflicted as a criminal, even though he had never touched any narcotic drug within the state or been guilty of any irregular behavior there, inflicts a cruel and unusual punishment in violation of the Fourteenth Amendment.[1]

In a significant concurring opinion, Mr. Justice Douglas regarded Robinson's conviction of being an addict as the specific "cruel and unusual punishment," not his confinement. Addicts, suggested Douglas, should be cured, not jailed.

1963: Clarence Earl Gideon's Right to Counsel Case. Of far greater significance, because of the sheer numbers of individuals affected, is the celebrated case of *Gideon v. Wainwright.*[2] It is probably the most famous "incorporation-decision" since *Palko.* In effect, it nationalized the right to counsel in *all* criminal cases, *be they capital or non-capital.* As indicated earlier, a good many observers had quietly assumed that Mr. Justice Sutherland's language in the *Scottsboro Case*[3] had fully intended to incorporate all aspects of the right to counsel in criminal cases. This understanding seemed to be confirmed by Mr. Justice Cardozo's choice of words—"the right of one accused of crime to the benefit of counsel"[4]—but the Court held to the contrary in the case of *Betts v. Brady*[5] in 1942. There, Mr. Justice Owen J. Roberts, speak-

---

[1] *Ibid.*, at 666-7.
[2] 372 U.S. 335 (1963).
[3] *Powell v. Alabama*, 287 U.S. 45 (1932).
[4] *Palko v. Connecticut*, 302 U.S. 319 (1937), at 324.
[5] 316 U.S. 455.

ing for a 6:3 majority, ruled that the due process clause of the Fourteenth Amendment did *not* require counsel to be furnished by a state,
here Maryland, in *non-capital* criminal cases, unless "special" or "ex-
ceptional" circumstances, such as "mental illness," "youth," or "lack
of education," were present. It was the *Betts* ruling that was specifically overturned by a unanimous Supreme Court, some 21 years later,
with the opinion delivered with great conviction and satisfaction by
the same man who had dissented in *Betts*—Mr. Justice Black.

The *Gideon* case, about which so much has been written,[1] and for
good cause, reached the highest tribunal as a result of a penciled
petition *in forma pauperis*,[2] written by Clarence Earl Gideon from
a Florida jail cell. Without a lawyer and penniless, he had been committed there as a result of a criminal conviction for "having broken
and entered a poolroom with intent to commit a misdemeanor" [3] on
the strength of testimony by a man who later turned out to have
been the culprit! Gideon's request for counsel to represent him at his
trial had been refused because of Florida's then valid requirement
under the *Betts* precedent, that court-appointed counsel be reserved
for capital criminal cases. To Gideon's pathetic plea in the courtroom,
"Your Honor, the United States Constitution says I am entitled to be
represented by Counsel," the trial judge could only say, in accordance with his Florida mandate, "I am sorry, but I cannot appoint
Counsel to represent you in this case." [4]

No knowledgeable observer of the judicial process and the Supreme
Court was surprised that the Court overturned the *Betts* decision so
decisively when Gideon managed to get his case "up." Briefs *amicus
curiae* [5] from only two states supported Florida's plea to the Court
that it leave *Betts v. Brady* [6] intact; yet 22 states argued, in Mr. Justice
Black's words "that *Betts* was an anachronism when handed down
and that it should now be overruled." "We agree," concluded Black
triumphantly, noting that in its *Betts* decision the Court had "de-

1 The best full-length book is Anthony Lewis, *Gideon's Trumpet* (New York:
Random House, 1964).

2 "In the form of a pauper; as a poor man."

3 A misdemeanor is an indictable offense, not usually serious enough to be
classified as a crime—but it is so in Florida.

4 *Gideon v. Wainwright, loc. cit.*, at 335-6.

5 A brief *amicus curiae*, i.e. "friend of the Court," enables an interested third
party to enter the case, with the consent of the other litigants and/or the Court.

6 316 U.S. 455 (1942).

parted from the sound wisdom upon which [its] holding in *Powell v.
Alabama* [1] rested." Ruling squarely that a state's failure to appoint
counsel in a non-capital case deprived the indigent defendant in a
criminal proceeding of due process of law under the Fourteenth
Amendment, as comprehended by the right to counsel requirements
of the Sixth, Black remarked that it was "an obvious truth" that

> in our adversary system of criminal justice any person hailed into court
> who is too poor to hire a lawyer cannot be assured a fair trial unless
> counsel is provided for him.[2]

Another long-overdue aspect of incorporation had thus been accomplished, one which, as will be demonstrated in the next chapter, was
to be significantly broadened in succeeding years.[3] And just around
the corner waited another contentious sector of the Bill of Rights,
the Fifth Amendment's stricture against compulsory self-incrimination.

1964: The Self-Incrimination Cases. The frequently predicted and
much publicized *self-incrimination safeguards* were incorporated in a
significant dual decision in the last days of the 1963-64 term. In two
cases [4] the Court dramatically overruled its 1908 decision in the *Twining* case [5] (see p. 48, *supra*), thus adopting the lone dissent in that
case by Mr. Justice Harlan, to make again a signal contribution to the
broadening concept of criminal jurisprudence.

The first case was from Connecticut and concerned one William
Malloy, who had been arrested during a gambling raid in 1959 by
Hartford police. Pleading guilty to the crime of "pool-selling," he was
sentenced to one year in jail and fined $500.00. Some 16 months
thereafter Malloy was ordered to testify in an official, court-sanctioned
inquiry into alleged gambling and other criminal activities in the
county. Asked a number of questions about events surrounding his
own arrest and conviction, Malloy refused to answer any question "on
the grounds it may tend to incriminate me." He was held in contempt

[1] 287 U.S. 45 (1932).
[2] *Gideon v. Wainright, loc. cit.,* at 355.
[3] See, for example, these decisions liberalizing even further the right to counsel:
Massiah v. United States, 377 U.S. 201 (1964); *Escobedo v. Illinois,* 378 U.S.
478 (1964); and the series of June 1966 cases expanding the *Escobedo* decision,
headed by *Miranda v. Arizona,* 384 U.S. 436.
[4] *Malloy v. Hogan,* 378 U.S. 1 (1964) and *Murphy v. Waterfront Commission
of New York Harbor,* 378 U.S. 52 (1964).
[5] *Twining v. New Jersey,* 211 U.S. 78.

and incarcerated "until he was willing to answer the questions." His appeal via a writ of *habeas corpus* was rejected all along the judicial hierarchy in Connecticut, its highest tribunal ultimately ruling, *inter alia*, that the Fifth Amendment's privilege against self-incrimination was not available to a witness in a state proceeding and that the Fourteenth Amendment "extended no privilege to him." The Connecticut courts relied, of course, on past Supreme Court rulings to that effect. But they were now to fall. Over vigorous dissenting opinions by Justices Harlan and Clark, who firmly rejected nationalization of the Fifth, and by Justices White and Stewart, who questioned the propriety of the privilege's invocation in the instant case, a majority of five members of the Court extended the "incorporated" side of the Cardozo table. Speaking for the Chief Justice, Justices Black, Douglas, Goldberg, and himself, Mr. Justice Brennan held that the Fourteenth Amendment, which assures all citizens due process of law, guaranteed the petitioner the protection of the Fifth Amendment's privilege against self-incrimination. In language redolent with appeals for a system of "nationalized" criminal justice, Brennan pronounced the *Twining* [1] and *Adamson* [2] decisions as wrong constitutional law and announced that, "*a fortiorari*":

> The Fourteenth Amendment secures against state invasion the same privilege that the Fifth Amendment guarantees against federal infringement—the right of a person to remain silent unless he chooses to speak in the unfettered exercise of his own free will, and to suffer no penalty . . . for such silence. [3]

The New York companion case turned on the refusal of William Murphy to give testimony to the New York Waterfront Commission which was then investigating a work stoppage at certain New Jersey piers. Murphy had been promised immunity from prosecution in return for his testimony, but he refused this offer, fearing that his answers might incriminate him under *federal* law to which the grant of immunity did not purport to extend. Overruling its own precedents,[4] the Supreme Court, without dissent this time, categorically rejected "the established rule that one jurisdiction within our federal

---

[1] *Ibid.*

[2] *Adamson v. California*, 332 U.S. 46 (1947).

[3] *Malloy v. Hogan, loc. cit.*, at 8.

[4] *United States v. Murdock*, 284 U.S. 141 (1931); *Feldman v. United States*, 322 U.S. 487 (1944); *Knapp v. Schweitzer*, 357 U.S. 371 (1958).

structure may compel a witness to give testimony which could be used to convict him of a crime in another." [1] Although two of the justices, in a concurring opinion by Harlan, joined by Clark, objected to the "mixing together" of the Fifth and the Fourteenth Amendments, the Court unanimously agreed with its spokesman, Mr. Justice Arthur J. Goldberg:

> We hold that the Constitutional privilege against self-incrimination protects a state witness against incrimination under Federal as well as state law and a Federal witness against incrimination under state as well as Federal law.[2]

Although the case featured three separate opinions [3]—two of these concurring on different grounds—and the individual justices may have accepted the Goldberg conclusion for different reasons, it nevertheless represented another broadening of the application of the Bill of Rights to the states.

1965: The Texas Confrontation of Witnesses Case. Next in line was the clause of the Sixth Amendment that provides: "In all criminal prosecutions, the accused shall enjoy the right . . . to be confronted with the witnesses against him. . . ." Did it, too, apply with equal effect to proceedings in state courts by virtue of the due process clause of Amendment Fourteen? Yes, held a unanimous Supreme Court, although the four opinions in the case were based on varying grounds, as we shall see.

Granville Pointer (and a cohort, Dillard) had been charged with robbing Kenneth W. Phillips of $375 "by assault, or violence, or by putting in fear of life or bodily injury." [4] At the preliminary hearing before a state judge, called the "examining trial" in Texas, Phillips gave detailed testimony including an identification of Pointer who, although present throughout the hearing, had no attorney and made no effort to cross-examine Phillips. At Pointer's trial the State submitted evidence that Phillips had recently moved to California and had no intention, whatever, of returning to Texas. The trial judge permitted the prosecution to introduce the transcript of Phillips' testimony at the preliminary hearing, over the repeated objections of Pointer's counsel. In each instance the trial judge overruled the de-

---

[1] *Murphy v. Waterfront Commission of New York Harbor, loc. cit.,* at 77.
[2] *Ibid.,* at 77-8.
[3] Those by Justices Goldberg, White, and Harlan.
[4] *Pointer v. Texas,* 380 U.S. 400 (1965).

fense objections on the ground that Pointer had had ample opportunity to cross-examine Phillips at the preliminary hearing stage. The Texas Court of Criminal Appeals affirmed Pointer's conviction—but the Supreme Court of the United States reversed it 9:0, though it was divided on the bases for its action.

Mr. Justice Black, speaking for the Court, referred to the spate of recent decisions holding applicable to the states various guarantees in the Bill of Rights, including the Sixth Amendment's right to counsel and the Fifth's guarantee against compulsory self-incrimination. He ruled:

> We hold today that the Sixth Amendment's right of an accused to confront the witnesses against him is likewise a fundamental right and is made obligatory on the States by the Fourteenth Amendment.[1]

Black then observed that the inclusion in the Sixth Amendment of *the right of confrontation* "reflects the belief of the Framers . . . that confrontation was a fundamental right essential to a fair trial in a criminal prosecution." [2] And he concluded that since the right of confrontation comprehended the right to cross-examine, reversal was mandatory. Henceforth, the same standards that protect litigants against federal encroachment of this right would be applicable and enforceable against the states. A precedent of more than six decades earlier thus stood overruled.[3]

Three concurring opinions were filed, each dealing with the "incorporation doctrine." Mr. Justice Goldberg, evidently concerned to go on record with his approach to the problem—for he had not been on the Court when the issue was joined in the *Adamson* case [4] in 1947—acknowledged that, on the record, the "incorporation doctrine" had never really commanded a majority of the Court. However, he sternly rejected both the Frankfurter case-by-case "was it due process?" approach and the *Palko* line of the "implicit in the concept of ordered liberty" test. In effect, he embraced the applicability to the states of the fundamental guarantees of the Bill of Rights, and he clearly did not particularly care *how* this was done by the Court or by what name the process would be known—just so long as the guar-

---

[1] *Ibid.*, at 403.
[2] *Ibid.*, at 404.
[3] *West v. Louisiana*, 194 U.S. 258 (1904).
[4] 332 U.S. 46.

antees were indeed made obligatory on the states via the Fourteenth Amendment.[1]

Mr. Justice Harlan, while concurring in the result of *Pointer*, nevertheless could not forbear to re-express his so deeply held conviction that the majority's holding here constituted deplorably "another step in the onward march on the long-since discredited 'incorporation' doctrine." [2] Exhorting the Court to return to a policy of "leaving room for differences among states," he wrote that *he* would have reversed Pointer's conviction on the basis that the procedure followed by Texas had deprived Pointer of due process of law guaranteed by the Fourteenth Amendment, "independently of the Sixth." [3] Harlan freely acknowledged that the right of confrontation is indeed "implicit in the concept of ordered liberty," which mandated its observance by Texas. But he lashed out at "incorporation" as being "incompatible with our constitutionally ordained federal system" as well as "unsound doctrine." [4] Once again he pointed to what he saw as the value of the states as "laboratories" that must not be "subordinated to federal power." Taking firm issue with that contention, Mr. Justice Goldberg wrote in his concurring opinion that while it was good that the states should be able to try social and economic experiments, he did not believe that this "includes the power to experiment with the fundamental liberties of citizens safeguarded by the Bill of Rights." [5]

In his brief concurring opinion, Mr. Justice Stewart took to task the Black opinion for the Court as a "questionable tour de force . . . entirely unnecessary to the decision of this case. . . ." [6] He said that *he* would have reversed Pointer's conviction on the simple ground that he had been clearly deprived of liberty without due process of law in express violation of the Fourteenth Amendment—which, of course, constitutes the case-by-case approach to the applicability question. But on the same day the Court proceeded to apply the new ruling in reversing a conviction in a similar case.[7]

As the Supreme Court of the United States prepared to return to

---

[1] *Pointer v. Texas, loc. cit.*, at 414.
[2] *Ibid.*, at 408.
[3] *Ibid.*
[4] *Ibid.*, at 409.
[5] *Ibid.*, at 413.
[6] *Ibid.*, at 410.
[7] *Douglas v. Alabama*, 380 U.S. 415 (1965), with the same Court "lineup," although Mr. Justice Brennan wrote the opinion here.

its labors in the fall of 1966, no further provisions of the Bill of Rights had been incorporated. However, the Court had agreed to decide during its 1966-67 term whether three as yet "un-incorporated" provisions of that Bill should indeed be made applicable to the states. One was the Sixth Amendment right "to a *speedy* . . . trial"; [1] the other the more controversial problem of the Fifth Amendment's double jeopardy rule [2]—to which the Court had said "no" on several occasions in the past [3]—and third, the Seventh Amendment's guarantee of a jury trial in *civil* cases involving a controversy in excess of twenty dollars. Given the decisions since *Mapp v. Ohio* [4] in 1961, and the demonstrably pro-incorporation attitude of at least three justices (Warren, Black, Douglas), and quite likely a fourth (Mr. Justice Abe Fortas who succeeded Arthur Goldberg as of the 1965-66 term of Court), and possibly even a fifth (Brennan), additional incorporation was quite possible. This belief is strengthened by a careful reading of the *Connecticut Birth Control* case [5] (see below). Whether the Bill of Rights will ever be incorporated *in toto* is doubtful because of the particularly delicate implications of federalism and "states' rights" in those segments of the Bill which are still unincorporated. This is especially true of those dealing with the Fifth Amendment guarantees to indictment by grand jury or those of trial by jury in the Sixth. But to say that total incorporation is "doubtful" is not to say that it is "impossible," given the increasingly strong belief on and off the bench that if there is anything at all that is "national" in scope and application under the United States Constitution, it must be our civil rights and liberties. In a sense, the extensive discussion of the problem by six justices in the 1965 *Birth Control* case [6] underscores both trend and belief.

"Incorporation" Re-Argued: The Connecticut Birth Control Case. As if to continue the "argument" among themselves on the incorpora-

[1] *Klopfer v. North Carolina*, 384 U.S. 959 (1966), certiorari granted. (Italics supplied.)

[2] *Cichos v. Indiana*, 383 U.S. 966 (1966), certiorari granted. But, after taking a closer look, the Court on November 14, 1966, voted 6:3 to *dismiss* the *Cichos* writ of certiorari as having been "improvidentially granted" (385 U.S. 76).

[3] See especially *Palko v. Connecticut*, 302 U.S. 319 (1937), *Brock v. North Carolina*, 344 U.S. 424 (1953), *Bartkus v. Illinois*, 359 U.S. 121 (1959), and *Abbate v. United States*, 359 U.S. 187 (1959).

[4] 367 U.S. 643, *op. cit.*

[5] *Griswold v. Connecticut*, 381 U.S. 479 (1965).

[6] *Ibid.*

tion controversy they had once again raised in the *Texas Confrontation* case [1] some weeks earlier in 1965, the Supreme Court justices addressed themselves to it with gusto in their controversial decision in *Griswold v. Connecticut*, now generally referred to as the *Birth Control* case.[2] Our concern here is less with the merits of the decision than with the reasoning of the six opinion writers on the incorporation problem (which, depending upon one's analysis of the case, either did or did not have something to do with the holding in the case itself). It suffices to note briefly that the Court, by a 7:2 vote, invalidated an old and generally unenforced Connecticut statute that made it a crime for any person, married or single, to use any drug or other article for the purpose of preventing conception. The Court's opinion was delivered by Mr. Justice Douglas and its judgment of reversal of the defendants' [3] conviction was agreed to by the Chief Justice and Associate Justices Clark, Harlan, Brennan, White, and Goldberg. But only Clark accepted Douglas's full reasoning (at least he wrote no opinion); Harlan, White, and Goldberg wrote separate concurring opinions, with the Chief Justice and Brennan joining in Goldberg's. Justices Black and Stewart wrote separate dissenting opinions, each specifically also joining the other's.

Douglas noted at the outset that the Court was here confronted with a *bona fide* controversy that it could properly decide, one involving "the constitutional rights of married people with whom [the defendants, leaders of the Planned Parenthood League] had a professional relationship." [4] He reviewed several Court decisions that, in his judgment, established "that specific guarantees in the Bill of Rights have *penumbras*, formed by emanations from those guarantees that help give them life and substance," [5] penumbras that reached areas not specifically mentioned in the Bill. He thereupon cited five (!) different amendments the "penumbras" of which "create zones of privacy," among them the First Amendment's protection of the

---

[1] *Pointer v. Texas,* 380 U.S. 400.

[2] 381 U.S. 479.

[3] They were Estelle T. Griswold, Executive Director of the Planned Parenthood League of Connecticut and Dr. Charles L. Buxton, a licensed physician who served as medical director for the League's New Haven Center. They gave information and medical advice to married persons on means of preventing conception, were found guilty of violating the Connecticut statute at issue, and were fined $100.00 each. Their appeal was on Fourteenth Amendment grounds.

[4] *Griswold v. Connecticut, loc. cit.,* at 481.

[5] *Ibid.,* at 484. (Italics added.)

right of association, the Third's prohibition of quartering of soldiers in homes, the Fourth's guarantee against unreasonable searches and seizures, the Fifth's against compulsory self-incrimination. He added, in a coup of interpretative trail-blazing, the *Ninth Amendment*, justifying its inclusion as a beacon to illuminate "the zone of privacy created by [the] several fundamental constitutional guarantees." [1]

Predictably, the concurring opinions raised the issue of "incorporation," and specifically whether—in the light of the expansive Douglas opinion—it was indeed limited to the Bill of Rights. Mr. Justice Harlan, in his solo opinion, saw the issue in terms of the requirement of basic values that are "implicit in the concept of ordered liberty" —the *Palko* and case-by-case approach to the scope of the due process clause of the Fourteenth Amendment rather than "incorporation." He was satisfied that the Connecticut statute did unconstitutionally infringe the due process clause which "stands . . . on its own bottom," and which is not dependent on "one or more provisions of the Bill of Rights . . . or any of their radiations. . . ." [2]

Mr. Justice Goldberg, whom the Chief Justice and Mr. Justice Brennan joined in his concurring opinion, was eager to make clear his conviction that the due process clause was neither limited to, nor necessarily as broad as, the Bill of Rights but rather that it "protects those personal rights that are fundamental." In sweeping language, he strongly emphasized the relevance of the Ninth Amendment to the Court's holding, contending that its language and history reveal that

> the Framers of the Constitution believed that *there are additional fundamental rights*, protected from governmental infringement, which exist *alongside those fundamental rights specifically mentioned in the first eight constitutional amendments.*[3]

In other words, he viewed the Ninth Amendment as a lever for the protection of all those "fundamental rights" not specifically protected by the first eight via the "liberty" protected in the due process clauses of both the Fifth and the Fourteenth Amendments. The Ninth, he reiterated several times in his opinion, "is surely relevant in showing

1 *Ibid.*, at 485.
2 *Ibid.*, at 500.
3 *Ibid.*, at 488. (Italics added.)

the existence of other fundamental personal rights now protected from state as well as federal infringement." [1]

He thus rejected the Black approach to incorporation because he believed—and Black would assuredly agree with this analysis of his views—that it would *limit the rights eligible for incorporation to those specifically listed* in the Bill of Rights.

Mr. Justice White's relatively brief concurring opinion saw a clear-cut violation of substantive due process by the Connecticut statute because of its "too sweeping" provisions which entered "a realm of family life which the state cannot enter." [2] In short, incorporation or no incorporation, the crux of the matter to White was that the due process clause, which prohibits states from depriving any person of "liberty" without due process of law, was clearly violated by the restrictions of the Connecticut law.

In dissenting, Mr. Justice Black took pains to announce his complete agreement with all of the "graphic and eloquent strictures and criticisms" leveled at what his colleague Stewart, dissenting with him, termed "this uncommonly silly law," but he rejected the majority's collective reasoning. Characteristically, he noted the absence of a *specific* constitutional provision that proscribed an invasion of privacy, and he warned that the Court's reliance on the Ninth Amendment together with the due process clause would give the "federal judiciary the power to invalidate any legislative act which the judges find irrational, unreasonable or offensive." [3] To accept such an approach, he believed, was to revive the doctrine rejected by the Court three decades earlier under which it had for so long struck down federal and state statutes in the *economic* realm because of alleged violations of substantive due process of law based on such notions as the sanctity of contracts. "Privacy," he declared, "is a broad, abstract, and ambiguous concept" that can be readily expanded or shrunken by later decisions. Lest he be misunderstood, he reiterated his belief that the Court does have the power, "which it should exercise," [4] to hold laws unconstitutional where they are forbidden by the Constitution, and that he fully believed now as before, that

[1] E.g. *ibid.*, at 493.
[2] *Ibid.*, at 502.
[3] *Ibid.*, at 511.
[4] *Ibid.*, at 520.

the specifics of that document are incorporated and made applicable
to the states via the due process clause of the Fourteenth Amendment. Yet, like Stewart in his dissenting opinion, he could find nothing in the Constitution and its amendments to forbid the passage
of the Connecticut law. Quoting from his dissenting opinion in
Adamson v. California[1] almost two decades earlier, he cautioned:

> ... to pass upon the constitutionality of statutes by looking to the
> particular standards enumerated in the Bill of Rights and other parts
> of the Constitution is one thing; to invalidate statutes because of ap-
> plication of "natural law" deemed to be above and undefined by the
> Constitution is another.[2]

To Black, the First Amendment protects freedom of *expression*, and
it does that absolutely. Yet it does not protect "conduct" (or "physical activities")—be that conduct a racial "sit-in"[3] or the sale and use
of contraceptive devices.[4] And he quoted with full agreement a
famous statement by Judge Learned Hand on the matter of judicial
invalidating of legislation offensive to the jurists' "personal prefer-
ences":

> For myself it would be most irksome to be ruled by a bevy of Platonic
> Guardians, even if I knew how to choose them, which I assuredly do
> not.[5]

But in the footnote giving the above statement's citation, Black had
to acknowledge that although he agreed with Hand's "criticism of
use of the due process formula, I do not agree with all the views he
expressed about construing the specific guarantees of the Bill of
Rights."[6] Of course, Black could not—for, ironically, in his 1958
book, *The Bill of Rights*[7]—which contains the "platonic Guardians"
statement so approvingly quoted by Black—Hand took considerable
pain to contend that the Court on which Black then served had gone
too far, in a number of cases, in holding legislation to be in violation
of *specific* guarantees of the Bill of Rights.[8]

---

[1] 330 U.S. 46 (1947), at 90-92.
[2] *Griswold v. Connecticut, loc. cit.*, at 525.
[3] See Chapter VII, *infra*.
[4] *Griswold v. Connecticut, loc. cit.*, at 507-8.
[5] *Ibid.*, at 526.
[6] *Ibid.*, fn. 23.
[7] Cambridge: Harvard University Press, 1958.
[8] *Ibid.*, pp. 35-45.

LEADING POSITIONS ON INCORPORATION

It may be useful to summarize the major judicial positions taken on the question of incorporation of the Bill of Rights by representative past and present members of the Supreme Court and their allies. Although close students of the problem can determine as many as eight or nine such positions, we can eschew fine distinctions and point to four chief ones.

The first position is the current doctrine of a majority of the Court: selective incorporation, or the concept of the "Honor Roll of Superior Rights." Since the *Palko* case [1] in 1937, this position has been adhered to by a majority of the members of the Court—a shifting majority, but a majority nonetheless. Among those who have labored to "incorporate" the gradually increasing string of rights from the Bill of Rights, without necessarily advocating *total* incorporation, have been Chief Justices Hughes, Stone, and Warren (although it is possible to make a good, but inconclusive, case for the acceptance of not only total incorporation by the latter two, but of total incorporation "plus"); Associate Justices Brandeis, Cardozo, Reed, Jackson, Burton, Clark (with reservations in the area of criminal procedural safeguards), Brennan (who may be leaning toward total incorporation or even total incorporation "plus" but has some doubts in the criminal procedure area); Stewart and White (both with reservations akin to Clark's). This majority position, which will complete its third decade in 1967, possesses both the virtues of flexibility and compromise and the vices of selectivity and uncertainty.

The second position on incorporation is the "fair trial" or "case by case" rule. This position was consistently and prominently advocated by Mr. Justice Frankfurter and has been faithfully continued, with some bows toward the Cardozo reasoning in *Palko* but not toward the *Palko* doctrine itself, by "F.F."'s jurisprudential student and companion, the younger John Marshall Harlan. To a lesser degree it has been favored by Mr. Chief Justice Vinson and Justices Sherman Minton and Charles E. Whittaker and, sporadically, by Justices Clark, Stewart, and White. It is essentially a "case-by-case" approach which closely examines on its own merits each individual claim of violation of due process of law, determines whether or not the common law as

[1] *Palko v. Connecticut*, 302 U.S. 319.

well as statutory law principles of "a fair trial" were accorded to the petitioner, and tests his claim against the requirement of "due process of law"—as that elusive concept may be viewed by a majority of the Court. It is here that the famous Frankfurter *quaere*, whether the governmental action does in effect "shock the conscience" or violate "common standards of civilized conduct," is asked. If the answer is yes, the partisans of the case-by-case approach will then hold due process of law to have been violated. For the adherents to this group of Justices, however, such a decision will be without any reference to incorporation of the Bill of Rights, wholly or partly. In short, the "fair trial" test adherents reject both the selective incorporation approach of the Cardozo test and the total incorporation approach of the elder John Marshall Harlan. They reject the total incorporation (and certainly total incorporation "plus") as an example of "judicial legislating," and as a clear-cut violation of the principles of federalism and the commands of the Constitution. They reject selective incorporation as an unwise and unworkable resort to the vague tenets of "natural law" and as the "slot machine approach," whereby, in Mr. Justice Frankfurter's words, "some are in and some are out," and as the creation of a hopeless, artificial, and unfair distinction among our basic rights and liberties. Yet to Mr. Justice Black the "due process" approach is itself plainly a "natural-law due process" formula.[1]

Pertinent illustrations of the Frankfurter "fair trial" approach are the *Adamson* case,[2] discussed earlier in this chapter, and the *Rochin* case.[3] In *Adamson*, the due process standards of Frankfurter's and his colleague Reed's majority [4] simply had not been violated and their consciences had not been shocked by California's statute that permitted official courtroom comment on the fact that the accused, Adamson, refused to take the stand in his defense. In *Rochin*, the conduct of certain Los Angeles County police officers so outraged their standards and consciences that the accused's conviction was unanimously reversed by the Court—although two justices, Black and Douglas, concurred on separate grounds: "incorporation" of the

---

[1] *Harper v. Virginia State Board of Elections*, 383 U.S. 663 (1966), at 677-9.
[2] *Adamson v. California*, 332 U.S. 46 (1947).
[3] *Rochin v. California*, 342 U.S. 165 (1952). See Ch. IV, *infra*.
[4] They were joined by Mr. Chief Justice Vinson and Associate Justices Jackson and Burton.

Bill of Rights safeguards involved. Also, in the 1964 self-incrimination cases, Mr. Justice Harlan's and his supporters' consciences were *not* "shocked" by Connecticut's procedures denying Malloy's self-incrimination claims,[1] but they *were* shocked by the New York Harbor Waterfront's treatment of Murphy's compulsory testimony claims.[2] In *Malloy*, Harlan's case-by-case approach thus enabled him to see due process accorded to the petitioner—while his five colleagues who constituted the Court majority here not only disagreed with his conclusions on the presence of due process, but, going further, incorporated the Fifth Amendment's self-incrimination issue. In *Murphy*, on the other hand, Harlan did see a violation of the petitioner's due process, and he thus joined his unanimous brethren to reverse Murphy's contempt conviction. This Frankfurter-Harlan position has the virtues of extensive judicial discretion and minute individual examination and the evident vices of unpredictability and subjectivity.

The third judicial posture, total incorporation of the Bill of Rights, was, of course, ardently and faithfully advocated by Mr. Justice John Marshall Harlan, the elder. It is a doctrine espoused after *Palko* most notably by Mr. Justice Black, with early support from Douglas, Murphy, and Rutledge, and later from Goldberg (all four of whom, however, wanted to go even beyond Black's incorporation to achieve maximum application of the federal Constitution to the states and eventually did so). Simply stated, the Black attitude asserts that not only does the due process clause of the Fourteenth Amendment— and probably its privileges and immunities clause—mandate the total incorporation of the *specific* commands of the Bill of Rights, but that even if history does not provide a foolproof guide, the logic of life in democratic society in our times dictates such a position as a matter of minimum fairness and necessity. But it should be remembered that the Black position of nationalization *in toto* extends only to those guarantees specifically spelled out in the Constitution and its amendments. To Black, for whom any kind of "natural law" formula is anathema, the first section of the Fourteenth Amendment not only incorporates the specifics of the first eight amendments, but *it is confined to them*. Time and again he made clear that natural law may *not* be employed either to expand or to limit state legislative powers

---

[1] *Malloy v. Hogan*, 378 U.S. 1 (1964).
[2] *Murphy v. Waterfront Commission of New York Harbor*, 378 U.S. 52 (1964).

beyond those limitations placed upon their exercise by the commands
of the Bill of Rights.[1] This approach possesses the undeniable virtues
of both simplicity and predictability and the vices of dogmatism and
questionable interpretation of the Fourteenth Amendment, in particular, and the United States Constitution, in general.

A fourth, and for our purposes last, position is really an extension
of the third: namely, that the Bill of Rights in all its majestic
guarantees may not suffice to ascertain full "due process of law," and
that therefore it may be necessary to draw on a kind of total incorporation "plus" approach in order to do full justice to the allegedly
aggrieved individual. Known as the "total incorporation plus theory,"
it was initially most notably expounded in the immediate post-*Palko*
era by Justices Murphy and Rutledge. In their dissenting opinion in
the famed *Adamson* case,[2] written by Murphy, the words and intent
are clear:

> We agree that the specific guarantees of the Bill of Rights should be
> carried over intact into the first section of the Fourteenth Amendment.
> But [we are] not prepared to say that the latter is entirely and neces-
> sarily limited by the Bill of Rights. *Occasions may arise where a pro-*
> *ceeding falls so far short of conforming to fundamental standards of*
> *procedure as to warrant constitutional condemnation in terms of a lack*
> *of due process despite the absence of a specific provision in the Bill of*
> *Rights. . . .*[3]

Justices Black and Douglas, who also dissented in *Adamson*—in the
former's celebrated opinion—did not then address themselves to the
issue raised by their two junior colleagues; they were simply content
to advocate total incorporation. However, while Black then as now
rejected the "incorporation plus" philosophy on the grounds that concepts of intrinsic justice may *neither be used to limit nor to expand*
individual rights *beyond what is spelled out in the Bill of Rights*,
Douglas did gradually draw closer to the Murphy-Rutledge position.
And only a few years later, after Murphy and Rutledge died in 1949,
Douglas had wholly embraced the "incorporation plus" doctrine.
"The Bill of Rights Is Not Enough" was the title of one of his essays,[4]

---

[1] See, for example, *Adamson v. California*, 332 U.S. 46 (1947), at 75; *Gris-*
wold v. Connecticut, 381 U.S. 479 (1965), at 511-13; and *Harper v. Virginia*
State Board of Elections, 383 U.S. 663 (1966), at 675-6.

[2] 332 U.S. 46 (1947).

[3] *Ibid.*, at 124. (Italics supplied.)

[4] 38 *New York University Law Review* 207 (April 1963).

symptomatic of this intriguing position, which might be called a "super-fair-trial" rule. Mr. Justice Goldberg demonstrated his sympathy toward that constitutional posture with his important concurring opinion in the *Connecticut Birth Control* case [1] in which he was significantly joined by Mr. Chief Justice Warren and also Mr. Justice Brennan. Goldberg, it will be recalled, made a point of stating that the due process clause was "neither limited to nor necessarily as broad as" the Bill of Rights, but rather that it "protects those personal rights that are fundamental." [2] Despite the theoretical loophole for a contraction of incorporation in view of the "nor as broad as" phrase of the statement just quoted, the Goldberg position, presumably now embraced also by Warren and Brennan, constitutes in effect the acceptance of "incorporation plus"—with the possibility of a retrenchment when deemed necessary (an unlikely assumption). Moreover, it accepts the spirit and letter of the Douglas position on the Ninth Amendment announced in the *Birth Control* case, which is patently the most advanced of all positions on the basic issue.[3]

A Guess and a Judgment. If the "total incorporation plus" policy is not in the offing, simple total incorporation of the Bill of Rights *could* become the law of the land in the not too distant future. The current philosophy of selective incorporation (Cardozo's *Palko* decision) has been steadily, if sporadically, broadened, and with increasing velocity of late. Thus it may resolve itself into an ultimate across-the-board nationalization of all aspects of the Bill of Rights in terms of the requirement of those basic values that are "implicit in the concept of ordered liberty," that constitute those "fundamental principles of liberty and justice which lie at the base of all our civil and political institutions." But with the possible exceptions of the right to counsel even in all *civil* cases, the concept of a "speedy" trial, and certain elements of the double jeopardy safeguards, the few federally ascertained rights that are still "out" of the due process of law concept of Amendment Fourteen, such as grand jury indictment and trial by petit jury, are likely to remain out, at least formally. And perhaps they should; the selective incorporation concept, coupled with the Court's increasing concern for a full measure of "due proc-

---

[1] *Griswold v. Connecticut*, 381 U.S. 479 (1965).
[2] *Ibid.*, at 493.
[3] *Ibid.*, at 485.

ess," and the obvious presence of the "double standard" in favor of basic human rights render plausible the argument *cum* plea that the federal principle might well be asked to continue to permit the states to pursue their own procedural standards in the remaining non-incorporated areas. If so, however, these standards must scrupulously meet, and adhere to, the demands of due process of law, or total incorporation with strict federal rules will almost certainly result.[1]

1 See the stringent rules regarding confessions, counsel, and police interrogation practices generally, laid down by the Court in the landmark series of cases decided 5:4 in June 1966. (*Miranda v. Arizona*, 384 U.S. 436, and four other cases.)

IV

The Fascinating World of
"Due Process of Law"

THE CONCEPT "due process of law" has been an integral part of much of what we have been discussing. It is both subordinate and co-ordinate to any consideration of "values and lines" in the realm of civil rights and liberties. No concept is mentioned more frequently in our judicio-legal process than "due process of law," for either its presence or its absence; its banner is now raised in more appellate cases at the level of the United States Supreme Court than any other. Its terminology, if not its meaning, is found in Amendments V and XIV of the Constitution. Both amendments issue clarion calls to national and state governments alike for the presence and main-tenance of "due process of law." In the words of Article V, ratified on December 15, 1791: "No person shall...be deprived of life, liberty, or property, *without due process of law*...";[1] and in the words of Article XIV, ratified on July 23, 1868: "No State shall... deprive any person of life, liberty, or property, *without due process of law*...."[2] Towering disagreements have plagued our polity as to the meaning of the command and will undoubtedly continue to do so. "Line drawing" is complicated by the problem of that meaning—as our analysis of the question of the incorporation of the Bill of Rights has demonstrated. Yet basic guidelines do exist, and, no matter how vexatious and hazardous the task at hand may well be, they enable us to come to grips with the meaning of "due process of law."

[1] Italics supplied.
[2] Italics supplied.

SOME BASIC GUIDELINES

Although it is as futile as it is unwise to attempt definitive interpretations of "due process of law," it is possible—indeed it is essential
—to delineate certain fundamentals. One basic requirement of the
concept "due process of law" is that government may not act in an
"arbitrary," "capricious," or "unreasonable" manner in performing
its task vis-à-vis the body politic. The judicial branch as the ultimate
or penultimate guardian of our civil rights and liberties has the delicate
and difficult task of ascertaining the constitutional appropriateness
of governmental action by weighing it against what amount to common-law notions of "arbitrariness," "capriciousness," or "unreason-
ableness."

Suffice it to say that opinions differ widely on the meaning of these
concepts. What may be "arbitrary" to some legislators may seem
entirely reasonable to others; what may be "capricious" police behavior in the eyes of a prisoner may be utterly fair in the eyes of the
apprehending and prosecuting authorities; and what may well seem
to be an "unreasonable" interpretation by an administrative agency
in the view of an affected business concern may appear entirely reasonable to the agency's commissioners. Does the matter, then, become
merely a matter of opinion, or are there ascertainable standards? The
answer cannot be conclusive: there *are* standards, of course—as we
have seen at some length in the discussion on incorporation, for example, and as we will see in the chapters to come—but unless and
until they have been judicially tested and pronounced, they remain
general standards based as much on hopefully civilized notions of
fairness and decency as on any written commands, be the latter at
the level of statutes, ordinances, or even constitutions, federal or
state. At the *federal* level, because of the specific commands of the
Constitution and the centralizing tendency of having only one final
arbiter, "due process" standards are both more predictable and more
ascertainable than at the *state* level. Fifty units of government, despite
the sturdy mandates and exhortations of the Fourteenth Amendment and of their own bills of rights, bring a more fluid, less predictable, and less "generous" interpretation of "due process of law"
to the individual. However, under the increasingly insistent orders

emanating from the United States Supreme Court, the states, too, have had to pay far more attention to those supports, "fairness and decency," which are necessary to "due process of law."

A *General Definition*. Any general definition must take into account the origin of the concept of "due process of law." The concept has been with us as such for eight centuries! To the surprise of no student of our jurisprudence, it was originally derived from English common law—probably during the reigns of Henry I (1100-1135) and Henry II (1154-89). Its more obvious antecedent is the Magna Charta of 1215. As it developed, "due process of law" restrained a head of government from adopting such arbitrary methods as to deprive a member of his realm of life, liberty, or property. In due course this notion of due process of law was embraced by the other departments of government as well; it has been an essential fact of governmental life on this side of the ocean from the moment of the Constitution's adoption in 1789.

Perhaps the best brief definition of due process of law was contained in Mr. Justice John Marshall Harlan's famed dissenting opinon in 1884, in *Hurtado v. California*.[1] Governments, he wrote, should be confined within the limits of those fundamental "principles of liberty and justice lying at the foundation of our civil and political institutions that no state can violate consistent with due process of law." [2] This noble phrase, then advanced on the losing side of the judicial ledger, became firmly implanted on the majority side with its well-known acceptance, clarification, and refinement by Mr. Justice Cardozo, more than half a century later, in *Palko v. Connecticut*.[3]

But what are those "fundamental principles of liberty and justice" which constitute the irreducible minimum of due process of law? We may discover them from a variety of sources:

from the body of constitutions;
from bills of rights;
from customs, conventions, and traditions;
from legislative enactments;
from executive ordinances, decrees, and practices;
from judicial interpretations and precedents;

[1] 110 U.S. 516.
[2] *Ibid.*, at 546.
[3] 302 U.S. 319 (1937). See Chapter III, *supra*.

and significantly,

from what one commentator has aptly termed "current views of right and wrong which collectively have come to be accepted as a part of the established law of the land." [1]

The concept of due process of law and its application to our federal and state governments is based on an extensive reservoir of *constitutionally expressed and implied limitations upon governmental authority*, ultimately determined by the judicial process, and upon those basic notions of fairness and decency which govern, or ought to govern, the relationships between rulers and ruled. Although Mr. Justice Frankfurter's record is, of course, based on the subjective case-by-case approach described earlier, rather than a clearly circumscribed one, he viewed this flexible concept of due process of law as:

... compounded by history, reason, the past course of decisions, and stout confidence in the democratic faith which we profess. . . . [2]

SUBSTANTIVE AND PROCEDURAL DUE PROCESS OF LAW

Any explanation of due process of law must consider its two "types" or aspects— *substantive* and *procedural*—for judicial disposition of due process litigation necessarily turns on the *kind* of violation that is alleged by a petitioner. Although neither is readily definable nor as clearly separable from the other as is sometimes claimed, it is essential to understand at least a general distinction between the two kinds of due process. We may broadly view *substantive* due process as referring to the *content or subject matter* of a law or an ordinance, whereas *procedural* due process—by far the more litigated of the two —refers to the matter in which a law, an ordinance, an administrative practice, or a judicial task is carried out. In both the substantive and procedural due process concepts the judicial test of constitutionality or legality is the same: is the governmental action "arbitrary," "capricious," or "unreasonable" either in content or in procedure? If it is, the action by government and/or its agent will then fall—and on occasion *both* substantive and procedural violations have been present.

---

[1] Professor Jesse T. Carpenter in the *Dictionary of American Politics*, Edward C. Smith and Arnold J. Zurcher, eds. (New York: Barnes & Noble, 1955), p. 128.
[2] *Joint Anti-Fascist Refugee Committee v. McGrath*, 341 U.S. 123 (1951), concurring opinion.

SUBSTANTIVE DUE PROCESS

As our discussion of the post-1937 "double standard" has demonstrated, the Supreme Court has largely abandoned substantive due process of law as a check on legislative economic-proprietarian regulation. This does not mean, of course, that legislatures are free to disregard the basic standards of substantive due process when legislating in the realm of the economy—indeed, the Court will permit no such obvious violations. But it does mean that in line with its latter-day canons of judicial self-restraint, the Court will bend over backward to uphold such legislation. In the area of civil liberties, however, judicial action in the substantive due process area is not only probable but relatively frequent. Although, as we saw in Chapters II and III, the Court, by virtue of the nature of substantive due process, is called upon to pass judgment far less often in that sphere than in the procedural one, no term of Court passes without some challenges to governmental enactments on substantive due process grounds. Many of these fall into the area of the First Amendment freedoms,[1] in particular the freedom of expression and religion which will be discussed in Chapters V and VI respectively. Another pertinent illustration is sterilization legislation.

Carrie Buck Loses. Carrie Buck, an 18-year-old feeble-minded white girl, the daughter of a feeble-minded mother, and the mother of a feeble-minded, illegitimate baby, found herself committed in 1924 to the Virginia State Colony for Epileptics and the Feeble Minded—where her mother had also been committed. An Act of Virginia, duly passed and approved, provided that the health of the patient and the welfare of society may be promoted in certain cases by the sterilization of mental defectives, under careful safeguard; that the sterilization may be effected in males by vasectomy and in females by salpingectomy, without serious pain or substantial danger to life; that the Commonwealth of Virginia "is supporting in various institutions many defective persons who if now discharged would become a menace but if incapable of procreating might be discharged with safety and become self-supporting with benefit to themselves and to society"; and that experience has shown that heredity plays an

[1] Space does not here permit a discussion of the following three basic substantive due process safeguards found in the *body* of the Constitution (Article I): the writ of *habeas corpus, ex post facto* law, and bills of attainder.

important part in the transmission of insanity, imbecility, idiocy, feeble-mindedness, or epilepsy.[1] The Virginia statute went on to state that whenever the superintendent of certain institutions, including the State Colony where Carrie and her mother were, shall be of the opinion that it is for the best interests of the patients and of society, he may have the operation "performed upon any patient afflicted with hereditary forms of insanity, imbecility," etc., if he complies with the very careful provisions by which the law protects the patients from possible abuse.[2]

Bell, the Superintendent of the State Colony, in scrupulous compliance with the terms of the statute, and after many months of close observation, recommended to his Board of Directors that Carrie Buck be sterilized. The Board, again in full compliance with the very succinctly drawn statute, ultimately ordered the sterilization. Carrie may have been feeble-minded, but she understood what was about to happen to her. Her lawyers, setting into motion the elaborate appellate procedure provided by the law, applied to the Circuit Court of the County for reversal of the order, but the Court affirmed the sterilization decree. Carrie's petitioners then appealed to the Virginia Supreme Court of Appeals; it granted the appeal, heard the case upon the record, yet agreed with the conclusion reached below that the application of the sterilization law in the case at issue would be a "blessing" for feeble-minded patients like Carrie. The next legal step was an appeal to the Supreme Court of the United States, the constitutional issues raised being alleged denial of *substantive* due process and the "equal protection of the laws," [3] both under the Fourteenth Amendment. Carrie's lawyers had no quarrel with the *procedural* aspects of the Virginia law, readily granting that they provided full due process of law; the attack was upon the *substance* of the legislation. In brief, counsel for the girl contended that not only was the sterilization order not justified on the existing grounds, but that "in no circumstances could such an order be justified" under substantive due process of law; it was on its face arbitrary, capricious, and unreasonable. Moreover, reasoned Carrie's attorneys in their brief, Virginia had violated Carrie's, and similarly afflicted candidates', equal protection of the laws because the law applied only to the

1 Act of March 20, 1924.
2 *Ibid.*
3 *Buck v. Bell,* 274 U.S. 200 (1927).

"small number who are in the institutions named and is not applied to the multitude outside." [1]

Over Mr. Justice Butler's dissent without a written opinion (an annoying idiosyncrasy), Mr. Justice Holmes upheld Virginia's statute and action, joined by Chief Justice Taft and Associate Justices Van Devanter, McReynolds, Brandeis, Sutherland, Sanford, and Stone. Holmes reasoned that since the public welfare has more than once called, and may at almost any time call, upon the best citizens for their lives, it would be "strange if it could not call upon those who already sap the strength of the State for these lesser sacrifices often not felt to be such by those concerned, in order to prevent our being swamped with incompetence." Having established that premise (and one wonders whether any Supreme Court justice on the bench today would employ such reasoning), the famed jurist continued with an oft-quoted passage:

> It is better for all the world, if instead of waiting to execute degenerate offspring for crime, or to let them starve for their imbecility, society can prevent those who are manifestly unfit from continuing their kind. The principle that sustains compulsory vaccination is broad enough to cover cutting the Fallopian tubes. . . . Three generations of imbeciles are enough.[2]

As to the allegations of denial of the equal protection of the laws, the Civil War veteran commented that "it is the usual last resort of constitutional arguments to point out shortcomings of this sort," i.e. that the Virginia statute did not reach "the multitude outside" state institutions. The answer to *that* argument, lectured the dedicated exponent of judicial self-restraint in concluding his opinion for the Court, is that

> the law does all that is needed when it does all that it can, indicates a policy, applies it to all within the lines, and seeks to bring within the lines all similarly situated so far and so fast as its means allow. Of course so far as the operations enable those who otherwise must be kept confined to be returned to the world, and thus open the asylum to others, the equality aimed at it will be more nearly reached. Judgment affirmed.[3]

[1] See Chapter VII for a discussion of the "equal protection clauses."
[2] *Ibid.*, at 207.
[3] *Ibid.*, at 208.

Although the philosophy of *Buck v. Bell* has been subjected to heavy and trenchant criticism—partly with the hindsight of socio-medical developments since the twenties— it still serves to illustrate well some of the problems inherent in the concept of substantive due process of law. Carrie Buck was ultimately sterilized. As of 1967 more than half of the states of the Union still carried sterilization statutes on their books,[1] yet the performed operations in 1964 totaled only 467. But fifteen years after Carrie's future chance of motherhood had been surgically terminated, one man *won* his battle against sterilization on both "substantive due process" and "equal protection" grounds, in a case often regarded as a sequel to *Buck v. Bell*. His name was Arthur Skinner—and he was not precisely a pillar of the community, either.

Arthur Skinner Wins. An Oklahoman, habitually in trouble with the law, Arthur Skinner was convicted in 1926 of the crime of stealing three chickens and was sentenced to the Oklahoma State Reformatory. Three years later he was convicted of the crime of robbery with fire-arms and was again sentenced to the Reformatory. In 1934 he was once more convicted of robbery with firearms, and was sent to the penitentiary, where he was when, in 1935, Oklahoma enacted a new statute that was to prove of considerable interest to him. It was known as the Habitual Criminal Sterilization Act, passed by the legislature in a burst of moralistic enthusiasm and fully confident not only of its wisdom but of its constitutionality. The intriguing law defined a "habitual criminal" as a person who, having been convicted two or more times for crimes "amounting to felonies involving moral turpitude" either in an Oklahoma or in any other state court, is *thereafter* convicted of a *third* such felony in Oklahoma and duly sentenced to a term of imprisonment in an Oklahoma penal institution. The statute then provided that the Oklahoma Attorney-General

---

[1] In March 1965 the Supreme Court refused to rule whether sterilization of a California man violated the Eighth Amendment's ban on "cruel and unusual punishment." (*In re Miguel Vega Andrada*, 380 U.S. 953.) He had agreed to the vasectomy, but later charged it was coerced and "inflicted" as punishment in a misdemeanor case in which he was charged with failure to provide for his four children by his first wife. Having later resumed payments to his ex-wife, and having married his common-law wife (by whom he had had a child out of wedlock), he subsequently sought to have the vasectomy "undone," a feat successful in only 50 per cent of such cases. Andrada's unsuccessful appeal to the Supreme Court left the matter more or less in limbo.

could institute "a proceeding against such a person in the Oklahoma courts for a judgment that such person be rendered sexually sterile." Continued the law:

> If the court or jury finds that the defendant is an "habitual criminal" and that he "may be rendered sexually sterile without detriment to his or her general health," then the court "shall render judgment to the effect that said defendant be rendered sexually sterile" by the operation of a vasectomy in case of a male and of a salpingectomy in case of a female.[1]

The Act went on to state that offenses arising out of the violation of "the prohibitory laws, revenue acts, embezzlement, or political offenses, shall *not* come or be considered within" its terms. In other words, one might commit a crime in these selected and selective areas and not have them "counted" as one of the three crimes that led to the knife for those who committed felonies[2] involving "moral turpitude."

Arthur Skinner was not so fortunate. He had already committed his three felonies involving "moral turpitude"—the chicken theft in 1926, the first robbery with firearms in 1929, and the second robbery with firearms in 1934. Thus he was a perfect candidate when the sterilization statute became law in 1935. For a year he seemed to have escaped, but in 1936 the Attorney-General of Oklahoma began proceedings against him. Properly following every prescribed aspect of procedural due process of law under the statute, the Attorney-General steered the case through the various stages, challenged at each by Skinner's attorneys. But by a 5:4 decision a judgment directing that the vasectomy be performed on Skinner was ultimately affirmed by the Oklahoma Supreme Court.[3] A now thoroughly frightened Arthur Skinner appealed the statute's constitutionality to the United States Supreme Court.

Of the members of the Court that had sealed Carrie Buck's fate fifteen years earlier, all except Mr. Chief Justice Stone had either died, resigned, or retired. As an Associate Justice who had sided with the 8:1 majority in that earlier case, Stone was to find himself again

---

[1] *Skinner v. Oklahoma,* 316 U.S. 535 (1942).
[2] A felony is a crime in general graver or more serious in nature and penal consequence than a misdemeanor.
[3] *Skinner v. Oklahoma,* 198 Okl. 235, 115 P. 2d 123.

on the side of the majority (indeed the Court was to render a unanimous decision), although he disagreed with certain aspects of the opinion written in 1942 by Mr. Justice Douglas.[1] Be it said at once that the Supreme Court did not *reconsider* its *Buck v. Bell*[2] decision —which still stands along with Virginia's statute. While, in a concurring opinion, Mr. Justice Jackson pointedly warned that there are "limits to the extent to which a legislatively represented majority may conduct biological experiments at the expense of the dignity and personality and natural powers of a minority,"[3] the Chief Justice, in his own concurring opinion, made quite clear (he used the term "undoubtedly") that he still considered *Buck v. Bell* to have been properly decided.[4]

The Douglas opinion for the Court, joined by Justices Roberts, Black, Reed, Frankfurter, Murphy, and Byrnes, was actually less concerned with "due process of law" than it was with what it viewed as Skinner's denial by Oklahoma of the "equal protection of the laws." Still, the lack of substantive due process was clearly implied, since Douglas, by continuous inference if not by language, demonstrated that, in fact, the law deprived Skinner of "a basic liberty" by its "inequality." And it was not difficult for him to find the manifold aspects of inequality that were indeed inherent in the Act. Directing his attention to the provision that *included larceny* but *excluded embezzlement* as a crime leading toward sterilization, he wrote with indignation:

> A person who enters a chicken coop and steals chickens commits a felony; . . . and he may be sterilized if he is thrice convicted. If, however, he is the bailee of the property and fraudulently appropriates it, he is an embezzler. . . . Hence no matter how habitual his proclivities for embezzlement are and no matter how often his conviction, he may not be sterilized.[5]

Douglas reminded Oklahoma and the nation that when the law "lays an unequal hand" on those who have committed intrinsically the same quality of offense and sterilizes one and not the other, it has made "as invidious a discrimination as if it had selected a particular race or nationality for oppressive treatment."[6] And he concluded

[1] *Skinner v. Oklahoma*, 316 U.S. 535.
[2] 274 U.S. 200 (1927).
[3] *Skinner v. Oklahoma*, 316 U.S. 535, at 546.
[4] *Ibid.*, at 544.
[5] *Ibid.*, at 539.
[6] *Ibid.*, at 541.

that while there had been "saving features" in the *Buck v. Bell* circumstances, none were present in the *Skinner* case:

> Sterilization of those who have thrice committed grand larceny with immunity for those who are embezzlers is a clear, pointed, unmistakable discrimination. Oklahoma makes no attempt to say that he who commits larceny by trespass or trick or fraud has biologically inheritable traits which he who commits embezzlement lacks. . . . The equal protection [of the laws] clause would indeed be a formula of empty words if such conspicuously artificial lines could be drawn. . . .[1]

To Stone, however, the most significant question of line-drawing involved was not one of "equal protection," but "of whether the wholesale condemnation of a class to such an invasion of personal liberty . . . satisfies the demands for due process." [2] To him and to the entire Court, it clearly did not. Arthur Skinner escaped the surgical reaches of the statute, which was thus declared unconstitutional. Of course, there is a limit on the kind of laws regulating life, liberty, and property that a legislature can make. Notwithstanding the high judicial regard for self-restraint vis-à-vis legislative activities, the demands of due process of law (here substantive due process) will continue to require the drawing of lines.[3] Such line-drawing is even more difficult in the realm of *procedural* due process of law.

---

[1] *Ibid.*, at 541, 542.

[2] *Ibid.*, at 544.

[3] An intriguing new twist to the sterilization problem, one that might ultimately reach the Supreme Court, is the case of one Nancy Hernandez, a 21-year-old mother of two, who faced jail in California in mid-1966 because she refused to submit to sterilization as a condition of probation on a misdemeanor offense. She had pleaded guilty to a minor narcotics charge and was given a suspended sentence and freed on probation by Municipal Court Judge Frank P. Kearney provided she agreed to sterilization. At first she agreed, then changed her mind, and her court-appointed lawyer obtained a writ of habeas corpus. Judge Kearney's order was subsequently overruled as "arbitrary and outside the law" by Superior Court Judge C. Douglas Smith. (See the articles in *The Philadelphia Evening Bulletin*, May 23, 1966; *The New York Times*, May 24, 1966; *ibid.*, May 29, 1966; *ibid*, June 9, 1966; and *Time*, June 3, 1966.)

On the other hand, early that June a 24-year-old unwed mother agreed to be sterilized in order to reduce her sentence for killing her four-day-old son (who was her fourth child born out of wedlock). The mother, who had an I.Q. of 62 and a mental age of 12, was asked by Philadelphia Common Pleas Judge Raymond Pace Alexander if she understood the meaning of sterilization. "Yes, sir," Miss Francine Rutledge replied, "I don't want no more babies." (*The Philadelphia Bulletin*, June 1, 1966.)

PROCEDURAL DUE PROCESS

The number of cases reaching the Supreme Court of the United States on grounds of alleged abridgment or denial of *procedural* due process of law far outweigh those concerned with alleged *substantive* infringements. This is entirely natural, for it is in the execution, administration, and interpretation of the meaning of statutes and executive ordinances that actions of the agents of the governmental process are likely to be challenged on due process grounds. "The history of liberty," once wrote Mr. Justice Frankfurter in a federal case "has largely been the history of observance of procedural safeguards." [1] Much is involved, of course, in the concept of procedural due process of law: it is almost impossible to provide a complete definition. It embraces a general standard of *fairness*. As a minimum, it denies to "governments the power to filch away private rights by hole-and-corner methods"; [2] a host of practices falls into that category. For example, deliberately "stacked" juries, coerced confessions, denial of counsel in criminal cases, and *unreasonable* searches and seizures. The obvious difficulty arises, of course, in a consideration of the question of when, for instance, a confession *is* coerced, or when a search and/or seizure *is* unreasonable. Continuing incorporation of federal standards in criminal justice cases has tended increasingly to narrow the scope of state (and federal) violations of the standard of fairness, but lines must still be drawn. Two well-known cases in the area of search, seizure, confession, and self-incrimination will illuminate both the difficulties involved and the differences of opinion on the meaning and requirements of procedural due process of law.

The Case of Antonio Richard Rochin. Rochin, habitually in difficulties with the Los Angeles police authorities—more often than not because of his exotic tastes in stimuli—lived in a modest two-story house with his mother, his common-law wife, and an assortment of brothers and sisters. For some time the County had tried to "get the goods," literally and figuratively, on Rochin. In June of 1949 the County received what its agents had reasonable ground to believe was reliable information that Rochin was selling narcotics. Hence,

---

[1] *McNabb v. United States*, 318 U.S. 332 (1943), at 347.
[2] J. A. Corry and Henry J. Abraham, *Elements of Democratic Government*, 4th ed. (New York: Oxford University Press, 1964), p. 267.

early on the morning of July 1, 1949, three deputy sheriffs appeared at the Rochin homestead. Finding the door open, they entered, called a soft "hello," walked to the second floor, and forced open the door of Rochin's room. The deputy sheriffs had neither search nor arrest warrants. Inside his room Antonio Richard was sitting partly dressed on the side of the sole bed, on which his spouse was lying. On the night table the deputies spied two morphine capsules. When they shouted "Whose stuff is this?," Rochin quickly grabbed them and put them in his mouth. The agents of the law thereupon "jumped upon him," kicking and pummeling, in the mistaken expectation that he would relinquish the pills. Mr. Rochin swallowed them. The underwriters of due process of law then administered a rather thorough beating to the by then prostrate Rochin, hoping, again unsuccessfully, that he would vomit the desired evidence. Ultimately, the deputies tied and gagged Rochin and took him to a hospital, where they ordered a compliant resident physician to administer to the immobile and irate Rochin an emetic through a stomach tube. That generally unfailing procedure did have the desired effect: Rochin vomited the two morphine capsules which the police agents then presented as the necessary evidence at his subsequent trial. Over the defendant's objections that the police methods of obtaining evidence were not precisely in accordance with Anglo-Saxon traditions of procedural due process of law, and despite the frank acknowledgment of the above-described facts by one of the participating deputies, he was convicted and sentenced to a 60-day prison stint.

Rochin immediately appealed this conviction to the proper appellate tribunal, the California District Court of Appeal. To his chagrin and surprise, that tribunal *affirmed* the trial court's holding, despite its judicial finding that the officers

> were guilty of unlawfully breaking into and entering defendant's room and were guilty of unlawfully assaulting and battering defendant while in the room . . . [and] were guilty of unlawfully assaulting, battering, torturing and falsely imprisoning defendant at the alleged hospital. . . .[1]

What more, must Rochin have asked himself, is necessary to establish rank violation of procedural due process of law and a reversal of the conviction? On the *federal* level, the recovered morphine capsules would clearly and unmistakably have been regarded as the fruit of

[1] *People v. Rochin,* 101 Cal. App. 2nd 140 (December 12, 1950).

an *unreasonable* search and seizure, forbidden by the Fourth Amendment. But it was not until the *Mapp* case [1] in 1961 that the United States Supreme Court ruled that all evidence obtained by searches and seizures in violation of the Fourth Amendment is inadmissible in *state* courts as well as in federal courts.

Since *Rochin* came almost a decade prior to *Mapp*, unless the defendant could demonstrate a violation of the due process of law clause of the Fourteenth Amendment he would have no case, for in 1952 neither the Fourth Amendment nor the compulsory self-incrimination safeguards of the Fifth was held applicable to the states. And California, in line with standing traditions of common law then in use by roughly one-half of the states, did *not* bar the admission at the trial stage of evidence obtained illegally. It enabled the aggrieved party to sue the offending officers, with scant hope of success, needless to add, but such an action in no manner affected his obligation to pay fines and go to jail. This accounts for the reasoning of the District Court of Appeal. Rochin next appealed to the California Supreme Court, which denied his petition for a hearing without opinion. But two of the seven justices dissented from this denial, and in doing so expressed themselves in significant language:

> ... a conviction which rests upon evidence of incriminating objects obtained from the body of the accused by physical abuse is as invalid as a conviction which rests upon a verbal confession extracted from him by such abuse. ... Had the evidence forced from the defendant's lips consisted of an oral confession that he illegally possessed a drug ... he would have the protection of the rule of law which excludes coerced confessions from evidence. But because the evidence forced from his lips consisted of real objects the People of this state are permitted to base a conviction upon it. [We two] find no valid ground of distinction between a verbal confession extracted by physical abuse and a confession wrested from defendant's body by physical abuse.[2]

When the unhappy Rochin then appealed to the Supreme Court of the United States, he was granted *certiorari* and, in due course, his conviction was unanimously reversed on grounds of rank violations of the very rudiments of procedural due process of law. In what was soon to be regarded as one of his most important opinions, Mr. Justice Frankfurter spoke for the Court. He not only outlined the "respon-

[1] *Mapp v. Ohio*, 367 U.S. 643.
[2] *People v. Rochin*, 101 Cal. App. 2nd 140, at 149, 150.

sibilities" of both the state and federal courts and wrote a significant essay on the meaning of due process of law, but he restated his own case-by-case approach to the question of the applicability of the commands of the Constitution.[1]

"The vague contours of the Due Process Clause do not leave judges at large," the eloquent jurist explained; rather, they place upon the Supreme Court the duty of exercising a judgment "within the narrow confines of judicial power in reviewing State convictions, upon interests of society pushing in opposite directions . . . duly mindful of reconciling the needs both of continuity and of change. . . ." [2] Frankfurter then sternly lectured California that the proceedings by which its agents had obtained Rochin's conviction "do more than offend some fastidious squeamishness about combatting crime too energetically." Then came the sentence that represented his test, his creed, in determining the presence or absence of due process of law: *"This is conduct that shocks the conscience."* [3] And he continued to prove why it did:

> Illegally breaking into the privacy of the petitioner, the struggle to open his mouth and remove what was there, the forcible extraction of his stomach's contents—this course of proceeding by agents of government to obtain evidence is bound to offend even hardened sensibilities. They are methods too close to the rack and the screw to permit of constitutional differentiation.[4]

Although Frankfurter went out of his way to assure the states that they had considerable leeway in their administration and enforcement of justice, he reminded them that it is, and must always be, axiomatic that "States in their prosecution respect certain decencies of civilized conduct." Reversing Rochin's conviction for the unanimous Court, Frankfurter terminated his memorable opinion in words symptomatic of his judicial posture on the entire incorporation problem:

> Due process of law, as a historic and generative principle, precludes defining, and thereby confining, these standards of conduct more precisely than to say that convictions cannot be brought about by methods than offend a "sense of justice." [5]

[1] See Chapter III.
[2] *Rochin v. California*, 342 U.S. 165 (1952), at 172, 173.
[3] *Ibid.*, at 172.
[4] *Ibid.*
[5] *Ibid.*, at 173.

Precisely because of the vagueness of that "sense of justice" and, of course, because of their deep commitment to the underdog, Justices Black and Douglas, although naturally voting for the reversal of Rochin's conviction, wrote separate concurring opinions, contending that, while the case was rightly decided, it was decided on wrong grounds. In a judgment which has been subsequently confirmed in the history of incorporation, the two justices held that the basic constitutional issue involved in *Rochin v. California* was not at all the one Frankfurter expressed, that is, a violation of the procedural due process guarantees of the Fourteenth Amendment. Rather, held Black and Douglas, it was that California's agents had, in fact, clearly and unmistakably violated the *specific* commands of the Fifth Amendment that "No person . . . shall be compelled in any criminal case to be a witness against himself," a command which, in their view, extended to the states via the due process of law clause of the Fourteenth Amendment. To base the reversal of Rochin's conviction on a violation of procedural due process was constitutionally a Pyrrhic victory in the eyes of these two advocates of total incorporation of the Bill of Rights. The "does it shock the conscience" test, based on a case-by-case approach to the presence or absence of due process of law, represented a travesty of justice to Black and Douglas. As Black put it in closing his concurring opinion: "I long ago concluded that the accordion-like qualities of this philosophy must inevitably imperil all the individual liberty safeguards specifically enumerated in the Bill of Rights." [1]

Nonetheless, the case was decided, and Rochin owed the reversal of his conviction to considerations of procedural due process. A related case, decided five years later, will illustrate both the assets and liabilities of the due process test approach.

The Case of Paul H. Breithaupt. While driving a pickup truck on a New Mexico highway, one Paul H. Breithaupt collided with a passenger car. Three occupants in the car lost their lives; Breithaupt was seriously injured but eventually recovered. When the police arrived on the scene of the collision they detected unmistakable alcoholic odors and, on investigating, not only found an almost empty pint bottle of liquor in the glove compartment of Paul's pickup truck but

---

[1] *Rochin v. California*, 342 U.S. 165, at 177.

also thought they detected damaging vapors on his breath. The three bodies were taken to the morgue, Breithaupt to the nearest hospital.

As he lay in the emergency room of the hospital, the smell of liquor on the unconscious Breithaupt's breath was unmistakable, and one of the state patrolmen who had been at the scene of the accident requested that a physician take a sample of the patient's blood. An attending physician, using a hypodermic needle, withdrew approximately 20 cubic centimeters of blood from the still unconscious man. The physician then turned the sample over to the patrolman in charge, who submitted it for the customary laboratory analysis. The analysis proved to be positive, indeed: it contained 0.17 per cent alcohol!

When Breithaupt was well enough to stand trial, the state charged him with involuntary manslaughter. The "clincher" proved to be the damaging sample analysis, which was submitted as New Mexico's chief evidence of the accused's culpability. An expert in toxicology and hematology testified that a person with 0.17 per cent alcohol in his blood was decidedly under the influence of intoxicating liquor. Over Breithaupt's objection on procedural due process grounds, the trial judge admitted the blood test results into evidence, and Breithaupt was duly convicted as charged. He accepted his conviction and sentence of imprisonment without appealing the case.

Subsequently, however, he had second thoughts, and sought release from his incarceration by petitioning the Supreme Court of New Mexico for a writ of habeas corpus. That tribunal did hear argument on his petition, but denied the desired writ as being groundless. Breithaupt then petitioned the United States Supreme Court for a writ of *certiorari*, which the Court granted. In essence, Breithaupt contended that his conviction was a *prima facie* violation of procedural due process of law, because it was based on an involuntary blood test which had been taken while he was unconscious. No one had asked him for his consent and he could not have responded in his "senseless condition," even if he had wanted to. Thus he pleaded violation of his liberty without the procedural due process of law guaranteed him by the Fourteenth Amendment to the Constitution. Relying on the Court's unanimous opinion in the *Rochin* case, he argued that the conduct of the state officers of New Mexico involved in his conviction offended that "sense of justice" of which the justices spoke in

Rochin, that here New Mexico's conduct, just as much as California's there, represented, in Mr. Justice Frankfurter's test phrase, "conduct that shocks the conscience."

But two-thirds of the members of the Court disagreed. Seeing an important distinction between the procedures utilized by agents of government in *Rochin* and *Breithaupt,* they were quite prepared to draw a line between the two cases. Speaking for the majority of six, Mr. Justice Clark began his explanation of the distinction by holding that there is nothing "brutal" or "offensive" in the taking of a sample of blood when done, as it was in this case, under the protective eye of a physician. He acknowledged that the driver of the death-truck was unconscious when the blood was taken, but that "the absence of conscious consent, without more, does not necessarily render the taking a violation of a constitutional right; and certainly the test as administered here would not be considered offensive by even the most delicate." Furthermore, Clark went on, endeavoring to explain the labyrinth of the due process test,

> due process is not measured by the yardstick of personal reaction or the sphygmogram [a tracing of curves corresponding with the beat of the heart] of the most sensitive person, but by that whole community sense of "decency and fairness" that has been woven by common experience into the fabric of acceptable conduct. *It is on this bedrock that this Court has established the concept of due process.* The blood test procedure has become routine in our everyday life.[1]

He went on to point out that

> as *against the right of an individual* that his person be held inviolable, even against so slight an intrusion as is involved in applying a blood test of the kind to which nearly millions of Americans submit as a matter of course nearly every day, *must be set the interests of society* in the scientific determination, one of the great causes of the mortal hazards of the road. And the more so since the test likewise may establish innocence, thus affording protection against the treachery of judgment based on one or more of the senses.[2]

Here again, we see the quest for the just line between the rights of an individual citizen and those of society at large—a line particularly difficult to draw when it comes to due process, in general, and *proce-*

---

[1] *Breithaupt v. Abram,* 352 U.S. 432 (1957), at 436. (Italics supplied.)
[2] *Ibid.,* at 439. (Italics supplied.)

dural due process, in particular. Three justices dissented vigorously from the reasoning of the majority of six. Speaking for himself and Associate Justices Black and Douglas—the latter also wrote a separate dissent—Mr. Chief Justice Warren dissented on the ground that *Rochin* was not distinguishable at all but should, in fact, be controlling. He observed that the majority's opinion suggests that an invasion of private rights—i.e. Breithaupt's body—is "brutal" or "offensive" only if the police use force to overcome a suspect's resistance. With deep conviction, the Chief Justice contended that he could not accept "an analysis that would make physical resistance by a prisoner [as in *Rochin*] a prerequisite to the existence of his constitutional rights." [1] Urging that Breithaupt's conviction be reversed, he rhetorically asked whether the taking of spinal fluid from an unconscious person would be condoned because such tests are commonly made and might be made as a scientific aid to law enforcement, and concluded that

> only personal reaction to the stomach pump and the blood test can distinguish them. To base the restriction which the Due Process Clause imposes on state criminal procedures upon such reactions is to build on shifting sands. We should, in my opinion, hold that due process means at least that law enforcement officers in their efforts to obtain evidence from persons suspected of crime must stop short of bruising the body, breaking skin, puncturing tissue or extracting body fluids, whether they contemplate doing it by force or by stealth.[2]

In a separate dissent, joined by his colleague Black, Mr. Justice Douglas stated as the simple crux of the whole matter his firm belief that, under our system of government, "police cannot compel people to furnish the evidence necessary to send them to prison." [3] To Black and Douglas a case such as *Breithaupt* merely confirmed the fears and reservations they expressed in *Rochin*, that the test of whether the conscience is shocked was so uncertain and so subjective that to render justice with an equal eye and an even hand was all but impossible. Their solution, of course, was to incorporate the entire Bill of Rights via the due process clause and thus make its specific provisions applicable to the states.

But *Breithaupt* was confirmed by a 5:4 majority in 1966 in *Schmer-*

---

1 *Ibid.*, at 441.
2 *Ibid.*, at 442.
3 *Ibid.*, at 443.

ber v. California [1] even in the face of the incorporation of the self-incrimination clause that had taken place two years earlier.[2] In the majority opinion, written by Mr. Justice Brennan and joined by Justices Clark, Harlan, Stewart, and White, the Court held that the privilege against self-incrimination does not permit a driver to balk at giving a sample of his blood, taken by medical personnel in a medical environment, for a test to determine if he is drunk. (Schmerber's blood sample showed a blood-alcohol level of 0.18 per cent; California and most other states consider 0.15 per cent as presumptive proof of drunkenness.) The Brennan opinion declared that the Fifth Amendment protected an accused person only from "the use of physical or moral compulsion" to extort "testimonial or communicative" evidence that could be used against him; but that "compulsion which makes the body of a suspect or accused the source of 'real or physical' evidence" that, like a blood sample, *did not involve personal communication or testimony*, did not violate the self-incrimination rule. He made it clear that arrested persons might be required by the police to submit to "fingerprinting, photographing or measurements, to write or speak for identification, to appear in court, to stand, to assume a stance, to walk or to make a particular gesture." [3] Dissenting opinions were written by the Chief Justice and Justices Black and Fortas, with Douglas joining Black's. (Warren, Black, and Douglas had been the three *Breithaupt* dissenters.) "To reach the conclusion that compelling a person to give his blood to help the state convict him," wrote Black, "is not equivalent to compelling him to be a witness against himself strikes me as quite an extraordinary feat." [4] With obvious feeling he concluded that he deeply regretted the Court's holding, and that he would continue to believe

with the Framers that these constitutional safeguards broadly construed by independent tribunals of justice provide our best hope for keeping our people free from governmental oppression.[5]

[1] 384 U.S. 757 (1966).
[2] *Malloy v. Hogan*, 378 U.S. 1.
[3] *Schmerber v. California, loc. cit.*, at 764. (Many states employ other methods of detecting inebriation, such as the drunkometer or breathing apparatus. Seventeen have "implied consent laws," meaning that anyone who drives there agrees to submit to a test of some sort or lose his road privileges. California now (1967) gives drivers a choice between blood, breath, and urine tests.)
[4] *Ibid.*, at 773.
[5] *Ibid.*, at 778.

The Dilemma

We know now, of course, that a majority of the Court has gradually, but still not wholly, moved toward incorporation, particularly in the past decade. Since *Breithaupt* in 1957, the following pertinent prohibitions and provisions of the Bill of Rights have been ruled applicable to the several states by way of the "due process of law" clause of the Fourteenth Amendment:

1961: evidence obtained as a result of unreasonable searches and seizures (Fourth Amendment); [1]

1962: cruel and unusual punishment (Eighth Amendment); [2]

1963: right to counsel in *all* criminal cases (Sixth Amendment); [3]

1964: compulsory self-incrimination (Fifth Amendment); [4]

1965: confrontation by adverse witness (Sixth Amendment). [5]

Admittedly, the incorporation of these various constitutional safeguards of procedural due process provides significant guidelines for applying the three famous adjectives, "arbitrary," "capricious," and "unreasonable." Yet differentiation in posture, analysis, and interpretation is still permitted; it is one thing to *forbid* coerced confessions, to use an obvious can-of-worms, but it is quite another to standardize the *concept* of "coerced confession." We know that it *is* forbidden *when* it *is* one, and that the Supreme Court has provided both the states and the federal government with considerable directions in interpreting the concept, of which the most important is the test of "voluntariness." But at what point does a confession in fact become involuntary? Because no tests, decisions, or guidelines can really gainsay the presence of procedural due process as a lodestar in both statutory and constitutional differentiation, the Court does need to test individual situations for the presence or absence of due process

---

[1] *Mapp v. Ohio*, 367 U.S. 643.

[2] *Robinson v. California*, 370 U.S. 660.

[3] *Gideon v. Wainwright*, 372 U.S. 355. (But evidently not yet to *misdemeanors*; the Supreme Court twice late in 1966 refused to grant review to lower court decisions limiting the *Gideon* decision to *felonies*.)

[4] *Malloy v. Hogan, loc. cit.*

[5] *Pointer v. Texas*, 380 U.S. 400.

of law. This is a judicio-legal fact of the first magnitude unless, of course, the alleged due process violation constitutes on its face an outright violation of an established, identifiable principle about which there is no longer any doubt. For example, the Supreme Court's decision in *Gideon v. Wainwright* [1] left no room for future doubt in its ringing mandate that, henceforth *and* retroactively, there exists an absolute right to have counsel in *all* criminal cases, be they federal or state, and indigents must be provided with counsel.[2] This is now a clear-cut, straightforward requirement of due process. Yet, even the *Gideon* decision has raised numerous problems; for instance, at what point in the judicial process must counsel be provided? [3] Both the complexity of the problem and the philosophical justifications of the inherent line-drawing need a much closer look, but first we shall attempt to summarize the minimum requirements of procedural due process of law.

Basic Procedural Due Process Requirements. The Bill of Rights contains certain concepts inherited from common law that we have always viewed as basic to our government, be it federal or state. They are, more or less in the words of the Constitution (with the appropriate Amendment indicated in parentheses): [4]

(a) the right of people to be secure in their persons, houses, papers, and effects against *unreasonable* searches and seizures (IV);

(b) the issue of a search and/or arrest warrant only upon *probable cause*, supported by oath or affirmation, and *particularly* describing the place to be searched and the person or things to be seized (IV);

(c) *indictment* by grand jury for capital or otherwise infamous crime (V);

(d) *no double jeopardy* (V);

(e) immunity against *compulsory* self-incrimination (V);

(f) the right to a *speedy and public trial*, by an impartial *jury*, in the state and district wherein the crime was committed (VI);

---

[1] 372 U.S. 335 (1963). See Chapter III, *supra.*
[2] *Ibid.*
[3] See, among others, *Miranda v. Arizona*, 384 U.S. 436 (1966); *Escobedo v. Illinois*, 378 U.S. 478 (1947); and *Massiah v. United States*, 377 U.S. 201 (1964). (See also fn. 3, p. 99, *supra*, concerning *misdemeanors.*)
[4] Taken verbatim, or paraphrased, from the Bill of Rights, Amendments Four through Eight. (Italics supplied.)

(g) the right to be *informed* of the nature and cause of the accusation (VI);

(h) the right of the accused to be *confronted* with adverse witnesses (VI);

(i) the right for compulsory process to *obtain witnesses* in the accused's favor (VI);

(j) *counsel* in criminal cases (VI);

(k) safeguards against *excessive bail, excessive fines,* and *cruel and unusual punishment* (VIII).

Although these safeguards, as outlined in the Constitution, are restrictions only upon the federal government, all but (c), (d), and (f) now also apply to the several states as a result of judicial interpretation. And even if a good many of the states do not provide the specific safeguards inherent in these three remaining areas, they are expected to provide procedures that, in their sum total, amount to *due process of law.* In other words, the concept of a "fair trial" demands *safeguards which may not fall below a certain minimum* even if it be that vague minimum of "due process." The freedoms from arbitrary arrest, questioning, and imprisonment, from unreasonable searches and seizures, from the third degree (be it physiological or psychological), from compulsory self-incrimination, from "stacked" juries, from "quickie" trials, are as national in scope, at least in theory, as they would be if they had been derived from just one basic document rather than from 51 documents.

Critical Reactions. Yet, precisely because our federal system is a multiple system of justice, particularly in the realm of criminal procedure, the United States Supreme Court has been increasingly called upon to adjudicate conflicting claims between individuals and society; and most public officials in most states feel that, in so doing, the Court has made it increasingly difficult for them to bring accused violators of the law to bay. The federal judiciary, in particular the Supreme Court, has been bitterly assailed—often in intemperate language, as "a bunch of do-gooders," "bleeding hearts," "criminal-coddlers." Law enforcement officers from J. Edgar Hoover to the lowliest deputy sheriff, raising their voices in protest against what they have viewed as "undue sentimentality toward lawbreakers," have charged the judiciary with making the job of the police authorities not only difficult but well-nigh impossible.

Nor have these charges and complaints been confined to the executive-administrative and legislative segments of the government; members of the judiciary itself have gone on record as viewing with alarm the tough due process standards imposed by the Court, particularly in the realm of procedure in criminal cases. In the Brune Report [1] 36 state chief justices protested what they considered "a dangerous development in Supreme Court adjudication." The Report expressed general alarm over what the majority regarded as the "erosion of the federal system," and, exhorting the Court to return to the "greatest of all judicial powers—the power of judicial self-restraint," addressed itself censorially to most of the controversies that have embroiled the Court in the recent past. The Report particularly criticized the steady evolution by Court mandate of the due process and equal protection clauses of the Fourteenth Amendment as criteria with which the states must comply in exercising their authority; it concluded that, by assuming legislative authority and acting without judicial restraint, the Court had expanded national power and contracted the power of the states. This is not the place to discuss and attempt to rebut the specific charges thus flung at the highest tribunal of the land—it has been well done by others [2]—but there is much to be said for Paul A. Freund's contention that all the Court has really demanded of the states under the due process concepts of Amendment Fourteen is that in order to "turn square corners" in dealing with sensitive areas of human liberty, they should follow procedures that are consistent with due process of law.[3] In his study of the Brune Report, Eugene V. Rostow concluded that its findings represent "not so much a protest against the Court as against the tide of social change reflected in the Court's opinions." [4]

Still, as we have seen, even some members of the Supreme Court itself have voiced serious alarm about the standards and requirements set by a majority of their fellow justices in certain instances, particu-

[1] Named after the Chief Judge of Maryland, who headed the "Committee on Federal-State Relationships as affected by Judicial Decisions," of the 1958 Conference of Chief Justices. The Brune Report is reprinted in full in numerous legal journals, among others, the *Harvard Law Record* of October 23, 1958.

[2] For example, E. V. Rostow's biting attack on the Report in Chapter 3, "The Court and Its Critics," in his fine book, *The Sovereign Prerogative: The Supreme Court and the Quest for Law* (New Haven: Yale University Press, 1962).

[3] *The Supreme Court of the United States: Its Justices, Purposes, and Performance* (Cleveland: The World Publishing Co., 161), p. 87.

[4] *Loc. cit.*, p. 111.

larly in regard to procedural due process. Thus, we have the angry dissenting opinion by Mr. Justice Byron White, joined by Justices Harlan and Clark, in the now famous case of *Massiah v. United States*.[1] The case involved questions of the Fifth Amendment's compulsory self-incrimination and the Sixth Amendment's right to counsel and, by implication, the Fourth Amendment's safeguards against unreasonable search and seizure.

Winston Massiah and the Law. Once again—and as is so often the case in civil liberty litigation, especially in the context of procedural due process—the petitioner was of the lower class of society. Winston Massiah, a merchant seaman on the crew of the S.S. *Santa Maria* in 1958, was engaged in a narcotics conspiracy according to data received by federal customs officials in New York. Indeed, he was about to transport a quantity of narcotics aboard the *Santa Maria* from South America to New York City. As a result of tips received by the customs officers the ship was searched on its arrival in New York. Parcels containing three and a half pounds of cocaine were found in the afterpeak of the vessel, and Massiah was connected with their presence. He was arrested, promptly arraigned, and then indicted for violating the federal narcotics laws; he retained a lawyer, pleaded not guilty, and was released on bail. All of these various steps fully met the requirements of due process of law. Indicted three months after Massiah as a co-conspirator, and charged with the same substantive offense, was one Jesse Colson.

In November 1959, while free on bail, Massiah met Colson, who was also "out" on bail. The two men went for a ride in the latter's automobile and soon parked on a New York street. There, Massiah began a lengthy discussion regarding his part in the narcotics transportation conspiracy, making innumerable incriminating statements— incriminating, that is, if they had been made in the presence of public officials. But, or so Massiah had every reason to believe, Colson was a co-conspirator—hardly a government agent!

However, his "buddy" Colson a few days after his indictment and subsequent bailing had decided to co-operate with government agents in their continuing investigation of the kind of activities in which the two had allegedly been engaged. Hence Jesse Colson permitted a federal agent named Finbarr Murphy to install a radio transmitter under

[1] 377 U.S. 201 (1964).

the front seat of the Colson car. By this means, Murphy, equipped with an appropriate receiving device, could overhear from some distance away conversations carried on in Colson's vehicle. And by prearrangement with Colson, Murphy was parked near the spot, but out of sight of the Colson automobile. Murphy was an eager and accurate listener to Massiah's talkathon.

At the subsequent trial, agent Murphy was permitted by the United States District Court judge to testify regarding the Massiah statements he had overheard. Massiah's defense counsel vigorously objected on two distinct and independent grounds: the alleged violation of the Fourth Amendment's proscription against the admission of evidence obtained as a result of unreasonable searches and seizures, and the alleged violation of Massiah's rights according to the Fifth *and* Sixth Amendments because of the admission in evidence of the *incriminating statements* he had made in the car *after he had been indicted* and *in the absence of his retained counsel.* The jury convicted Massiah and he was sentenced to nine years in prison. His conviction was affirmed by the U.S. Circuit Court of Appeals, and he appealed to the U.S. Supreme Court, which granted *certiorari*.[1]

Addressing himself to the second argument and concentrating upon the underlined portions of the defendant's claims, Mr. Justice Stewart's majority opinion for six members of the Court did not reach the *Fourth* Amendment question at all, although it was implicit in the litigation, of course. Stewart, hardly classifiable as a doctrinaire "libertarian activist" or a "bleeding heart," very simply pointed out for himself, the Chief Justice, and Associate Justices Black, Douglas, Brennan, and Goldberg that Massiah had been denied the basic protections of the Sixth and Fifth Amendments' guarantees of the right of counsel and against compulsory self-incrimination, respectively; the information that convicted him had been "deliberately elicited from him" by federal agents "*after* he had been indicted and in the absence of his counsel." Winston Massiah "did not even know that he was under interrogation by a government agent." Concluded Stewart:

> *Fourth* Amendment problems aside . . . all that we hold is that a defendant's own incriminating statements, obtained by federal agents

[1] 374 U.S. 805 (1963).

under the circumstances here disclosed, could not constitutionally be used by the prosecution as evidence against *him* at his trial.[1]

And Massiah's conviction was thus reversed—which, since it had been based on what was now held to have been illegally obtained and illegally admitted evidence, meant that he went scot-free.

The majority's reasoning infuriated Mr. Justice White. His lengthy dissenting opinion for himself and Justices Clark and Harlan asked precisely the sort of questions the average observer of criminal justice might ask himself:

> Undoubtedly, the evidence excluded in this case would not have been available but for the conduct of Colson in cooperation with agent Murphy, but *is it this kind of conduct which should be forbidden to those charged with law enforcement?* It is one thing to establish safeguards against procedures fraught with the potentiality of coercion and to outlaw "easy but self-defeating ways in which brutality is substituted for brains as an instrument of crime detection." [2]

But in the *Massiah* case, he continued, there was no "substitution of brutality for brains, no inherent danger of police coercion justifying the prophylactic effect of another exclusionary rule." The petitioner, White went on, had not been interrogated in a police station, had not been surrounded by numerous officers, questioned in relays, or been forbidden access to others. "Law enforcement," commented President Kennedy's first appointee to the highest bench, "may have the elements of a contest about it, but it is not a game." [3]

The White dissent was replete with admonitions and exhortations lest the line drawn in criminal justice between the rights of society and those of the accused be drawn too much in favor of the accused. It was a pungent broadside attack on the whole approach of the Court's majority, not just in *Massiah* but in numerous other cases in this field of adjudication, in the judicial quest for a balance of interests between fairness for the criminal suspect and adequate protection for the public at large. White expressed grave concern lest the *Massiah* decision discourage both the ordinary citizen and the confessed crim-

---

[1] *Massiah v. United States*, 377 U.S. 201 (1964), at 207. (Italics supplied for "Fourth" only.)

[2] *Ibid.*, at 213 (Italics supplied.)

[3] *Ibid.*, at 213.

inal "from reporting what he knows to the authorities and from lend-
ing his aid to secure evidence of crime":

> Certainly after this case the Colsons will be few and far between, and
> the Massiahs can breathe much easier, secure in the knowledge that
> the Constitution furnishes an important measure of protection against
> faithless compatriots. . . .[1]

And, seconding a contention so frequently voiced by those charged
with the prosecution of crime and law enforcement, White warned
that "meanwhile, of course, the public will again be the loser and law
enforcement presented with another serious dilemma." [2] Less than
five weeks later Mr. Justice White was to have occasion to become
even more alarmed, although this time he gained the vote of Mr.
Justice Stewart as well as the continued support of Justices Clark and
Harlan.

Danny Escobedo's Right to Counsel. On the dark night of January
19, 1960, Manuel Valtierra was shot in the back and died. He was
the brother-in-law of a 22-year-old, 5 ft. 5 in., 106 lbs. Chicago laborer
of Mexican extraction, named Danny Escobedo. At 2:30 A.M. on the
following morning Danny, his now-widowed sister, Grace, and two
of Danny's friends, Bobby Chan, 17, and Benni DiGerlando, 18, were
arrested by Chicago police *without* warrants and questioned inten-
sively at headquarters. Danny refused to make any statement whatever to his questioners. At 5:00 P.M. on that afternoon, after a full
fourteen and a half hours of interrogation, he was released together
with the others pursuant to an Illinois state court writ of habeas
corpus, obtained by attorney Warren Wolfson, who had once before
represented Escobedo in a personal injury case and who had been
called into the present case by Chan's mother. But on January 30,
DiGerlando allegedly voluntarily confessed to his part in the crime
and informed the police authorities that Danny was the one who had
fired the fatal shots on the night of the murder. Between 8:00 and
9:00 P.M. on the day of DiGerlando's assertions Danny Escobedo was
accordingly re-arrested and, his hands manacled behind his back,
taken to police headquarters together with Grace and Chan who
were also placed under arrest.

En route to the police station, one of the arresting officers told

---

[1] *Ibid.*, at 212.
[2] *Ibid.*

Danny that DiGerlando had named him as the one who had shot his brother-in-law. At his subsequent trial, Danny swore—without any contradiction from the officers involved—that "the detectives said they had us pretty well, up pretty tight, and we might as well admit to this crime," to which, Danny testified, he replied, "I am sorry but I would like to have advice from my lawyer." On arrival at the police station around 9:00 P.M. Danny had been taken to the Homicide Bureau for questioning, after having been in the "lockup" for a while. In vain Danny asked to see his lawyer, Wolfson. The latter, having been told of the re-arrest by Chan's mother, had immediately gone to the police station, where he arrived a few minutes after Danny. Mr. Wolfson at once asked to see Danny, but the police told Wolfson, "Danny doesn't know you." Wolfson unsuccessfully repeated the request to see his client on some five or six separate occasions throughout the evening, but each was denied politely by the authorities, although Wolfson quoted to Homicide Bureau Chief Flynn the pertinent section of the Illinois Criminal Code which allows an attorney to see his client "except in cases of imminent escape." Wolfson and Danny did chance to catch a glimpse of one another "for a second or two" when the lawyer spotted Danny through a half-open door, waved to him, and was greeted by a similar wave by Danny—whereupon the door was quickly closed. At 1:00 A.M., realizing that he was not going to get anywhere, Wolfson signed an official complaint with Commissioner Phelan of the Chicago Police Department and went home.[1]

The interrogation of Danny Escobedo went apace, amidst his repeatedly unsuccessful pleas to see his attorney. At the trial the defendant and his interrogators disagreed on Danny's assertion that a Spanish-speaking interrogator, Officer Montejano, had offered to let his sister, Chan, and him "go home" if Danny "pinned it on DiGerlando." But the record showed that when DiGerlando and Danny were confronted with each other during the course of the night, Danny called DiGerlando a liar and said, "I didn't shoot Manuel, you did." In this manner, of course, Danny for the first time admitted to some knowledge of the crime, at least indirectly. Then, in the face of Montejano's alleged promise that a full statement would free him, Grace, and Chan, Danny further implicated himself as well as the other three accused in the murder plot. At this point, an Assistant

---

[1] *Escobedo v. Illinois*, 378 U.S. 478 (1964).

State's Attorney, Theodore J. Cooper, was summoned by the inter-rogating officers " to take" a full statement. Mr. Cooper, an able and experienced lawyer, not only failed to advise Danny of his roster of constitutional rights before, during, or after "taking" the statement, but his questions were obviously carefully framed so as to ascertain admissibility into evidence at the trial. In any event, the record stands undisputed that no one during the interrogation advised Danny of his rights and that at no time during the long evening, despite re-peated requests by Danny and Wolfson, was he allowed legal counsel. Danny, Grace, and Chan were all indicted for murder, but Grace was later acquitted for lack of evidence and the charges against Chan were dropped. DiGerlando, who later charged that his confession was beaten out of him, received a life sentence. As for Danny, his defense moved, both before and during his trial, that the incriminating state-ment he had given to Cooper be suppressed; but the trial judge de-nied each motion, holding the confession to have been voluntary. Danny Escobedo was accordingly convicted of murder and sentenced to a 20-year term in prison. He, of course, appealed his conviction to the Supreme Court of Illinois on grounds of due process of law.

That tribunal reversed the conviction of the troubled young man, who had known previous arrests, on February 1, 1963, holding that the defendant understood that "he would be permitted to go home if he gave the statement and would be granted an immunity from prose-cution." [1] But the State petitioned for, and the Illinois Supreme Court granted, a rehearing—whereupon the latter reversed itself and the conviction below, ruling:

> [t]he officer [Montejano] denied making the promise and the trier of fact believed him. We find no reason for disturbing the trial court's finding that the confession was voluntary.[2]

Danny Escobedo's counsel then appealed to the United States Su-preme Court for review—his last hope—and won the first round when the Court granted a writ of *certiorari* in order to consider whether the petitioner's statement to Cooper was in fact constitutionally admis-sible at his trial.[3] On June 22, 1964, in the narrowest possible division,

[1] *Ibid.*, at 483.
[2] *Ibid.*, at 484.
[3] *Escobedo v. Illinois*, 375 U.S. 902 (1964).

5:4, the Court responded "no," reversed Danny's conviction and remanded it to the Illinois trial court "for proceedings not inconsistent with this opinion." But the State of Illinois decided that it could not obtain a conviction without the now inadmissible statement, dropped the charges, and Danny was released from jail where he had spent almost four and a half years.

To understand the Supreme Court's majority opinion by Mr. Justice Goldberg for himself, the Chief Justice, and Associate Justices Black, Douglas, and Brennan, it is necessary to remember not only the increasingly general "toughening and tightening" of due process standards demanded by the Court of the states, but also what it had done concerning both the right to counsel and the use of confessions between the day of Danny's arrest in 1960 and his appeal to the court of last resort in 1964. Regarding the right to counsel, the Supreme Court in 1961 overruled the capital criminal conviction of Charles Clarence Hamilton on the *sole* ground, and for the first time, that the defendant had not been represented by counsel at the *arraignment*,[1] a "critical stage." [2] Two years later the *Gideon* case [3] was decided which, as we have already seen, extended the absolute right of indigents to have counsel assigned in *all* criminal cases—although so far apparently exempting *misdemeanors*—by making the Sixth Amendment's requirements of "the Assistance of Counsel" obligatory upon the states via the due process of law clause of the Fourteenth Amendment. And two weeks after *Gideon*, the Court reversed the capital conviction of one Robert Galloway White *solely* because the defendant had not been represented by counsel at an even earlier stage than arraignment, namely the "preliminary examination." [4] The *White* decision was based on the "critical stage logic" of the *Hamilton* case.[5] Regarding the problem of "voluntary confessions" which was so crucial in the *Escobedo* ruling, the Court had for some

---

[1] That stage of the proceedings in criminal justice when a prisoner is called to the bar of the court of jurisdiction to be identified, to hear the formal charges against him, and to make an appropriate plea.

[2] *Hamilton v. Alabama*, 368 U.S. 52 (1961).

[3] *Gideon v. Wainwright*, 372 U.S. 335 (1963).

[4] *White v. Maryland*, 373 U.S. 59 (1963). In the "preliminary examination" stage, following arrest, the apprehended is brought before a magistrate or a commissioner to determine whether he shall be released or *be held to answer* for the alleged offense.

[5] *Hamilton v. Alabama*, loc. cit.

time shown increasing concern about their use as the basis for convictions in criminal cases. Until the late 1950's, the failure to bring an accused in promptly for a preliminary examination, the number of hours of interrogation, the refusal to allow communication with counsel, and long incommunicado detention had not in and of themselves been considered enough to violate due process of law on the *state* level. [1] However, by the beginning of the 1960's, the stringent new judicial approach became readily apparent; one well-known instance of the reversal of a conviction based on a "voluntary confession" occurred in the case of Raymond L. Haynes because the State of Washington authorities had refused to permit him to telephone his wife, who would then have called an attorney.[2] Then, of course, came the decision in *Massiah*.[3]

In reversing Danny Escobedo's appeal conviction, the five-man Supreme Court majority stated the requirements for *early* implementation of the now "nationalized" right to counsel in all criminal cases *and* a confirmed, fundamental, judicially established, distrust of confessions. The basic effect of Mr. Justice Goldberg's opinion for the slender majority was, as the *Defender Newsletter* phrased it, to cause "the adversary system, traditionally restricted to the trial stage, [to be] hauled back slowly into the earlier stages of criminal proceedings." [4] Goldberg's specific point in *Escobedo* was quite simply and unequivocally that a person can consult with a lawyer *as soon as* a police investigation makes him a prime subject. Anticipating the heavy professional and lay criticism that was to come as a result of the decision, and combatting the four dissenters, Goldberg concluded that the *Escobedo* decision did not affect the powers of the police to investigate "an unsolved crime," but when, as in Danny's case, "the process shifts from investigatory to accusatory—when its focus is on the accused and its purpose is to elicit a confession—our adversary system begins to operate, and, under the circumstances here, the accused must be permitted to consult with his lawyer." [5] Earlier, Goldberg had spelled out the majority's specific holding as follows:

1 E.g. *Lisenba v. California*, 314 U.S. 219 (1941); *Crooker v. California*, 357 U.S. 433 (1958); *Cicenia v. Lagay*, 357 U.S. 504 (1958).
2 *Haynes v. Washington*, 373 U.S. 503 (1963).
3 *Massiah v. United States*, 377 U.S. 201 (1964).
4 November 2, 1964.
5 *Escobedo v. Illinois*, 378 U.S. 478 (1964), at 492.

We hold, therefore, that where, as here, the investigation is no longer a general inquiry into an unsolved crime but has begun to focus on a particular suspect, the suspect has been taken into police custody, the police carry out a process of interrogations that lends itself to eliciting incriminating statements, the suspect has requested and been denied an opportunity to consult with his lawyer, and the police have not effectively warned him of his absolute constitutional right to remain silent, the accused has been denied "the Assistance of Counsel" in violation of the Sixth Amendment to the Constitution as "made obligatory upon the States by the Fourteenth Amendment"... and that no statement elicited by the police during the interrogation may be used against him at a criminal trial.[1]

The four dissenting justices, however, were not convinced. Three separate dissenting opinions were written: one by Mr. Justice Harlan, one by Mr. Justice Stewart—who had been on the other side and, in fact, wrote the majority opinion in *Massiah* [2]—and one by Mr. Justice White, who was joined by Mr. Justice Clark and, again, by their colleague Stewart. The over-all tenor of the dissenting opinions was one of genuine concern and worry lest the decision hamper criminal law enforcement. Harlan wrote that he regarded the new rule formulated by the majority as "most ill-conceived and that it seriously and unjustifiably fetters perfectly legitimate methods of criminal law enforcement." [3] Stewart reasoned that the decision would have an extremely "unfortunate impact" on the fair and adequate administration of criminal justice. He explained his *Massiah* stand on the basis of what he deemed the overriding fact that Massiah had already been arraigned and indicted, after which the incriminating evidence was elicited from him by trickery while he was free on bail.[4] The longest dissent was White's who argued that the new ruling would cripple law enforcement and would render its tasks "a great deal more difficult." Bitterly, he asserted that from now on an accused's right to counsel would require "a rule wholly unworkable and impossible to administer unless police cars are equipped with public defenders and undercover agents and police informants have counsel at their side." [5] After pleading for more "reasonableness" and a more balanced ap-

[1] *Ibid.*, at 490-91.
[2] *Massiah v. United States*, 377 U.S. 201 (1964).
[3] *Escobedo v. Illinois*, 378 U.S. 478 (1964), at 493.
[4] *Ibid.*
[5] *Ibid.*, at 496.

proach that would eschew such a stringent and "nebulous" rule, the one-time Deputy Attorney-General of the United States concluded wistfully:

> I do not suggest for a moment that law enforcement will be destroyed by the rule announced today. The need for peace and order is too insistent for that. But it will be crippled and its task made a great deal more difficult, all in my opinion, for unsound, unstated reasons, which can find no home in any of the provisions of the Constitution.[1]

Across the country the police and prosecuting authorities alike echoed the four dissenting jurists. Thus John Collins, Counsel for Los Angeles County, attacked the Supreme Court for giving "the criminal one more advantage." And Police Chief Hobson McGill of Houston, Texas, contended that the police would "naturally" like to talk to "a person before his lawyer does, because we know that many a lawyer is unscrupulous and will advise his client to say nothing, even when he knows that his client is guilty." [2] Yet two years later many of the nation's top prosecutors conceded that law enforcement had not suffered from *Escobedo*.

There is no question, however, that the *Escobedo* decision, far more than *Massiah*, presented both the legal profession and the police authorities with what can only be styled as an enormous challenge. To interrogate a suspect behind closed doors in order to secure a confession was a concept not only based on the custom and usage of centuries, but it had quite logically become a deeply entrenched police practice, strongly supported by both "traditional" and "reform" elements in the ranks of those charged with the administration of criminal justice. Fully aware of this apprehensiveness and the general unpopularity of the decision, Mr. Justice Goldberg endeavored to put matters into their proper focus by appealing for a return to the obligations and commands of law enforcement by a government in democratic society:

> We have ... learned the ... lesson of history that no system of criminal justice can, or should, survive if it comes to depend for its continued effectiveness on the citizens' abdication through unawareness of their constitutional rights. No system worth preserving should have to *fear* that if an accused is permitted to consult with a lawyer, he will become aware of, and exercise these rights. *If the exercise of constitu-*

[1] *Ibid.*, at 499.
[2] As quoted in *Time* magazine, July 3, 1964.

tional rights will thwart the effectiveness of a system of law enforcement, then there is something very wrong with that system.[1]

Escobedo Extended. By January 1966 two United States Courts of Appeals had interpreted *Escobedo* in diametrically opposite ways. Duty-bound to referee such a conflict, the Supreme Court sifted fully 170 confession appeals and accepted for review five involving six defendants. On June 12, 1966, came the Court's 5:4 answer: far from totally unexpected, the *Escobedo* rule was extended significantly so as to prohibit police interrogation of any suspect in custody, without his consent, unless a defense attorney is present.[2] In effect, the Supreme Court thus answered two years of bitter criticism over its *Escobedo* ruling with a sweeping libertarian opinion that mandated important changes in police interrogation as that had been practiced in most of the states. "Instead of backing off," a pro-*Escobedo* attorney exulted, "the Court has put a full-dress suit on Danny Escobedo. All that's left are the spats and the boutonniere!"[3] While the Court did not outlaw confession, and stopped short of an absolute requirement that a lawyer be present before a suspect can be questioned, there is no doubt that the majority opinion, written by the Chief Justice himself, joined by Justices Black, Douglas, Brennan, and Fortas, intended to extend *Escobedo.* Over the bitter dissents by Justices Clark, Harlan, Stewart, and White, who denounced the decision (Harlan termed it "dangerous experimentation" at a time of a "high crime rate that is a matter of growing concern"[4]) the Court in effect laid down the following rules which police must follow before attempting to question an arrested criminal suspect:

1. He must be told he has the right to stay silent.

2. He must be told anything he says may be used against him in court.

3. He must be told he has the right to have an attorney with him before any questioning.

[1] *Escobedo v. Illinois, loc. cit.,* p. 492.
[2] *Miranda v. Arizona, Vignera v. New York, Westover v. United States, California v. Stewart*—all 384 U.S. 436 (1966).
[3] As quoted by Sidney E. Zion in "Beyond Escobedo Case," *The New York Times,* June 14, 1966, p. 25.
[4] Oral comment from the bench by Mr. Justice Harlan in the lead case, *Miranda v. Arizona (The New York Times,* June 14, 1966, p. 1).

4. He must be told that, if he wants an attorney but cannot afford one, an attorney will be provided for him free.[1]

5. If, after being told this, an arrested suspect says he does not want a lawyer and is willing to be questioned, he may be, provided he reached his decision "knowingly and intelligently."

6. If, after being told all his rights, a suspect agrees to be questioned, he can shut off the questions any time after they have started, whether or not he has an attorney with him.

Apprised of the Court's decision, Danny Escobedo said, "I think it was very nice of them. Something good." [2]

And that, of course, brings us back to the basic dilemma of values and lines. Perhaps their presence and the need to draw them wisely and well is more pressing and more widely perceived in the realm of criminal justice than in any of the other areas under discussion.

DUE PROCESS OF LAW IN PERSPECTIVE

No one challenges the basic contention that both the individual and society are entitled to "due process of law." The balance, however, has of late shifted to the side of the potential or actual lawbreaker—in the opinion of a good many observers. The Supreme Court, as we have seen, has come under heavy fire because of its tightening of due process concepts in recent decisions, particularly in the field of criminal justice. Has the Court gone too far—or not far enough? There is no answer that will please both sides of the question, let alone its manifold subdivisions. But it is certainly possible to consider some fundamental points.

"THE CRIMINAL GETS THE BREAKS"

This caption in an article in *The New York Times Magazine* late in 1964 was written by Dean Daniel Gutman of the New York Law

---

[1] A warning in the language of the Court's opinion would thus read: "The law requires that you be advised that you have the right to remain silent, that anything you say can be used against you in a court of law, that you have the right to the presence of an attorney, and that if you cannot afford an attorney one will be appointed for you prior to any questioning if you so desire." (*Miranda v. Arizona, loc. cit.*, at 479.)

[2] *The New York Times*, June 19, 1966.

School.[1] With unassailable statistics demonstrating a continued upward trend in crime, Dean Gutman warned that "we do not solve the problem of dealing with those who make crime their business by providing procedural methods of escape for the guilty, to the detriment of the law-abiding who are victimized by the lawless." After reciting a number of the more controversial Supreme Court decisions "in favor of criminals"—among them the *Massiah* and *Escobedo* rulings —the author called for a series of steps to be taken "within the framework of the Constitution and the Bill of Rights" to remedy the situation. Among them were (1) legislation to permit wiretapping, pursuant to court order, for evidence of major crimes; (b) "recodification" of procedural requirements for search and seizure, "which are distinctive for ancient strictures no longer valid"; (c) extension of the right to detain and interrogate, with due safeguards against coercion or other violation of constitutional rights; (d) clarification of the "extent and application" of the concept of right to counsel; and (e) "relaxation of the rule excluding all evidence improperly obtained, so as to vest discretion as to admission in the trial judge." [2] Such a list prompts recognition of the paradox that the administration of justice poses to thoughtful and committed Americans like Dean Gutman, the members of the Supreme Court, and their respective supporters and detractors. The paradox demands an answer, but there may well be none—certainly none to satisfy all—and all too often it depends upon whose ox is being gored at a particular time and place! In 1965, in an attempt to find at least a partial solution, the American Bar Association began a three-year $750,000 study and search for "minimum standards of criminal justice for both state and federal courts." The program was being conducted by a distinguished 18-member committee, headed by J. Edward Lumbard, Chief Judge of the United States Court of Appeals for the Second Circuit. But even in the event of utopian conclusions in 1968, and their even less likely acceptance by all federal and state agencies concerned, the basic issues and doubts raised by men like Dean Gutman are likely to remain.

Has the Court Been Too Lenient? It is entirely natural to ask—as, for example, Lewis F. Powell, Jr., the 1965 President of the American Bar Association has done—whether the Supreme Court of the United

---

[1] November 29, 1964, p. 36. (The New York Law School is not to be confused with the New York University School of Law.)
[2] *Ibid.*, p. 123.

States has not in fact tipped the balance of justice in favor of the criminal to the detriment of the public? Given a rise in crime from 1958 to 1967 at a rate five times faster than the not inconsiderable growth of America's population, it is indeed understandable why professionals and laymen alike should be fond of quoting Mr. Justice Cardozo's well-known observation that "Justice is due the accused, but it is also due the accuser." Or, as Mr. Justice Robert H. Jackson pointed out in a case involving the question of due process in connection with the composition of a "blue ribbon" [1] jury: "Society also has a right to a fair trial. The defendant's right is a neutral jury. He has no constitutional right to friends on a jury." [2]

Yet in insisting upon strict standards of decency and fairness in governmental law-making, law-enforcing, and prosecuting, the Court simply performs its historic function of protecting the rights of the individual against the alleged unlawful acts of government. After all, as Mr. Justice Brennan once put the matter so well in speaking for the 7:1 Court in a reversal of the conviction of union leader Clinton E. Jencks, a suspected perjurer of Communist persuasion, who had not been permitted to attempt to impeach testimony given to the F.B.I. on the basis of which he had been found guilty and convicted in the trial court below:

> ... the interest of the United States [and any of the several states] "is *not that it shall win a case, but that justice shall be done."* [3]

There is no doubt that this philosophy is "hard-to-take" in specific instances—but can there really be any compromise with it under our form of government? The answer must be a firm "NO"!

True, indeed, that men and women like Rochin, Jencks, Mapp, Massiah, Escobedo, Robinson, Malloy, Murphy, and Miranda are neither paragons of citizenship nor likely to "stay out of trouble" despite their "victories" at the bar of the Supreme Court. Indeed, almost all of them did again run afoul of the law. That, however, is beside the main issue; what *is* very much the issue is the need to provide justice in accordance with the commands of our constitutional principles, in this case due process of law.

---

[1] A special jury which in some jurisdictions—e.g. Manhattan—may be selected by the jury commissioner from those qualified as trial jurors on the basis of special or superior qualifications.

[2] *Fay v. New York*, 332 U.S. 261 (1947), at 288-9.

[3] *Jencks v. United States*, 353 U.S. 657 (1957), at 668, quoting from *Berger v. United States*, 295 U.S. 78, at 88. (Italics supplied.)

But to give some thought to certain of the specific attacks upon Supreme Court rulings, *just which* of the more recent, controversial issues would we have the Court or—failing its acquiescence—the legislative branches alter, if not negate? The famed *Gideon* decision that guaranteed counsel in state criminal proceedings for indigent defendants in all criminal cases? [1] Or its subsequent extension to the preliminary hearing stage? [2] Or its farther extension to the interrogation stage following arrest? [3] Can any member of a democratic society *honestly* argue the point that counsel in a criminal case is a luxury, that he who cannot afford it is not entitled to it? Or that, as in Danny Escobedo's situation, a request to consult with one's attorney prior to a police interrogation is somehow loading the dice against the government?

Or, to consider an allied area of due process, are we really prepared to oppose or even reverse the Court's 1964 decision that the Fifth Amendment's tradition-heavy guarantee against compulsory self-incrimination is applicable to the states as well as the federal government? [4] Totalitarian societies may well approve incrimination, coercion, star-chambers, forced confession—but how can we justify it under our system? Admittedly, there are matters of degree involved here—as there are in all of these areas—and perhaps the aforementioned A.B.A. study will result in some viable line-drawing; but there can hardly be any compromise with the elementary command that a suspect need not "sing" unless he so desires. [5] It is understandably revolting to find obvious, confessed murderers go scot-free (indeed, the phrase "getting away with murder" applies here literally) as, for

[1] *Gideon v. Wainwright*, 372 U.S. 335 (1963).
[2] *Escobedo v. Illinois*, 378 U.S. 478 (1964).
[3] *Miranda v. Arizona*, 384 U.S. 436 (1966).
[4] *Malloy v. Hogan*, 378 U.S. 1 (1964).
[5] Cf. *Miranda v. Arizona, loc. cit.* Following the uproar caused by this and the other *Miranda* rules, the findings of a major statistical study were disclosed by Evelle E. Younger, the District Attorney of Los Angeles County (which has the largest case load in the country). The survey, which covered 4000 felony cases, and the results of which frankly "amazed" Mr. Younger, showed that confessions were needed for successful prosecution in fewer than 10 per cent of the 4000 cases, and that 50 per cent of the suspects were confessing *despite* the warning by the police. "The most significant things about our findings," commented Younger (a former F.B.I. agent), "are that suspects will talk regardless of the warning and furthermore it isn't so all-fired important whether they talk or not." (*The New York Times*, August 21, 1966.) The Younger study confirmed similar findings by Brooklyn Supreme Court Justice Nathan R. Sobel and by Detroit's Chief of Detectives, Vincent W. Piersante. (See Sidney Zion, "So They Don't Talk," *The New York Times, loc. cit.*)

example, one Arthur Culombe did in a grisly, multiple-murder case in Connecticut.[1] But the partially demented Culombe's confession had been *coerced* by Connecticut authorities in the most devious and patently illegal manner, involving the accused's family. True, one may well ask why the State was not justified in utilizing *any* methods that would bring such a criminal to justice? The answer is simple: because of our civilized standards of decency, fair play, and due process, our Constitution simply and resolutely proscribes such methods.

There is neither the intention nor the available time and space to survey each of the various contentious and so difficult areas in which the lines of private and public rights converge. But one last illustration: the complex matter of search and seizure. Under the Fourth Amendment, *unreasonable* searches and seizures are forbidden; out of this grew the so-called exclusionary rule, applied to the federal government as of 1914 [2] and, as we noted in the *Mapp* case,[3] to the states in 1961. The exclusionary rule forbids the use of any illegally obtained evidence to convict an accused in court; "fishing expeditions" on the part of police in search of evidence are thus out. Before asking for an arrest warrant, the police officer must convince the warrant-issuing magistrate of his "personal knowledge" of "probable cause." To obtain a search warrant, the place to be searched *and* the object(s) to be seized must be described "particularly." Warrants are not issuable for "general" searches. But there are—because there must be—situations in which the search of a person or the immediate surroundings is lawful *if* it is "incidental" to a legal arrest—i.e. one with an arrest warrant or one on the basis of probable cause. And there are certain situations in which it is considered "reasonable" to search without warrants provided there *is* "probable cause"—mere "suspicion" is not enough: for example, in case of a valid arrest with a proper arrest warrant,[4] in case of *moving* vehicles,[5] to discover weapons and/or to prevent destruction of evidence,[6] and the common-law right of a police agent to search *if* he has "probable cause" that a crime is being committed. Despite the increasingly stringent judicial requirements,

---

[1] *Culombe v. Connecticut*, 367 U.S. 568 (1961).
[2] *Weeks v. United States*, 232 U.S. 383.
[3] *Mapp v. Ohio*, 367 U.S. 643.
[4] *United States v. Rabinowitz*, 339 U.S. 56 (1950).
[5] *Carroll v. United States*, 267 U.S. 132 (1925).
[6] *Agnello v. United States*, 269 U.S. 20 (1925).

in the search-and-seizure field the cards are still heavily stacked in favor of the agents of government—and perhaps they have to be. But here, too, frustrating as it may be, the rules of the constitutional game must be observed.

To illustrate further: wire-tapping, one of the most vexatious of the due process problems, is *not* unconstitutional—or at least has not yet been held to be. The famous 5:4 *Olmstead* case of 1928 declared it *not* to be a Fourth Amendment violation because it "does not involve a physical intrusion on the defendant's premises"—over Mr. Justice Holmes's vigorous dissent that it is "dirty business"—and this decision has never been overruled.[1] But what then *is* "wire-tapping"? The Federal Communications Act of 1934 (and many state statutes[2]) expressly forbids it, yet the courts have held that mere "interception" is not a violation of the Act's famous Section 605 *unless there is also "divulgence."* Hence we have something that is proscribed yet goes on constantly! But wire-tapping makes the citizen prey to the very kind of "fishing expedition" which is theoretically forbidden under the Fourth Amendment. Modern scientific "advances" in the realm of detection are rapidly reducing privacy to a shibboleth. Thus, as was demonstrated in 1965 and 1966 to a subcommittee of the United States Senate's Committee on the Judiciary, headed by Senator Edward V. Long (D.-Mo.), we now have available such eavesdropping devices as tiny radio transmitters that can be concealed in a martini olive, with the toothpick serving as the antenna; in a pencil; in a wrist watch or a tie clasp; in a pack of cigarettes or just a cigarette butt; in a picture frame; in a boutonniere or a cigarette lighter; or a woman's purse—even in the cavity of a tooth of an intimate associate![3] Then there is the laser, a device which can transmit a concentrated beam of light to a room several blocks away so as to reflect back a television picture of everything happening in the room, including the sound! Perhaps it was specters such as these that caused Mr. Justice Nathan R. Sobel of the New York State Supreme Court (Brooklyn Division) to declare unconstitutional on March 1, 1965, the New York State law that had author-

---

[1] *Olmstead v. United States*, 277 U.S. 438. (Italics supplied.)

[2] In January 1967, outright bans, *including* agents of government, existed in California, Florida, Illinois, Kentucky, Michigan, New Jersey, Pennsylvania, and Wisconsin—which did not necessarily mean that the bans were in fact enforced.

[3] E.g. *The Evening Bulletin* (Philadelphia, Pa.), February 19, 1965; *The New York Times*, February 28, 1966; *Life*, May 20, 1966.

ized court-approved electronic eavesdropping on a suspect's private premises. In his 32-page opinion, Justice Sobel held the law invalid because the eavesdropping orders it authorized could not, in his judgment, meet the standards required for the issuance of search warrants under the Fourth Amendment.[1] Just a year later, the Federal Communications Commission issued an order prohibiting private citizens from using radio devices to eavesdrop. Theoretically, the F.C.C. order made illegal such equipment as the tiny radio transmitters described above (unless everyone present knew the equipment was being used). Yet it did *not* affect the use of a miniature tape recorder directly connected to a small camouflaged microphone, since no radio transmission is involved—although the same kind of eavesdropping may take place. Nor did the ban affect law-enforcement agencies, such as the F.B.I., the Internal Revenue Service, or state and local police and similar authorities.

On the other hand, a number of legal experts became convinced that the Supreme Court's intriguing *Griswold* ruling [2] in June 1965 which, as we saw in Chapter III, invalidated Connecticut's birth control statute by enunciating a new "right of privacy," had laid the basis for an eventual judicial outlawing of wire-tapping and other forms of electronic eavesdropping. It was argued that the new right of privacy could be held to override the technical distinction of a physical intrusion that the Court made both in the *Olmstead* case [3] and in subsequent decisions involving other electronic eavesdropping,[4] and thus declare all such intrusions unconstitutional.[5]

---

[1] *People v. Grossman*, 257 N.Y.S. 2nd 266. Reversed by the Appellate Division on December 28, 1966, the case was appealed to the New York Court of Appeals, the state's highest court, whence it was expected to go to the U.S. Supreme Court in 1967.

[2] *Griswold v. Connecticut*, 381 U.S. 479.

[3] *Olmstead v. United States*, 277 U.S. 438 (1928). The vote in that case, as noted earlier above, was 5:4; the majority opinion was written by Mr. Chief Justice Taft and joined by Associate Justices Van Devanter, McReynolds, Sutherland, and Sanford. The dissenters, in addition to Holmes and Brandeis, were Justices Butler and Stone.

[4] E.g. *Goldman v. United States*, 316 U.S. 129 (1942) and *On Lee v. United States*, 343 U.S. 747 (1952).

[5] Such a ruling would presumably reach the so-called distinction between "wire-tapping" and "bugging," a distinction that sees the latter as not proscribed. It has been embraced by sundry law-enforcement officials, apparently including ex-U.S. Attorney-General Robert F. Kennedy. (See David Lawrence, "Rightful Bugging," *The New York Herald-Tribune* [International Edition], July 9, 1966.)

Still it may be asked, could not and should not the kind of search-and-seizure represented by wire-tapping be authorized under our Constitution? Although wire-tapping and electronic eavesdropping are clear-cut invasions of the basic rights of privacy, perhaps they *are* necessary in cases of subversive activities, seditious conduct, espionage, kidnapping, and certain other major crimes. Perhaps a good case *can* be made for eavesdropping in the fields just mentioned when the act is duly requested *and judicially authorized before the fact,* notwithstanding the reprehensible nature of the incursions of privacy involved. On the other hand, it would be much harder to make a viable case for such intrusions on privacy in crimes like fraud, racketeering, prostitution, and gambling, or for the "investigation" of public and private employees in anything but highly secret positions.[1] In the final analysis, our response must turn first on the constitutionality of any such proposed action and second on its wisdom. And even assuming the former—now a doubtful assumption, despite the *Olmstead* precedent [2]—any thoughts on the wisdom of such action must confront the basic issues raised by Mr. Justice Brandeis in his memorable dissent in that very case, when he wrote:

> The makers of our Constitution undertook to secure conditions favorable to the pursuit of happiness. They recognized the significance of man's spiritual nature, of his feelings and of his intellect. They knew that only a part of the pain, pleasure and satisfactions of life are to be found in material things. They sought to protect Americans in their beliefs, their thoughts, their emotions and their sensations. They conferred, as against the Government, *the right to be let alone—the most comprehensive of rights and the right most valued by civilized men.* To protect that right, every unjustifiable intrusion by the Government upon the privacy of the individual, whatever the means employed, must be deemed a violation of the Fourth Amendment. . . .[3]

An Alternative? There are no shortcuts to regulation or conviction or prosecution. The game must be played according to its constitutional rules—no matter how difficult it may well become thereby. But it would be sophistry to gainsay the genuine public concern,

[1] An interesting case for such a balancing approach to the use of wire-tapping and electronic eavesdropping was made by Alan Westin in "Surveillance, Privacy, and the Free Society," a paper delivered at the 1965 Annual Meeting of the American Political Science Association, Washington, D.C., September 8-11, 1965.
[2] *Loc. cit.*
[3] *Ibid.,* at 478. (Italics supplied.)

both lay and professional, over the recent augmentation of judicial supervision in the realm of criminal justice and the resultant tough new rules of procedure that have evolved. Given the increasing rate of crime, is there an alternative to "easy" apprehensions, prosecutions, and convictions that either circumvent, dilute, or wink at basic constitutional guarantees? One suggestion may be hazarded: Since, according to the most recent statistics,[1] some 73 per cent of those booked on criminal charges in 1965, for example, were "repeaters," it seems reasonable to ask whether our courts could, and indeed should, be more severe in the type and length of sentences meted out to repeaters. The public has the right to be protected from habitual criminality; and perhaps longer, less readily commutable, and less generously parolable sentences may well be in order.[2] It does seem that trial judges and parole officers have often been guilty of the kind of lenience in criminal cases involving repeat-offenders that may be appropriate only for an *initial* offense.

Because "bigger and better" prison sentences will not solve the problem of crime, a plea for toughness in sentencing must carry with it a plea for *much* more effective rehabilitation work in prison than exists at present; for *much* more modern institutional facilities; and for *much* better trained professional personnel. There is a limit to the type of rehabilitation that the walls of a prison can provide—but infinitely more can be done than is done at present. Of course, the public, in turn, must be willing to foot the bill for such measures. All too often that public, while insisting on more protection, has been resolutely opposed to paying for it. The old saw of not being able to have one's cake and eat it too applies in this realm also.

Whether or not the suggested "alternative" represents a basis for assuaging the fears of the lay and professional public, when it comes to the fundamental standards of due process of law under our Constitution, there can be no compromises, no shortcuts. "The interest of ... [the government]," to reiterate a memorable statement by Mr. Justice Brennan, "is not that it shall win a case, but that justice shall be done." [3] There is no reason why in our democratic society well-trained, professional agents of the law cannot apprehend and convict

---

[1] E.g., *The Philadelphia Inquirer*, September 28, 1965, *et seq.*

[2] In saying this, the writer is acutely aware of the criticism he is unquestionably courting from his colleagues in such disciplines as sociology and psychology.

[3] *Jencks v. United States,* 353 U.S. 657 (1957), at 660.

alleged criminals without, in the process, becoming criminals them-selves. As Arnold S. Trebach put it so well in his *The Rationing of Justice*,[1] the argument *against* greater protection for the rights of the accused reduces itself to an argument *for* violation of the law in order to enforce it. It is a crime to violate the rights of *any* person," [2] whether he be a criminal or a saint.

As he did so frequently, Mr. Justice Brandeis went to the heart of the matter with language both appropriate and stirring in the con-cluding paragraph to his dissenting opinion in the *Olmstead* case some four decades ago:

> Decency, security, and liberty alike demand that government officials shall be subjected to the same rules of conduct that are commands to the citizen. In a government of laws, existence of the government will be imperiled if it fails to observe the law scrupulously. Our govern-ment is the potent, the omnipresent, teacher. For good or for ill, it teaches the whole people by example. Crime is contagious. If the gov-ernment becomes a lawbreaker, it breeds contempt for law; it invites every man to become a law unto himself; it invites anarchy. *To declare that in the administration of the criminal law the end justifies the means—to declare that the government may commit crimes in order to secure the conviction of a private criminal—would bring terrible retribution.* Against that pernicious doctrine this court should resolutely set its face.[3]

He could not be certain then—but today he would know that in the main the Supreme Court has for some time now been setting its face against that pernicious doctrine, and that it has done so regardless of the winds that have buffeted it.

[1] Subtitled *Constitutional Rights and the Criminal Process* (New Brunswick, N.J.: Rutgers University Press, 1964), p. 233.

[2] *Ibid.*, p. 233.

[3] *Olmstead v. United States*, 277 U.S. 438 (1928), at 485. (Italics supplied.)

V

The Precious Freedom of Expression

IF WE AMERICANS have, and practice, "ambivalence" [1] as our primary ideology, the area of the precious freedom of expression is a case in point. The commonplace expression "It's a free country, isn't it—so I can darn well say what I please!" is in fact sincere, for its underlying philosophy is ingrained in the body politic's notion of what democratic America means. But its paradox is that throughout history we so often permit, wink at, even encourage, its violation in practice. Thus we have been quite willing to curb the "dangerous," the "seditious," the "subversive," the "prurient," the "obscene," the "libelous," and a host of other presumably undesirable modes and manners of expression that—at a particular time and place—seemed to justify repression. Yet, unless we accept the absolutist approach advocated so consistently by Mr. Justice Black and his supporters, the need to draw some line is primary.

Black observed in a famous 1941 dissenting opinion:

> Freedom to speak and write about public questions is as important to the life of our government as is the heart of the human body. In fact, this privilege is the heart of our government! If that heart be weakened, the result is debilitation; if it be stilled, the result is death.[2]

Mr. Justice Brandeis, whose last two years of service on the bench of the highest court coincided with Black's first two, tried to provide a memorable guideline when, in a concurring opinion joined by his

---

[1] This was cogently suggested by Professor Robert G. McCloskey of Harvard University in "The American Ideology," an essay in Marian D. Irish, ed., *Continuing Crisis in American Politics* (Englewood Cliffs, N.J.: Prentice-Hall, 1963).
[2] *Milk Wagon Drivers Union v. Meadowmoor Dairies*, 312 U.S. 287, at 301-2.

colleague Holmes, he defended the "chance-taking" aspects of freedom of expression in ringing terms:

> [Those who won our independence] believed that freedom to think as you will and to speak as you think are means indispensable to the discovery and spread of political truth; that without free speech and assembly, discussion would be futile; that with them, discussion affords ordinarily adequate protection against the dissemination of noxious doctrine; that the greatest menace to freedom is an inert people; that public discussion is a political duty; and that this should be a fundamental principle of the American government. . . .[1]

To draw the line in freedom of expression is an enormously difficult task; yet, as they have done elsewhere, the courts have valiantly endeavored to find and draw that line.

Some Basic Concepts

Since we cannot attempt to cover all, or even most, aspects of "freedom of expression," we shall concentrate on those which illustrate the fundamental problem and are of topical interest.

A *Basic Definition.* In its over-all context, freedom of expression connotes the broad *freedom to communicate*—a concept that far transcends mere speech. It embraces the prerogative of the free citizen to express himself—verbally or on paper—without *previous* restraint, and, if the expression meets the test of truth, the prerogative necessarily extends to the post-utterance period. It is vital to recognize at the outset that the freedom of expression extends not only to speech, but also to such areas as press, assembly, petition, and even lawful picketing.

Yet, since none of these freedoms can be absolute, in any basic definition we must consider the inevitability of limits—limits that recognize the rights of the minority in a majoritarian system, without, however, subscribing to a philosophy of the "tyranny of the minority." Thus, there is no doubt that picketing, for example, is a vital prerogative of the freedom of expression; mass picketing, however, or picketing that applies physical force to those who might wish to exercise their equal rights of freedom of expression by disregarding the picket line, is not. Screaming "fire" in a crowded theater—to use the famed Holmesian illustration—upon discovery of a blaze is not only "free-

[1] *Whitney v. California*, 274 U.S. 357 (1927), at 375.

dom of speech" but a dutiful exercise of citizenship—provided there really is a fire; if there is none, the call is not freedom of expression but license. *Actual, overt* incitement to the overthrow of the government of the United States by force and violence, accompanied by the language of direct incitement, is not freedom of expression, but a violation of Court-upheld legislative proscriptions; yet the *theoretical* advocacy of such overthrow, on the other hand, has been a judicially recognized protected freedom since 1957.[1] Publicly addressing someone as "damned Fascist" and "God-damned racketeer" can hardly be considered as freedom of speech,[2] but calling a duly convicted thief "thief" or "crook" presumably is—at least until the epithet's target has paid his debt to society.

Throughout our history, lawmaking and judicial authorities have had to wrestle with these and similar questions, and a welter of both common and statutory law is the result. Limitations, today almost entirely of a statutory nature, are thus present on both the national and state levels of government—a phenomenon almost unknown prior to World War I.

There is thus scant doubt that Congress has the authority to guard against sedition and subversion and has employed it rather widely, especially in periods of national emergency and the Cold War.[3] Since 1940 it has enacted three significant pieces of legislation: the Smith Act of 1940, the Internal Security Act of 1950 (passed over President Truman's veto), and the Communist Control Act of 1954. The problem implicit in this legislation is, of course, where to draw the line between the individual's cherished right to espouse and express unpopular, even radical, causes and the right of the community to protect itself against the overthrow of government. As the courts have ultimately been called upon to demonstrate time and again, democratic society has the right and duty to maintain concurrently both freedom of expression and national security.

To allude briefly to another era, one in which the states have pre-

---

[1] See *Yates v. United States,* 354 U.S. 298, particularly Mr. Justice Harlan's opinion for the 7:1 Court.

[2] *Chaplinski v. New Hampshire,* 315 U.S. 568 (1942), involving a narrowly and carefully drawn New Hampshire law.

[3] *Sedition* consists of publications, utterances, or other activities, short of treason, which are deemed to encourage resistance to lawful authority. *Subversion* comprehends participation in or advocacy of any organized activity to overthrow an existing government by force.

dominated, what of the matter of prohibiting the sale and dissemination of "obscene" literature? Statutes abound, many, as we shall
presently note, quickly running afoul of First and Fourteenth Amendment safeguards of freedom of expression—yet may the community
not protect itself against "obscenity"? Do particular publications possess the "redeeming social value" which underlies the exercise of
responsible freedom? Is demonstrable obscenity a "civil right"? But
the anticipated negative chorus to that rhetorical question must be
discounted (a) by hypocrisy and (b) by the fiendishly difficult definition of the "obscene." Hence, here again the judicial branch has
had to endeavor to draw lines—which it has more than once done
by reading the allegedly "obscene" book, or going to the movies to
determine whether or not a film is indeed "obscene" in whole or in
part.[1]

The following capsule illustrations, hopefully, will serve to indicate
topically the at once fascinating and frustrating line-drawing problem
involved in freedom of expression—one the Supreme Court, in particular, has been repeatedly called upon to solve amidst the inevitable
jeers and cheers.

DRAWING LINES: SOME BRIEF EXAMPLES

1. *Press Freedom and Fair Trial.* Where does one draw the line
between the right of a free press to comment and criticize and the
duty of the judiciary to ensure a fair trial? In *Pennekamp v. Florida* [2]
the publisher and the associate editor of the *Miami Herald* were
fined for contempt because they had printed a cartoon and written
an editorial designed to demonstrate that a Miami trial judge had,
by certain rulings, favored criminals and gambling establishments.
Their conviction was justified by Florida on the grounds that their
actions had reflected upon and impugned the integrity of the trial
court, had tended to create public distrust for it, and had obstructed
the fair and impartial justice of pending cases. In a unanimous decision, written by Mr. Justice Reed, the Supreme Court reversed their

---

[1] E.g. the "Miracle" decision (concerning Roberto Rossellini's controversial
movie) *Burstyn v. Wilson*, 343 U.S. 495 (1952) and that of the film "Lady
Chatterley's Lover," *Kingsley Corporation v. Regents of the University of New
York*, 360 U.S. 684 (1959).
[2] 328 U.S. 331 (1946).

conviction, holding that their rights of freedom of speech and press had been violated. Reed admitted that some of the *Herald's* comments were directed at pending cases and, moreover, were not even truthful. In drawing a necessarily generous line here, he ruled that "in the borderline instances where it is difficult to say upon which side of the line the offense falls, we think the specific freedom of public comment should weigh heavily against a possible tendency to influence pending cases. Freedom of discussion should be given the widest range compatible with the essential requirement of the fair and orderly administration of justice." [1]

But in *Irvin v. Dowd* [2] a unanimous Supreme Court struck down a state conviction solely on the ground of prejudicial pre-trial publicity. Nothing happened to the offending newspapers or their "roving reporters" in Gibson County, Indiana, nor to the Evansville radio and television stations that blanketed the county with the news of petitioner Irvin's alleged crime of six murders in the vicinity of Vandenburgh County. But the accused's detention and death sentence were vacated and remanded in an opinion by Mr. Justice Clark, replete with criticism of an irresponsible press. However, it was Mr. Justice Frankfurter, in a concurring opinion, who administered the most telling lecture to the news media, exhorting them warmly that freedom implies responsibility:

> ... this is, unfortunately, not an isolated case that happens in Evansville, Indiana, nor an atypical miscarriage of justice due to anticipatory trial by newspaper instead of trial in court before a jury. ... But, again and again, such disregard of fundamental fairness is so flagrant that the Court is compelled, as it was only a week ago, to reverse a conviction in which prejudicial newspaper intrusion has poisoned the outcome. ... This Court has not yet decided that the fair administration of criminal justice must be subordinated to another safeguard of our constitutional system—freedom of the press, properly conceived. The Court has not yet decided that, while convictions must be reversed and miscarriages of justice result because the minds of jurors or potential jurors were poisoned, the poisoner is constitutionally protected in plying his trade.[3]

[1] *Ibid.*, at 347.
[2] 366 U.S. 717 (1961).
[3] *Ibid.*, at 729, 730. We should note here that—perhaps as a precursor of the *Estes* decision (see pp. 129-32, *infra*.), the Court, in *Rideau v. Louisiana*, 373 U.S. 723 (1963), voided, on due process grounds, the murder conviction of a defendant whose confession to a sheriff had been televised and thrice beamed at potential jurors throughout the area.

Here, then, we see clearly the vexatious line implicit in press freedom. It is difficult enough to find the line when responsibility obtains, but how much more so when the press ignores its responsibility? Must we really continue to believe that there is an unlimited right to conduct *ex parte* public trials in the press, on the radio, and on television? The British have long since answered that fundamental question in the negative. There, any publication of information about a defendant in a criminal case before the trial starts leads to punishment for contempt of court. Nothing that might conceivably affect the attitude of a potential juror may be published unless and until it is formally disclosed in court. Large fines have been meted out to newspapers that have violated the so-called Judges Rules, some of which have been enacted into formal statutes. To cite just one example, a Scottish newspaper, *The Daily Record* of Edinburgh, was fined £7,500 ($21,000) for using on its front page a picture of a soccer star charged with "indecent exposure." In addition, Chief Assistant Editor Robert Johnson—who was in charge when the issue went to press—was fined £500 ($1,400); and the only reason no individual was sent to jail for contempt was that the responsible editor had been at home sick that night. "How is a judge or jury to know," asked the presiding judge in the case, "that the witness is identifying the man seen on the occasion of the crime and not the man whose photograph has been blazoned on the front page of a newspaper?" [1]

Yet the future does not augur well for a similar strictness in our own institutions—given our traditions of reporting and publishing, the failure of the media to arrive at a workable code of conduct, and the competitiveness of the trade. Still, fundamental fairness would seem to cry out for a "balance" between freedom of the press and the right of the public to be informed, on the one hand, and the responsibilities of freedom and the right of the accused, on the other.

A notable step in that general direction may have been heralded by—once again—Supreme Court decisions in 1965 and 1966. The first ruling involved the conviction for swindling of Texas financier and "wheeler-dealer" Billie Sol Estes, who had been tried and convicted (among several other earlier convictions) in a Tyler, Texas, courtroom in 1962. During the pre-trial hearing extensive and ob-

[1] As reported by the Associated Press in the *New York Herald Tribune*, February 12, 1960. See also "British Verdict On Trial-by-Press," by Anthony Lewis, in *The New York Times Magazine*, June 20, 1965.

trusive television coverage took place: "The courtroom," reported
The New York Times, "was turned into a snake-pit by the multiplicity
of cameras, wires, microphones and technicians milling about the
chamber." [1] Estes' appeal to the United States Supreme Court alleged
denial of his constitutional rights of "due process of law." In a six-
opinion, 5:4 decision, the Court laid down a rule that televising of
"notorious" criminal trials is indeed prohibited by the "due process
of law" clause of Amendment Fourteen, and it reversed Estes' conviction.[2] But it was a far from clear decision insofar as the basic problem of freedom of the press and fair trial goes. Four justices,[3] through
Mr. Justice Clark, said that "the time honored principles of a fair
trial" are violated when television is allowed in any criminal trial. A
fifth, Mr. Justice Harlan—supplying the winning vote—agreed, but
only because the Estes trial was one of "great notoriety," and he
made clear that he would reserve judgment on more routine cases.
Four dissenting justices [4] objected on constitutional grounds to the
blanket ban at this stage of television's development, holding that
there was insufficient proof that Estes' rights had here been violated.

The second case involved the Court's striking down of the 1954
second-degree-murder conviction of a Cleveland, Ohio, osteopath, Dr.
Samuel H. Sheppard, for the bludgeon-murder of his pregnant
wife.[5] Dr. Sheppard has been in jail until 1964 when a federal district
judge in Dayton granted a writ of habeas corpus and released him
from the Ohio penitentiary, ruling that prejudicial publicity had
denied him a fair trial. Two years later the Supreme Court affirmed
that action by a vote of 8:1, giving Ohio authorities a choice of retry-
ing him or of dismissing the case against him. (Ohio decided to retry
him on the murder charge; the jury acquitted him in November 1966
after a trial that was a model of courtroom decorum!) Mr. Justice
Clark's majority opinion pointed to the circus atmosphere that attended Dr. Sheppard's sensationalized trial. For example, the trial
judge, Edward Blythin, positioned the press inside the lawyer's rail
so close to the bench that it was in effect impossible for defense at-

[1] June 9, 1965.
[2] *Estes v. Texas,* 381 U.S. 532 (1965).
[3] Clark, Warren, Douglas, and Goldberg.
[4] Stewart, Black, Brennan, and White.
[5] *Sheppard v. Maxwell,* 384 U.S. 333 (1966).

torneys to consult with either their client or the judge without being overheard. When the jurors viewed the scene of the murder at Dr. Sheppard's home, a representative of the press was included in the group, while other reporters hovered overhead in a press helicopter. Radio and television commentators, among them Bob Considine and Walter Winchell, kept up a drum-fire of accounts of alleged illicit liaisons of the defendant. Television broadcasts spewed forth from the room adjacent to the jury deliberation chamber. Jurors were photographed and interviewed by the news media as were witnesses. In setting aside the conviction of Dr. Sheppard, Clark's opinion restated the Court's concern that had led it to void Billie Sol Estes' conviction just a year earlier: that the presence of a large, ill-controlled news media contingent can deny a defendant that "judicial serenity and calm" which the "due process of law" guarantees of the Constitution mandate for a fair trial—even in the absence of proof that the jury was in fact prejudiced by the publicity. And Clark added significantly that although the various officials involved could probably stifle most sources of prejudicial trial publicity, he would not rule out the possibility that *a judge could take direct action* against a newspaper, for example, if it persisted in violating defendant's rights.[1]

Thus the dilemma remains, but the Court may well have given it a new twist, in *Estes* and *Sheppard*, in the direction of considerably more concern for fairness to those on trial.[2] Such a trend was also indicated by the actions taken by the bar associations and jurists in a number of states, among them New Jersey, New York, and Pennsylvania,[3] during 1964, 1965, and 1966 and, perhaps most significantly,

[1] *Ibid.,* 357-62.

[2] In October 1966 the Texas Court of Criminal Appeals reversed the murder conviction of Jack Ruby, who had been sentenced to death in 1964 for the slaying of Lee Harvey Oswald, presumed assassin of President Kennedy. The Court cited the rampant publicity (as well as inadmissible evidence) and, for Ruby's new trial, ordered a change of venue from Dallas County where the shooting took place. But Ruby's fatal illness intervened.

[3] Thus the Philadelphia Bar Association in 1965, by a 6:1 margin, endorsed a code to limit disclosure of information in criminal cases. Among its suggested safeguards it prohibits lawyers from making public statements, granting press interviews, or preparing statements for others to make about pending criminal cases. But Philadelphia's Mayor James H. J. Tate immediately announced that he would *not* direct the Police Department to comply. He said the adoption of the code looked to him like a minority move by "some lawyers representing criminals." (*The New York Times,* January 6, 1966.)

by a widely circulated 226-page Report by the American Bar Association's Advisory Committee on Fair Trial and a Free Press.[1] The group recommended a drastic tightening of the canons of legal ethics to limit sharply the release and publication of information about persons accused of crime. Yet we are very likely still far from a solution!

2. *Free Speech and Freedom from Noise.* During the 1948 presidential elections, two interesting cases involving sound trucks caused the Court to draw two different lines between "freedom and order."

In the first case, *Saia v. New York*,[2] the petitioner was a minister of the Jehovah's Witnesses—who are persistent, and usually successful, litigants at the bar of the Supreme Court.[3] Wishing to broadcast his gospel in Lockport, New York, Samuel Saia had run afoul of a city ordinance forbidding the use of sound-amplification devices except "public dissemination . . . of items of news and matters of public concern . . . provided that the same be done under permission obtained from the Chief of Police." Refused a new permit on the ground that complaints had been made about his prior sound-amplified speeches on religious (and, we might add, not very popular) subjects, Saia nevertheless decided to proceed to lecture, by means of loud-speakers, in a small city park used for recreation purposes. He was convicted, fined, and sentenced to jail. Speaking for a closely divided Court (5:4),[4] Mr. Justice Douglas held the ordinance "unconstitutional on its face, for it establishes a *previous* restraint on the right of free speech."[5] The right to be heard, concluded Douglas, was here placed impermissibly at the "uncontrolled discretion of the Chief of Police." To the four dissenting justices, however—Frankfurter, Reed, Jackson, and Burton—this was not a free speech issue at all since no one, they contended, had stopped Saia from using his voice; rather, it was a question of the protection of society's unwilling listeners by a non-arbitrary, non-capricious, non-discriminatory ordinance. But they lost.

They *won*, however, only eight months later in *Kovacs v. Cooper*,[6]

---

[1] See *The New York Times*, October 2, 1966, for excerpts of its tentative proposals, pp. 1, 81.

[2] 334 U.S. 558 (1948).

[3] See Chapter VI, *infra*, for details.

[4] He was joined by Mr. Chief Justice Vinson and Associate Justices Black, Murphy, and Rutledge.

[5] *Saia v. New York, loc. cit.*, at 559-60. (Italics supplied.)

[6] 336 U.S. 77 (1949).

a case involving the validity of a Trenton, New Jersey, ordinance. This time it was Henry Wallace's Progressive Party which was involved. The case went 5:4 the opposite way, Mr. Chief Justice Vinson switching sides and thus providing the key vote for the upholding of the Trenton law, which prohibited the use on the city's "public streets, alleys or thoroughfares" of any "device known as a sound truck, loud speaker or sound amplifier..." that "emits therefrom loud and raucous noises...." Speaking for the new majority, Mr. Justice Reed distinguished *Kovacs v. Cooper* from the *Saia* case on the grounds that the Trenton ordinance was carefully drawn and that the kind of discretionary power that the Court had found fatal to the Lockport ordinance was not present in Trenton's. The four dissenters, who, with the Chief Justice, had made up the majority in the *Saia* case, saw a rank violation of Charles Kovacs' right to freedom of expression under Amendments One and Fourteen, and raised the interesting question of how sound trucks can be other than "loud and raucous"? [1]

3. *Freedom of Street Corner Exhortation.* Two famous decisions, illustrating how specific facts in particular court cases are significant in line-drawing, were decided by the Supreme Court on the same "Opinion Monday" in its 1951 term. The first, which went in favor of the free-speech claimant, concerned the verbal calisthenics of one Carl Jacob Kunz, an ordained Baptist minister of rather unsavory reputation and long a thorn in the side of New York City police authorities because of his penchant for inflammatory addresses against Jews and Catholics in areas abounding with these two groups (minorities in most areas of the country, but certainly not in New York City.) Preaching under the auspices of what he called the "Outdoor Gospel Work," of which he was the self-appointed director, Kunz had in 1946 asked for and received a permit under a New York City ordinance that made it unlawful to hold public worship meetings on the streets without first obtaining a permit from the City Commissioner of Police. After having seen what Kunz had done with his 1946 permit—which was revoked after a hearing—the Commissioner sev-

[1] The issue has a habit of recurring. Thus in 1966 U.S. District Court Judge Alfred L. Luongo ruled that the city of Chester, Penna., was within its rights in establishing certain controls over operation of a sound truck, but could not charge a $25 fee for its operation. His decision came in a suit brought by the NAACP against the city. (*The Philadelphia Bulletin*, April 28, 1966.)

eral times refused a new one to Kunz, each time pointing to the fact
that the 1946 revocation was based on evidence that Kunz had publicly ridiculed and denounced other religious beliefs in his meetings.
In 1948 Kunz, having decided to hold one of his meetings *without* a
permit, was arrested for speaking at Columbus Circle, and fined
$10.00 for violating the New York City ordinance in question. In an
8:1 opinion for the Court, Mr. Chief Justice Vinson addressed himself exclusively to the matter of prior suppression of free speech,
concluding that

> it is sufficient to say that New York cannot vest restraining control over
> the right to speak on religious subjects in an administrative official
> where there are no appropriate standards to guide his action.[1]

There was a lengthy and vigorous dissenting opinion by Mr. Justice
Jackson, who expressed the fear that with decisions such as this it
"may become difficult to preserve here what a large part of the world
has lost—the right to speak, even temperately, on matters vital to
spirit and body." [2] He pointed to the kind of "preachings" Kunz
made, which, on his arrest in 1948, included the following observations:

> The Catholic Church makes merchandise out of souls ... [Catholi-
> cism] is a religion of the devil ... [the Pope] is the anti-Christ. ...
> The Jews ... are Christ-killers. ... All the garbage [the Jews] that
> didn't believe in Christ should have been burnt in the incinerators.
> It's a shame they all weren't.[3]

To Jackson, the American Prosecutor at the Nürnberg War Crimes
Trials, this public speech was too "intrinsically incendiary and divi-
sive," given the delicate and emotional nature of the two subjects of
"race and religion," to permit the type of constitutional protection
claimed by Kunz and confirmed by Jackson's eight fellow judges.
"The consecrated hatreds of sect," concluded the lone dissenter,

> account for more than a few of the world's bloody disorders. These
> are the explosives which the Court says Kunz may play with in the
> public streets, and the community must not only tolerate but aid him.
> I find no such doctrine in the Constitution.[4]

[1] *Kunz v. New York*, 340 U.S. 290 (1951), at 295.
[2] *Ibid.*
[3] *Ibid.*, at 296.
[4] *Ibid.*, at 314.

Yet on that same day of Court, just a few pages along in the same *United States Reports*,[1] the majority adopted—at least apparently— the very ideas that Jackson alone expressed in the *Kunz* case! Involved here was the free speech claim of one Irving Feiner, an adolescent sidewalk orator, who, using derogatory language about public officials and certain interest groups, had harangued a crowd of some 75 to 80 white and colored persons in a predominantly Negro residential area of Syracuse, New York. He was publicizing a "Young Progressives" meeting to be held that evening in a local hotel rather than in the public school auditorium originally scheduled, because the permit granted for the latter had been revoked as a result of local pressure-group activities. In the course of his speech Feiner referred to President Truman as a "bum"; to Mayor Costello of Syracuse as a "champagne-sipping bum" who "does not speak for the Negro people"; to Mayor O'Dwyer of New York City as a "bum"; to the American Legion as "a Nazi Gestapo"; and, in what the record described as "an excited manner," yelled: "The Negroes don't have equal rights; they should rise up in arms and fight for them." [2]

Feiner's statements "stirred up a little excitement," and one of the bystanders called out that if the police did not get that "s...o... b..." off the stand, he would do so himself. (The police later admitted that there was "not yet a disturbance," but there did occur "angry muttering and pushing.") At this point one of the police officers stepped forward and arrested Feiner to "prevent [the events] from resulting in a fight," since Feiner had disregarded two requests by the policeman to stop speaking. Evidently, it was more convenient to stop one unpopular orator than to control a fairly sizeable crowd of rather angry people! The New York State trial judge concluded that the police officers were justified in taking the action "to prevent a breach of the peace," and the intermediate appellate tribunal concurred. New York State's highest court, the Court of Appeals, then affirmed the findings below, stating that Feiner,

> with intent to provoke a breach of the peace and with knowledge of the consequences, so inflamed and agitated a mixed audience of sympathizers and opponents that, in the judgment of the police officers present, a clear danger of disorder and violence was threatened.[3]

[1] The official volumes reporting all Supreme Court decisions.
[2] *Feiner v. New York*, 340 U.S. 315 (1951), at 330.
[3] *Ibid.*, at 319, n. 2.

Speaking for himself and five of his colleagues—Associate Justices Reed, Frankfurter, Jackson, Burton, and Clark—Mr. Chief Justice Vinson agreed with the findings of "three New York courts" that Feiner's free speech claims were spurious; that, indeed, his right to hold his meeting and utter the derogatory remarks was uncontested and uncontestable; *but* that the police officers were justified in making the arrest because they

> were motivated solely by a proper concern for the preservation of order and protection of the general welfare, and that there was no evidence which could lend color to a claim that the acts of the police were a cover for suppression of [Feiner's] views and opinions. Petitioner was thus neither arrested nor convicted for the making or the content of his speech. Rather, *it was the reaction which it actually engendered.*[1]

It was precisely from this last sentence that Justices Black, Douglas, and Minton dissented strongly in two separate opinions, Black writing his own. In brief, they rejected the majority's key points: that danger of a riot existed and that a breach of the peace had been perpetrated by Feiner. They denied that the facts demonstrated "any imminent threat of riot or uncontrollable disorder," [2] and declared [3] that the record merely showed "an unsympathetic audience and the threat of one man to haul the spaker from the stage. *It is against that kind of threat that speakers need police protection*," [4] concluded Mr. Justice Douglas, joined by Minton.

And there, of course, lies the dilemma: at what point should speech be prohibitable? When it stirs to anger? When it creates opposition? When it creates disorder? But who is to say that the latter cannot be artificially stimulated, even created? Could not a strong point be made that the police have an obligation to protect the *maker* of the speech *against* a hostile audience? To raise these fundamental questions is to recognize the difficulty of any all-embracing response! Does it depend not only upon the *content* of a speech but how it is *delivered*? "Incitement," too, is a double-edged sword. After all, as Mr. Justice Holmes put it so perceptively in his memorable dissenting opinion in the *Gitlow* case,[5] "[E]very idea is an incitement. . . . The only dif-

---

1 *Ibid.*, at 319-20. (Italics supplied.)
2 *Ibid.*, Black, dissenting opinion, at 325.
3 *Ibid.*, Douglas, dissenting opinion, at 331.
4 *Ibid.* (Italics supplied.)
5 *Gitlow v. New York*, 268 U.S. 652 (1925).

ference between the expression of an opinion and an incitement in the narrower sense is the speaker's enthusiasm for the result. Eloquence may set fire to reason." [1] Whatever the elusive answer, democratic society demands that it be a generous one. If that means taking chances, so be it.[2]

4. *Free Expression and Subversive Activity.* Many books have been written—and will undoubtedly continue to be written—on the problem of national security. Here we can simply touch on it as one more illustration of the problem of line-drawing in the exercise of freedom of expression. The fact and concept of subversive activity and how to meet it has concerned the nation, more or less sporadically, ever since its birth. From the hated Alien and Sedition Acts of 1798 through the trying eras of the Civil War, World War I, the Red Scare of the 1920's, post–World War II, McCarthyism and the cold war, the legislative and administrative remedies adopted to deal with the problem of national security have often been dominant concerns. And the resultant statutes, executive orders, legislative investigations have all, sooner or later, found themselves in judicial hot water, heated by the clash between freedom of expression and national security. Answers given by the judicial branch in this area—if answers they be—have understandably been more cautious, more circumspect, than in any other aspect of the freedom at issue. Nonetheless, as the 1950's turned into the 1960's, the courts became increasingly generous toward the individual's claims as against those of majoritarian society. Hence, while necessarily recognizing the right and duty of Congress (and, by implication of state legislatures) to keep itself informed in order to legislate more wisely, keep an eye on the executive branch, and inform the public, the Supreme Court has also recognized that there are, and must be, limits on the right, or perhaps more correctly the power, to investigate. Among these are the witness's right to decline to respond by invoking the Fifth Amendment's privilege against self-incrimination; to refuse to reply if the question is beyond the investigating committee's mandate; [3] and to have "explicit and

---

[1] *Ibid.*, at 673.

[2] An interesting—and troublesome—case demonstrating that very problem is *Terminiello v. Chicago,* in which the Court, dividing 5:4, reversed the breach-of-peace conviction of a professional rabble-rouser, who had *really* caused a riot. But the year was 1949—with Justices Murphy and Rutledge still alive. (337 U.S. 1.) And Douglas's majority opinion was based on a dubious statutory analysis.

[3] E.g. *United States v. Rumely,* 345 U.S. 41 (1953).

clear" knowledge of the subject to which the interrogation is deemed pertinent.[1] Yet as other decisions of the Court have shown, great difficulties here are the matters of "pertinency" [2] and just what constitutes "exposure for the sake of exposure." [3]

Similarly troublesome has been the matter of "loyalty and security." Again, while recognizing the right and obligation of both legislative and executive authorities to ascertain loyalty to the state by its employees and quasi-employees, the Court has been called upon repeatedly to draw the lines between the rights of the individual according to the Bill of Rights, which he assuredly does not surrender simply because he works for government, and the rights of the state which has a basic obligation to protect its citizenry from subversion by disloyal elements. Grave problems have surrounded the nature and meaning of the terms "loyalty" and "security," as well as the compatibility of such legislation and ordinances with the prerogatives of free citizens. Avoiding the constitutional issues whenever possible, the Court has handed down several significant guidelines, chiefly by statutory interpretation, but also when it has come to the states rather than to the national government, by constitutional adjudication. Thus, federal employee loyalty-security programs, which initially seemed to have a rather free rein, have found themselves increasingly confined in coverage and held to ever more strict requirements of procedural due process.[4] And some state statutes and allied requirements have fallen on grounds of both substantive and procedural due process, often in concord with freedom of expression guarantees. Thus, while some programs have been upheld as valid exercises of the state police power,[5] others have fallen, more often than not because of the "vice of vagueness"—the sweeping implications of such terms as "subversive organizations," "subversive persons," or "sympathetic association with. . . ." [6] Here, again, the advocates of maximum security and those who believe that democratic society must take risks for the sake of

[1] E.g. *Watkins v. United States*, 354 U.S. 178 (1957).
[2] E.g. *Barenblatt v. United States*, 360 U.S. 109 (1959).
[3] E.g. *Braden v. United States*, 365 U.S. 431 (1961).
[4] *Peters v. Hobby*, 349 U.S. 341 (1955); *Cole v. Young*, 351 U.S. 356 (1956); *Service v. Dulles*, 354 U.S. 363 (1957); *Vitarelli v. Seaton*, 359 U.S. 353 (1959); *Greene v. McElroy*, 360 U.S. 374 (1959).
[5] *Garner v. Board of Public Works of Los Angeles*, 341 U.S. 716 (1951); *Adler v. Board of Education of New York*, 342 U.S. 485 (1952).
[6] *Wieman v. Updegraff*, 344 U.S. 183 (1952); *Shelton v. Tucker*, 364 U.S. 479 (1960); *Baggett v. Bullitt*, 377 U.S. 360 (1964); *Elfbrandt v. Russell*, 384 U.S. 11 (1966); *Keyishian v. Board of Regents* (decided January 23, 1967).

freedom are at loggerheads. It is far easier to criticize than to solve. And it has been understandably rare for the Court to be unanimous in any cases where the restrictions involved were not clearly and patently unconstitutional.[1]

In the three major federal statutes that have been enacted since 1940 to combat subversion and increase national security, heavy judicial involvement was inevitable, given the nature of the controversy and the delicacy and difficulty of producing legislation that would achieve the desired goal without impinging upon fundamental individual liberties. The triumvirate of laws, in the order of their enactment, are the Smith Act of 1940, the Subversive Activities Control (McCarran) Act of 1950, and the Communist Control Act of 1954. We need not here be concerned with this last, hastily enacted, largely floor-legislated statute since it has been more or less ignored by the Department of Justice as a basis for possible prosecution; and although it did figure tangentially in two cases in 1956 and 1961,[2] it had not been meaningfully tested by the Court as of January 1967.

The first major test of anti-Communist legislation involved the Smith Act: the celebrated 1951 case of *Dennis v. United States*,[3] now a household word in cold war litigation. Here, in a 6:2 decision, featuring five separate opinions (the opinion for the Court by Mr. Chief Justice Vinson, two separate concurring opinions by Justices Frankfurter and Jackson, and two separate dissenting opinions by Justices Black and Douglas), the Supreme Court upheld the Smith Act's constitutionality. It did so against the contentions by Eugene Dennis and his ten co-leaders of the Communist Party, U.S.A., that the statute infringed on First Amendment guarantees of freedom of expression, in addition to violating substantive due process guarantees under the Fifth Amendment because of vagueness. The eleven top leaders had been indicted and tried in United States District Court Judge Harold Medina's tribunal, and after a sensational nine-months' trial were found guilty of a conspiracy[4] to teach and advocate the overthrow of the United States Government by force and violence,

[1] E.g. *Wieman v. Updegraff, loc. cit.,* in which the Court unanimously struck down an Oklahoma loyalty-oath law that made even *innocent* membership in a proscribed organization an offense.

[2] *Pennsylvania v. Nelson,* 350 U.S. 497 (1956), and *Communist Party v. Catherwood,* 367 U.S. 389 (1961).

[3] 341 U.S. 494.

[4] A conspiracy is commonly regarded as any combination of two or more persons to do an unlawful act or accomplish some lawful purpose by illegal means.

and a conspiracy to organize the Communist Party, U.S.A., to teach and advocate the same offenses proscribed and rendered criminal by the terms of the Smith Act. Their appeal to the United States Court of Appeals for the Second Circuit had been unanimously rebuffed by the intermediate appellate tribunal. In upholding the challenged segments of the Act, the Chief Justice, speaking for himself and Associate Justices Reed, Burton, and Minton,[1] focused on what the majority regarded as the conspiratorial nature of the defendants' activities. Calling upon the "clear and present danger" formula—a judicial doctrine utilized in freedom of expression cases which we shall discuss below—Vinson ruled that these activities transgressed the permissible line between the exercise of individual rights of peaceful advocacy of change and the right of society to ascertain national security as viewed by the Smith Act. But in invoking the concept that the activities of the eleven did indeed constitute a clear and present danger that Congress had a right and duty to prevent, he added an important qualification originally expressed by Chief Judge Learned Hand in the same case in the Court of Appeals:

> In each case [courts] must ask whether the gravity of the "evil," discounted by its improbability, justifies such invasion of free speech as is necessary to avoid the danger.[2]

"We adopt this statement of the rule," the Chief Justice went on, because it is "as succinct and inclusive as any other we might devise at this time. It takes into consideration those factors which we deem relevant, and relates their significance. More we cannot expect from words." [3] Explaining the community's justification for its national security policy, he continued:

> The formation by [the convicted Communist Party leaders] of such a highly organized conspiracy, with rigidly disciplined members subject to call when the leaders, these petitioners, felt that the time had come for action, coupled with the inflammable nature of world conditions, similar uprisings in other countries, and the touch-and-go nature of our relations with countries with whom the petitioners were in the very least ideologically attuned, convince us that their convictions were justified on this score.[4]

[1] Mr. Justice Clark, who, as President Truman's Attorney-General, had brought the indictments in the case, did not participate.
[2] *Dennis v. United States*, 183 F. 2d 201 (1950), at 212.
[3] *Dennis v. United States*, 341 U.S. 494 (1951), at 510.
[4] *Ibid.*, at 510-11.

"And this analysis," wrote the Chief Justice determinedly,

> disposes of the contention that a conspiracy to advocate, as distinguished from the advocacy itself, cannot be constitutionally restrained, because it comprises only the preparation. *It is the existence of the conspiracy which creates the danger.*[1]

Earlier, he had disposed of one anticipated objection by commenting that "clear and present danger" cannot mean that before the "Government may act, it must wait until the *putsch* is about to be executed, the plans have been laid and the signal is awaited." [2] And he rejected success or probability of success as a criterion.

Mr. Justice Frankfurter's concurring opinion was characteristic of his jurisprudential philosophy: to him, the decisive consideration was the Court's obligation to exercise judicial self-restraint by recognizing that the legislative assumption in passing the Smith Act was a reasonable one, consummated by reasonable representatives of the body politic. He was troubled by the law, however, and warned that "it is a sobering fact that in sustaining the conviction ... we can hardly escape restriction on the interchange of ideas"; that without "open minds there can be no open society." [3] Yet he emphatically held to his cardinal belief that even "free-speech cases are not an exception to the principle that we are not legislators, that direct policy-making is not our province." [4] Only if the legislative determination on how competing interests might best be reconciled is clearly "outside the pale of fair judgment," would the Court be justified in exercising its veto. The obvious difficulty, of course, remains: how and when to judge what is "outside." On the other hand, Mr. Justice Jackson, in his concurring opinion, pursued a different tack; waving aside the intricate free speech problem line *per se*, he concentrated almost exclusively on what he chose to see as *the* crux of the case—a conviction of and for *conspiracy*. Eleven times in two paragraphs of his opinion he used the noun "conspiracy," commenting in rather typical Jacksonian language, that the "Constitution does not make conspiracy a civil right." [5]

Justices Black and Douglas dissented vehemently. Once again, they

[1] *Ibid.*, at 511. (Italics supplied.)
[2] *Ibid.*, at 509.
[3] *Ibid.*, at 556.
[4] *Ibid.*, at 539.
[5] *Ibid.*, at 572.

found themselves alone on the individual's side of the line between individual and community, between democratic society's ability, even willingness, to confront risk and its quest for safety and security. In their separate opinions, but with each joining the other's, they *denied* the existence of a danger either clear or present enough to justify what they regarded as a rank invasion of the prerogatives of freedom of expression; charged that the Court's majority had, in effect, introduced a formula far less "tough" for the Government to meet than the "clear and present danger" concept Mr. Chief Justice Vinson ostensibly employed; and fervently argued for "full and free discussion even of ideas we hate." Mr. Justice Black—once a United States Senator from Alabama—closed his opinion with the observation that

> Public opinion being what it now is, few will protest the conviction of these Communist petitioners. There is hope, however, that in calmer times, when present pressures, passions and fears subside, this or some later Court will restore the First Amendment liberties to the high preferred place where they belong in a free society.[1]

Whatever the substantive merits of the Black position, this statement proved to be correct both as an analysis and as a prophecy. By June 1957, the federal authorities had obtained 145 indictments and 89 convictions under the Smith Act. But then, a six-man majority of the Supreme Court [2]—with only Mr. Justice Clark in dissent—drastically and dramatically limited the application of the Act by handing down a series of significant amendatory interpretations in the difficult case of *Yates v. United States*.[3] Writing for the Court in an intriguingly intricate opinion, Mr. Justice Harlan narrowed the meaning of the term "to organize"—one that Congress, clearly in retaliation, again broadened in 1962—and endeavored to establish an important legal distinction under the Smith Act between the *statement of a philosophical belief and the advocacy of an illegal action.* The Court took pains to make clear that the Smith Act still stood and there was no attempt to overrule the *Dennis* case, but it was obvious that the federal government would now no longer be statu-

---

[1] *Ibid.*, at 581.

[2] Justices Black and Douglas concurred in part *and* dissented in part—the latter because they wanted to declare the statute *unconstitutional*, not just inapplicable in the case at bar. Justices Brennan and Whittaker did not participate in the case.

[3] 354 U.S. 298 (1957).

torily able to punish members of the Communist Party, U.S.A., such as Oleta O'Connor Yates and her co-defendant "second string Communists," *for expressing a mere belief in the "abstract idea"* of the violent overthrow of the government. It would now have to prove that individuals on trial for alleged violations of the Smith Act had *actually intended*, now or in the future, to overthrow the government by force and violence, or to persuade others to do so. Moreover, the government would still have to demonstrate that the language employed by the advocates of actual overthrow was in fact "calculated to incite to action . . . to *do* something, now or in the future, rather than merely *believe* in something." [1] This, of course, it should be observed, was no longer the Vinson Court of 1951; the Chief Justice had died, to be replaced by Earl Warren; in his grave also was Robert Jackson, replaced by John Marshall Harlan; and although they took no part in the consideration or decision of *Yates*, William Brennan and Charles Whittaker had replaced the resigned Sherman Minton and the retired Stanley Reed. Remaining were Tom Clark, who had not participated in *Dennis* and now dissented in *Yates*; Felix Frankfurter and Harold Burton, who made up part of the *Yates* majority; and the *Dennis* dissenters, Hugo Black and William Douglas.

The public reaction to *Yates* was adverse; the line created by the Court between "theoretical" and "actual" advocacy did not assuage the uneasy feelings of the opponents or the recognition by the decision's proponents that it would prove to be a vexatious distinction, indeed. Hence it came as less than a total surprise that four years later the Court, in *Scales v. United States*,[2] in the first test involving the so-called membership clause [3] of the Smith Act, upheld that clause in the face of stringent constitutional challenges on the grounds of First and Fifth Amendment infringements. Mr. Justice Harlan speaking for the 5:4 majority (to "make amends at the bar of the public for Yates," as one bitter commentary charged) ruled that a person who was a "knowing, active" member of a subversive group, and who personally had a "specific intent to bring about violent overthrow of the government, could be convicted under the statute—and Junius

[1] *Ibid.*, at 325.
[2] *Scales v. United States*, 367 U.S. 203 (1961).
[3] The Act, among other things, made a felony the acquisition or holding of knowing membership in any organization which advocates the overthrow of the Government of the United States by force or violence. (18 U.S.C. #2385, 18 U.S.C.A. #2385.)

Irving Scales went to jail.[1] Yet in a companion case decided on the very same day, also testing the validity of a conviction under the "membership clause," Mr. Justice Harlan, adhering to his *Yates* dichotomy between a philosophical belief and advocating an illegal action, *switched* sides to bring about a 5:4 majority *against* the culpability of one John Francis Noto.[2] Noto, held Harlan for himself, the Chief Justice, and Justices Black, Douglas, and Brennan—the latter four having dissented from the *Scales* decision [3]—did not meet the "knowing, active" membership test necessary for conviction. Again we see the difficult and delicate balancing problem in freedom of expression—for which there is assuredly no easy answer.

As if to demonstrate that fact of governmental life, on the very day of the two 5:4 decisions in *Scales* and *Noto*, another 5:4 verdict upheld the registration requirements of the second national security statute, the McCarran or Subversive Activities Control Act of 1950.[4] Under that statute, the Subversive Activities Control Board (SACB) could, after a due hearing, order any Communist "action" or "front" group to register—and it had so ordered the Communist Party, U.S.A. For more than a decade the Party had refused to register. It challenged the order as a violation of the freedom of expression and association under the First Amendment and (in view of the Smith Act's criminal stricture) as compulsory self-incrimination under the Fifth. In one of the longest opinions in the history of the Court, Mr. Justice Frankfurter, speaking for himself and his colleagues Clark, Harlan, Whittaker, and Stewart, upheld the forced disclosure of Communist Party members' names. With characteristic caution, and deference to the legislative branch, the Frankfurter opinion failed to consider such a difficult constitutional question as self-incrimination under Amendment Five or any of the several others raised by the defense. Rather, he based his ruling strictly upon the considered judgment that the "registration requirement of #7 [of the McCarran Act], on its face and as here applied, does not violate the First Amendment." [5] Dis-

---

[1] After having served 15 months of his six-year sentence, he was pardoned by President Kennedy on Christmas Day 1962. Ironically, he had broken with the Communist Party four years before he went to jail.

[2] *Noto v. United States*, 367 U.S. 290 (1961).

[3] These four now concurred; they would have preferred to discuss the indictment, not merely to have reversed the conviction.

[4] *Communist Party v. Subversive Activities Control Board*, 367 U.S. 1 (1961).

[5] *Ibid.*, at 105.

senting, Warren, Black, Douglas, and Brennan, in three separate opinions, not only flayed the Court majority for ducking the crucial self-incrimination issue, but they also exhorted it to recognize, in Mr. Justice Douglas's words, that "our Constitution protects all minorities, no matter how despised they are." [1]

Yet the Court's hand was forced on the compulsory self-incrimination issue little more than two years later when, in December 1963, the United States Court of Appeals for the District of Columbia *did* squarely meet that aspect of the registration issue by *reversing* the Communist Party's conviction in a federal trial court for its failure to register under the McCarran Act's commands. The reversal [2] was on narrow grounds and did not necessarily settle the self-incrimination matter,[3] but it did uphold the Communist Party's constitutional argument that since the Smith Act treats it as a criminal conspiracy, compelled registration would *ipso facto* be self-incriminating. Since "mere association with the party incriminates," thus ruled the unanimous intermediate appellate tribunal in its opinion by Chief Judge Bazelon, statutory registration would indeed force self-incrimination in the face of Fifth Amendment guarantees to the contrary. When the United States Government appealed this adverse decision to the Supreme Court, the highest tribunal eschewed the opportunity to expound on the problem and, by refusing without comment to review the decision at that time, maintained the Government's defeat.[4] Two weeks later, however, the Court did, fairly and squarely, come to constitutional terms with another section of the McCarran Act, which it had also purposely ignored in the 1961 decision: the denial of passports to members of the Communist Party, U.S.A., and its "fronts." In a 6:3 decision, written for the Court by its most junior member in point of service, Mr. Justice Goldberg, the majority ruled the provision "unconstitutional on its face" as a deprivation of liberty guaranteed by the "due process of law" concept of the Fifth Amendment.

[1] *Ibid.*, at 190.
[2] *Communist Party v. United States*, 331 F.2d 807 (1963).
[3] "We hold only that the availability of someone to sign the forms was an element of the offense; that the officers, who should otherwise have signed, were unavailable by reason of their valid claim of the privilege against self-incrimination; that the government had the burden of showing that a volunteer was available; and that its failure to discharge this burden requires reversal of this conviction." (331 F.2d 807, at 815.)
[4] *United States v. Communist Party*, 377 U.S. 968 (1964).

The Court held that it "too broadly and indiscriminately restricts the right to travel." [1] And a scant year later, the Court, in a bullish mood, granted *certiorari* in two cases again challenging the McCarran Act requirement of *individual members* of the Communist Party, rather than the Party itself, to register with the Government.[2]

In November 1965 the Court's decision was announced—and it was unanimous. Speaking through Mr. Justice Brennan, it held *unenforceable* the Justice Department orders requiring two alleged subversives, William Albertson and Roscoe Quincy Proctor, to register under the McCarran Act, ruling that such registration would expose them to prosecution under other federal laws "in an area permeated with criminal statutes." [3] The opinion stopped short of declaring the "individual membership registration" provision of the Act *unconstitutional,* because a party member could still waive his self-incrimination privilege and register. But the obvious effect of the Court's holding was to make the registration requirement unenforceable and thus unusable in the hands of the government. In an area of freedom of expression in which unanimity, as we have seen, is indeed hard to attain, the Court stood as one with Brennan's holding that

> . . . the requirement to accomplish registration by completing and filing [the required form] is inconsistent with the protection of the self-incrimination clause [of the Fifth Amendment to the Constitution of the United States].[4]

Communists, too, have constitutional rights under our system of government.

Foreshadowing its increasing strictness vis-à-vis legislative experimentations in that realm, the Court—shortly prior to its adjournment of its eventful 1964-65 term—had entered virgin territory in the battleground between freedom of expression and national security by declaring unconstitutional for the very first time a *congressional* statute on

---

[1] *Aptheker v. Secretary of State,* 378 U.S. 500 (1964), at 514.

[2] *Albertson v. Subversive Activities Control Board,* 381 U.S. 910, and *Proctor v. Subversive Activities Control Board,* 381 U.S. 910 (1965). Earlier, the Court had vacated two orders requiring Communist "fronts" to register, ruling that the record in the cases was "too stale" for a serious constitutional adjudication. *American Committee for Protection of Foreign Born v. S.A.C.B.,* 380 U.S. 503, and *Veterans of the Abraham Lincoln Brigade v. S.A.C.B.,* 380 U.S. 513 (1963).

[3] *Albertson v. Subversive Activities Control Board,* 382 U.S. 70 (1965).

[4] *Ibid.,* at 76.

grounds of First Amendment freedom of speech. Although federal statutes had heretofore fallen on other grounds, frequently because of due
process violation, for one, and many a state law had been struck down
on the freedom of expression issue by its incorporation via Amendment
Fourteen, this was truly a novel development. Unanimously, the Court
now threw out a 1962 federal law that had required persons to whom
"Communist political propaganda" from abroad was addressed to
make a special request to the Post Office to deliver it. Under the statute—which did not cover sealed letters—the Customs Bureau gave
the Post Office Department a list of countries from which printed
Communist propaganda emanated. At the eleven entry points postal
officials examined the material and, if they decided that it was "Communist political propaganda," intercepted it. The Department then
notified the persons to whom it was addressed that they could receive
it only if they returned an attached reply card within twenty days; if
they did not respond, the mail was destroyed! Wrote Mr. Justice
Douglas for himself and his colleagues:

> We conclude that the act as construed and applied is unconstitutional
> because it requires an official act [returning the reply card] as a limita-
> tion on the unfettered exercise of the addressee's First Amendment
> rights. . . . The addressee carries an affirmative obligation which we do
> not think the Government may impose on him. . . . The regime of this
> *act is at war with the "uninhibited, robust, and wide-open" debate*
> *and discussion that are contemplated by the First Amendment.*[1]

Not only were the two petitioners grateful to the Court, but so also
was Postmaster-General John A. Gronouski,[2] who had been deeply
troubled "by the implications of this program on freedom of speech." [3]
(Moreover, the decision would free forty postal employees for other
work at an estimated savings of $250,000 a year!)

Perhaps more than any of the other examples of "line-drawing,"
that of the potent and pervasive riddle of national security in the days
of the cold war may serve to demonstrate that there are no easy answers to the problem of the balance between freedom of expression
and the security and safety requirements of the state. Dedicated democrats may well find themselves on opposite sides of the proverbial

[1] *Lamont v. Postmaster-General and Fixa v. Heilberg,* 381 U.S. 301 (1965).
(Italics supplied.)
[2] A Ph.D. from the University of Wisconsin.
[3] As quoted in *The New York Times,* May 25, 1965.

ledger.[1] A less vital but intriguing question concerns freedom of expression and "obscenity."

5. *What Is Obscene and When Is It?* The temptation to wallow a bit in this interesting section of the line-drawing vineyard is strong, but we shall confine ourselves to some fundamental considerations. The obvious difficulty is again the problem of definition: what is "obscenity" to some is mere "realism" to others; what is "lascivious" in the eyes of one reader is merely "colorful" in those of another; what is "lewd" to one parent may well be "instructive" to another. New York's Board of Regents—that state's official censor of movies —was never troubled by the charming little movie, "The Moon is Blue," in which its actors used such commonplace terms as "pregnant" and "virginity"; but Maryland and the United States Navy deemed it "lewd" and "lascivious," and accordingly banned the showing of the film—lest it have dire effects on the viewers. On the other hand, New York banned the distribution of "Lady Chatterley's Lover," charging that "the whole theme of this motion picture is immoral [under the applicable New York statute], for that theme is the presentation of adultery as a desirable, acceptable and proper pattern of behavior."[2] In unanimously reversing the New York action, the Supreme Court issued a number of opinions,[3] but they are turned, more or less specifically, on the vagueness of the concept "immorality" and the problem of censorship generally. In his concurring opinion, Mr. Justice Frankfurter stated the crux of the matter—differences of opinion as to the meaning of terms and differences of taste:

> As one whose taste in art and literature hardly qualifies him for the *avant-garde*, I am more than surprised, after viewing the picture, that the New York authorities should have banned "Lady Chatterley's Lover." To assume that this motion picture would have offended Victorian moral sensibilities is to rely only on the stuffiest of Victorian conventions. Whatever one's personal preferences may be about such matters, the refusal to license the exhibition of this picture . . . can only mean that [the portion of the New York statute in question] forbids the public

---

[1] Carl Friedrich, a close student of the problem, is convinced that it defies satisfactory solution by the judiciary—let alone the legislature! Hence he has suggested a *constitutional* amendment be passed specifically to deal with the security issue. (See his "Rights, Liberties, Freedoms: A Reappraisal," 57 *American Political Science Review* 853 [December 1963].)

[2] *Kingsley International Pictures v. Regents*, 360 U.S. 684 (1959).

[3] By Justices Stewart, Black, Frankfurter, Douglas, Clark, and Harlan—the latter five all concurring in the result, but on varying grounds.

showing of any film that deals with adultery except by way of ser-
monizing condemnation or depicts any physical manifestation of an
illicit amorous relation. . . .[1]

In general, the trend has been to throw out, on constitutional or statutory grounds, most state censorship laws, or, if not the laws themselves, the procedures involved. At the end of 1966 only Maryland,
Kansas, and Virginia still had such state-wide laws, and the *procedures*
used by Maryland had been declared unconstitutional one year earlier.[2] A good many cities still do have censorship ordinances, but
where the requirement is for licensing *in advance* of exhibition, only
four were still enforced in 1965.[3] These statistics do not, however,
cover state criminal statutes against the showing of obscene films *not
subject to prior censorship*; these are still widespread and, of course,
raise a different, no less difficult, issue. Whereas there is no consensus
about the illegality of *prior* censorship, whatever the medium of expression, there seems to be agreement that obscenity, at least in
public, is of "no redeeming social value" and must be both inter-
dictable *and* punishable. The increase in printed smut throughout the
country that seems to have accompanied judicial reversals of state
obscenity convictions has given rise to fairly widespread outcries—
both genuine and hypocritical—from citizens and citizen groups, and
demands for curbs. If only we could agree on just what is obscene!
How to protect ideas and morality concurrently demands a veritable
Solomon.

It ought to be noted that it is not only America that must wrestle
with this problem. Our sister democracies throughout the world have
encountered similar considerations, admittedly under different national and cultural traditions, and their solution has been far from
easy. For example, the *Chambre de Droit Public* of Switzerland's
highest tribunal, the *Tribunal Fédéral Suisse*, had to deal with "indecency" charges against one Werner Kunz, a Zürich producer of
three "naturalist" films, who found himself censored because he had
shown "nudism" on the beaches and on snow-covered mountains.
Now, did this showing of nudity constitute "naturalist beauty" or
"indecent character"? The seven jurists rendered a split decision on
each count: Yes, 5:2, it was indecent publicly to exhibit nudity on the

---

[1] *Loc. cit.*, at 691-2.
[2] *Freedman v. Maryland*, 380 U.S. 51 (1965).
[3] *The New York Times*, March 21, 1965.

white snow; but no, 4:3, it was not indecent to show it publicly on the beach.[1] And henceforth similar "naturalist" or "vacation" films by Mr. Kunz would carefully have to bear the distinction in mind.

Attempts to censor *written publications* have often turned on the use of certain infamous Anglo-Saxon four-letter words. Generally, books and allied media have found at least as much judicial protection against unbridled censorship as have movies. Obviously, obscenity, or, more precisely, "hard-core pornography"—as it has been increasingly classified by the Court—may be forbidden, but the problems of classification, sanctions, and punishment are indeed vexatious. Mr. Justice Stewart, for one, who backs censorship solely if the material represents "hard-core pornography," threw up his judicial hands when asked its meaning, responding "[all I can say is that] I know it when I see it. . . ." [2] And he has stuck to this position ever since.[3] Justice Harlan tried to be more precise when he explained that, to him, "hard core" signifies "that prurient material that is patently offensive or whose indecency is self-demonstrating" [4]—which is not crystal clear either, as definitions go!

One man's smut may well be another one's Chaucer! But, rather logically, as the Supreme Court held 8½:½ (Mr. Justice Harlan concurred in part and dissented in part) in the significant decision of *Smith v. California*,[5] the proprietor of a bookstore cannot constitutionally be punished for offering an "obscene" book, here *Sweeter than Life*, for sale—an act banned by the terms of a Los Angeles City ordinance—if he was *unaware* that the book is in fact obscene. And Eleazar Smith was thus absolved of the charges against him. Yet, it may be asked, if the book had already been adjudged "obscene" in another jurisdiction, could Mr. Smith really plead ignorance, or lack of *scienter*,[6] regarding continued sales of the volume? At least one student of the field observed that he certainly could not.[7] Actually, the Court ruled on the matter only tangentially by placing the burden

---

[1] *Chambre de Droit Public*, P110/CG, Séance du 7 décembre 1960.

[2] *Jacobellis v. Ohio*, 378 U.S. 184 (1964), at 197, concurring opinion.

[3] E.g. *Ginzberg v. U.S.*, 383 U.S. 463 (1966), dissenting opinion at 499.

[4] *A Book Named "John Cleland's Woman of Pleasure" v. Massachusetts*, 383 U.S. 413 (1966), dissenting opinion.

[5] 361 U.S. 147 (1959).

[6] *Scienter* means having such knowledge as charges a man with the consequences of his actions.

[7] Paul G. Kauper, *Civil Liberties and the Constitution* (Ann Arbor: University of Michigan Press, 1962), p. 71.

of proof of criminal violation upon the state. The highest tribunal has gone further to condemn on constitutional grounds the kind of "informal censorship" by the "Rhode Island Commission to Encourage Morality in Youth," which was statutorily created and empowered to educate the public

> concerning any book, picture, pamphlet, ballad, printed paper or other thing containing obscene, indecent or impure language, or manifestly tending to the corruption of the youth . . . and to investigate and recommend the prosecution of all violations of [the statute involved]. . . .[1]

Such action, held Mr. Justice Brennan for the 8:1 Court, constituted "in fact a scheme of state censorship effectuated by extra-legal sanctions; they acted as an agency not to advise but to suppress." [2]

That the Court's search for a viable standard has been extremely difficult is illustrated by some additional examples. In a well-known 1957 case, *Butler v. Michigan*,[3] it held unconstitutional a Michigan law that forbade "any person" to sell or give away anything "containing obscene, immoral, lewd or lascivious language . . . tending to incite minors to violent or depraved or immoral acts, *manifestly tending to the corruption of the morals of youth*." Speaking for the unanimous Court, Mr. Justice Frankfurter set aside the conviction of Alfred E. Butler who had sold such a book (*The Devil Rides Outside*) to another adult, here a policeman. (The book is a story of a young American's visit to a Benedictine monastery in France to study Gregorian chants. As a result of his observations of the monks he aspires to resemble them, particularly in the virtue of chastity, although he is obsessed by sex and indulges in several sordid amours.) The Court's ruling was on the ground that the state could not, under its police power, quarantine "the general reading public against books not too rugged for grown men and women in order to shield juvenile innocence. . . . Surely, *this is to burn the house to roast the pig*." [4] Frankfurter, who was not usually against reasonably drafted, tightly drawn [5] police-power legislation, continued:

---

[1] *Bantam Books, Inc. v. Sullivan*, 372 U.S. 58 (1963), at 59-60.
[2] *Ibid.*, at 72.
[3] 352 U.S. 380 (1957). (Italics in following quotation supplied.)
[4] *Ibid.*, at 383. (Italics supplied.)
[5] E.g. see his opinion for the Court in *Kingsley Books, Inc., v. Brown*, 354 U.S. 436 (1957).

We have before us legislation not reasonably restricted to the evil with which it is said to deal. The incidence of this [law] is to reduce the adult population of Michigan to reading only what is fit for children. It thereby arbitrarily curtails one of those liberties of the individual, now enshrined in the due process clause of the Fourteenth Amendment, that history has attested as the indispensable conditions for the maintenance and progress of a free society.[1]

A few weeks later, a divided Court attempted to provide a yardstick which has since proved to be but partly successful. In the combined *Roth* and *Alberts* cases,[2] featuring five opinions, the justices who joined in the majority's holding [3] did their best to "balance" the rights involved by establishing the "prurient interest" test.[4] Here, speaking through Mr. Justice Brennan—who has been frequently called upon by Mr. Chief Justice Warren to write opinions in this sphere—[5] the Court upheld both a federal statute forbidding the transportation through the mails of "obscene, lewd, lascivious, indecent, filthy or vile" materials *and* a state statute forbidding the sale or advertisement of "obscene or indecent matter" on the strength of the new "prurient interest" concept. This test, as described by Brennan, was to determine *"[w]hether to the average person, applying contemporary community standards, the dominant theme of the material, taken as a whole, appeals to prurient intersts,"*[6] and whether, in addition, the material "goes substantially beyond the customary limits of candor." That Brennan cited "impure sexual thoughts" as one example of "prurient interests" ought to demonstrate the intriguingly difficult nature of the test. On the other hand, he made clear that by "obscenity" the Court had in mind only material that was *"utterly without redeeming social importance."* [7]

What Brennan himself regarded as the "difficult, recurring and unpleasant task" of setting a national moral criterion for a heterogeneous

[1] *Butler v. Michigan, loc. cit.,* at 383-4.

[2] *Roth v. United States* and *Alberts v. California,* 354 U.S. 476 (1957).

[3] Justices Brennan, Frankfurter, Burton, Clark, and Whittaker. The Chief Justice concurred separately, Justice Harlan concurred in *Alberts* but dissented in *Roth.* Justices Black and Douglas dissented in both.

[4] "Prurient," according to *Webster's,* signifies "Itching; longing; of persons, having lascivious longings; of desire, curiosity, or propensity, lewd."

[5] Some Justices seem to become regarded by the Chief Justice and the other members of the Court as "specialists" in certain fields.

[6] *Roth v. United States* and *Alberts v. California,* 354 U.S. 476 (1957) at 489.

[7] On this point see his fine article, based on the 1965 Meiklejohn Lecture at Harvard University, "The Supreme Court and the Meiklejohn Interpretation of the First Amendment," 79 *Harvard Law Review* 1-20 (November 1965).

people such as the citizenry of the United States, was accentuated by
the wistful dissenting opinion by Mr. Justice Douglas, joined by his
colleague Black. He questioned "prurience" as a viable standard, commenting that "the arousing of sexual thoughts and desires happens
every day in normal life in dozens of ways." [1] He cited a questionnaire sent to college and normal school female graduates in the late
1920's which asked "what things were most stimulating sexually?" Of
409 replies, 218 responded "man"—not an unreasonable answer.[2]
After a lengthy lecture on the First Amendment guarantees of free
expression, he concluded that he, for one,

> would give the broad sweep of the First Amendment full support. I
> have the same confidence in the ability of our people to reject noxious
> literature as I have in their capacity to sort out the true from the false
> in theology, economics, politics, or any other field.[3]

This, of course, goes to the very heart of one's own democratic *Weltanschauung*.

Yet the Court did manage to arrive at some standards with its
"prurient interest" test; and it further refined, perhaps liberalized, it
in 1962 in *Manuel Enterprises, Inc. v. Day:* [4] Mr. Justice Harlan, writing for the 6:1 Court majority—which was badly split, however, on
just what was being decided—held that the matter challenged must
be not only "so offensive as to affront current community standards
of decency," but that the indecency must be "self-demonstrating."
In other words, Harlan joined "patently offensive" to "prurient interest" in an attempt to find a more viable line.[5] Another explanation
cum refinement came in a multiple 1964 decision. There it was Mr.
Justice Brennan who, speaking for a majority of six, made clear that
the *Roth-Alberts* test reference to "contemporary community standards" was intended to establish a *national* standard rather than a "particular local community standard." [6]

Thus the Court by 1964 had established a basic constitutional requirement that material attacked on grounds of "obscenity," or any

---

[1] 354 U.S. 476, at 509.
[2] Douglas quoted from Leo M. Alpert, "Judicial Censorship of Obscene Literature," 52 *Harvard Law Review* 40 (1938), at 73. Ninety-five girls said "books";
40 "drama"; 29 "dancing"; 18 "pictures"; 9 "music."
[3] *Roth v. United States* and *Alberts v. California, loc. cit.,* at 514.
[4] 370 U.S. 478.
[5] *Ibid.,* at 482.
[6] *Jacobellis v. Ohio,* 378 U.S. 184, at 193.

other similar concepts, *must be judged not by its isolated parts, but by the dominant theme of the material as a whole.* The Court had demonstrably made clear that freedom of expression carries with it the inherent privilege of "unconventional," "controversial," even "immoral" advocacy, *provided* the manner in which this is done is not "obscene" under the established guidelines. Moreover, the Court would obviously not permit loosely drawn administrative and/or legislative procedures, nor would it assume automatic *scienter* of possession of obscene matter on the part of vendors.

However, in March of 1966 along came the rather surprising *Ginzberg* decision.[1] There, in a welter of fourteen opinions by seven justices in three cases decided together,[2] the Court, narrowly dividing 5:4 in the lead case (*Ginzberg*), demonstrated that, notwithstanding its recent "liberalizing" decisions in the obscenity field, it was also by no means necessarily averse to "toughening" its *Roth-Alberts*[3] test: Ralph Ginzberg, publisher of the magazine *Eros* and other erotic literature[4] stood convicted of 28 counts of violating the federal obscenity statute at issue in the *Roth* case, not because the material in itself was obscene, but *because of the manner in which it was "exploited," i.e. advertised.* As Mr. Justice Brennan, the Court's "obscenity expert," put the matter for himself, the Chief Justice, and Associate Justices Clark, White, and Fortas (with Justices Black, Douglas, Stewart, and Harlan dissenting in four separate opinions):

> Where an exploitation of interests in *titillation by pornography* is shown with respect to material lending itself to such exploitation through pervasive treatment or description of sexual matters, such evidence may support the determination that the material is obscene even though in *other contexts* the material would escape such condemnation.[5]

In other words, in "close cases," evidence of pandering may be "probative with respect to the nature of the material."[6] But to Mr. Justice

[1] *Ginzberg v. United States,* 383 U.S. 463.
[2] *Ibid.* (decided 5:4); *Mishkin v. New York,* 383 U.S. 502 (decided 6:3); and *A Book Named "John Cleland's Woman of Pleasure" v. Massachusetts,* 383 U.S. 413 (decided 6:3).
[3] *Op. cit.*
[4] *Eros,* a hard-cover magazine of expensive format; *Liaison,* a bi-weekly newsletter; and *The Housewife's Handbook on Selective Promiscuity,* a short book.
[5] *Ginzberg v. United States,* 383 U.S. 463 (1966), at 475. (Italics added).
[6] *Ibid.,* at 474. (Italics added.)

Black, the majority's stance fatally misinterpreted the First Amendment, for, as he put it:

> I believe that the Federal Government is without power whatever under the Constitution to put any type of burden on speech and expression of ideas of any kind (as distinguished from conduct).[1]

What all this means, in effect, is that we may well expect continued, close, independent, case-by-case judicial review of findings of "obscenity." [2] Censors will continue to find it difficult, indeed, to obtain judicial confirmation or support. On the other hand, it must not be assumed that government has been, or is being, denied the authority to ban the sale and/or "pandering" of "hard-core pornography," genuine smut, which, by self-demonstration, is patently offensive to current national community standards of decency, and thereby clearly appeals to prurient interests, particularly if advertised in "titillating" or "pandering" fashion. Presumably that type of filth and its method of dissemination—a new factor since the *Ginzberg* case—could hence be classified as "hard-core pornography," [3] and it is rather difficult to make a good case for its free advocacy! Sex, which Mr. Justice Brennan dubbed "a great and mysterious motive force in human life," has indeed "indisputably been a subject of absorbing interest to mankind through the ages; it is one of the vital problems of human interest and public concern." [4] And, as he pointed out in the key *Roth* and *Alberts* cases,[5] "sex and obscenity are not synonymous. On the other hand, obscene material is material which deals with sex in a manner appealing to prurient interests." [6] Moreover, since *Ginzberg*, a book or film need *not* have a "prurient appeal" to the public at large to be declared obscene. It can now be so judged even if it pan-

[1] *Ibid.*, at 476.

[2] Indeed, the Court's 1966-67 docket listed three obscenity cases for argument during the first two days of its term: *Redrup v. New York, Austin v. Kentucky,* and *Gent v. Alabama,* 385 U.S. 804, *certiorari* granted. And at least ten other cases awaited review disposition in February 1967.

[3] Under the heading "Ginzberg: The Fallout," *Civil Liberties,* the monthly publication of the American Civil Liberties Union, reported in October 1966 that the effects of the *Ginzberg* case were being felt in crackdowns throughout the country.

[4] *Roth v. United States* and *Alberts v. California,* 354 U.S. 476 (1957), at 487.

[5] *Loc. cit.*

[6] *Ibid.*, at 487.

ders merely to a "clearly defined deviant sexual group," such as homo-sexuals or masochists.[1] An otherwise obscene book is *not* obscene, to be sure, if it has "a modicum of social value." But this anti-censorship rule may be vitiated by evidence of a publisher's pandering.[2] Thus, the post-*Roth-Alberts* history, without settling the matter—especially in view of the narrow divisions and multiple opinions that have characterized the cases—has brought us somewhat closer to the possibility of drawing some lines. To be sure, these lines or rules may well have to be necessarily unsatisfactory and wavering, for they *are* so vitally concerned with sex, a subject that, in Mr. Justice Black's dissenting words in the *Ginzberg* case, is "pleasantly interwoven in all human activities and involves the very substance of life itself." [3]

In the visual media, such as movies, the over-all problem is considerably less complicated than in the realm of the printed word. For one thing, the movie-maker is usually acutely conscious of what he perceives as the public consensus and the public's pocketbook; and he is not likely to venture forth in the unconventional or the experimental, although movies have become quite a bit more daring lately. Moreover, the movie industry does have a bureau, at various times known as the Hays or Johnson Office, through which movies receive— or do not receive—the industry's seal of approval. It was not until some four decades after the office's establishment, that a film was released without the seal of approval.[4] Self-policing is not, of course, a guarantee of good taste, but it does place responsibility and judgment where it ought to lie: with the industry itself. (The same may be said for the press.) Still, the matter essentially comes down to the public, who should be free to patronize or to refuse to patronize the visual as well as the written media without governmental interference or injunction by administrative or legislative fiat or as a response to a powerful or vocal pressure group. If a movie is offensive to the sensibilities of a minority or majority group, that group is free, of course, to advise and campaign against its patronization. But it is emphatically not free to prevent those who desire to patronize it from so doing. Freedom of expression and advocacy is a two-edged sword.

[1] *Mishkin v. New York*, 383 U.S. 502 (1966).

[2] *A Book Named "John Cleland's Woman of Pleasure" v. Massachusetts*, 383 U.S. 413 (1966).

[3] *Ginzberg v. United States, loc. cit.*, at 481.

[4] *The Man with the Golden Arm*, produced in 1955, dealing with the narcotics problem (Producer Otto Preminger, United Artists Release).

There remains one additional word to be said here: much of the agitation and fear surrounding the problem at issue stems from the fear and misgivings of parents of minors. Yet it would seem that it is precisely they who must shoulder the responsibility for the ventures of their children. Far too many protests from those of us who are parents represent an abdication of responsibility, be it for supervision or education or both. Perhaps the state should help parents, as it does in the United Kingdom [1] and in Scandinavia, by "classifying" movies into those fit only for adults; those that may be seen by children under a certain age, usually 16, if accompanied by adults; and those open to all. We might also note that many private organizations and journals here at home do "classify"; it may be more appropriate for them to do so than the state. But neither device, however helpful, can be a substitute for the ultimate parental or personal responsibilities.

Judicial Line Formulae

Throughout the preceding discussions the enormity of the difficulty in any attempt to establish viable lines or standards in the realm of freedom of expression has been apparent. Yet, as the five key example-areas should have readily indicated, attempts at judicial tests, doctrines, or formulae have been as continuous as they are necessary. Much depends on the definition of terms which determine a particular judicial decision. Yet we can isolate at least two, perhaps three, judicial "tests," all of them post–World War I phenomena.

The "Clear and Present Danger" Test

Certainly the best-known is the "clear and present danger" test. Credit for its authorship has generally been given to Mr. Justice Holmes, actively supported by Mr. Justice Brandeis, although there are some observers who would credit famed United States Court of Appeals' Judge Learned Hand with an important assist in the birth of the doctrine, if not its central idea. It was first used in 1919 in the

---

[1] The British categories, as established and supervised by a Board of Census, are: "A" for adults and children with adults; "U" for universal viewing; "H" for horror films; and "X" for adults only and not for any children under sixteen. The Board is without statutory power, and the exhibition of films not passed by it is not an offense *per se*. Nevertheless, the classifications are given legal effect under the Cinematograph Act of 1909, which allows revocation of the exhibitor's license for failure to enforce the classification.

Schenck case, a case which is known to all students of government and politics.

Schenck v. United States.[1] In 1917 Charles T. Schenck, General Secretary of the Socialist Party, and some of his associates, sent out some 15,000 leaflets to potential and actual draftees under the Conscription Act, urging the young men to resist the draft. Under the Espionage Act of June 15, 1917, which specifically proscribed the kind of activities in which Schenck and his colleagues had engaged, the federal government indicted them on three counts: (1) conspiracy to cause insubordination in the military service of the United States; (2) using the mails for the transmission of matter declared to be non-mailable under the Espionage Act; and (3) the unlawful use of the mails for the transmission of the matter under (2). Schenck and his co-defendants were convicted in a federal trial court over their objections that the pertinent provisions of the Espionage Act constituted a violation of the freedom of speech and press guaranteed by the First Amendment. Unanimously rejecting the petitioners' contentions, the Supreme Court, speaking through Mr. Justice Holmes, enunciated its new "clear and present" doctrine. As the then 78-year-old jurist explained it in a memorable passage:

> We admit that in many places and in *ordinary times* the defendants in saying all that was said in the circular would have been within their constitutional rights. *But the character of every act depends upon the circumstances in which it is done.* . . . The most stringent protection of free speech would not protect a man in *falsely* shouting fire in a theatre and causing a panic. It does not even protect a man from an injunction against uttering words that have all the effects of force. . . . *The question in every case is whether the words used are used in such circumstances and are of such a nature as to create a clear and present danger that they will bring about the substantive evils that Congress has a right to prevent.* When a nation is at war many things that might be said in time of peace are such a hindrance to its effort that their utterance will not be endured so long as men fight and that no Court could regard them as being protected by any constitutional right.[2]

The doctrine was designed to draw a sensible and viable line between the rights of the individual and those of society at the point where the former's actions or activities tended to create a danger to organ-

[1] *Schenck v. United States*, 249 U.S. 47.
[2] *Ibid.*, at 52. (Italics supplied.)

ized society, so "clear and present" that government, the servant of the people—here the representative legislative branch by way of a wartime emergency statute—had a right to attempt to prevent the individual's actions or activities in *advance*. Schenck and his associates deemed such a statute to be an unconstitutional invasion of their First Amendment rights. But the highest tribunal of the land, resorting to its new doctrine, concurred with the government that the exigencies of wartime provided sufficient justification for its passage; that, indeed, any government worthy of the name would protect itself against the danger "clear and present" of interference with the so basic element of conscription for military service. It would be difficult to quarrel with that contention. And just one Opinion Day after *Schenck*, with Holmes again the author of two unanimous opinions for the Court upholding the Act of 1917 anew, the "clear and present danger" test again was invoked. One of the cases involved a pro-German newspaperman,[1] the other the famous Socialist leader Eugene V. Debs.[2] Not entirely happy with the nomenclature, Brandeis preferred to categorize the doctrine as a "rule of reason"—which, of course, it has to be. As he saw the test, correctly applied it would preserve the right of free speech both from "suppression by tyrannous, well-meaning majorities, and from abuse by irresponsible, fanatical minorities."

Abrams v. United States.[3] As if to demonstrate almost immediately the difficulties inherent in the "clear and present danger" formula, its two leading champions found themselves in the minority in the celebrated *Abrams* case barely six months after the *Schenck* decision. This time the Sedition Act of 1918, which went considerably beyond its predecessor, the Espionage Act of 1917, was at issue. It made punishable what two subsequent observers have justly called "speech that in World War II would have been deemed mere political comment."[4] It thus rendered punitive any "disloyal, profane, scurrilous, or abusive language about the form of government, the Constitution, soldiers and sailors, flag or uniform of the armed forces," and it also made unlawful any "word or act [favoring] the cause of the German Empire . . . or [opposing] the cause of the United States."

[1] *Frohwerk v. United States*, 249 U.S. 204 (1919).
[2] *Debs v. United States*, 249 U.S. 211 (1919).
[3] 250 U.S. 616 (1919).
[4] Alpheus T. Mason and William M. Beaney, *American Constitutional Law*, 3rd ed. (Englewood Cliffs, N.J.: Prentice-Hall, 1964), p. 476.

Under the statute, Jacob Abrams, a 29-year-old self-styled "anarchist-Socialist," and five young associates—one a girl—all aliens, were apprehended for distributing certain English- and Yiddish-language leaflets from rooftops on New York City's Lower East Side late in August 1918. These leaflets urged the "workers of the world" to resist the Allied and American military intervention against the Bolsheviki in Russia's Murmansk and Vladivostok areas during the summer of 1918. Bitterly, the leaflets denounced President Woodrow Wilson for his decision to intervene and exhorted "the workers of the world" to a general strike in order to prevent future shipment of munitions and other war materials to the anti-Soviet forces. The English leaflet closed with the following observation: "P.S. It is absurd to call us pro-German. We hate and despise German militarism more than do your hypocritical tyrants. We have more reasons for denouncing German militarism than has the coward in the White House." [1]

Four of the five defendants were found guilty in the United States District Court for the Southern District of New York. Visiting Trial Judge Henry DeLamar Clayton of Alabama [2] sentenced three of them, including Abrams, to the maximum of twenty-years' imprisonment in a federal penitentiary and a $4,000 fine each; the girl received fifteen years and a $500 fine; and one defendant got three years. (Four years later President Harding commuted their sentences on condition that they would all embark at once for the Soviet Union—which they did.) When their appeal reached the Supreme Court, Mr. Justice John H. Clarke, in a 7:2 opinion, agreed that the defendants had intended to "urge, incite, and advocate" curtailment of production deemed necessary to the conduct of the war effort, a crime under the Sedition Act and its predecessor statute. Clarke granted that the "primary purpose and intent" of the petitioners "was quite obviously to aid the cause of the Russian Revolution"—which was not forbidden *per se* under either of the statutes involved. But, he ruled,

the plan of action which they adopted necessarily involved, before it could be realized, defeat of the war program of the United States, for the obvious effect of this appeal, if it should become effective, as they

[1] As quoted by Zechariah Chafee, Jr., in his classic *Freedom of Speech in the United States* (Cambridge: Harvard University Press, 1954), p. 110. See his Chapter III for a fascinating account of the *Abrams* case.

[2] He authored the Clayton Anti-Trust Act of 1914 when a member of Congress from Alabama.

hoped it might, would be to persuade persons . . . not to aid government loans and not to work in ammunition factories. . . .[1]

The question that arises at once, of course, is whether the advocacy of a general strike constituted the kind of direct threat to the war effort that the laws under which they were indicted and sentenced envisaged. A plausible case could certainly be made, as indeed it was made by Professor Chafee, that "interference with the war was at the most an incidental consequence of the strikes [they clamored for], entirely subordinate to the longed-for consequences of all this agitation, withdrawal from Russia . . ." and should certainly *not* be made the main basis for punishments restricted open discussion.[2]

And while the majority of seven saw a "clear and present" danger, the doctrine's authors dissented in an opinion written by Mr. Justice Holmes which has become the classic exposition of the necessary balance implicit in the First Amendment. With Brandeis concurring, Holmes penned the best that he (or anyone else, we may add) could say on the matter, as the following impassioned excerpt testifies:

> . . . when men have realized that time has upset many fighting faiths, they may come to believe even more than they believe the very foundations of their own conduct that the ultimate good desired is better reached by *free trade in ideas*—that the best test of truth is the power of the thought to get itself accepted in the competition of the market, and that *truth is the only ground* upon which their wishes can be safely carried out. That at any rate is the theory of our Constitution. *It is an experiment, as all life is an experiment.* Every year if not every day we have to wager our salvation upon some prophecy based upon imperfect knowledge. While that experiment is part of our system I think that we should be *eternally vigilant against attempts to check the expression of opinions that we loathe and believe to be fraught with death,*

—and here, of course, he draws the line—

> *unless they so imminently threaten immediate interference with the lawful and pressing purposes of the law that an immediate check is required to save the country. . . .*[3]

Holmes and Brandeis saw no such interference in what Holmes called the "surreptitious publishing of a silly leaflet" by an unknown man.

---

[1] *Abrams v. United States,* 250 U.S. 616 (1919), at 621.
[2] *Freedom of Speech in the United States,* p. 134.
[3] *Abrams v. United States, loc. cit.,* at 630. (Italics supplied.)

Assuredly, noted Holmes, this did in no sense constitute "a present danger of immediate evil," and he warned his fellow countrymen and their legislators that

> Only the emergency that makes it immediately dangerous to leave the correction of evil counsels to time warrants making any exception to the sweeping command, "Congress shall make no law abridging freedom of speech." [1]

Holmes was not speaking of *acts*, but of the five young radicals' "expressions of opinions and exhortations, which were all that were uttered here." He concluded that beyond any shadow of doubt they "were deprived of their rights under the Constitution of the United States." [2]

The "Bad Tendency Test"

If the *Abrams* majority did not modify the "clear and present danger" doctrine, it assuredly sidetracked it. The *official* modification came six years later in the *Gitlow* case.

Gitlow v. New York.[3] The facts and circumstances surrounding this famous decision have been amply outlined and discussed in Chapter III on "incorporation." However, we must examine here the Supreme Court majority's holding, over the dissenting opinion by Mr. Justice Holmes, in which once again Mr. Justice Brandeis concurred, that "certain writings" of Benjamin Gitlow constituted a *"bad tendency"* to "corrupt public morals, incite to crime, and disturb the public peace." The majority thus affirmed Gitlow's conviction under New York State's Criminal Anarchy Act of 1902, which prohibited the "advocacy, advising, or teaching the duty, necessity or propriety of overthrowing or overturning organized government [New York's] by force or violence" and the publication or distribution of such matters. Despite the fact that there was no evidence, whatsoever, of any effect from the publication of Gitlow's "Left Wing Manifesto," Mr. Justice Sanford, speaking for the Court, contended that the "State cannot reasonably be required to measure the danger from every such utterance in the nice balance of a jeweler's scale" [4] and ruled that because a

---

1 *Ibid.*, at 630-31.
2 *Ibid.*, at 631.
3 *Gitlow v. New York*, 268 U.S. 652 (1925).
4 *Ibid.*, at 669.

single revolutionary spark may kindle a fire that, smoldering for a time, may burst into a sweeping and destructive conflagration . . . [the State] . . . may, in the exercise of its judgment, suppress the threatened danger in its incipiency.[1]

Obviously, this was no longer the "clear and present danger" test. When the State is empowered to suppress a mere *threat* in its very *incipiency*, the line is being drawn on the basis of a "bad tendency" rather than at that of a danger "clear and present." There was hardly anything very "clear" or "present" in Gitlow's activities, confined as they were to the written exhortations—Holmes called them "redundant discourse" in his dissent—of a rather pathetic individual.

In asking itself whether Gitlow's activities had created, or constituted, *a "bad tendency" to bring about a danger* (a phrase from the *Schaefer* [2] decision five years earlier), the majority shifted the balance between the individual and the state toward the latter. Holmes and Brandeis were not amused. Thundered Holmes:

If what I think the correct test is applied it is manifest that there was no present danger of an attempt to overthrow the government by force. . . . It is said that this manifesto was more than a theory, that it was an incitement. *Every idea is an incitement.* It offers itself for belief and if believed it is acted on unless some other belief outweighs it or some failure of energy stifles the movement at its birth. The only difference between the expression of an opinion and an incitement in the narrower sense is the speaker's enthusiasm for the result. *Eloquence may set fire to reason.*[3]

Holmes pointed out, as he had in similar circumstances in his *Abrams* dissent, that the charges against the defendant alleged *publication*, and nothing more. And, calling a democratic spade a democratic spade, he commented:

If in the long run the beliefs expressed in proletarian dictatorship are destined to be accepted by the dominant forces of the community, the only meaning of free speech is that they should be given their chance and have their way.[4]

He was naturally confident, as was Mr. Justice Douglas in his dissenting opinion in the *Dennis* case [5] a quarter of a century later, that "the

1 *Ibid.*
2 *Schaefer v. United States,* 251 U.S. 466 (1920).
3 *Gitlow v. New York, loc. cit.,* at 673. (Italics supplied.)
4 *Ibid.*
5 *Dennis v. United States,* 341 U.S. 494 (1951).

American people want none of Communism [whose] doctrine is exposed in all its ugliness . . . its wares unsold." [1] In a very real sense the issue for both men came down to a matter of faith in the ability of the American people to decide, in the absence of demonstrable, overt, illegal *actions*.

EXPANDING "CLEAR AND PRESENT DANGER"

Holmes and Brandeis recognized that some amplification of their "clear and present danger" test was needed to prevent its demotion to the "bad tendency" level. Their opportunity came some two years following the *Gitlow* decision in the too often neglected case of *Whitney v. California*.[2]

Whitney v. California. Miss Charlotte Anita Whitney was an interesting individual, indeed. A niece of one of the pillars of *laisser faire* American capitalism, Mr. Justice Stephen J. Field, whose wealthy and conservative family was repulsed by their relative's radicalism, Miss Whitney was one of the band of disenchanted adventurers who, in 1919, helped to organize the Communist Labor Party of California. Motivated largely by her passionate espousal of the cause of the poor, she readily permitted herself to be elected as a member of the C.L.P.C. during its 1919 convention held in Oakland. The Party's constitution was quite clear on its affiliation with both the Communist Labor Party of America and the Communist International of Moscow. Miss Whitney's activities brought her into conflict with California's Criminal Syndicalism Act of 1919. She soon found herself indicted on five counts, and subsequently convicted of one: that on November 28, 1919, she "did then and there unlawfully, willfully, wrongfully, deliberately and feloniously organize and assist in organizing, and was, is, and knowingly became a member of an organization, society, group and assemblage of persons organized and assembled to advocate, teach, aid and abet criminal syndicalism." [3]

On appeal, Charlotte Anita protested, as she had during her trial, that at no time did she wish her Party to engage in any acts of violence or terror, but the intermediate appellate tribunal affirmed her conviction and the State Supreme Court refused to review her case, which then went on to the United States Supreme Court. At issue was the association between due process of law and First Amendment

1 *Ibid.*, at 588-9.
2 274 U.S. 357 (1927).
3 *Ibid.*, at 358.

guarantees, against the basic charge of a criminal conspiracy, which is naturally an activity outside the protection of free speech. Again, Miss Whitney lost. Mr. Justice Sanford, here writing the opinion for a unanimous Court that included Justices Holmes and Brandeis, agreed that the State of California had an inherent right to guard statutorily against the alleged conspiracy, and neither Holmes nor Brandeis disputed the Court's finding that there was sufficient evidence to point to the existence of such a conspiracy to violate the Criminal Syndicalism Act. However, in a highly significant concurring opinion, joined by Holmes, Brandeis rejected the majority's interpretation of a section of the law that not only made it a crime to advocate or teach or practice criminal syndicalism, or conspire to do so, but also to be in "association with those who proposed to teach it." Here Brandeis and Holmes saw a lurking and grave threat to the concept of "clear and present danger" as they had conceived of it and, with the *Gitlow* "bad tendency" doctrine in mind, the two jurists endeavored not only to resurrect their original "clear and present danger" concept but to strengthen it. In a ringing admonition— which reportedly so moved the then Governor of California, C. C. Young, that he later pardoned Miss Whitney—Brandeis's concurrence attempted to clarify, expand, and liberalize the doctrine by joining to its basic test the requirement of *"imminence"*:

> Fear of serious injury cannot alone justify suppression of free speech and assembly . . . there must be reasonable ground to fear that serious evil will result if free speech is practiced. There must be reasonable ground to believe *that the danger apprehended is imminent.* There must be reasonable ground to believe that the evil to be prevented is a serious one. . . . In order to support a finding of clear and present danger *it must be shown either that immediate serious violence was to be expected or was advocated, or that the past conduct furnished reason to believe that such advocacy was then contemplated.*
>
> Those who won our independence were not cowards. They did not fear political change. They did not exalt order at the cost of liberty. To courageous, self-reliant men, with confidence in the power of free and fearless reasoning applied through the processes of popular government, *no danger flowing from speech can be deemed clear and present, unless the incidence of the evil apprehended is so imminent that it may befall before there is opportunity for full discussion. If there be time to expose through discussion the falsehood and fallacies, to avert the evil by the processes of education, the remedy to be applied is more speech, not enforced silence.*[1]

1 *Ibid.*, at 377. (Italics supplied.)

In his and Holmes's opinion, "such . . . is the command of the Constitution." [1]

Thus, we again see the basic dilemma inherent in the two approaches to freedom of expression in democratic society. No matter what the language employed, no matter what the rationalization by individuals in specific situations, it comes down to a matter of reading the Constitution in its historical-evolutionary setting, against what Holmes called "the felt necessities of the times." And underlying the entire problem is, inevitably and necessarily, the faith one has in a free people's willingness and ability to experiment, to take chances, to govern themselves in democratic society.

"Preferred Freedoms" and Beyond. We noted in Chapter II that the Supreme Court in the late 1930's and much of the 1940's—in line with the Brandeis-Holmes philosophy expressed in *Whitney* and other cases—adopted the view that there should be "more exacting judicial scrutiny" of First Amendment freedoms. Here the Court determined a constitutionally protected area of "preferred freedom," based upon the famous footnote by Mr. Justice Stone in *United States v. Carolene Products Co.*,[2] where the future Chief Justice called for a special niche for "legislation which restricts the political processes." [3] A concept enthusiastically embraced by Justices Black, Douglas, Murphy, and Rutledge when they served together with Stone on the Court from the time of Rutledge's appointment in 1943 to the deaths of Stone, Rutledge, and Murphy in 1943, 1949, and 1949, respectively, it was to be joined to the "clear and present danger plus imminence" doctrine.

But when Harlan Stone died in 1946, Fred Vinson replaced him as Chief Justice, foreshadowing trouble for the new "line" established by the civil libertarians. And when Murphy and Rutledge both died in the summer of 1949, their replacements, Justices Clark and Minton, together with the new Chief Justice and the "holdovers"—Justices Reed, Frankfurter, Jackson, and Burton—constituted a new majority that almost at once departed from the philosophy of "preferred freedom." Indeed, in the internal security case of *Dennis v. United States* [4] even the "clear and present danger" doctrine underwent a rather dramatic transformation into what some observers

---

[1] *Ibid.*
[2] 304 U.S. 144 (1938).
[3] *Ibid.*, at 152.
[4] 341 U.S. 494 (1951).

viewed as a "grave and probable" test patterned upon Judge Learned Hand's opinion,[1] an opinion on which Mr. Chief Justice Vinson leaned very heavily in his *Dennis* majority opinion.[2] Others felt that in fact the Court had adopted as its new freedom of expression doctrine a "possible and remote danger" test! [3] Unquestionably, "bad tendency" had taken over from "clear and present danger." However, soon after Earl Warren became Chief Justice on Vinson's death in 1953, the Court returned to the "clear and present danger" test, even restoring its "imminence" appendage in such areas as racial discrimination, freedom of religion, and standards of criminal procedure. Indeed, some even felt that the new Court adopted a "super-preferred" standard vis-à-vis claims of racial discrimination and due process standards of criminal justice. It did retain the "bad tendency" test in the national security field for a while longer but, by the *late* 1950's, in cases such as *Yates v. United States*,[4] the Court, after some wavering and broken-field strategy, returned to the "clear and present danger" test for the national security field also.

SOME CONCLUDING THOUGHTS

No other branch of our government is as qualified to draw lines between the rights of individuals and the rights of society as the Supreme Court of the United States. All too easily do the legislative and executive branches yield to the politically expedient and the popular. Admittedly, the "clear and present danger" approach to freedom of expression, however amended and augmented, is far from perfect. But the sole alternative to it would be an almost total absence of immunity in the face of legislative actions. Freedom of expression cannot, in the nature of things, be absolute; but it can be protected to the widest degree humanly feasible under the Constitution. And there are giants of liberal democracy who bridle at any restraint on free expression. Thus we have Mr. Justice Black in his absolutist approach to the problem [5] and, almost as absolute, the famed educator-philosopher, the late Alexander Meiklejohn, who

[1] *Dennis v. United States*, 183 F. 2d 201 (1950), at 212.
[2] *Loc. cit.*, at 510 ff.
[3] Alfred H. Kelly and Winfred A. Harbison, *The American Constitution: Its Origins and Development*, 2nd ed. (New York, W. W. Norton & Co., 1955), p. 893.
[4] 354 U.S. 298 (1957). See the discussion of the case, *supra*.
[5] E.g. his "The Bill of Rights," 35 *New York University Law Review* 865-81 (April 1960).

held that while the First Amendment "does not forbid the abridging of speech ... it does forbid the abridging of freedom of speech." [1]

For Alexander Meiklejohn, who rejects the "clear and present danger" approach, there is thus *never*, under the First Amendment, any right or reason to curb or abridge freedom of speech; dangers, even in war time, are irrelevant; and the time of danger is precisely the time to show people that one means what one says and has the right to say it:

> If, then, on any occasion in the United States it is allowable to say that the Constitution is a good document it is equally allowable, in that situation, to say that the Constitution is a bad document. If a public building may be used in which to say, in time of war, that the war is justified, then the same building may be used in which to say that it is not justified. If it be publicly argued that conscription for armed service is moral and necessary, it may likewise be publicly argued that it is immoral and unnecessary. If it may be said that American political institutions are superior to those of England or Russia or Germany, it may, with equal freedom, be said that those of England or Russia or Germany are superior to ours. These conflicting views may be expressed, must be expressed, not because they are valid, but because they are relevant. If they are responsibly entertained by anyone, we, the voters, need to hear them. When a question of policy is "before the house," free men choose it not with their eyes shut, but with their eyes open. To be afraid of ideas, any idea, is to be unfit for self-government.[2]

This stirring language should serve as a beacon to us all; but the fact remains that there *are* limits to the precious freedom and that we do need some such doctrine as "clear and present danger." Meiklejohn, however, proposed a different solution: He created a dichotomy of *public speech* and *private speech*, "public" speech pertaining to any matter that concerns politics—i.e. public policy and public officials. This type of speech, Meiklejohn holds, is given absolute protection in the interests of self-governing free and democratic society by the First Amendment and the "privileges and immunities" clause of the Fourteenth, and cannot be abridged at all. *"Private"* speech, he contends, pertains to speech that concerns only private individuals in their personal, private concerns, and can therefore be regulated or

[1] *Free Speech and Its Relation to Self-Government* (New York: Harper & Brothers, 1948), p. 19.
[2] *Ibid.*, p. 27.

restricted—but *only* in accordance with the "due process of law" safeguards under the Fifth and Fourteenth Amendments. Noble as well as intriguing the Meiklejohn dichotomy may be, but it is burdened with what is clearly an unresolvable dilemma: how to draw the line pragmatically between "public" and "private" speech. Much speech is private but has definite public ramifications—a viable line seems impossible to attain. Yet shortly before he died in 1965 Meiklejohn voiced the belief that the Supreme Court had, in effect, adopted his "public speech" approach because of its developing stance on litigation concerning libel, slander, and defamation of character, highlighted by the 1964 decision in *New York Times Co. v. Sullivan*.[1] There the Court held that a *public* official cannot recover libel damages for criticism of his official performance unless he proves that the statement was made with deliberate malice. "It is an occasion for dancing in the streets," exclaimed Meiklejohn, according to Mr. Justice Brennan—who, however, preferred to leave to his readers "to say how nearly Dr. Meiklejohn's hope has been realized." [2]

A stanch supporter of the Holmes-Brandeis "clear and present danger plus imminence" doctrine, Zechariah Chafee, Jr., another towering advocate of free expression, had all but scolded his revered teacher and friend Meiklejohn in 1949, in a well-known and often quoted book review.[3] Reviewing Meiklejohn's *Free Speech and its Relation to Self Government*,[4] Chafee charged that Meiklejohn, in his repeated challenge to Holmes and the "clear and present danger" doctrine,[5] simply showed no realization of the long uphill fight which Holmes had to wage in order to secure free speech. After all, as Chafee explained correctly in his review, it *was* Holmes who

> worked out a formula which would invalidate a great deal of suppression, and won for [free speech] the solid authority of a unanimous Court. Afterwards, again and again, when the test was misapplied by the majority, Holmes restated his position in ringing words which, with

[1] 376 U.S. 254.
[2] William J. Brennan, Jr., "The Supreme Court and the Meiklejohn Interpretation of the First Amendment," 79 *Harvard Law Review* (November 1965) at 17, 20.
[3] 62 *Harvard Law Review* 891 (1949).
[4] *Op. cit.*
[5] See also Meiklejohn's "charges which I would bring against the 'clear and present danger' theory," in another important work on the freedom of speech problem, *Political Freedom: The Constitutional Powers of the People* (New York: Harper and Bros., 1948 and 1960), pp. 75-6.

the help of Brandeis and [later, after he had become Chief of Justice] Hughes, eventually inspired the whole Court.[1]

Of course, to support the "clear and present danger" doctrine, or that of "clear and present danger plus imminence," is not to ignore its inherent dilemmas—as the preceding discussion demonstrates. The very adjectives "clear" and "present" raise problems of great magnitude—e.g. clear and present danger of what? Still, both in its basic philosophy and its application, the doctrine's overriding tenets are realistic in approach and reflect an attitude which is both liberal *and* conservative in the classic connotations of those two so often misunderstood and misapplied terms. It is simply not possible to get away from the concept of "balancing"—a contentious term in some quarters [2]—liberty and authority, freedom and responsibility.[3] But when "balancing" is called for, and in the absence of a danger clear, present, and imminent, we must presume the scale to be weighted on the side of the individual.

In a liberal democracy, it must be remembered that the majority has an eternal obligation to leave open all those political channels by which it can be replaced when it is no longer able to command popular support. As the author has had occasion to say elsewhere,[4]

[1] *Loc. cit.*, p. 901.

[2] See, for example, the intriguing law-review debate between Professors Laurent Frantz and Wallace Mendelson over the validity of "balancing" as a technique in free spech cases: Frantz, "The First Amendment in the Balance," 71 *Yale Law Journal* 1424 (1962); Mendelson, "On the Meaning of the First Amendment: Absolutes in the Balance," 50 *California Law Review* 821 (1962); Frantz, "Is the First Amendment Law? A Reply to Professor Mendelson," 51 *California Law Review* 729 (1963); and Mendelson, "The First Amendment and the Judicial Process: A Reply to Mr. Frantz," 17 *Vanderbilt Law Review* 479 (1964). Speaking broadly, Professor Frantz was anti-, Professor Mendelson pro-"balancing" —but the reader is cautioned against over-simplification. See also the challenging article by Dean Alfange, Jr., "The Balancing of Interests in Free Speech Cases: In Defense of an Abused Doctrine," 2 *Law in Transition Quarterly* 1 (1965).

[3] In his interesting position essay on the over-all question, *Freedom of Speech: The Supreme Court and Judicial Review* (Englewood Cliffs, N.J.: Prentice-Hall, 1966), Professor Martin Shapiro contends that although balancing "may still occasionally be useful in particular instances, it cannot be maintained as a general formula for a Court bent on fulfilling its First Amendment responsibilities" (p. 105). Issuing a clarion call for judicial activism, he sees the "preferred freedom" position as the only viable formula, one that he insists must "again become the dominant First Amendment doctrine of the Supreme Court" (p. 172). Again and again calling for judicial activism, judicial policy-making, in the freedom of speech sphere, he argues that American democracy "not only permits but invites and requires a strong measure of judicial activism here."

[4] J. A. Corry and Henry J. Abraham, *Elements of Democratic Government*, 4th ed. (New York: Oxford University Press, 1964), pp. 262 ff.

the philosophical test to be applied is clear: Will the forbidding of freedom of expression further or hamper the realization of liberal democratic ideals? The sole manner in which to moderate, remedy, or remove rankling discontent is to get at its causes by education, remedial laws, or other community action. Repression of expression will only serve to sharpen the sense of injustice and provide added arguments and rationalizations for desperate, perhaps reckless measures. Surely the loyalty of the mass of men to liberal democracy has been immensely strengthened by the right to free expression and the consequent feeling of a genuine stake in society, a society that allows the expression of our deepest and most rankling grievances. Hence repressive laws will fail to maintain "loyalty." While they may give a false sense of security, at least for a time, since we would be excused from arguing the case for our ideals and for the carefully developed procedures for pursuing them, we must also recognize that freedom of utterance, even though it be rebellious, constitutes a safety valve that gives timely warning of dangerous pressures in our society. Committed to the principles of Western liberal democracy, we have a lasting obligation always to leave open the political channels by which a governing majority can be replaced when it is no longer able to command popular support. However, to plead for a generous approach to freedom of expression is not to say that it is absolute. It is not; it cannot be. In the final analysis we must confidently look to the Court to draw a line steeped in constitutional common sense. No other agency of government is equally well qualified to do so.

VI

Religion

IF LINE-DRAWING in the realm of due process is difficult because of the ambiguity of the concept, and if it is elusive in determining the freedom of expression, it is pre-eminently delicate and emotional in the matter of religion. Religion, like love, is so personal and irrational that no one has either the capacity or justification to sit in judgment.[1] (This is not to say that people do not try—be they plain citizens, members of the cloth, or eminent psychiatrists!) Any attempt by society to find and draw a line here is bound to be frustrating. Our own society is certainly no exception—although it is to America's credit that in probably no other area of civil rights and liberties have our agencies and agents of government maintained such a consistently good record. More even than the hallowed freedom of the press has the freedom of religion been safeguarded from governmental interference. This is not to say, of course, that we have a perfect record; our early history is replete with both public and private discrimination against religious creeds, particularly Catholics, Quakers, and Jews. However, as we grew and developed as a nation, discrimination *by government* declined perceptibly and fairly rapidly. *Private* religious discrimination is no longer, if it ever was, affirmatively encouraged or even sanctioned by government, and when it occurs it is pre-eminently of a "social" rather than a "religious" nature. The problems arise when attempts are made to commingle matters of religious

[1] Still, the author feels tempted to profess a modicum of "expertise": a product of secular secondary schools, he spent one year at a Roman Catholic university; was graduated from an Episcopal college; married a Christian Scientist; his children go to Quaker schools; and he is a member of the Board of Trustees of an old Reform Jewish Congregation.

belief with matters of state and to conduct policy in line with spiritual commitments.

The election of the first Roman Catholic President of the United States in 1960; the rise to public prominence and power of a host of members of religious minority groups; and the steadily increasing official proscription of public or quasi-public discrimination because of race, religion, color, and national origin—brought to such a dramatic climax in the Civil Rights Act of 1964—all augur well for a continuing increase in understanding and a continuing decline of the barriers built of religious discrimination. Nevertheless, problems of religious freedom still do arise and lines must be drawn. Our concern here lies predominantly in the public sector, and in how and where lines are drawn between the prerogatives of free exercise of religion, and all the concept entails, and the right of society to guard against activity that would infringe upon the rights of other members of that society. The distinction is compounded by the unique collateral problem of the constitutional command against the "establishment" of religion, and *it* has proved to be a hornets' nest, indeed!

SOME BASIC CONSIDERATIONS

Basic to our understanding of the problem are three constitutional facts.

1. *The Proscription of Religious Tests in Article VI of the Constitution.* It is often forgotten that there exists in the body of our Constitution an important provision dealing directly with a crucial religious right, the forbidding of religious tests as qualifications for public office. The third section of Article VI, following the famed supremacy clause,[1] reflects the concern for religious liberty of four Virginians to whom, although not all participants in the Constitutional Convention, is due chief credit for our constitutional theory of freedom of religion: Thomas Jefferson, James Madison, George Mason, and, perhaps with an occasional aberration, Patrick Henry.[2] The Journal of the Convention for August 30, 1787, bears the follow-

[1] "This Constitution, and the Laws of the United States which shall be made in Pursuance thereof; and all Treaties made, or which shall be made, under the Authority of the United States, shall be the supreme Law of the Land; and the Judges in every State shall be bound thereby, any Thing in the Constitution or Laws of any State to the Contrary notwithstanding."

[2] Anson Phelps Stokes and Leo Pfeffer, *Church and State in the United States,* rev. one-vol. ed. (New York: Harper & Row, 1964), pp. 65 ff.

ing entry: "It was moved and seconded to add ... —'but no religious test shall *ever* be required as a qualification to *any* office or public trust under the authority of the United States;' which passed unanimously in the affirmative." [1] Only North Carolina voted against the adoption of this clause.[2] Later, referring to the significance of the clause, the great Mr. Justice Joseph Story commented: "The Catholic and the Protestant, the Calvinist and the Armenian [sic], the infidel and the Jew, may sit down to the Communion-table of the National Council, without any inquisition into their faith or mode of worship." [3]

Although this ban against religious test-oaths settled matters at once insofar as public office under the federal government was concerned, it did become an issue in state and municipal public employment, and remained so for a good many years. Most states removed their mandated disqualifications against Jews and members of other theistic religions, but others, such as Arkansas, Maryland, Pennsylvania, and Tennessee, retained constitutional provisions compelling all would-be public office-holders to take an oath or make an affirmation of their belief in God. Inevitably, however, judicial nationalization of civil rights and liberties via the "due process of law" clause of the Fourteenth Amendment ultimately did reach the area of religion,[4] as we have seen in Chapter III. In 1961 the Supreme Court addressed itself specifically to the religious oath clause in the Maryland case of *Torcaso v. Watkins*.[5]

In that case one Roy Torcaso, an aspirant for the minor state office of notary-public in Maryland, refused to abide by his state's requirement, imbedded in a clause of its Constitution, that all office-holders declare their belief in the existence of God as a part of their oath of office. On Torcaso's refusal to take the oath his application was denied, and he appealed to the Maryland courts for a reversal of that ruling, alleging violation of the religious liberty guaranteed to him

---

[1] Jonathan Elliot, *The Debates in the Several State Conventions*, Vol. I, 2nd ed. (Philadelphia: Lippincott & Co., 1854), pp. 277. (Italics supplied.)

[2] With the substitution of a semicolon for the dash before "but" and of a period for the semicolon after "States," it became the last phrase of Article VI, Section 3.

[3] As quoted in Phelps and Pfeffer, *loc. cit.*, p. 91.

[4] See, *inter alia*, Hamilton v. Board of Regents of California, 293 U.S. 245 (1934); Cantwell v. Connecticut, 310 U.S. 296 (1940); and Everson v. Board of Education of Ewing Township, 330 U.S. 1(1947).

[5] 367 U.S. 488.

by the United States Constitution. When the state courts sided with Maryland, Torcaso took his case to the United States Supreme Court, which not only agreed with Torcaso's contentions, but declared the oath requirement unconstitutional as a violation of the "free exercise of religion" clause of the First Amendment of the federal Constitution. Unanimously, the Court, without any inquiry into what belief, if any, Roy Torcaso held dear (he was an atheist), declared that the state test oath constituted a clear invasion of "freedom of belief and religion." Moreover, wrote Mr. Justice Black for himself and the entire Court, in placing Maryland on the side of "one particular sort of believer," namely, theists—those who believe in the existence of God—the constitutional requirement imposed a burden on the free exercise of the faiths of *non-believers* in violation of the free exercise clause.[1] To emphasize this point, Black appended what has become a well-known footnote in constitutional law: "Among religions in this country which do not teach what would generally be considered a belief in the existence of God are Buddhism, Taoism, Ethical Culture, Secular Humanism and others." [2] In other words, the Court made categorically clear that not only were religious test oaths barred, but that theistic belief could not be a requirement for religious belief. Put somewhat differently, the Court affirmed what has been, or should have been, apparent all along: that the Constitution of the United States, in guaranteeing freedom of religion, by implication also guarantees freedom of *irreligion*. Four years later, the Maryland Court of Appeals specifically extended that guarantee to invalidate a requirement that all Maryland jurors declare a belief in God.[3]

2. *The "Nationalization" of the Religion Clauses.* As we already know from Chapter III, the wording of the First Amendment, of which the religion phrases constitute the opening statements, confined the inherent prohibitions against governmental action to the *federal* government. This made particular sense in the case of religion, for at the time of the adoption of the Constitution of the United States many of the original thirteen *states* had specific religious establishments or other restrictive provisos. In fact, in the earliest days of the fledgling nation only Virginia, led by Jefferson and Madison, and Rhode Island conceded full, unqualified freedom; New

[1] *Ibid.*, at 495.
[2] *Ibid.*, n. 11.
[3] *Schowgurow v. Maryland*, 213 A2nd 475 (1965).

York almost did the same.[1] Two states, Delaware and Maryland, demanded Christianity, Delaware also insisting on assent to the doctrine of the Trinity; four, Delaware, North Carolina, Pennsylvania, and South Carolina, called for assent to the divine inspiration of the Bible, with Pennsylvania and South Carolina further requiring a belief in heaven and hell, and South Carolina—the only one among the thirteen—still speaking of religious "toleration"; three, Maryland, New York, and South Carolina excluded all ministers, even Protestants, from any civil office; five, Connecticut, Maryland, Massachusetts, New Hampshire, and South Carolina insisted on "Protestantism," or "Christian Protestantism"; and six, Connecticut, Georgia, New Hampshire, New Jersey, North Carolina, and South Carolina, specifically adhered to religious establishments—one of its Protestant forms.[2] Hence it is not surprising that the First Amendment was widely regarded as a protection of state establishments *against* Congressional action. By 1833, however, following the capitulation of the Congregationalists in Massachusetts, the fundamental concepts of freedom of religion had, to all intents and purposes, become an established and recognized fact, with only minor aberrations, throughout the young United States of America.

It was thus but a matter of time for religious freedom and its attendant safeguards for the separation between Church and State to become legally as well as factually binding under our Constitution. As the "incorporation," "absorption," or "nationalization" of the Bill of Rights guarantees became a judicially recognized reality, beginning with the Sanford opinion in *Gitlow v. New York* [3] in 1925, the Court ultimately would, given the proper opportunity, address itself to religion. And it did so address itself, first to the free exercise of religion in 1934 and 1940,[4] then to the separation of Church and State in 1947.[5]

3. *The Two Aspects of the Religion Clause.* One of the difficulties in the interpretation of the religion clause is that its language speaks

1 In addition to barring ministers from public office, New York required naturalized citizens to abjure allegiance in all foreign ecclesiastical as well as civil matters.

2 See Stokes and Pfeffer, *op. cit.*, Ch. 3, for a full account.

3 268 U.S. 252.

4 *Hamilton v. Regents of University of California*, 293 U.S. 245, and *Cantwell v. Connecticut*, 310 U.S. 296.

5 *Everson v. Board of Education*, 310 U.S. 1.

of both the "establishment" of religion and the "free exercise" of religion. Certainly the two clauses are interrelated, but they are separable.[1] The author of the language of the First Amendment, usually regarded as Madison, even separated the two by a comma: "Congress shall make no law respecting an establishment of religion, or prohibiting the free exercise thereof...."When the Supreme Court first undertook to nationalize the religion clauses in the *Hamilton* case [2] in 1934, Mr. Justice Butler's opinion confined itself to Albert Hamilton's claim of free exercise; the matter of "establishment," or separation of Church and State was not properly at issue. Nor did it play a meaningful role in the next great freedom of religion case to be decided by the Supreme Court six years later, *Cantwell v. Connecticut*,[3] which elaborated upon the *Hamilton* [4] rationale. It was not until the famed *New Jersey Bus case*,[5] seven years after Cantwell, that the Court, speaking through Mr. Justice Black, held that the First Amendment's prohibition against legislation respecting an establishment of religion is also applicable to the several states by virtue of the language and obligations of the Fourteenth Amendment. Thus, by 1947, both aspects of the religion guarantee had been judicially interpreted to apply to both the federal government and the several states of the Union. Far more complicated, however, was the determination of the meaning, range, and extent of the famous clauses.

Attempting To Define "Religion"

To state the problem is to see its complications. Yet in a government under law, whatever an individual's personal viewpoint of religion might be, definitions have to be ventured, if for no other reason than to protect the right of conscientious objectors to avoid conscription! Each individual does, of course, possess the basic right, now one universally guaranteed and protected under our Constitution, to believe what he chooses, to worship whom he pleases and how he pleases, provided that he does not impermissibly interfere with the

[1] This is not to say that commentators and students have not at times been puzzled both as to the choice determined by the judiciary in specific cases and as to the viability of a distinction in others.

[2] *Hamilton v. Regents of California, loc. cit.*

[3] 310 U.S. 296 (1940).

[4] *Loc. cit.*

[5] *Everson v. Board of Education of Ewing Township,* 330 U.S. 1 (1947).

right of others. Hence we have those who believe in nothing; those who believe but doubt; those who believe without questioning; those who worship the Judeo-Christian God—in innumerably different ways; those who adhere to Mohammed's creed; those who worship themselves; those who worship a cow or other animals; those who worship several gods—to mention just a few of the remarkable variety of expressions of belief that obtain.

Webster's New Collegiate Dictionary gives us the following choices under the heading "religion":

> 1. The service and adoration of God or a god as expressed in forms of worship. 2. One of the systems of faith and worship. 3. The profession or practice of religious beliefs; religious observances collectively; *pl.*, rites. 4. Devotion or fidelity; conscientiousness. 5. An awareness or conviction of the existence of a supreme being, arousing reverence, love, gratitude, the will to obey and serve, and the like; as, man only is capable of *religion*.[1]

At best such a definition can offer a broad guideline of a non-binding nature. The same is more or less true of the kind of psychological guideline furnished by such thoughtful commentators as Professor Gordon W. Allport, for example, who wrote that religion encompasses a value that every democrat "must hold: the right of each individual to work out his own philosophy of life, to find his personal niche in creation as best he can."[2] He further elaborated that

> A man's religion is the audacious bid he makes to bind himself to creation and to the Creator. It is his ultimate attempt to enlarge and to complete his own personality by finding the supreme context in which he rightly belongs.[3]

Although it is not difficult to agree with Allport's approach to a definition or interpretation, the authoritative definition ultimately had to come from the highest tribunal in the land, acting either upon a congressional definition or within the confines of its common law responsibilities.

The Supreme Court Defines Religion. The classic definition was penned by that devotee of rugged individualism Mr. Justice Stephen

---

[1] Sixth ed. (Springfield, Mass.: G. & C. Merriam Co., 1961), p. 715, col. 1.
[2] Gordon W. Allport, *The Individual and His Religion* (New York: The Macmillan Co., 1962), p. vii.
[3] *Ibid.*, p. 142.

Johnson Field. In 1890 the Court unanimously upheld [1] a lower court judgment that one Samuel Davis, a Mormon residing in the then Territory of Idaho, should be disqualified as a voter for falsifying his voter's oath since, as a Mormon, he believed in polygamy. Polygamy was considered a disqualifying offense under the territorial voting and other statutes. Field wrote for the Court:

> [T]he term "religion" has reference to one's views of his relations to his Creator, and to the obligations they impose of reverence for his being and character, and of obedience to his will. It is often confounded with the cultus or form of worship of a particular sect, but is distinguishable from the latter. . . . With man's relations to his Maker and the obligations he may think they impose, and the manner in which an expression shall be made by him of his belief on those subjects, no interference can be permitted, provided always the laws of society, designed to secure its peace and prosperity, and the morals of its people are not interfered with. . . .[2]

Thus, although giving religion the widest feasible interpretation in terms of individual commitment, Field found that Davis had violated the reservation of the last qualifying clause.

As the years went by, this Supreme Court definition of religion was most often tested in cases dealing with military exemptions and conscientious objectors. Exemption from the draft and/or combat service for those who oppose war on religious grounds is deeply rooted in American tradition and history. Much litigation has attended this problem, frequently involving the Jehovah's Witnesses, who—in addition to being conscientious objectors as a group—contend that every believing Witness is a "minister" and as such ought to be exempt from service. Both the Society of Friends (the Quakers) [3] and the Mennonites have made pacifism a dogma. And there has, of course, been a continuous stream of individual conscientious objectors, coming chiefly from small Protestant sects but from other faiths as well. Congress has been increasingly generous in recognizing *bona fide* conscientious objectors and in exempting these from military service.

[1] *Davis v. Beason,* 133 U.S. 333 (1890).

[2] *Ibid.,* at 342.

[3] Thus in June 1966 United States District Judge John W. Lord sentenced Jeremiah T. Dickinson, 18, a Haverford College freshman and devout Quaker, who had refused to register for the draft, to work two years at the Friends Hospital, a mental institution operated by Quakers in Philadelphia. (*United States v. Jeremiah Dickinson,* Crim. No. 22377, June 7, 1966.)

The two major draft statutes of this century, those of 1917 and 1940, both included exemption provisions, and amendments to the latter, enacted in the 1950's, have expanded them.[1]

But, again the problem in granting these exemptions has been, and is, the distinction between *bona fide* and not so *bona fide* claims. It is axiomatic in democratic society that men of abiding religious conviction, who are members of pacifist sects whose creeds proscribe participation in war or related strife, should neither be compelled to participate nor be jailed for refusing to do so. Yet, just as clearly, those whose objections are not of a *bona fide* religious nature, but are merely sociological or political, should not be permitted to set their own personal judgments above that of society as a whole. In March 1965 the Supreme Court handed down a momentous decision in three cases involving the most recent provisions in the draft law exempting religious objectors from combat training and service. At issue was the restriction established by Congress of exemption to "persons who by reason of religious training and belief are conscientiously opposed to any participation in war." The definition spelled out "religious training and belief" as follows:

> Religion and belief in this connection means an individual belief in a relation to a Supreme Being involving duties superior to those arising from any human relation, but does not include essentially political, sociological or philosophical views, or merely a personal moral code.[2]

Three men were involved in these 1965 *Draft Act Cases*,[3] Daniel A. Seeger, Arno S. Jakobson, and Forest B. Peter. Seeger and Jakobson had been convicted by the United States District Court in New York, and Mr. Peter by the United States District Court in San Francisco, of refusing to submit to induction. Both New York convictions were reversed by the United States Court of Appeals for the Second Circuit, but the Appeals Court for the Ninth Circuit upheld the Peter conviction. Seeger had told the Selective Service authorities that he was conscientiously opposed to participation in war in any form because of his "religious" belief; but that he preferred to leave

---

[1] For the best treatment of the subject, although a bit out of date, see Mulford Q. Sibley and Philip E. Jacob, *Conscription of Conscience: The American State and the Conscientious Objector, 1940-1947* (Ithaca, N.Y.: Cornell University Press, 1952).

[2] 50 App. U.S.C.A., § 456(j) (1951).

[3] *United States v. Seeger.* 380 U.S. 163 (1965).

open the question of his belief in a Supreme Being rather than answer "yes" or "no." Jakobson asserted that he believed in a Supreme Being who was "Creator of Man," in the sense of being "ultimately responsible for the existence of" man, and who was the "Supreme Reality" of which "the existence of man is the result." Peter said the source of his conviction was "our democratic American culture, with its values derived from the Western religious and philosophical tradition." As to his belief in a Supreme Being, Peter added that he supposed "you could call that a belief in the Supreme Being or God. These just do not happen to be the words I use." [1]

In affirming the reversals by the Second Circuit Court of Appeals and in reversing the decision of that of the Ninth Circuit, the United States Supreme Court, while sidestepping constitutional questions, clearly broadened construction of the statutory provision quoted above. The test of belief "in a relation to a Supreme Being," the Court held, is whether a sincere and meaningful belief which occupies in the life of its possessor a place parallel to that filled by the God of those admittedly qualifying for the exemption comes within the statutory definition.[2] Applying this liberalizing test, the Court ruled that the beliefs expressed by the three men involved in the cases before it consequently entitled them to the exemption. Thus they created a new definition of the concept of religion, at least for statutory purposes under the Constitution. However, mindful of its role as educator of the public, the Court, in a unanimous opinion written by its foremost religious layman, Mr. Justice Clark, added:

> We also pause to take note of what is not involved in this litigation. No party claims to be an atheist or attacks the statute on this ground. The question is not, therefore, one between theistic and atheistic beliefs. We do not deal with or intimate any decision on the situation in this case.[3]

Indeed, the Clark opinion, and a concurring one by Mr. Justice Douglas, as *The New York Times* commented on the morning after,[4] read like a short course in theology. The majority opinion quoted Paul Tillich, the Bishop of Woolwich, John A. T. Robinson, and the schema of the most recent Ecumenical Council at the Vatican to

[1] *Ibid.*, at 165.
[2] *Ibid.*, at 176.
[3] *Ibid.*, at 173.
[4] March 9, 1965.

prove, as Clark put it, the "broad spectrum of religious beliefs found among us." These quotations, the opinion went on,

> demonstrate very clearly the diverse manners in which beliefs, equally paramount in the lives of their possessors may be articulated. They further reveal the difficulties inherent in placing too narrow a construction on the provisions [of the particular section of the Draft Act here at issue] and thereby lend conclusive support to the [broad] construction which we today find that Congress intended.[1]

Whether or not Congress really did intend such a broad interpretation or construction of the Act, there was little criticism of this particular Court decision—a remarkably different state of affairs than, as we shall see presently, that which had greeted (if that is the word!) the Court's memorable decision in the *New York Prayer* case [2] and the *Bible Reading* cases [3] several years before.[4] What the 1965 *Draft Act Cases* do prove conclusively is that there is less certainty of and less emphasis on a strictly construed traditional definition of religion. Instead, and without—just yet, perhaps—getting into the matter of distinctions between theistic and atheistic creeds and dogmas, a unanimous Supreme Court struck a blow for broadened concepts of religious liberty and conscience by declaring that a conscientious objector need not believe in the orthodox concept of a Supreme Being. But a "religious motivation," however vague or existential, is apparently still required.[5]

THE FREE EXERCISE OF RELIGION

"Free exercise" brackets freedom of religious belief and freedom of religious action. As such they have a close link with those other bastions of the First Amendment, freedom of speech, of the press, of

[1] *Ibid.*, at 183.

[2] *Engel v. Vitale*, 370 U.S. 421(1962).

[3] *Abington School District v. Schempp* and *Murray v. Curlett*, 374 U.S. 203 (1963).

[4] 1963 and 1962 respectively.

[5] An intriguing new aspect of the problem slowly began to wind its way through the courts late in 1966: Could an individual claim exemption from the draft because of conscientious objection to *a particular war*—e.g. Viet-Nam—without, however, being opposed to *all wars?* (See Sidney E. Zion, "A.C.L.U. Asks Draft Exemption for Objectors to a Particular War," *The New York Times,* March 3, 1966.)

assembly, and of petition. Indeed, any reading of the religion clause guarantee of the First Amendment that does not consider its dependence upon the other four guarantees spelled out in that provision of the Bill of Rights, and now carried over to the states via the Fourteenth Amendment, does a distinct disservice to constitutional analysis and interpretation. The interrelationship is as real as it is significant.

A Basic Dilemma

The very language of the "free exercise" segment of the religion phrase poses a dilemma. The phrase militates against any governmental action ". . . prohibiting the free exercise thereof." Unquestionably, the phrase is designed to mean what it says: Congress—and by interpretation the states—may not interfere with the sacred rights of freedom of religious "belief" and "exercise." But, as Mr. Justice Roberts pointed out in his opinion for a unanimous Court in the 1940 *Cantwell* case, while "freedom of exercise" embraces both the freedom to *believe* and the freedom to *act*, "the first is absolute but, in the nature of things, the second cannot be. *Conduct* remains subject to regulation for the protection of society. The freedom to act must have appropriate definition to preserve the enforcement of that protection." [1]

In every case, Roberts continued, "the power to regulate must be so exercised as not, in attaining a permissible end, unduly to infringe the protected freedom." [2] This, of course, raises as many *practical* questions as it settles. But the general line is at least perceivable in *Cantwell*, and it remains a landmark chiefly for three reasons: It embraces the dual aspects of "belief" and "action"; it reaffirms the absorption or incorporation of the freedom of religion guarantees into the Fourteenth Amendment; and it emphasizes the close link of the free exercise of religion with the other freedoms spelled out in the First Amendment.

The Jehovah's Witnesses. The *Cantwell* case was the first freedom of religion case involving the Jehovah's Witnesses to be decided by the Supreme Court. Actually, the initial litigation concerning that fundamentalist sect had come two years earlier, but it was decided under

[1] *Cantwell v. Connecticut*, 310 U.S. 296 (1940), at 303. (Italics supplied.)
[2] *Ibid.*, at 304.

the freedom of speech and press rather than those of the freedom of religion.[1] The Jehovah's Witnesses have won over 90 per cent of the host of significant cases which have come before the Court since the mid-1930's. Their success is due in no small measure to the superb talents of their chief legal counsel, Hayden C. Covington. A dedicated and growing sect of approximately 800,000 members throughout the world who believe that Armageddon is more or less just around the corner, their creed is based on what they regard as utter obedience to the Bible. They accept the Biblical prophecy that Satan will be defeated in the cataclysm of Armageddon, followed by eternal life for the righteous. (Other Christians share this belief, but disagree sharply with the assertion by the Witnesses that they alone, as the "only true followers of the Bible," will be saved.) The Jehovah's Witnesses' movement began in 1872, largely as the result of the efforts of one Charles Taze Russell, a Pittsburgh merchant, who had become disenchanted with his Congregationalist Church. Russell began to preach the Adventist doctrine that the imminent second coming of Christ will trigger Armageddon, which he finally pegged at 1914. He might have come close with that date—but nuclear warfare had not yet raised its ugly head! With a rapidly increasing following, Russell incorporated in 1884 the Watch Tower Bible and Tract Society, now generally known as the Jehovah's Witnesses ("Ye are my Witnesses, saith Jehovah," Isaiah 43:10). They deem Abel the first Witness, Christ the Chief Witness, and themselves direct descendants, from whose ranks Jehovah will select 144,000 (at last count) members who will reign in heaven after Armageddon.

An impressively organized hierarchy with totalitarian overtones, the Witnesses are fiercely evangelistic, and publicly so. Although inevitably polite, they persistently solicit and proselytize, push their two journals, *Awake!* and the *Watchtower*, and, if given permission, play their gramophone records. To the Witnesses, the chief villains on earth are the leaders of organized religion in general, and the Roman Catholic Church in particular: The Witnesses' notorious gramophone record "Enemies" characterizes the Roman Catholic Church as "a great racket." It is no wonder then, that they often find

---

[1] *Lovell v. Griffin*, 303 U.S. 444 (1938). The next Jehovah's Witnesses case, also decided under the freedom of speech and press guarantees, was *Schneider v. Irvington, New Jersey*, 308 U.S. 137 (1939)—one year prior to *Cantwell*, which was thus the third Supreme Court case involving the Witnesses.

themselves in considerable litigation involving such matters as leaflet distribution, local and state censorship ordinances, parade permits, flag salutes, license taxes, conscientious objection to the draft, public meetings, and blood transfusion requirements.[1] The United States Reports for the past three decades list some thirty cases involving the Witnesses in one or more of the above problems. And *Cantwell v. Connecticut*[2] was *not* one of the very few they lost.

Cantwell v. Connecticut. Jesse Cantwell and his two sons approached two pedestrians on Cassius Street in New Haven, an area whose inhabitants were 90 per cent Roman Catholic, and asked their permission to play them a record on their portable phonograph. Obtaining that permission, the Cantwells put on "Enemies." One portion of the record stated in particular that the Roman Catholic Church was an instrument of Satan which had for fifteen hundred years brought untold sorrow and sufferings upon mankind by means of deception and fraud. The two pedestrians were, according to their own testimony, "rather tempted to strike the Cantwells," but confined themselves to an exhortation to "shut the damn thing off and get moving"—which the Cantwells did as soon as they were requested to do so. No violence of any kind occurred, nor was it alleged. Nonetheless, the Cantwells were arrested, indicted, charged with, and convicted of two separate violations of Connecticut law.

One count of a five-count indictment charged them with soliciting funds and subscriptions for the Witnesses' cause without obtaining in advance—as required by statute—a "certificate of approval" from the Secretary of the Connecticut Public Welfare Council, who was specifically empowered to determine, again in advance, whether the cause was either a "religious" one or one of a "*bona fide* object of charity." The second charge against the Cantwells was a breach of the peace, based on their stopping pedestrians on New Haven's public streets and asking them for permission to play the described phonograph record. The Cantwells appealed their several convictions to the United States Supreme Court on both substantive and pro-

[1] See, *inter alia, Minersville School District v. Gobitis,* 310 U.S. 596 (1940); *Cox v. New Hampshire,* 312 U.S. 569 (1941); *Martin v. Struthers,* 319 U.S. 141 (1943); *Jones v. Opelika,* 316 U.S. 584 (1942); *Prince v. Massachusetts,* 321 U.S. 158 (1944); *Marsh v. Alabama,* 326 U.S. 501 (1946); *Niemotko v. Maryland,* 340 U.S. 268 (1951); and many others. The listing here is designed merely to be representative and is not intended to be exhaustive, of course.
[2] 310 U.S. 296 (1940).

cedural grounds, alleging infringement of freedom of religion rights under both the First and Fourteenth Amendment on the first (substantive) count and violations of the Fourteenth Amendment alone on the second (procedural) ground. The Court agreed with their contentions and reversed their convictions unanimously as constituting unconstitutional violations of the free exercise of religion. Mr. Justice Roberts was assigned the opinion for the Court by Mr. Chief Justice Stone. It provided the Court with the already briefly described opportunity to comment upon and to try to explain the difficulties of drawing the line between freedom of religious belief and freedom of religious action in the realm of the free exercise of religion.

The Roberts opinion emphasized that there can be no doubt that a state has the right to guard against breaches of the peace and thus punish those who would incite to, or be guilty of, such breaches— even as a result of religious motivations or considerations. Yet just because an individual, in his religious fervor, resorts to exaggeration and even vilification, thereby arousing public anger and ill will, does not per se render him liable to punishment unless there is a demonstrably clear and present danger to public peace. In the instance of the Cantwells there was no such danger or menace: no assault took place; there was no intentional discourtesy; no threatening bearing; no personal abuse. Hence, there existed no such clear and present danger to public peace—and the Cantwells' arrest was patently unconstitutional. The challenged Connecticut statute, which gave such broad prior censorship powers to an official of Connecticut's government, was held to constitute on its face an impermissible infraction of religious freedom guaranteed by the First Amendment, as absorbed by the Fourteenth. The Court ruled that for religious groups such as the Jehovah's Witnesses, Connecticut's requirement as applied here represented a "censorship of religion as a means of determining its right to survive," a clear violation of the basic guarantee. Roberts took pains to acknowledge that nothing he had said for the Court was "intended even remotely to imply that, under the cloak of religion, persons may, with impunity, commit frauds upon the public." Endeavoring to establish a general line, he observed that, certainly, penal laws are properly available to punish such proscribed conduct, and emphasized that even the exercise of religion may be at some slight inconvenience in order that the State may protect its citizens from injury:

Without doubt a State may protect its citizens from fraudulent solicitation by requiring a stranger in the community, before permitting him to solicit funds for any purpose, to establish his identity and his authority for the cause which he purports to represent. The State is likewise free to regulate the time and manner of solicitation generally, in the interest of public safety, peace, comfort or convenience. But to condition the solicitation of aid for the perpetuation of religious views or systems upon a license, the grant of which rests in the exercise of a determination by state authority as to what is a religious cause, is to lay a forbidden burden upon the exercise of liberty protected by the Constitution.[1]

The Cantwells had won an important victory not only for themselves, but for the cause of religious liberty. And although the Witnesses were to find themselves increasingly at the bar of the highest Court as the years went by, *Cantwell* provided a lodestar for future triumphs.

The Flag Salute Cases. But two weeks later, the next Jehovah Witnesses case to be decided did not augur well for the future of a generous interpretation of the religious liberty clause. As a condition of attending the public schools of the metropolis of Minersville, Pennsylvania, all children had to salute the national flag as part of a daily school exercise. Twelve-year-old Lillian Gobitis and her brother William, aged ten, the children of Walter Gobitis, a member of the Jehovah's Witnesses, were expelled from the public schools for refusing to comply with the flag salute requirement. To them any compliance with the flag salute requirement would have been tantamount to paying homage to a graven image—a mortal sin under the precepts of the Witnesses.[2] For a while Walter Gobitis bore the burden of sending them to private schools which did not require the flag salute. But unable any longer to afford that expense, Gobitis sued to enjoin the public authorities from continuing to exact participation of Lillian and William in the daily flag-salute ceremony as a condition of their public school attendance. To his surprise and gratification the United States District Court in Philadelphia granted his plea on the grounds that the expulsions violated the First, and through it the

---

[1] *Ibid.*, at 306.

[2] The daily ceremony, in which all teachers, as well as the students participated, was a familiar one. The right hand was placed on the breast and the following pledge recited in unison: "I pledge allegiance to my flag, and to the Republic for which it stands; one nation indivisible, with liberty and justice for all." While the words were spoken, teachers and pupils extended their right hands in salute to the flag.

Fourteenth, Amendment's guarantees of religious liberty. Now it was the Minersville School District's turn to appeal, and it did so to the Supreme Court which granted *certiorari*. The nation awaited its decision with considerable interest; both the Committee on the Bill of Rights of the American Bar Association and the American Civil Liberties Union had sought, and been granted, permission to enter the case in behalf of the Witnesses as *amici curiae*.[1]

But to the astonishment of many—including some of those who consider themselves experts on the Court and its personnel—the Court *reversed* the judgment below and upheld the Minersville flag salute requirements by a resounding 8:1 vote.[2] Delivering the Court's opinion, Mr. Justice Frankfurter contended that religious liberty does not exempt citizens from obedience to general laws applicable to all and not designed to restrict religious beliefs as such. Explaining that "we live by symbols," Frankfurter exhorted the country that the "flag is the symbol of our national unity, transcending all internal differences, however large, within the framework of the Constitution."[3] He rejected the plea that the Gobitis children should be excused from "conduct required of all other children in the promotion of national cohesion," adding that "we are dealing with an interest inferior to none in the hierarchy of legal values. National unity is the basis of national security. . . ."[4] He acknowledged that many might well doubt the effectiveness of the compulsory flag salute in the promotion of national unity and loyalty, but he insisted—characteristically for one so committed to the doctrine of judicial self-restraint—that, lest the Supreme Court become "the school board of the country,"[5] this was a decision to be made by the elected school officials. Mr. Justice Frankfurter was joined in his opinion by Mr. Chief Justice Hughes, Associate Justices McReynolds, Roberts, and—amazingly—by Associate Justices Black, Douglas, and Murphy, whom prognosticators would have expected confidently to side with the sole dissenter, Mr. Justice Stone.

[1] Literally, "friends of the court"; see the author's *The Judicial Process* (New York: Oxford University Press, 1962), pp. 209-12, for a brief explanation of the brief *amicus curiae*.

[2] *Minersville School District v. Gobitis*, 310 U.S. 586 (1940).

[3] *Ibid.*, at 596.

[4] *Ibid.*, at 595.

[5] *Ibid.*, at 598.

Conceding that the personal liberty guarantees under the Constitution are by no means "always absolutes," and that "Government has a right to survive," Stone's dissent nonetheless bitterly assailed the majority's opinion as doing violence to "the very essence of liberty . . . the right of the individual to hold such opinions as he will and to give them reasonably free expression, and his freedom, and that of the state as well, to teach and persuade others by the communication of ideas." [1] He continued that the very essence of the liberty which the freedom of the human mind and spirit and the freedom of reasonable opportunity to express them guarantee is

> the freedom of the individual from compulsion as to what he shall think and what he shall say, at least where the compulsion is to bear false witness to his religion. If these guarantees are to have any meaning they must . . . be deemed to withhold from the state any authority to compel belief or the expression of it where that expression violates religious convictions, whatever may be the legislative view of the desirability of such compulsion.[2]

His noble spirit simply could not see how any inconveniences that might attend what he called "some sensible adjustment of school discipline" would present a problem "so momentous or pressing as to outweigh the freedom from compulsory violation of religious faith which has been thought worthy of constitutional protection." [3] He did not have to wait long, however, to see his reasoning become the majority opinion of the Court and thereby the law of the land!

To realize that constitutional turnabout, some crucial developments took place—all significant elements in the judicial process. One was the retirement of Mr. Chief Justice Hughes in 1941 and his replacement by Attorney-General Robert H. Jackson—although as an Associate Justice, President Roosevelt having seen fit to elevate Mr. Justice Stone to the Chief Justiceship. A closely related denouement was the retirement of Mr. Justice McReynolds early in 1943 and his replacement by the one-time Dean of the University of Iowa School of Law, Wiley B. Rutledge. On paper, at least, the two new appointees could be expected to be more sympathetic to the Stone

[1] *Ibid.*, at 604.
[2] *Ibid.*
[3] *Ibid.*, at 607.

point of view than to that of Frankfurter. The third important development was a dramatic announcement by Justices Black, Douglas, and Murphy, who joined in a separate memorandum of dissent—written by Murphy—in a case that upheld (5:4) the validity of a license tax on bookselling levied upon Jehovah's Witnesses, as well as other activities considered "commercial" by the city of Opelika, Alabama.[1] (In 1942, just one year later that ruling was reversed on rehearing [2] in conjunction with another decision favoring the Witnesses.[3]) Written by Black, the six-sentence, one-paragraph memorandum simply stated, *inter alia*, that "since we joined in the opinion in the *Gobitis* case, we think this is an appropriate occasion to state that *we now believe that it was also wrongly decided.*" [4] The test of these developments came but a few months later in 1943, when the Court overruled the *Gobitis* precedent in another flag-salute case, *West Virginia State Board of Education v. Barnette.*[5]

Following the Court's decision in *Gobitis* [6] three years earlier, the State of West Virginia legislature had amended its statutes to require all of its schools to conduct courses of instruction in history, civics, and both the federal and West Virginia Constitutions "for the purpose of teaching, fostering and perpetuating the ideals, principles and spirit of Americanism, and increasing the knowledge of the organization and machinery of government." [7] In 1942, the Board of Education adopted a resolution based largely on the Supreme Court's *Gobitis* opinion, which ordered the salute to the Flag to become "a regular part of the program of activities in the public schools"; that all teachers and pupils "shall be required to participate in the salute honoring the Nation represented by the Flag; provided, however [sic], that refusal to salute the Flag be regarded as an Act of insubordination, and shall be dealt with accordingly." [8] The "accordingly" meant expulsion—with readmission denied by the statute until compliance. Meanwhile, the expelled child was considered "unlawfully absent,"

---

[1] *Jones v. Opelika*, 316 U.S. 584 (1942).
[2] *Jones v. Opelika*, 319 U.S. 105 (1943).
[3] *Murdock v. Commonwealth of Pennsylvania*, 319 U.S. 105.
[4] 316 U.S. 584, at 623. (Italics supplied.)
[5] 319 U.S. 624 (1943).
[6] 310 U.S. 586 (1940).
[7] *West Virginia State Board of Education v. Barnette, loc. cit.*, at 625.
[8] *Ibid.*, at 626.

was subject to delinquency proceedings, and his parents or guardians were liable to prosecution and punishment by fine and/or imprisonment. Members of the Jehovah's Witnesses like the Gobitis family, Walter Barnette and his relatives, Paul Stull and Mrs. Lucy Barnette McClure, would not comply and saw their seven children expelled from school for "insubordination." The crucial difference between their and the Gobitis's fortunes was that the Barnette families won!

They won because the two new Associate Justices, Jackson and Rutledge, added to the three "mind-changers," Black, Douglas, and Murphy, and the one steady holdover from the *Gobitis* decision, the now Chief Justice Stone, constituted a new six-man majority! Three *Gobitis* holdovers continued to cling to their then majority reasoning in that case: Associate Justices Frankfurter, Reed, and Roberts. The Barnettes won a victory for a liberal construction of the line between the individual's freedom of conscience and the state's claims for conformance to majority policy in regard to symbols. It was a significant victory—one that is not likely to be overturned.

It would have been fitting had Mr. Chief Justice Stone assigned the majority opinion to himself, being the only member on that side of the decision who had consistently supported it. Yet, characteristically, he chose to let someone else write it—and, at least in terms of the power and beauty of language, he could not have chosen a more appropriate spokesman than Mr. Justice Jackson. The latter held that the guarantees of freedom of speech and conscience imply the freedom *not* to speak and *not* to make any other symbolic expression, even the saluting of the national flag. He acknowledged that public officials did naturally have the right to foster national unity and might well employ a symbolic public ceremony to achieve this, but that they may not render participation in such ceremonies compulsory. To the dissenters' contention that if laws such as those of Pennsylvania and West Virginia were unwise, the manner to alter or abolish them was not through court action but through the electoral process—what Mr. Justice Frankfurter, the author of the dissenting opinion, was later on several occasions [1] to call the "searing

[1] Particularly on the "political question" in redistricting and reapportionment cases, such as *Colegrove v. Green*, 328 U.S. 549 (1946), and, especially, in his last signed opinion (appropriately in dissent—running to more than sixty pages) in *Baker v. Carr*, 369 U.S. 186 (1962).

of the legislators' conscience"—Jackson responded it depended necessarily upon the type of claim involved. In situations like *Barnette*,
judicial action was not only necessary but essential, because, "[o]ne's
right to life, liberty, and property, to free speech, a free press, freedom
of worship and assembly, and other fundamental rights may not be
submitted to vote; they depend on the outcome of no elections." [1]

The closing paragraphs of the Jackson opinion for the Court contain some of the most significant language ever used by an opinion-
assignee. Stressing the futility of compelling conformity and coher-
ence in such sacred First Amendment guarantees as the freedom of
belief, conscience, and expression, Jackson warned that

> Those who begin coercive elimination of dissent soon find themselves
> dissenters. Compulsory unification of opinion achieves only the una-
> nimity of the graveyard.

And he concluded:

> If there is any fixed star in our constitutional constellation, it is that
> no official, high or petty, can prescribe what shall be orthodox in poli-
> tics, nationalism, religion, or other matters of opinion or force citizens
> to confess by word or act their faith therein.[2]

The Barnette families and the nation were the richer for Jackson's
eloquent opinion and its implications.

Predictably, and justly, the dissenting opinion was written by the
author of the *Gobitis* majority opinion, Mr. Justice Frankfurter—and
it was one of his most important and longest, representing, as it did,
his passionate dedication to the creed of judicial self-restraint, the
raison d'être of his judicial career. Probably quoted only slightly less
than the Jackson passages outlined above are the haunting opening
passages of Frankfurter's exhortation:

> One who belongs to the most vilified and persecuted minority in his-
> tory is not likely to be insensible to the freedoms guaranteed by our
> Constitution. Were my purely personal attitude relevant I should
> whole-heartedly associate myself with the general libertarian view in
> the Court's opinion, representing as they do the thought and action
> of a lifetime. But as judges we are neither Jew nor Gentile, neither

[1] *West Virginia State Board of Education v. Barnette, loc. cit.*, at 641.
[2] *Ibid.*, at 642.

Catholic nor agnostic. We owe equal attachment to the Constitution and are equally bound by our judicial obligations whether we derive our citizenship from the earliest or the latest immigrants to these shores. As a member of this Court I am not justified in writing my private notions of policy into the Constitution, no matter how deeply I may cherish them or how mischievous I may deem their disregard. . . . Most unwillingly, therefore, I must differ from my brethren with regard to legislation like this. I cannot bring my mind to believe that the "liberty" secured by the Due Process Clause gives this Court authority to deny to the State of West Virginia the attainment of that which we all recognize as a legitimate legislative end, namely, the promotion of good citizenship, by employment of the means here chosen.[1]

Frankfurter did not prevail, yet some schoolboards have continued to read his dissent as a majority opinion: Thus in 1966, the New Jersey Supreme Court had to rule unanimously, quoting *Barnette*, that children cannot be suspended from school if they refuse to salute the flag on the grounds of conscientious scruples! [2]

A *Catalogue of Line Decisions*. So manifold have been the Supreme Court's decisions concerning the free exercise of religion that it is impossible here to give each, or even most of these, detailed consideration in the limited space available. But the tables below will at least serve to indicate a pattern—a pattern of increasing liberality on the part of the highest tribunal, a liberality based, in large measure, on the kind of basic convictions about individual freedom of conscience so well expressed by Mr. Justice Jackson in his *Barnette* opinion. Table I illustrates those instances in which the Court held *against* constitutional claims of freedom of religion and thus in favor of society's constitutional prerogative to promulgate and enforce the official statutes, ordinances, or practices involved. Table II, in turn, demonstrates those instances in which the highest tribunal held in favor of the individual's contentions *versus* those of the state. Neither table is intended to be, nor could it be, exhaustive; rather, each will simply indicate the kind of pattern or catalogue of values which America has pursued through the instrumentalities of the legislative and judicial processes.

---

[1] *West Virginia State Board of Education v. Barnette, loc. cit.,* dissenting opinion, at 646, 647. Associate Justices Roberts and Reed were the other two dissenters in the case.

[2] *Holden v. Board of Education, Elizabeth,* 46 N.J. 281 (1966).

TABLE I

"Free Exercise" Cases Decided Against the Individual

DATE	CASE	VOTE	CONST'L ISSUES DECIDED	COMMENTARY
1878	*Reynolds v. United States,* 98 U.S. 145.	9:0	Validity of Congressional statute proscribing practice or advocacy of polygamy against claim of freedom of religious practice.	The first of the *Mormon* cases, holding religious beliefs not to justify polygamy.
1890	*Davis v. Beason,* 133 U.S. 333.	9:0	Validity of Idaho Territorial statute requiring an "Oath abjuring bigamy or polygamy as a condition to vote."	Bigamy and polygamy regarded as crimes, not religious exercise.
1890	*The Late Corp. of the Church of Jesus Christ of Latter-Day Saints v. United States,* 136 U.S. 1.	9:0	Validity of 1887 Congressional statute annulling charter of the Mormon Church and declaring all its property forfeited save for a small portion used exclusively for worship.	Law came as a result of the continued defiance of the Mormon Church regarding the practice of polygamy.
1929	*United States v. Schwimmer,* 279 U.S. 644.	6:3	Denial of naturalization-application to 50-year-old Hungarian Quaker woman for refusing to pledge to "take up arms" on behalf of U.S.	First of the naturalization cases. Holmes, Brandeis, and Sanford dissented from the Butler opinion (*Overruled in 1946.*)
1931	*United States v. Macintosh,* 283 U.S. 605.	5:4	Denial of naturalization-application to Canadian Baptist minister, a professor of theology and chaplain at Yale, for refusal to agree to defend U.S. by arms unless he were convinced of "moral justification."	Second of the naturalization cases. Hughes, Holmes, Brandeis, and Stone dissented from the Sutherland opinion. (*Overruled in 1946.*)

1934	Hamilton v. Regents of the University of California, 293 U.S. 245.	9:0	Refusal of Hamilton (and others) on grounds of conscience to take state-required courses in military science and tactics of state university.	Concurring opinion by Cardozo, joined by Brandeis and Stone, warned against carrying compulsion too far but joined in Court's decision.
1940	Minersville v. Gobitis, 310 U.S. 586.	8:1	Validity of compulsory flag salute contested by Jehovah's Witnesses.	Discussed above in Chapter VI. (Overruled in 1943.)
1941	Cox v. New Hampshire, 312 U.S. 569.	9:0	Validity of N.H. statute requiring a permit to hold a procession or parade on a public street, but considering only time, manner, and place of the parade.	Jehovah's Witnesses failed to apply for a permit; engaged in a parade.
1942	Chaplinsky v. New Hampshire, 315 U.S. 568.	9:0	Validity of narrowly drawn N.H. law proscribing the "address [of] any offensive, derisive or annoying word to any other person who is lawfully in any street or other public place or call[ing] him by any offensive or derisive names."	A Jehovah's Witness called city marshal "God damned racketeer" and "damned Fascist." Murphy wrote opinion.
1942	Jones v. Opelika [I], 316 U.S. 584.	5:4	Validity of Opelika ordinance imposing license taxes on bookselling—here by Jehovah's Witnesses.	Stone, Black, Douglas and Murphy dissented. (Overruled in 1943.)
1944	Prince v. Massachusetts, 321 U.S. 158.	8:1	Validity of Mass. statute forbidding boys of under 12 and girls of under 18 to sell newspapers or periodicals on streets or in other public places. Jehovah's Witness Prince allowed her under-age children and ward to help sell and distribute J. W. literature.	Freedom of religious exercise here must give way to state's interest and right to protect the health and welfare of children. Murphy dissented.

TABLE I (*continued*)

DATE	CASE	VOTE	CONST'L ISSUES DECIDED	COMMENTARY
1945	*In re Summers*, 325 U.S. 561.	5:4	Validity of Illinois' denial of admission to the bar of an otherwise qualified applicant who was a conscientious objector to war and who would therefore not serve in the state militia if called upon to do so under the State's constitutional provisions.	Black, Douglas, Murphy and Rutledge dissented on grounds that a state has no right to "bar from a semi-public position, a well-qualified man of good character solely because" of his religious conviction.
1949	*State v. Bunn*, 336 U.S. 942.	No vote	Validity of North Carolina prohibition of handling of poisonous snakes in a "religious ceremony."	One of several of such state laws upheld by Court via denial of writ of *certiorari*.
1951	*Breard v. City of Alexandria*, 341 U.S. 622.	7:2	Validity of ordinance banning the practice of summoning occupants of a residence to the door *without prior consent* for the purpose of soliciting orders for the sale of goods.	Distinguished from other solicitation cases because of the presence of the commercial element. Dissent by Black joined by Douglas.
1961	The Four Sunday Law Cases: a) *McGowan v. Maryland*, 366 U.S. 420. b) *Two Guys from Harrison-Allentown, Inc. v. McGinley*, 366 U.S. 582. c) *Braunfeld v. Brown*, 366 U.S. 599. d) *Gallagher v. Crown Kosher Market*, 366 U.S. 617.	8:1 8:1 7:2 6:3	Validity of a series of so-called state Blue Laws, variously forbidding sales on Sundays. Challenges were brought on several grounds, including "due process of law" and "equal protection" of the laws, and the individual facts and circumstances of the cases varied. However, in all cases both the religious liberty *and* the establishment of religious claims were raised, particularly the former, in the attacks on the statutes' constitutionality.	Chief Justice Warren, who wrote the opinion in each of the four cases, disposed of the constitutional challenge mainly on the ground that the purpose and effect of the laws was "pre-eminently secular" and could thus be upheld as general welfare regulations under the state police power. Numerous concurring and wholly or partly dissenting opinions—a total of between 8 and 12 opinions being written (depending upon one's count).

TABLE II

"Free Exercise" Cases Decided in Favor of the Individual

DATE	CASE	VOTE	CONST'L ISSUES DECIDED	COMMENTARY
1892	*Church of Holy Trinity v. United States*, 143 U.S. 226.	9:0	Did a Congressional statute prohibiting the importation of foreigners "under contract or agreement to perform labor in the United States" forbid a New York Church from contracting with an English clergyman to migrate to the U.S. and act as its rector and pastor?	Marshaling much evidence that "we are a religious people," the Court held that such a restrictive intent as claimed could not be validly imputed to the statute by the Government. Has overtones of Church-State problem.
1940	*Cantwell v. Connecticut*, 310 U.S. 296.	9:0	(a) Validity of Conn. statute requiring State Secretary of Welfare before soliciting funds, to let him determine whether the "cause is a religious one." (b) Cantwell's conviction for breach of the peace.	Both aspects discussed in body of text above. First case under the "freedom of religion guarantees" clause decided by Court to be applicable to states as well as government. Jehovah's Witness Cantwell won on both counts (a) and (b).
1943	*Jones v. Opelika* [II], 319 U.S. 103.	5:4	Reconsideration of the *Jones v. Opelika* decision (see Table I) of 1942, questioning validity of Opelika's ordinance imposing license tax on bookselling, here by Jehovah's Witnesses.	Made possible largely by the new stance of Black, Douglas and Murphy, and the constancy of Stone.
1943	*Murdock v. Commonwealth of Pennsylvania*, 319 U.S. 105. (See also *Follett v. McCormick*, 321 U.S. 573 [1944]).	5:4	Validity of statute requiring payment of a tax ranging from $1.50 to $20.00 a day for three weeks for the privilege of canvassing or soliciting orders for articles, as here applied to Jehovah's Witnesses.	Douglas opinion, joined by Stone, Black, Murphy, and Rutledge, held statute inapplicable to Witnesses, for "a person cannot be compelled to purchase, through a license fee or a license tax, a privilege freely granted in Constitution."

TABLE II (continued)

DATE	CASE	VOTE	CONST'L ISSUES DECIDED	COMMENTARY
1943	*Martin v. Struthers*, 319 U.S. 141.	5:4	Validity of Struthers, Ohio, ordinance forbidding knocking on door or ringing of doorbell of a residence in order to deliver a handbill to occupant without his invitation.	Ordinance held an unconstitutional abridgement of freedom of religion as applied to Jehovah's Witnesses who distribute their literature in this way.
1943	*Douglas v. City of Jeannette*, 319 U.S. 157.	5:4	Can public evangelism and proselytizing be stopped by police on Sundays, acting on numerous citizens' complaints?	Douglas opinion again joined by Stone, Black, Murphy, and Rutledge, held "no"—that Jehovah's Witnesses had right to do so. Angry dissent written by Jackson.
1943	*West Virginia State Board of Education v. Barnette*, 319 U.S. 624.	6:3	Validity of W.Va. compulsory flag salute—upheld in *Minersville* case (see above)—again contested on free exercise grounds.	Famed overruling of the *Minersville* decision. (Discussed in detail above in body of chapter.)
1943	*Taylor v. Mississippi*, 319 U.S. 583.	6:3	Validity of Mississippi statute making it unlawful to urge people, on religious grounds, not to salute the flag.	If the Constitution bans enforcement of a flag salute regulation, held the Court, it also prohibits the imposing of punishment for advising and urging that, on religious grounds, citizens refrain from saluting the flag.
1943	*Jamison v. Texas*, 318 U.S. 413.	6:2	Validity of Dallas ordinance prohibiting distribution of handbills in city streets.	A state may not prohibit distribution of handbills in city streets in the pursuit of a clearly religious activity—merely because the handbills invite purchase of books or promote raising of funds for religious purposes.

198

Year	Case	Question/Facts	Vote	Holding
	...*322 U.S. 78.*	...may secular authority—in connection with alleged mail fraud—determine the truth of religious claims and beliefs, here the "I am" movement?	5:4	No matter now "preposterous" or "incredible" they may be, religious beliefs are not subject to findings of "truth" by fact-finding bodies.
1946	*Girouard v. United States,* 328 U.S. 61. (See also *Cohnstaedt v. Immigration and Naturalization Service,* 339 U.S. 901 [1950].)	Re-examination of the *Schwimmer* and *Macintosh* question (see Table I, *supra*) regarding denial of naturalization to conscientious objectors.	5:3	Court overruled its 1929 and 1931 decisions adopting the then dissenting opinions of Justices Holmes and Hughes that religiously motivated refusal to bear arms does not manifest a lack of attachment to the U.S. Constitution.
1946	*Marsh v. Alabama,* 326 U.S. 501. (See also companion case of *Tucker v. Texas,* 326 U.S. 517 [1946].)	Validity of Alabama statute making it a crime to enter or remain on private premises—here the privately owned shipbuilding wharf of Chickasaw—after having been duly warned by the owner not to do so.	5:3	Distribution of religious literature by Jehovah's Witnesses cannot be banned even on the privately owned streets of a company town. First and Fourteenth Amendments.
1951	*Niemotko v. Maryland,* 340 U.S. 268.	Validity of city of Havre de Grace ordinance allowing use of public parks for public meetings, including religious groups, by custom requiring an advance permit to be issued by City Council.	9:0	Denial of permit by City Council to Jehovah's Witnesses evidently based on their "unsatisfactory responses", to questions concerning their views of flag salutes, military service, Roman Catholicism, etc. Denial held to be prior censorship violative of First and Fourteenth Amendments.
1953	*Fowler v. Rhode Island,* 345 U.S. 67.	Application of Pawtucket public-park-meetings ordinance that, by interpretation, did not forbid church service in public parks to Catholics and Protestants, but did ban the Jehovah's Witnesses.	9:0	By treating the religious services of the Witnesses differently than those of other faiths, Pawtucket had unconstitutionally abridged the religious freedom commands of the First Amendment.

TABLE II (continued)

DATE	CASE	VOTE	CONST'L ISSUES DECIDED	COMMENTARY
1961	*Torcaso v. Watkins,* 367 U.S. 488.	9:0	Validity of Maryland Constitution's provision of test oath of belief in the existence of God as prerequisite to holding public office.	Held a fatal invasion of freedom of belief and religion, violative of both the free exercise and establishment concepts. (See discussion above in body of text.)
1963	*Sherbert v. Verner,* 374 U.S. 398.	7:2	Legality of South Carolina State's ruling that Seventh Day Adventist Sherbert's refusal to work on Saturdays (her Sabbath Day), a refusal for which she was discharged by her employers, did not constitute "good cause" under the law, and therefore did not entitle her to unemployment compensation benefit payments.	Despite its earlier (1961) precedents in the *Blue Law Cases* (see Table I above and discussion, *infra*), the Court held that the denial of benefits to Sherbert constituted infringement of her constitutional rights under the First Amendment because her disqualification imposed a burden on the free exercise clause by forcing her to choose between adhering to her religious precepts and forfeiting benefits for abandoning these precepts and accepting employment.
1965	*United States v. Seeger, et al.,* 380 U.S. 163.	9:0	Validity of claim by Seeger and two others, alleging their exemptability under Draft Act provision governing conscientious objection "by reason of religious training and belief."	Delicate question of meaning of "an individual's belief in a relation to a Supreme Being" interpreted broadly and liberally by unanimous Court. (See discussion above n text.)

The Dilemma Compounded

Before considering the far more intricate concept of the "establishment" of religion, its close relationship with the "free exercise" aspect may be demonstrated—following the above tabular analysis—by pointing to at least one complex example.[1] This example concerns the handling of the 1961 *Blue Laws Cases*[2] as seen against the Court's perhaps rather astonishing subsequent decision, just two years later, in *Sherbert v. Verner*,[3] a case involving South Carolina unemployment compensation claims.

The Sunday Law Cases and Sherbert v. Verner. The underlying principle of the manifold "Sunday" or "Blue Laws"—which exists in 37 states in various forms and contains some incredible inconsistencies and incongruities—is the right of a state, under its police power, to enact legislation providing for the Sunday closing of certain business enterprises, while permitting others to remain open. Undoubtedly there must be some logic to such intriguing provisions as those that—under the very same state laws—ban the sale of hosiery in hosiery shops on Sundays yet do not forbid it in drugstores; or those that permit the sale of "antiques," but not "reproductions"; or those that require candy stores to be closed but permit road-side candy counters to be open; or those that allow clam-digging but forbid

---

[1] Space does not permit an examination of the tragic problem of drawing lines between the rights of parents and the right of the state, in *loco parentis*, when the parents' faith precludes submittal to medical treatment. It is clearly established in statutory law that parents have the right to determine treatment—of whatever type or kind. Since Christian Science Practice, for example, *is* legal in every state of the Union, such parents have the right to determine the nature of the medical care, if any, their minor children are to receive. What then if a Christian Science child dies as a result of the parents' deliberate decision not to submit the child to orthodox medical treatment? For a pertinent illustration, see the case of *Commonwealth of Pennsylvania v. Cornelius*, Quarter Sessions, April Term, #105(1956), which was *nolle prossed* at the request of the then district attorney, Victor H. Blanc. Numerous other examples could be readily cited, of course, involving particularly Jehovah's Witnesses and Seventh Day Adventists who have frequently refused—with varying degrees of success—to submit to such standard medical practices and/or legal requirements as blood transfusions or compulsory smallpox vaccinations. For a case involving the latter, see *Jacobson v. Massachusetts*, 197 U.S. 11 (1905).

[2] *McGowan v. Maryland*, 366 U.S. 420; *Two Guys from Harrison-Allentown, Inc. v. McGinley*, 366 U.S. 582; *Gallagher v. Crown Kosher Super Market of Massachusetts*, 366 U.S. 617; and *Braunfeld v. Brown*, 366 U.S. 599.

[3] 374 U.S. 398 (1963).

oyster-dredging! [1] Yet such logic, if any, is rather difficult to detect and is certainly subject to some question! It was just such questioning and reasoning that finally, in 1961, brought a spate of Sunday Law litigation to the bar of the Supreme Court. In addressing itself to the basic constitutional question, the Court combined four cases coming to it, some of them reaching the Court with diametrically opposed judgments from lower federal tribunals! Two of the cases [2] involved owners of highway discount department stores that were open for business seven days a week; the other two concerned smaller stores, owned and operated by Orthodox Jews who, given their religious convictions, closed their establishments on Saturdays but wanted them open on Sundays. [3] The four cases came from three different "Blue Law states," Maryland, Massachusetts, and Pennsylvania, and in all of them the constitutionality of the several statutes involved was under attack on the grounds that they infringed upon religious liberty in violation of the First Amendment; that they contravened the First's constitutional proscription against the establishment of religion; and that they constituted an unreasonable, arbitrary, and capricious classification and thus denied to the merchant involved the equal protection of the laws guaranteed under the Fourteenth Amendment.

Depending upon how one wishes to count or number opinions that are listed as "concurring and dissenting in part," at least eight and perhaps a dozen separate opinions were handed down in these four cases by a rather obviously uncomfortable and unhappy Court. For our present purposes, it suffices to point to the fact that the prevailing majority opinion—where one could be said to exist at all—in each one of the four cases was written by Mr. Chief Justice Warren, whereas Mr. Justice Douglas dissented in each. The other justices ranged across an opinion spectrum that varied from 8:1 to 6:3. It is clear that the Court did not believe that a demonstrable case for the laws' unconstitutionality had been made; nor did it wish to strike down legislation that, to such a large degree, was based upon either legislative discretion or popular demand, legislation that not only varied

---

[1] For an illuminating analysis of this crazy-quilt pattern of exemptions and exceptions, see Richard Cohen, *Sunday in the Sixties* (New York: Public Affairs Committee, 1962).

[2] *McGowan v. Maryland* and *Two Guys from Harrison-Allentown, Inc. v. McGinley*, loc. cit.

[3] *Gallagher v. Crown Kosher Super Market of Massachusetts* and *Braunfeld v. Brown*, loc. cit.

so widely in character and substance but that also was enforced only sporadically for the simple reason that so many consumers evidently did not wish it enforced—legislation that, moreover, was in some cases at least based upon popular referenda.[1] Hence, although avowedly recognizing the "religious origin" of Sunday laws, the Chief Justice, in his four opinions, hit hard upon the general theme that, in effect, their religious purposes were no longer present; that the present-day purpose of a legislature in enacting such laws was to set aside a day not for religious observance but for "rest, relaxation, and family togetherness," with the motivation thus being "secular rather than religious"; that—with an eye toward the Orthodox Jewish merchants —although the freedom to hold religious beliefs and opinions is absolute, what was involved in the cases at issue was not freedom to hold religious beliefs or opinions *but freedom to act*; and that such freedom, even when motivated by *bona fide* religious convictions, is not wholly free from legislative restrictions, duly enacted under the state police power. The Chief Justice indicated strongly that, although the Court would have wished that the states had passed laws designating Sunday as a day of rest while providing an exemption, or the choice of another day (as New York and some others have done in a modified manner), it obviously could not compel the states to adopt such legislation in their sovereign discretion. Wisdom could not be the issue; constitutionality was—and it was deemed to have been met in view of what the Court regarded as the overridingly secular nature of the various laws. To Mr. Justice Douglas and his supporters in dissent, however, there was a patent violation of both the free exercise and the establishment clauses. Rejecting the majority's finding of predominating "temporal considerations," Douglas contended with feeling that when the laws are applied to Orthodox Jews or to "Sabbatarians" their absence of justice is accentuated. As he put it:

> If the Sunday laws are constitutional, Kosher markets are on a five-day week. Thus those laws put an economic penalty on those who observe Saturday rather than Sunday as the Sabbath. For the economic pressures on these minorities, created by the fact that our communities are predominantly Sunday-minded, there is no recourse. When, however, the State uses its coercive powers—here the criminal law—to

[1] See the discussion by Murray S. Stedman, Jr., in his *Religion and Politics in America* (New York: Harcourt, Brace and World, 1964), especially pp. 71-4.

compel minorities to observe a second Sabbath, not their own, the
State undertakes to aid and "prefer one religion over another—" contrary to the command of the Constitution. . . .[1]

Whatever the realities of the Sunday Closing Laws, and their degree
of enforcement, there can be little doubt that, as Mr. Justice Stewart
wrote in dissent in the pertinent Pennsylvania case,[2] the Orthodox
Jew is forced into "a cruel choice . . . between his religious faith and
his economic survival . . . a choice which . . . no State can constitutionally demand. . . . [T]his is not something that can be swept under
the rug and forgotten in the interest of enforced Sunday togetherness." [3] To Justices Stewart, Brennan, and Douglas this was a gross
violation of the constitutional right to the free exercise of religion.

If the majority's reasoning in the *Sunday Closing Law* cases raised
professional and lay eyebrows, they were *really* raised by the Court's
opinion and decision in *Sherbert v. Verner* [4] two years later. As indicated on Table II above, this free exercise of religion case dealt with
one Mrs. Adell H. Sherbert, a member of the Seventh Day Adventist
Church. She was a textile-mill worker, whose employer initially had
permitted her to work a five-day week, thus enabling her to have her
Sabbath on Saturdays in accordance with the Church's precepts. Yet
in 1959 the same employer changed the work week to six days for
all three shifts that operated in his mill. When she refused to work
on Saturdays her employer fired her, and she found herself unable to
find similar work because of her refusal to labor on Saturdays. Consequently she filed a claim for unemployment compensation under the
South Carolina Unemployment Compensation Act; but the State
Employment Security Commission found that Mrs. Sherbert's restriction upon her availability for Saturday work disqualified her for benefits under the Act because it denies benefits to any insured workers
who fail, "without good cause, to accept suitable work when offered
by the employment office or the employer." The South Carolina Supreme Court sustained the Commission's finding because, in its judgment, no restriction was placed upon Mrs. Sherbert's freedom of religion since she remained free to observe her religious beliefs in accordance with the dictates of her conscience.

[1] Dissenting opinion in *McGowan v. Maryland*, 366 U.S. 420, at 577.
[2] *Braunfeld v. Brown*, 366 U.S. 599, dissenting opinion.
[3] *Ibid.*, at 616.
[4] 374 U.S. 398 (1963).

In language that could have been applied in the *Sunday Closing Law Cases* to obtain *opposite* results from those obtained here, the majority of seven, speaking through Mr. Justice Brennan, who had been unhappy about at least two of the *Sunday Closing Law Cases*,[1] now *reversed* the South Carolina authorities! It did so on the ground that the denial of benefits to Mrs. Sherbert constituted a clear infringement of, and burden upon, her constitutional rights of free exercise of religion under the First Amendment. Explained Brennan:

> *The ruling forces her to choose between following the precepts of her religion and forfeiting benefits, on the one hand, and abandoning one of the precepts of her religion in order to accept work, on the other hand.* Governmental imposition of such a choice puts the same kind of burden upon the free exercise of religion as would a fine imposed against appellant for her Saturday worship.[2]

Mr. Justice Stewart wrote a separate concurring opinion, and Mr. Justice Harlan dissented in an opinion joined by his colleague White.

The disappointed owners of the Braunfeld and Crown stores had much cause to wonder why the Brennan language—particularly the underlined portions—did not also fit *their* cases. Yet although Justices Stewart, Harlan and White did indeed believe that the *Sherbert* decision had the effect of overruling the *Braunfeld* and *Crown* judgments, Brennan's majority opinion *distinguished* the former on the ground that the same practical difficulties and considerations arising from the granting of exemptions in Sunday Closing Laws did not apply and were not present in the South Carolina Unemployment Insurance problem. It is quite obvious that what the Court did here was to try to draw a line: to balance considerations of public policy against infringement on religious liberty. In the *Sunday Closing Law Cases* the Court was *not* willing to make exemptions in laws of general application on grounds of claims of religious liberty *versus* economic hardship—in the *Sherbert* case it was. And this distinction was emphatically not due to changes in personnel since Justices White and Goldberg, the successors to retired Justices Whittaker and Frankfurter, did not numerically or substantively affect the different results in the 1963 decision. Although the facts in the settings of the two cases differed, the difference was surely but one of kind rather than

---

[1] *Braunfeld v. Brown*, 366 U.S. 599, and *Gallagher v. Crown Kosher Market of Massachusetts*, 366 U.S. 617.

[2] *Sherbert v. Verner, loc. cit.*, at 404. (Italics added.)

of substance. The conclusion is inevitable that the distinction made in the *Sherbert* case is neither very logical nor very convincing.[1] The distinction advanced by Brennan that in the applicable *Blue Law Cases* there was a "less direct burden upon religious practices" is highly questionable—or as Mr. Justice Stewart put it in his concurring opinion, in which he strongly criticized the Brennan rationale, "[W]ith all respect, I think the Court is mistaken, simply as a matter of fact. . . ." [2] If anything, the secular purpose of the South Carolina statute was clearer than that of Pennsylvania's and Massachusetts's. The line the Court endeavored to establish here is simply not viable as a basic rule of law.

Yet if the results in *Sherbert* signify a more generous interpretation of the free exercise phrase, it is to be welcomed in the light of the fundamental question of whether more harm is done to the democratic process by permitting an eccentricity of personal code or behavior, as long as no valid law is broken, than by tramping upon the non-conformist in the interest of the power of majoritarianism. Since lines must be drawn along the way, and the drawing usually seems to fall to the Court, it is not surprising then, that the high tribunal would be guided on occasion, as it evidently was here, by certain judgments based on considerations of realistic subjectivity that inevitably characterize the political process. After all, the Supreme Court of the United States is a body at once legal, governmental, and political. With this thought we now turn to the Pandora's Box of "establishment."

"Establishment": The Separation of Church and State

If the clause "Congress shall make no law respecting an establishment of religion" is commanding in tone and clear in syntax, it is utterly unclear in its intention. What does it mean? What does it forbid? References to history only intensify the riddle. And because the "establishment" and "free exercise" clauses are closely related, the riddles of establishment simply cannot be understood if they are treated or considered in isolation from the central problem of religious liberty itself.

[1] See the interesting analysis of this general problem in Paul G. Kauper, *Religion and the Constitution* (Baton Rouge: Louisiana State University Press, 1964), Ch. 2, "Religious Liberty: Some Basic Considerations."

[2] *Sherbert v. Verner, loc. cit.*, at 477.

A Glance into History

Initially responsible among America's revolutionary and post-revolutionary leaders for the concept of non-establishment and its incorporation into the Bill of Rights were Thomas Jefferson, James Madison, George Mason, Patrick Henry (on a somewhat different plane), and the Reverends Samuel Davies and John Leland.[1] Virginians all, they led and fought the good fight in the struggle which took place during Virginia's last days as a colony and early days as a state, a struggle similar to that which took place almost a century-and-a-half earlier in Rhode Island and neighboring areas under Roger Williams. Williams, who has been appropriately called "the most advanced and effective advocate of religious freedom in colonial times,"[2] and his supporters fought less on the specific matter of "establishment" than on the general one of "freedom." Hence it is the Virginians, under the leadership of two future Presidents of the United States, who must receive chief credit for the notion and coinage of American theories of the separation of Church and State. Their influence was decisive and their debates and writings on establishment are still valuable sources of reference even though they can be differently interpreted. A matter on which there is agreement, however, is that the Virginia battlers for religious liberty strove, above all, for separation of Church and State in the sense that there should not be an Established Church—as the Episcopal Church was in Virginia at the time—and that there should never be "the preferred position of a favored Church." To achieve those minimum aims, Jefferson, Madison, Mason, and their allies, struggled for more than a decade until they succeeded in bringing about the "disestablishment" of the Episcopal Church as the State Church in Virginia. This they achieved, with the enactment, after a nine-year struggle, of Jefferson's great Bill for Establishing Religious Freedom in 1786. The effect of this monumentally significant legislation—hereafter commonly referred to as the Disestablishment Bill—was far-reaching and cataclysmic: Virginia's victory over establishment decisively influenced not only the ultimate course of action of her sister states but also that of the federal gov-

[1] Of course, others, who labored long before the Virginians (such as Roger Williams and the Reverend John Clarke), have carved their niche in the history of religious liberty, but at a different moment in history, under different circumstances, and with different impact.

[2] Stokes and Pfeffer, *op. cit.*, p. 65.

ernment. No wonder that Jefferson requested notation of his role in the epic struggle for religious freedom on his tombstone, along with the other two achievements he considered of far greater significance than his eight-year Presidency: his authorship of the Declaration of Independence and his founding of the University of Virginia.

Moreover, Madison's widely circulated and highly influential "Memorial and Remonstrance" of 1775 against the proposal of Virginia's House of Delegates to provide, through assessments, for teachers of the Christian religion is as classic a statement as may be found anywhere in support of the separation of Church and State. Supported by Jefferson, the eloquent and lengthy 15-point document argued persuasively that the state as the secular authority must have jurisdiction over *temporal* matters; that such authority does not extend over *spiritual* matters, which lie in the domain of private belief and the churches (note: "churches," not Church"). He warned persuasively that once they look to government for the achievement of their various purposes, the churches invite the sacrifice of their spiritual independence; and that when government enters upon the religious scene, it, in turn, enters into competition with the churches in seeking favors —thereby incurring the risk of ecclesiastical domination, with the attendant dangers of coercion of belief and persecution of dissenters.

Thus, to Jefferson and Madison, "children of the Enlightenment [who] represented the secular and humanistic view that supported religious liberty and the separation of church and state," [1] the principle of separation was absolutely indispensable to the basic freedoms of belief, conscience, and dissent. They were in no sense hostile to religion; they simply regarded it as an entirely private matter. Overridingly determined to keep religion out of the domain of private affairs, they were as much concerned with "freedom *from* religion as with freedom *of* religion." [2]

Difficulties of Historical Application to Contemporary Problems. Following the *obvious* intent of Jefferson and Madison, it is clear that there can be neither an *official* Church nor even an especially *favored* Church in the United States or in any of its constituent subdivisions. What is far less clear, however, is the matter of state *aid* to religious activities and that of state *co-operation*. If government treats *all* religions with an equal eye and an even hand, may it not, wholly in conformity with the Jefferson-Madison injunction, aid in furthering

[1] Paul G. Kauper, *op. cit.*, p. 48.
[2] *Ibid.*

the spiritual development of Americans, whom the Supreme Court has repeatedly styled "a religious people?" [1] Is the government, in the words of an experienced student of philosophy and politics, "furthering a legitimate purpose when it acts to encourage, support, or aid the institutions of religious life," or is it "precisely the point of the 'no establishment' clause that it precludes government action to this end"? [2] How authoritative and decisive can the intent of men who wrote and lived almost two centuries ago be regarded when applied to the current scene? The principle of "separation" *is* demonstrably present in both the spirit and the letter of the Constitution. Once again, then, we are faced with the ubiquitous line-drawing problem, and once again we must look to the Court, even if its role has evolved as much by default as by affirmation. And the Court has had a devilish time in finding and drawing a line.

A Solution That Is No Solution. Striving for a solution, the Court seized upon Jefferson's concept of the "wall of separation between Church and State," which he expressed in a letter to the Danbury Baptist Association in 1785. The idea that the clause against establishment of religion by law was intended to erect "a wall of separation between Church and State" was first expounded in the *First Mormon Polygamy* case [3] in 1879 by Mr. Chief Justice Waite, who wrote for a unanimous Court. (However, that case essentially rested on the free exercise question.) The "wall of separation" clause reappeared in a far more significant, highly contentious, opinion by Mr. Justice Black for a 5:4 Court in the *New Jersey Bus* case [4] in 1947, when the narrow majority found that wall had *not* been breached by granting state-subventions for bus fares to parents of non-public, if non-profit (which here meant Roman Catholic parochial schools only), as well as public school children. As we shall have occasion to note again, Black here reaffirmed the "wall" principle but announced that it had *not* been breached; his colleague Frankfurter, however, was not so sure and saw the wall "not as a fine line easily overstepped"; Mr. Justice Jackson quipped that that wall may become as winding as Jefferson's celebrated "serpentine wall" on the campus of his beloved University of Virginia; Mr. Justice Reed objected to drawing a rule of

[1] E.g. Mr. Justice Douglas's majority opinion in *Zorach v. Clauson*, 343 U.S. 306 (1952), at 313.
[2] Joseph Tussman, *The Supreme Court on Church and State* (New York: Oxford University Press, 1962), p. xv.
[3] *Reynolds v. United States*, 98 U.S. 145 (1879), at 164.
[4] *Everson v. Board of Education of Ewing Township*, 330 U.S. 1 (1947).

law from what he viewed as "a figure of speech"; and, to compound
the problem for generations yet unborn, fifteen years later one of the
five wall-upholders in that *New Jersey Bus* case, Mr. Justice Douglas,
seized upon the opportunity of the *New York Bible Reading* case [1] to
announce from the bench that he *now* (1962) believed the *Bus* case
to have been wrongly decided by him and his four colleagues who
then (1947) constituted the majority!

Obviously, then, that famous "wall of separation" seems to be
made of different stuff and be of rather different height depending on
who is viewing it, be they Supreme Court justices, other jurists, or
subjective or objective commentators, lay or professional. Yet Mr.
Justice Black firmly insisted that in the instance of the New Jersey bus
subsidies to the children attending the Township's non-profit parochial schools, the wall stood high and unbreached:

> The "establishment of religion" clause of the First Amendment means
> at least this: Neither a state nor the Federal Government can set up
> a church. Neither can pass laws which aid one religion, aid all religions,
> or prefer one religion over another. Neither can force or influence a
> person to go or remain away from church against his will or force him
> to profess a belief or disbelief in any religion. No person can be
> punished for entertaining or professing religious beliefs or disbeliefs,
> for church attendance or nonattendance. No tax in any amount, large
> or small, can be levied to support any religious activities or institutions,
> whatever they may be called, or whatever form they may adopt to teach
> or practice religion. Neither a state nor the Federal Government can,
> openly or secretly, participate in the affairs of any religious organiza-
> tions or groups and vice versa. In the words of Jefferson, the clause
> against establishment of religion by law was intended to erect a "wall
> of separation between Church and State." [2]

In the light of the above manifesto, Black's concluding passage in
his opinion must have come as a bit of a surprise to some of his
readers:

> The First Amendment has erected a wall between church and state.
> That wall must be kept high and impregnable. *We could not approve
> the slightest breach. New Jersey has not breached it here.*[3]

[1] *Engel v. Vitale,* 370 U.S. 421(1962).

[2] *Everson v. Board of Education of Ewing Township, loc. cit.,* at 15-16.

[3] *Ibid.,* at 18. (Italics added.) The Court thus *affirmed* the judgment of the
tribunal whence the case had come, the New Jersey Court of Errors and Appeals,
which in turn had *reversed* a lower New Jersey court.

Had it not? In a lengthy, troubled dissent (in which his colleagues Frankfurter, Jackson, and Burton joined), and to which he appended Madison's "Memorial and Remonstrance Against Religious Assessment," Mr. Justice Rutledge found, on the contrary, that the "wall" had not only been breached, but breached flagrantly and inexcusably. Rejecting the majority's so-called "child benefit" theory that New Jersey's subsidy was meant for, and went to, the *child* rather than to the Church, Rutledge warned the majority that separation must be strictly construed. It is only by observing the prohibition against establishment rigidly, he contended, that

> the state can maintain its neutrality and avoid partisanship in the dissensions inevitable when sect opposes sect over demands for public moneys to further religious education, teaching or training in any form or degree, *directly or indirectly*.[1]

And in response to the many who have argued long and persistently that such aid would be no more than simple equity to atone for the fact that people whose children go to non-public schools must pay public taxes and often tuition too, Rutledge observed:

> Like St. Paul's freedom, religious liberty with a great price must be bought. And for those who exercise it most fully, by insisting upon religious education for their children mixed with secular, *by the terms of our Constitution the price is greater than for others*.[2]

The divergent views of such devotees to the Constitution and the basic freedoms of man as Justices Black, Douglas, and Rutledge are proof positive that the doctrine of the "wall" is no solution *per se*— for its size and consistency evidently depend upon the builder's intentions! Like so many other problems, the "wall" approach fails essentially because the necessary line depends overridingly on public policy considerations—and, alas, upon whose ox is being gored.

Some Principal Theories of Separation

Since the "wall" approach fails us as a viable guidepost, it may well be wise to analyze those theories of separation which have made themselves felt in the interpretation of that clause. Again, in considering these theories we ought to keep in mind that a strict segre-

[1] *Ibid.*, at 59. (Italics added.)
[2] *Ibid.*

gation between the two prongs of the freedom of religion concept of the First Amendment is not only an oversimplification, but that it is misleading and causes a distinct disservice to the discussion of the basic problem.

A close reading of the major Supreme Court opinions specifically governing the issue of "establishment" or separation of Church and State,[1] rather than the specific issue of "free exercise"—assuming that dichotomy can ever be thus clearly delimited—presents three more or less identifiable Court theories.[2]

1. *The Strict Separation or "No Aid" Theory.* Presumably incorporating the "wall" approach to the problem, this theory holds that there must be a strict separation of Church and State, and that Government may not constitutionally provide support of religion or religious interests. The theory was demonstrably applied in the "released time" case of *McCollum v. Board of Education,*[3] where the Supreme Court ruled 8:1—the majority opinion written by Mr. Justice Black, the dissenting one by Mr. Justice Reed—that the "no aid" concept had been violated. At issue was Mrs. Vashti Cromwell McCollum's challenge[4] of the constitutional validity of a practice by the Board of Education of Champaign, Illinois, which enabled the interfaith Champaign Council on Religious Education to offer classes in religious instruction to public school children, on public school premises. The religious classes were attended from 30 to 45 minutes on Wednesdays by those public school students whose parents submitted written authorizations. Teachers were provided by the Council at no charge to the Board, but they were subject to the approval of Champaign's Superintendent of Schools. The classes were conducted in the regular school classrooms during school hours; those students who did not wish to stay for the religious sessions were required to go elsewhere in the building to pursue "meaningful secular studies." Evidently, these were not very meaningful in the case of those few students— such as young James Terry McCollum, whose family were professed agnostics—who did not stay for the Protestant, Catholic, or Jewish

[1] These major opinions are indicated in Tables III and IV, *infra*. Probably the most significant ones for our present purposes are the *Everson, McCollum, Zorach, Sunday Closing, Engel,* and *Schempp* cases. (See Tables III and IV for citations.)
[2] These are discussed in detail in Kauper, *op. cit.,* Ch. 3.
[3] *Illinois ex rel McCollum v. Board of Education,* 333 U.S. 203 (1948).
[4] See her interesting book on the case, *One Woman's Fight* (Boston: Beacon Press, 1961).

classes. Attendance at both the religious and lay classes was enforced strictly by secular teachers.

Strongly reiterating the "wall" principle which he pronounced as the author of the majority opinion in the *Everson Bus* case,[1] Mr. Justice Black found clear violations here of the First and Fourteenth Amendments. He rejected the Board of Education's argument that for the Court to hold that a state cannot consistently with those two Amendments utilize its public school system to aid any or all religious faiths or sects in the dissemination of their doctrines and ideals would "manifest a governmental hostility to religion or religious teachings." Black pointed to *Everson*, repeating its—his—language: ". . . the First Amendment has erected a wall between Church and State which must be kept high and impregnable." Since there was considerable evidence, however, that pointed to much lingering doubt as to just what had really happened to that wall in *Everson*, Black evidently felt constrained to spell out his conclusions on the violation of separation of Church and State again, and he closed his opinion with this admonition:

> Here [in McCollum] not only are the State's tax-supported public school buildings used for the dissemination of religious doctrines. The State also affords sectarian groups an invaluable aid in that it helps to provide pupils for their religious classes through use of the State's compulsory public school machinery. This is not separation of Church and State.[2]

Mr. Justice Reed, on the other hand, believed in solitary dissent that the principle of *Everson* could accommodate the facts in *McCollum*. Sounding the frequently-voiced argument that "devotion to the great principle of religious liberty should not lead us into a rigid interpretation of the constitutional guarantee that conflicts with accepted habits of our people," he observed sadly that here was

> an instance where, for me, the history of past practices is determinative of the meaning of a constitutional clause not a decorous introduction to the study of its text.[3]

Justices Reed and Black had been on the same side in the *Everson* case although it will be recalled that Reed, perhaps sensing the ex-

[1] *Loc. cit.*
[2] *Illinois ex rel McCollum v. Board of Education*, 333 U.S. 203, at 212.
[3] *Ibid.*, dissenting opinion, at 256.

pansiveness *cum* uncertainty of the "wall" doctrine, and reflecting the fear of those who well recognized that it could "give" in either direction, had there objected to "drawing a rule of law from a figure of speech."

In the light of his position in the separation cases that were yet to come [1] when *McCollum* was decided in 1948—barely a year after *Everson*—Black's position in the *New Jersey Bus* case can best be explained in terms of a distinction he was willing to make under the strict separation theory between "indirect" aid to religion and "direct" aid. The situation in the *Bus* case was for him an entirely viable example of *indirect* aid. He reasoned that since the purpose of the New Jersey ordinance was to provide nothing more than safe transportation of school children who were attending school under compulsory education laws, the fact that they happened to attend Roman Catholic parochial schools was, if not beside the point, certainly not constitutionally fatal. For Black and his (then) supporters, the purpose of the aid was "secular" and "incidental" to the requirements of the compulsory school attendance statute, *hence appropriately directed to secular objectives.* In other words, the aid given to the parochial school students was "aid," but it was not the kind of "aid" that was forbidden under the "wall" doctrine of the *Everson* decision itself. A cynic pondering the explanation or rationalization inherent in this analysis might be pardoned for commenting—with apologies to Gertrude Stein: "Aid is no aid until no aid becomes aid."

Some fifteen years after the *Everson* and *McCollum* cases, Black returned to the fray to write what quickly became one of the most contentious and most misunderstood opinions of our time in the *New York Prayer* case. [2] Here, writing for a 6:1 majority, Black made clear that the principle of the separation of Church and State could not permit the recitation in the public schools of a rather innocuous, 22-word, non-denominational daily prayer that had been drafted by the New York State Board of Regents, a state agency composed of state officials. The prayer read as follows:

> Almighty God, we acknowledge our dependence upon Thee, and we beg thy blessings upon us, our parents, our teachers, and our country.

[1] See text and Tables III and IV below, especially the *Zorach, Engel,* and *Schempp* cases, decided in 1952, 1962, and 1963, respectively.
[2] *Engel v. Vitale,* 370 U.S. 421 (1962).

It was recommended, although not required, for *viva voce* reading by teachers and students in the classrooms of the New York State public schools at the beginning of each school day. Numerous school boards adopted the recommendation, among them that of Hyde Park, Long Island, which did so in 1958. Five parents [1] of ten children attending the school involved brought suit on the ground that the use of the official prayer in the public schools violated both separation of Church and State and freedom of religion. In his neither very lengthy nor very complex opinion for the Court, Mr. Justice Black agreed with the contentions of the parents and held the practice unconstitutional as a violation of the First and Fourteenth Amendments' ban on establishment of religion. "We think," he wrote,

> that by using its public school system to encourage recitation of the Regents' prayer, the State of New York has adopted a practice wholly inconsistent with the Establishment Clause. *There can, of course, be no doubt* that New York's program of daily classroom invocation of God's blessing as prescribed in the Regents' prayer is a religious activity. It is a solemn avowal of divine faith and supplication for the blessings of the Almighty.[2]

Anticipating, perhaps, the public outcry that was to follow the decision—and it proved to be quite an outcry—he tried hard to put into words that the public might accept, and perhaps even appreciate, the manifold problems of personal commitments and drawing lines in cases of majority-minority religion that continue to bedevil these controversies. Thus, he explained,

> [T]he constitutional prohibition against laws respecting an establishment of religion must at least mean that in this country it is no part of the business of government to compose official prayers for any group of the American people to recite as part of a religious program carried on by government.[3]

And over the objections of the one dissenter, Mr. Justice Stewart, who contended that the Court "has misspelled a great constitutional principle" by ruling that "an 'official religion' is established by letting

---

[1] One of these was a Unitarian; one a non-believer; one a member of the Ethical Culture Society; and two were Jewish.
[2] *Ibid.,* at 424. (Italics added.)
[3] *Ibid.,* at 425.

those who want to say a prayer say it," [1] Black concluded on a frank, terse, and hardly illogical note:

> It is neither sacrilegious nor antireligious to say that each separate government in this country should stay out of the business of writing or sanctioning official prayers and *leave that purely religious function to the people themselves and to those the people look to for religious guidance.*[2]

In an important footnote, generally and unfortunately ignored by the news media, Black tried to make clear—as he also did in two additional remarks he made orally from the bench on that Opinion Monday in June 1962—that, contrary to his colleague Douglas's concurring opinion, he in no sense of the term intended his opinion for the Court to extend to ceremonial functions and observations with religious mottos or religious characteristics.

The *New York Prayer* decision seemed an enormously significant confirmation of the Court's adherence to an even stricter interpretation of the separation of Church and State concept than heretofore pronounced. Additional confirmation came just one year later with the extension of the *New York Prayer* case in two momentous decisions that fall under the second principal theory of separation of Church and State.

2. *The Governmental Neutrality Theory.* Under this theory, the establishment clause is viewed as requiring government to be resolutely "neutral" regarding religious matters. So neutral, in fact, that, in the interesting interpretation and application of the theory advanced by Professor Philip B. Kurland of the University of Chicago Law School, government cannot do anything which *either aids or hampers religion.*[3] Professor Kurland reads the freedom and separation segments of the religion phrases as "a single precept that government cannot utilize religion as a standard for action or inaction because these clauses prohibit classification in terms of religion *either to confer a benefit or to impose a burden.*" [4] This, of course, leaves

---

[1] *Ibid.*, dissenting opinion, at 445.

[2] *Ibid.*, at 435. (Italics supplied.)

[3] He has expressed this thesis frequently and in various media. See, for example, his essay in Dallin H. Oaks, ed., *The Wall Between Church and State* (Chicago: University of Chicago Press, 1963), entitled "The School Prayer Cases," p. 160.

[4] *Ibid.*, n. 83. (Italics supplied.)

us with the rather delicate and intriguing question as to the meaning of not only "benefit" and "burden" but of "neutral." It also leaves us with the suspicion that the suggested doctrine might well be rather hard on individual religious dissenters, which is something Kurland seems to acknowledge but does not quite concede.[1]

The Supreme Court resorted to the neutrality theory most obviously—and indeed avowedly—in the *Bible Reading* cases of 1963, *Abington School District v. Schempp* and *Murray v. Curlett*,[2] which were "follow-up" cases to the *New York Prayer* case. Briefly, the *Schempp* portion of the two cases—which were decided together in a 144-page, five-opinion compendium—challenged the validity of a Pennsylvania law requiring the reading without comment of 10 verses from the King James Version of the Holy Bible on the opening of public school each day, although provision was made for a child to be excused from the exercises on the written request of a parent or guardian. The Schempps were faithful members of the Unitarian religion; Mrs. Madalyn E. Murray and her son, William J. Murray, III—who brought the Maryland suit—were avowed atheists, contesting rulings of the Baltimore School Board that required reading of a Bible chapter "and-or the Lord's Prayer" at daily opening exercises in the public schools of that state. William had apparently been subjected to taunts and even physical assault in school because of his consistent opposition to these morning exercises. An interesting, although not uncommon, by-product of the two cases involved was that the two different lower courts, through which the cases passed to the United States Supreme Court, reached opposite conclusions on the same constitutional issues.

The Chief Justice assigned the cases to Mr. Justice Clark, a devout Presbyterian active in his church, who wrote an opinion redolent with diplomacy and acknowledgement of the significant place religion is presumed to hold in American society. He clearly endeavored to avoid the hostile, however uninformed, outcries that followed the Black opinion in the *Engel* decision. In the 8:1 ruling—from which only Mr. Justice Stewart dissented but, unlike his *Engel* dissent, now on almost wholly *procedural* grounds—Clark chose to rest both the decision and the burden of the opinion on a different tack, that of *gov-*

[1] See his *Religion and The Law* (Chicago: Aldine Publishing Co., 1962), esp. pp. 40 ff.

[2] 374 U.S. 203.

ernmental neutrality. How well he succeeded is perhaps tellingly illustrated by the fact that dozens of newspapers selected as the decisive
segment of opinion the following explanation *cum* exhortation:
Wrote Clark:

> The place of religion in our society is an exalted one, achieved through
> a long tradition of reliance on the home, the church and the inviolable
> citadel of the individual heart and mind. We have come to recognize
> through bitter experience that *it is not within the power of govern-
> ment to invade that citadel, whether its purpose or effect be to aid or
> oppose, to advance or retard. In the relationship between man and
> religion, the state is firmly committed to a position of neutrality.*[1]

Not only was the opinion in which the eight justices concurred, written by a devout Protestant, but lengthy, separate concurring opinions
were delivered by the Court's Roman Catholic, Mr. Justice Brennan,
whose comments embraced 77 pages, and its Jewish member, Mr.
Justice Goldberg. All five authors went to great pain to acknowledge
the hallowed place of religion, yet all five firmly, and indeed repeatedly, referred to governmental neutrality as the *sine qua non* of the
problem. Thus, the Court's emphasis was clearly on the theory of
neutrality, a requirement based—as Mr. Justice Clark put it—on the
possibility that "powerful sects or groups might bring about a fusion
of governmental and religious functions or a concert or dependency
of one upon the other." [2] The language, although evidently not the
full intent, of the application of the principle of neutrality thus becomes that advanced by Professor Kurland, discussed above. It asks
whether the "purpose or primary effect" of an enactment is "either
the enhancement or inhibition of religion":

> [T]o withstand the strictures of the Establishment Clause there must
> be a secular legislative purpose and a primary effect that neither ad-
> vances nor inhibits religion. . . . [and] the fact [advanced by Pennsyl-
> vania and Maryland] that individual students may absent themselves
> upon parental request . . . furnishes no defense to a claim of constitu-
> tionality under the Establishment Clause.[3]

The religious practices authorized by Pennsylvania and Maryland,
and challenged by the Schempps and Murrays, thus failed to meet

---

[1] For example (from the conclusion of the opinion), "Quotation of the Day,"
in *The New York Times,* June 18, 1963. (Italics supplied.)

[2] *Abington School District v. Schempp* and *Murray v. Curlett,* 374 U.S. 203
(1963), at 222.

[3] *Ibid.,* at 222, 224.

the demands of the "neutrality" test, a test under which *both* religion clauses of the First Amendment place the government in a "neutral position" vis-à-vis religion. As for the allegation that a logical concomitant of that "neutrality" policy would be, in effect, to render government hostile to religion, Mr. Justice Clark explained that the Court—and through it the country's constitutional framework—

> . . . cannot accept that the concept of neutrality, which does not permit a State to require a religious exercise even with the consent of the majority of those affected, collides with the majority's right to free exercise of religion. While the Free Exercise Clause clearly prohibits the use of state action to deny the right of free exercise to *anyone*, it has never meant that a majority could use the machinery of the State to practice its beliefs.[1]

What Clark says here is surely a basic premise of our government under law: that majorities, even near-unanimous ones, cannot violate the Constitution! When Florida attempted to continue required prayers and Bible-reading in its public schools, a practice approved by its state supreme court, the United States Supreme Court, without even hearing argument, promptly condemned the practice and reversed the tribunal by an 8:1 vote one year later.[2] And when in 1965 the principal of P.S. 184 in Queens, New York, ruled that not even a "voluntary" recitation of a nursery school prayer in public schools could be said, the Supreme Court upheld him by refusing to review an appeal from his ruling.[3]

The concept of governmental neutrality can be interpreted in various ways, depending upon the interpreter and his philosophy. Thus, to Wilbur Katz, Northwestern University's Rosenthal Lecturer of 1963, it means that in order to be truly neutral, the government is in some instances *obliged* to give aid to religion in order to avoid restricting the complete enjoyment of religious liberty.[4] To some, anything but total neutrality is anathema;[5] to others, a neutrality that

[1] *Ibid.*, at 225-6.
[2] *Chamberlin v. Dade County Board of Instruction*, 377 U.S. 402 (1964).
[3] *Stein v. Oshinsky*, 382 U.S. 957. The prayer, said before eating cookies and drinking milk: "God is great, God is good, and we thank him for our food, Amen."
[4] *Religion and American Constitutions* (Evanston: Northwestern University Press, 1964), *passim*.
[5] E.g. Professor Leo Pfeffer, a distinguished student of the field.

prevents a "just measure of governmental aid" is a violation of "the old American principles" of freedom of religion;[1] and to again others, it signifies that since government and religion both have roles to play in public life and the public order, and since they share some overlapping concerns and functions, neutrality can only mean that government policy must place religion neither at a *special advantage* nor a *special disadvantage*.[2]

How, then, does the "no aid" theory expounded in the *Everson Bus* case[3] differ from the "neutrality" theory expounded in the *Public School Prayer* cases?[4] Although the response depends upon interpretation, we *can* with some assurance say that the "no aid" test inquires whether government is acting *in aid of religion* (in *Everson* the Court found that New Jersey's subsidy aided the *child* rather than the *Church*), whereas the "neutrality" test inquires whether government is placing religion at a patent advantage or disadvantage (which the Court answered in the former in the *Public School Prayer* cases). There remains the third theory, whcih frankly recognizes governmental "accommodation."

3. *The Governmental Accommodation Theory.* Although he was on the side of the eight-man majority in both of the *Public School Prayer* cases, Mr. Justice Brennan felt constrained to write an enormously long concurring opinion in the *Pennsylvania/Maryland* decisions.[5] There, while acknowledging that the accommodation theory had no place in the particular cases at issue, he was moved to explain that only a concept such as that of "accommodation" could effectively reconcile the natural clash between the free exercise and separation clauses. He listed a series of permissible accommodation practices and categories to illustrate that we do as a matter of necessity accept, even demand, *some* accommodation between government and religion and between Church and State.[6] Readily acknowledging that Pennsylvania and Maryland had gone beyond "accommodation" with their Bible reading and public prayer legislation, and thereby violated

[1] Father John Courtney Murray, S.J., "Law and Prepossessions?" 14 *Law and Contemporary Problems*, 23 (1949).

[2] Professor Paul G. Kauper, *op. cit.*, Ch. 3, *passim.*

[3] *Everson v. Board of Education of Ewing Township*, 330 U.S. 1 (1947).

[4] *Engel v. Vitale*, 370 U.S. 421 (1962), and *Abington School District v. Schempp* and *Murray v. Curlett*, 374 U.S. 203 (1963).

[5] 374 U.S. 203 (1963).

[6] *Ibid.*, concurring opinion, Brennan.

the basic concept of governmental neutrality required by the Constitution, he listed activities that could not, in his opinion, be held to be constitutional violations,[1] such as: activities that, although religious in origin, have ceased to have religious meaning, e.g. the motto "In God We Trust" on currency and the belief expressed in the Pledge of Allegiance that the nation was founded "under God";[2] provisions for churches and chaplains in the armed forces and in penal institutions; draft exemptions for ministers and divinity students; the recital of invocational prayers in legislative assemblies; and the appointment of legislative chaplains; teaching *about* religion in the public schools, i.e. the *study* of the Bible and other religious literature; *uniform* tax exemptions incidentally available to religious institutions;[3] other public welfare benefits which government makes available to educational, charitable, and eleemosynary groups that *incidentally* aid individual worshippers; excuse of children from required school attendance on their respective religious holidays; the temporary use of public buildings by religious organizations when their own facilities have become unavailable because of disaster or emergency.

As if to indicate the difficulty of drawing such lines, Mr. Justice Douglas, in *his* concurring opinion in the *Pennsylvania/Maryland* decisions essentially reiterated his strong stand in the *New York Prayer* case, where he had said that the "First Amendment. . . . prevented secular sanctions to *any* religious ceremony, dogma, or rite."[4] But lest he be misunderstood, he emphasized his now firm conviction that the concept of the Wall brooked no infraction or circumvention, whatever the circumstances, whatever the rationale:

> . . . the First Amendment does not say that some forms of establishment are allowed; it says that "no law respecting an establishment of

[1] *Ibid.*, at 296-303.

[2] Indeed, late in 1964 the Court refused to review—and thereby let stand— a ruling by the Appellate Division of the New York Supreme Court that upheld the use of the words "under God" in the Pledge of Allegiance (*Lewis v. Allen*, 379 U.S. 923).

[3] In October 1966 the Supreme Court seemed to reaffirm that sensitive issue by declining to review a unanimous decision by the Maryland Court of Appeals that the time-honored state tax exemptions for church buildings were *not* an unconstitutional "establishment of religion." *Cree v. Goldstein*, 385 U.S. 816, and *Murray v. Goldstein ibid.*

[4] *Engel v. Vitale*, 370 U.S. 421 (1962), at 442, n. 7.

religion" shall be made. What may not be done directly may not be done indirectly lest the Establishment Clause become a mockery.[1]

This stand, of course, rejects *any* theory of "accommodation." Ironically, Mr. Justice Douglas had not only provided the necessary fifth vote that upheld New Jersey's public funds subsidy to students attending Catholic parochial schools, a position he publicly repudiated in *Engel v. Vitale*,[2] but it was he, who had written (a decade prior to the *Public School Prayer* cases) the majority opinion in *Zorach v. Clauson*, the *New York Released Time* case,[3] which best illustrates the accommodation theory!

Zorach v. Clauson presented a situation ostensibly different from the one that faced the Court in the *Champaign, Illinois, Released Time* case [4] four years earlier in 1948. It will be recalled that the Court's 8:1 decision in that Illinois case struck down as a clear-cut violation of the separation of Church and State the Champaign School Board's practice of permitting the use of its public school facilities for weekly "released time" religious classes. The New York released time arrangement differed on its face principally in that those public school students whose parents requested their attendance at religious instruction classes were in fact *released* from classes at school to journey outside to the site of the religious classes. Those who did not participate in the released time program were required to remain in the public school buildings for instructional or study-hall purposes. Theoretically, the public school teachers took no attendance of the student releasees, but the religious teachers *did* take attendance and filed it, although more or less *sub rosa*, with the individual's home room teacher.

The Supreme Court's six-man majority,[5] per the Douglas opinion, found critical differences between *McCollum* and *Zorach*. Douglas, while acknowledging that the public school teachers "co-operated" with the program to the extent of enabling voluntary attendance at the religious classes, held that the New York program, unlike that struck down in Illinois, involved neither religious instruction in the

---

[1] *Loc. cit.*, at 230, concurring opinion. He took pains publicly to reiterate that posture late in 1964 in the *Chamberlin* case, cited *supra*, p. 219, n. 2.

[2] 343 U.S. 307 (1952).

[3] *Ibid.*

[4] *McCollum v. Board of Education*, 333 U.S. 203 (1948).

[5] Douglas, with Mr. Chief Justice Vinson, and Justices Reed, Burton, Minton, and Clark.

public school classrooms nor the expenditure of public funds *per se*. He insisted that the Court was indeed following the *McCollum* case, but he added that this did not mean that the Court had to read into the Bill of Rights a "philosophy of hostility to religion." Musing that the constitutional standard of the separation of Church and State, like many problems in Constitutional Law, "is one of degree," he declared that Church and State need not be hostile to one another. Although granting that "[g]overnment may not finance religious groups nor undertake religious instruction or blend secular and sectarian education nor use secular institutions to force one or some religion on any person," [1] he added in language that has since come to haunt him in light of his concurring opinions in the *Public Prayer* cases of 1962 and 1963:

> But we find no constitutional requirement which makes it necessary for government to be hostile to religion and to throw its weight against efforts to widen the effective scope of religious influence. . . .[2]

The First Amendment, he had said earlier in his opinion, "does not say that in every and all respects there shall be separation of Church and State"; [3] and he elaborated later in a phrase much quoted by those opposed to later decisions by the Court, in general, and Douglas opinions, in particular, that "we are a religious people whose institutions presuppose a Supreme Being." [4]

But three dissenters, Justices Black, Frankfurter, and Jackson, not only regarded the majority's findings as going far beyond any constitutionally permissible "accommodation," but saw no difference (in the words of Mr. Justice Black, the author of the *McCollum* opinion) "even worthy of mention" between the Illinois and New York programs, except for the use of public school buildings. Black especially objected to what he regarded as the compulsory processes aspects of the New York practice: "New York," he wrote angrily, "is manipulating its compulsory education laws to help religious sects get pupils. *This is not separation but combination of Church and State*." [5] As for the different use of the school buildings, Black wrote: "As we attempted to make categorically clear, the *McCollum* decision

[1] *Zorach v. Clauson*, 343 U.S. 306 (1952), at 314.
[2] *Ibid.*
[3] *Ibid.*, at 312.
[4] *Ibid.*, at 313.
[5] *Ibid.*, at 318. (Italics supplied.)

would have been the same if the religious classes had *not* been held in the school buildings." [1] He concluded his opinion with an impassioned warning:

> State help to religion injects political and party prejudices into a holy field. It too often substitutes force for prayer, hate for love, and persecution for persuasion. Government should not be allowed, under cover of the soft euphemism of "co-operation," to steal into the sacred area of religious choice.[2]

To Mr. Justice Frankfurter, "the pith of the case" was that under New York's program, formalized religious instruction is substituted for other school activity which those who do not participate in the released time program are *compelled* to attend. He suggested that this coercion might well be met, and met constitutionally, if the public schools were to close their doors completely for an hour or two, leaving the pupils to go where they will, "to God or Mammon." This practice, known as "dismissed time," was then in vogue in three states, and readily upheld by the courts. Caustically, Mr. Justice Jackson, the third dissenter, commented that "my evangelistic brethren confuse an objection to compulsion with an objection to religion." [3] In his view the New York program operated to make religious sects beneficiaries of the power to compel children to attend secular schools, holding that the public school thereby "serves as a temporary jail for a pupil who will not go to Church." [4] He cautioned that "the day this country ceases to be free for irreligion it will cease to be free for religion—except for the sect that can win political power." [5] He ended his dissent on a note of combined alarm and sarcasm:

> ... the *McCollum* case has passed like a storm in a teacup. The wall which the Court was professing to erect between Church and State has become even more warped and twisted than I expected. Today's judgment will be more interesting to students of psychology and of the judicial processes than to students of constitutional law.[6]

The *Zorach* decision, however, has not yet been overruled, nor have any of the above cases, regardless of whether they reflected a theory

---

[1] *Ibid.*, at 316. (Italics supplied.)
[2] *Ibid.*, at 320.
[3] *Ibid.*, at 324.
[4] *Ibid.*
[5] *Ibid.*, at 325.
[6] *Ibid.*

of "strict separation," of "neutrality," or of "accommodation." Of the three, of course, the latter is clearly the only "pragmatic" one. That does not necessarily make it the "best," either in terms of constitutional application or in terms of public acceptability. But it does seem to serve as a viable bridge between the two religion clauses of the First Amendment; it takes notice of seemingly firmly established traditional practices, such as some of those outlined by Mr. Justice Brennan in his concurring opinion in the *Schempp* case; [1] and it [2] would probably "win" a clear majority in any popular referendum on the question—if one could ever be phrased so as to comprehend all of its vexatious aspects! [3] But conceding the "popularity" of the "accommodation" theory does not necessarily imply either its wisdom or its ultimate constitutionality if it is expanded appreciably. It will be fascinating to see what, if anything, the Court will do in that connection when—as assuredly it will sooner or later—the 1965 Federal Aid to Elementary and Secondary Education Act, with its partial subventions to parochial as well as public elementary and secondary schools, reaches the high tribunal for review of the basic constitutional problems involved.

Meanwhile, it may be helpful to provide a tabular recapitulation of the more significant decisions the Supreme Court of the United States has handed down to date (January 1967) on separation of Church and State. (See Tables III and IV on pages 226-9.)

Separation and the Problem of Aid to Non-Public Schools

Tables III and IV and the textual discussion hopefully make clear that of all the questions posed by the delicate and emotion-charged issue of non-establishment, the leading one has been the type, the

[1] *Abington School District v. Schempp* and *Murray v. Curlett*, 374 U.S. 203 (1963). But there must be a limit to these "traditional practices."

[2] Harold D. Hammett, in an article entitled "Separation of Church and State: By One Wall or Two?," 7 *Journal of Church and State*, suggests a "two-walls" solution that would more or less embrace this doctrine. It resembles strongly the Kurland approach, discussed above.

[3] In addition to the fact that the latter is more than doubtful, the writer hastens to add that he knows that our Constitution does not provide for referenda, or any other form of what is known as "direct democracy" on the *federal* level; on the other hand, many states do, of course, provide for it in one or more forms. On "direct democracy" see J. A. Corry and Henry J. Abraham, *Elements of Democratic Government*, 4th ed. (New York: Oxford University Press, 1964), pp. 410-14.

Table III

"Separation of Church and State" Cases * in Which the Court Found No Constitutional Violation

DATE	CASE	VOTE	CONST'L ISSUES DECIDED	COMMENTARY
1872	Watson v. Jones, 13 Wallace 679.	5:2	Decision of Kentucky state courts as to which of two Louisville Presbyterian church factions had the legal right to possess and operate a local church held binding on the churches by U.S. Supreme Court.	The U.S. Supreme Court recognized here that the freedom and independence of churches would be in grave danger if it undertook to define religious heresy or orthodoxy or to decide which of two factions was the "true faith."
1899	Bradfield v. Roberts, 175 U.S. 291.	9:0	May Congress appropriate funds ($30,000) for a District of Columbia hospital, operated by a sisterhood of the Roman Catholic Church but chartered by Congress?	Peckham held for unanimous Court that the 1st Amendment was not violated, since the hospital, as a corporation chartered by Congress, is a "purely secular agency", and does not become a religious one merely because its members are Catholic nuns.
1908	Quick Bear v. Leupp, 210 U.S. 50.	9:0	Could U.S. Government legally disburse treaty and other funds of which it was trustee for Indians (their real owners) to private religious schools at the designation of the Indians to defray their tuition costs?	Arrangement held constitutional on grounds that the U.S. Government is necessarily "undenominational" and cannot make any law respecting an establishment of religion. It merely held the funds in a fiduciary capacity for the Indians.

* Some cases, such as The Sunday Closing Cases, in which the "free exercise" issues predominated, are found in Table I.

1930	*Cochran v. Louisiana State Board of Education*, 281 U.S. 370.	8:0	Validity of a Louisiana statute providing for purchase of *secular* textbooks for use by public *and* non-public, including parochial, school children.	Initial application of the *"child benefit"* approach. Here, Court held that benefits went to the "children of the state," not to the "private schools *per se*." Due process decision.
1947	*Everson v. Board of Education of Ewing Township*, N.J., 330 U.S. 1.	5:4	Validity of N.J. statute authorizing bus fare reimbursement to parents of private (non-profit) and here parochial, as well as public, school students.	Statute upheld. The famed "wall" decision. (See body of chapter for discussion and analysis.)
1952	*Zorach v. Clauson*, 343 U.S. 306.	6:3	Validity of New York's "released time" program in New York City's public schools.	Upheld because of its special circumstances. (See body of chapter for discussion and analysis.)

TABLE IV

"Separation of Church and State" Cases * in Which the Court Did Find Constitutional Violation

DATE	CASE	VOTE	CONST'L ISSUES DECIDED	COMMENTARY
1815	*Terrett v. Tyler,* 9 Cranch 43.	5:0	Validity of Virginia recession statute that rescinded the charter of the Virginia Episcopal Church as a corporation and directed that its parish lands be sold and its proceeds used for the poor of the parish.	Not *truly* a "separation" issue, for case was decided under principles of general corporate law. Nonetheless, case established the principle that a state cannot deny to members of a religious corporation the right to retain a corporate charter and continue to act as a corporation.
1925	*Pierce v. Society of Sisters of the Holy Names of Jesus and Mary,* 268 U.S. 510.	9:0	Constitutionality of Oregon's Compulsory Education Act of 1922 requiring every child from eight to sixteen to attend *public* school. (The "Sisters" conducted a group of *private* schools, according to the tenets of the Roman Catholic Church.)	The Act held to interfere "unreasonably," with the liberty of parents and guardians to direct the upbringing and education of children under their control. (Also not purely a "separation" case issue, but related to it.) Similarly, see *Meyer v. Nebraska,* 262 U.S. 390 (1923).
1948	*Illinois ex rel McCollum v. Board of Education,* 333 U.S. 203.	8:1	Validity of Champaign, Ill., arrangements permitting "released time" programs on public school property under attendance sanctions.	Struck down as violative of separation concepts inherent in Amendments One and Fourteen. (See body of chapter for discussion and analysis.)

* Some cases, such as *Forcaso v. Watkins,* involving *both* issues, are found in Table II.

1952	*Kedroff v. Saint Nicholas Cathedral*, 344 U.S. 94.	8:1	Authority of New York State to deprive the Moscow hierarchy of the Russian Orthodox Church of control over all its Church property in New York by forceful transfer to the local "Russian Church in America."	A state is no more allowed than the federal government to enact a law impairing the separation of Church and State. Government has no capacity to intervene in religious controversies or determine which is "the true faith."
1962	*Engel v. Vitale*, 370 U.S. 421.	8:1	Constitutionality of New York State composed and administered 22-word non-denominational prayer in public schools.	"The New York laws officially prescribing the Regents' prayer are inconsistent with both the purposes of the Establishment Clause and with the Establishment Clause itself." (See Ch. VI.)
1963	*Abington School District v. Schempp* and *Murray v. Curlett*, 374 U.S. 203.	8:1	Validity of Pennsylvania's statutory requirement of reading of 10 verses from Holy Bible in public schools and Maryland's practice of daily Bible reading and Lord's Prayer recitation in public schools.	All three procedures held to violate the establishment clause, following *Engel.* (See Ch. VI for discussion and analysis.)

degree, and the conditions under which governmental aid can be constitutionally extended to non-public schools. To all intents and purposes, this means predominantly Roman Catholic schools. Regardless of which of the three theories of separation one may regard as most appropriate, there are no easy answers—either on procedural or substantive grounds. The facts of life (1967), on the other hand, are plain: The parents of almost 6,000,000 parochial school children, 93 per cent of them Roman Catholic, are members of the body politic and wield political power. When all is said and done, the issue ultimately falls into the *policy-field*, heavily surcharged with considerations of public welfare in a pluralistic society with a democratic base. The sole remaining question then becomes that of the *constitutionality* of such programs as government, be it state or federal, chooses to adopt. *Is* the program a violation of the pertinent aspects of the First and/or Fourteenth Amendments?

As we have had ample opportunity to see, the judiciary, and the Supreme Court of the United States in particular, have not been able to provide a clear-cut response to the constitutional question. At times they have upheld certain policies, at others they have struck them down. It must never be forgotten, however, that an additional consideration at the bar of judicial decision-making is the strong predisposition of the Court to exercise judicial self-restraint vis-à-vis legislative enactments. The Court's avowed purpose, given at least some doubt about a measure's legitimacy, is to *save*, not to destroy. It is our recognition of this basic maxim of judicial self-restraint that will enable us to understand decisions that, at least on paper, would seem to be diametrically opposite. Hence we have witnessed three levels of approach which the Court has taken here:

Level 1. The Court *strikes down* a measure or practice as a clearly and demonstrably unconstitutional infringement of the no establishment clause—*because* it is simply and patently unconstitutional (and usually so regarded by a heavy majority, if not always unanimity of the justices). Some obvious examples are:

> the *Illinois Released Time* case,[1] where the released time programs were held on public school property (8:1);
>
> the *Oregon Compulsory Education Law* case,[2] where that State *required* attendance at *public* schools (9:0);

[1] *Illinois ex rel McCollum v. Board of Education*, 333 U.S. 203 (1948).
[2] *Pierce v. Society of Sisters of the Holy Names*, 268 U.S. 510 (1925).

the *New York Prayer* case,[1] where the New York State-composed and administered public school prayer was declared unconstitutional (8:1);

the *Pennsylvania and Maryland Bible Reading* cases,[2] where statutes and practices requiring public school reading of Bibles and the Lord's Prayer met a like fate (8:1).

Although fully aware of the relative unpopularity of its decisions, especially in the last two illustrations—which evoked a violent popular reaction that was often uninformed and sometimes absurd, given the clear limits of the decisions involved [3]—the Court did not hesitate to do what it clearly considered its duty under the commands of the Constitution. And it did so with but 3 of 36 votes in dissent, 1 of these coming on procedural rather than substantive grounds.

Level 2. The Court perhaps somewhat uncomfortably at times, and often severely divided, *upholds* a measure or practice because it believes that it can stand under the principle of "auxiliary" rather than "primary" governmental aid to a non-public school situation. This we have seen rationalized earlier under the controversial "child benefit theory." Appropriate illustrations are:

the *Louisiana Textbooks to All* case,[4] which enabled use of public-funds-purchased textbooks by pupils of public *and* non-public schools (8:0), although this case was actually decided on "due process" grounds rather than on the religious issue *per se*;

the *New Jersey Bus* case,[5] the famous "wall" decision, upholding public subventions for transportation of parochial as well as public school students (5:4);

the *New York Released Time* case,[6] where religious classes were held *outside* public schools buildings during the school

---

[1] *Engel v. Vitale*, 370 U.S. 421 (1962).

[2] *Abington School District v. Schempp* and *Murray v. Curlett*, 374 U.S. 203 (1963).

[3] Shouted Representative George Andrews (D.-Ala.) on the floor of the U.S. House of Representatives: "They let the Negroes in and now they have thrown God out!" For a catalogue of public, private, and press reactions, see Philip B. Kurland in Oaks, *op. cit.*, "The School Prayer Cases," pp. 142 ff, esp. pp. 142-7.

[4] *Cochran v. Louisiana State Board of Education*, 281 U.S. 370 (1930).

[5] *Everson v. Board of Education of Ewing Township*, 330 U.S. 1 (1947).

[6] *Zorach v. Clauson*, 343 U.S. 306 (1952).

day for those wishing to attend, with the others continuing secular education (6:3).

Here, although sharply split with seven of twenty votes in dissent (one-third compared with one twelfth in the Level #1 group), the Court believed itself justified to accommodate public policy that raised questions about, but was not regarded as violative of, separation.

Level 3: The Court, on the basis of the principle of judicial self-restraint or because it adjudges the matter *res judicata*, either refuses to accept a case for review or simply affirms the decision below. This judicial practice may well have the effect of sanctioning practices in one state that are unconstitutional in another, since in each separate instance they were so held by the state courts concerned; but considerations of federalism are far from absent in the judicial process! Some random instances are:

> Despite its decision confirming Louisiana's free textbooks for parochial schools law, the Court denied *certiorari* in an Oregon case,[1] thereby upholding a 6:1 decision by Oregon's Supreme Court that school districts must *stop* providing free textbooks to parochial schools, and it even re-confirmed that decision one year later.

> Despite its decision in the *New Jersey Bus* case of 1948, the Court has refused to review innumerable state court decisions declaring *unconstitutional*, as violative of the respective state constitutions, free transportation provisions for parochial as well as public school children in, among others, Alaska, Iowa, Missouri, New Mexico, Oklahoma, Washington, and Wisconsin. In fact, all of these came after the *New Jersey Bus* case—and by 1967 in only two states, Connecticut and Pennsylvania, had courts *upheld* that type of law since the United States Supreme Court spoke in 1948. Obviously, the issue is far from settled insofar as some of the states go,[2] but the federal tribunal has not been eager to become re-

---

[1] *Dickman v. School District, Oregon City*, 371 U.S. 823 (1962).

[2] In 1967, state *constitutions* expressly prohibited the following: establishment of any religion by law (8); compelling any person to support a religion (7); expenditures of public monies for "religious establishment" (11); and expenditures of public funds for sectarian schools(34).

involved. Yet a multiple challenge to the new Pennsylvania Bus Law was on its way to the Supreme Court as these pages went to press in February 1967.

Despite other state precedents *to the contrary,* the Court refused to review,[1] and thereby upheld, a Vermont Supreme Court decision holding unconstitutional the use of public funds for tuition payable to children attending either public or private schools of their own choice in the instance of towns that had no high schools of their own.

Again, despite other state practices to the contrary, the Court refused to review,[2] and thus upheld, a 4:3 Court of Appeals of Maryland decision that declared unconstitutional as a violation of the *First* Amendment the subvention of matching state grants for construction purposes to two Maryland Roman Catholic colleges (Notre Dame and St. Joseph) and one Methodist college (Western Maryland), while upholding similar grants to Hood College. It had regarded Hood's character "essentially secular," but deemed the other three as clearly projecting a religious "image." (On the other hand, as we noted above,[3] the Court *also* affirmed a decision by Maryland that *upheld* state tax *exemptions* for church buildings!)

In terms of experience these three "levels" are readily explainable, and just as readily serve to re-emphasize the difficulty, if not perhaps the utter impossibility, of creating and drawing a viable, predictable line between the permissible and the impermissible in the realm of the establishment clause, in general, and in that of the subsection of public and private education, in particular. Still, some outlines are perceptible in general terms—if not in specific Court judgments —and they are identifiable, with no claim to clairvoyance as to future Court policy, particularly when the Court confronts, as surely it will sooner or later, aspects of the Federal Aid to Education Act of 1965.

---

[1] *Anderson v. Swart,* 366 U.S. 925 (1961).
[2] *Board of Public Works of Maryland v. Horace Mann League of U.S.,* 385 U.S. 97 (1966), and *Horace Mann League of U.S. v. Board of Public Works of Maryland,* 385 U.S. 97 (1966).
[3] See p. 221, n. 3, *supra.*

Some Over-all Policy Positions. A handful of these outlines have clearly emerged and thus may be stated broadly as follows:

First, because it is intended to serve pupils of all religious faiths, a public school in democratic society is *ipso facto* a secular institution. This, of course, does not mean that the public school either is, should be, or is intended to be anti- or irreligious—and the judiciary as well as the legislature have made this amply clear.

Second, freedom of conscience in all its religious aspects and concepts must be, and is, protected.

Third, although it is axiomatic that it is incumbent upon the federal government to protect freedom of religion and ascertain the separation of Church and State in the several states of the Union, responsibility for public school curriculum and administration lodges with the latter—although the Federal Aid to Elementary and Secondary Education Act of 1965 may well have a far-reaching amendatory impact upon that tradition.

Fourth, public education in the several states is controlled preeminently by duly appointed and/or elected public state officials.

Fifth, although attendance at public schools is inevitably one of the hallmarks of the body-politic in the several states, no state may compel school age students to attend public schools as distinct from private or parochial schools, and no state has tried to do so since Oregon's defeat at the hands of a unanimous Supreme Court in the *Pierce Case* [1] in 1925.

Sixth, either by constitutional provision or by statute almost all of the fifty states have endeavored to prevent the "direct" disbursement or subvention of any funds from the public state treasury to any parochial or otherwise denominational school. On the other hand, some states, in fact most, have permitted or even encouraged the providing of one or more, or even all, of the following "auxiliary" services to be extended to accredited non-public schools: tax exemptions; free lunches; free medical care; free protective services; free school nurse services; free textbooks; free bus transportation; and other similar services usually termed "indirect," "general," or "auxiliary." It should be noted again here, however, that many of these practices have either been specifically forbidden in some states and/or

[1] *Pierce v. Society of Sisters of the Holy Names,* 268 U.S. 510.

held to be unconstitutional by their state courts, while the precise *opposite* has been held in others.[1]

Seventh, even prior to the *Illinois Released Time* case,[2] the type of denominational or sectarian teaching there at issue was specifically forbidden by most states. Yet a number always did, and some now do since the *New York Released Time* case,[3] permit the kind of "released time" practiced in New York.

Eighth, state-mandated religious observances in the public schools such as prayers, Bible reading, recitation of the Lord's Prayer, used widely in various states [4] and banned in a good many others [5] prior to the New York, Pennsylvania and Maryland 1962 and 1963 Supreme Court decisions,[6] are no longer legal. And as it has already demonstrated repeatedly,[7] the Supreme Court no doubt will make short shrift of any subterfuges. The collateral question of the observance in the public schools of Christmas and other religious holidays has never reached the Supreme Court, although it well may. At the state court level, this matter—which raises such emotion-prone, difficult social issues—has seen one adverse [8] and one qualifiedly adverse ruling.[9]

The above eight guidelines to policy on the separation of Church and State vis-à-vis aid to non-public schools, and/or recognition of sectarian practices therein, are firmly established and should continue to be generally accepted, if not necessarily universally approved. But a new complexion may well have been introduced into the picture with the passage of the 1965 Federal Aid to Elementary and Second-

[1] The continuing controversy is demonstrated by the successful *veto* by Delaware Governor Charles L. Terry, Jr., early in 1966 of a bill that would have provided free bus transportation for parochial and other private school students. At approximately the same time Governor W. W. Scranton of Pennsylvania *signed* a similar measure. Both chief executives acted—or at least professed to act—in accordance with constitutional mandates governing such aid.

[2] *Illinois ex rel McCollum v. Board of Education,* 333 U.S. 203 (1948).

[3] *Zorach v. Clauson,* 343 U.S. 306 (1952).

[4] E.g. Alabama, Arizona, Indiana, Idaho, Maine, New Jersey.

[5] E.g. Alaska, Illinois, Nevada, Wyoming, Washington.

[6] *Engel v. Vitale,* 370 U.S. 421 (1962), and *Abington School District v. Schempp* and *Murray v. Curlett,* 374 U.S. 203 (1963).

[7] See footnotes 2 and 3, p. 219 *supra.*

[8] Florida: *Chamberlain v. Dade County Board of Public Instruction,* 143 So. 2d 21 (Fla., 1962).

[9] *Baer v. Kolmorgen,* 14 Misc. 2d 1015 (N.Y., 1960).

ary Education Act, with its controversial provisions of potentially crucial importance to the meaning of the First Amendment.

The 1965 Federal Aid to Elementary and Secondary Education Act. The concept of federal aid to education is not, of course, new. What is new is the revolutionary departure from precedent contained in the 1965 bill: Breaking historic ground, it has provided subventions of *federal money for elementary and secondary instruction for children in both public and parochial schools.* Sundry measures in the field of education, in which private schools and colleges participated, had been passed prior to 1965, but none of these had tackled the ticklish instructional federal aid to non-public schools below the college level. Among them were: the "G.I. Bill," the National School Lunch Act, the Special Milk Program, college housing, the Higher Education Facilities Act, the National Defense Education Act, the College Housing Loan Program, the National Science Foundation Program, and Atomic Energy Commission Fellowships. But because of the lasting opposition of educators, lawyers, and churchmen instructional aid was never included—and as a result no general federal aid to education measure ever saw the light of day until it reached the hands of Lyndon B. Johnson, who submitted his bill in 1964 and saw it enacted into law in 1965.

To the surprise of many, notwithstanding the recognition of President Johnson's political *savoir faire,* the bill went through both houses of Congress without a big Church-State fight, without a Conservative-Liberal battle, without a racial row. Indeed, it passed Congress without a single major change after it had been first introduced for the Johnson Administration by Representative Carl D. Perkins (D.-Ky.). It passed because the President had managed to convince most, if not all, of those either involved or interested that the entire scheme would collapse if anyone were to tinker with his bill. Although it truly pleased really no one, all the traditional protagonists supported the measure or at least did not oppose it: the National Education Association, the National Catholic Welfare Conference, the American Federation of Teachers, the American Jewish Congress, Americans for Democratic Action, Baptists, Methodists, and a coterie of other religious, educational, labor, and civil rights organizations. Heretofore, every past effort to see a general federal aid to education bill pass Congress had faltered for three overriding reasons: the opposition of the hard core of anti-big-government, conservative members of Congress; the opposition of the die-hard Southerners whose districts were in dire need of the kind of financial aid only the federal kitty could provide, but who had steadfastly opposed the legislation because of the perennial "Powell Amendment" that barred segregated use of the funds; and the opposition engendered by the delicate religious issue, with almost all Roman Catholics opposed to any bill that by-passed their parochial schools, and most Protestants and Jews opposed to any bill which did *not* by-pass aid to parochial schools.

President Johnson licked all three problems. The first was eliminated by the drastic reduction of conservative senators and congressmen as a result of the 1964 election. The race issue was by-passed in view of Title VI of the Civil Rights Act of 1964, banning the use of federal funds for segregated activities. The religious issue was the most difficult, of course, yet as a superb and experienced parliamentarian and tactician, Johnson was equal to the task. It was a task that his Roman Catholic predecessor in office had been unwilling even to consider: President Kennedy believed the inclusion of direct federal financial assistance to elementary and secondary schools to be of extremely doubtful constitutionality—or at least he chose to give that impression publicly in the famous Ribicoff Administration Brief of 1961.[1]

Determined to get a general aid-to-education measure through the Eighty-ninth Congress, and blessed with a two-thirds Democratic majority that might not soon again be available to him, President Johnson, however, was not to be stopped by the religious issue. He met it in several ingenious ways: First, he drafted his program as one in line with the Supreme Court's "child benefit" approach. Second, he more or less restricted the bill to the poor and needy; its primary benefits were assigned to counties and school districts with ten or more children of families with a yearly income of less than $2000. Next, the United States Office of Education was authorized to allocate grants, initially to the tune of $100 million, to the states for the purchase of textbooks and library materials to go to Church-controlled and other private non-profit as well as public schools. The language of this particular provision was closely tailored to the Louisiana statute that, as we noted above in the *Cochran* case,[2] successfully survived a constitutional onslaught in 1930—although it had turned

[1] See its reproduction in *The New York Times*, March 29, 1961.
[2] *Cochran v. Louisiana*, 281 U.S. 370 (1930).

predominantly on "due process." To the irrefutable argument that some states expressly *forbid* that type of bookgrant or even loan, the Administration's response was that *it*, rather than the states, would be the "owner" of the books and could, of course, loan them to the children concerned.[1] The last aspect of the Administration's strategy in defeating or isolating the religious issue as a factor of opposition to the over-all program, was an on-the-record promise by President Johnson to a number of balky, key Northern urban and suburban members of Congress to go "all out" to alleviate the overcrowded classrooms and half-day sessions so prevalent there. In typically forceful language he assured these critical legislators in March 1965 that he would

> use every rostrum and every forum and every searchlight that I can to tell the people of this country and their elected representatives that we can no longer afford over-crowded classrooms and half-day sessions.[2]

On the morning following this clinching declaration, the House Committee on Education and Labor reported the bill out favorably. The House ultimately passed it by a vote of 263:153, and the Senate, where the bill had been entrusted to Senator Wayne Morse (D.-Ore.), followed suit early in April by a vote of 73:18. For the first time, both houses of Congress had thus approved a broad ($1.3 billion) federal program to aid elementary and secondary education, regardless of the school's secular or non-secular character. The President triumphantly signed the bill into law on April 11, 1965. The proverbial fat was now in the fire!

---

1 That this reasoning would not necessarily be universally acceptable was demonstrated rather quickly: Late in August 1966, New York State Supreme Court Justice T. Paul Kane ruled in violation of the New York State Constitution a new state law, passed as a result of the 1965 federal statute, providing funds to public schools for the purchase of textbooks to be "loaned" to parochial school students. Moreover, he pointed to *both* the free exercise and establishment clauses of the First Amendment in the *federal* Constitution as proscribing any such arrangement. Answering those supporters who had advanced the "child benefit" theory, Kane said that "pupils are part of the school" and aid to them was the same as aid to the school (*Board of Education of East Greenbush v. Allen*, 51 Misc. 2d 297). The State then appealed Kane's decision to its higher tribunal, the Appellate Division, whose five justices *reversed* Kane in a split decision on Dec. 31, 1966. The case was then appealed to the highest New York Court and, whatever its decision, an ultimate U.S. Supreme Court test was probable.

2 As re-quoted in *The Philadelphia Evening Bulletin*, April 9, 1965.

The Constitutional Attack on the 1965 Act. Exactly two days later the first steps were taken to mount the anticipated constitutional attack on the revolutionary measure. The National Governing Council of the American Jewish Congress, which has a record of close alliance with liberal Protestant denominations on the Church-State issue, announced that it would seek a court test of the three most controversial and most precedent-departing provisions of the Act. Urging that the "grave issues that have been raised during the long debate on the [statute] must be resolved promptly—before the church-state separation guarantee in the Bill of Rights is eroded to the point of extinction," [1] the A.J.C. thus moved to ask for constitutional tests on the following:

(1) The dual enrollment or "shared time" arrangements authorized under the bill—to the extent that these result in the "commingling" of public and parochial school faculties, facilities, and/or administration. (Under "shared time" programs the time of parochial school children is divided between public and parochial schools; i.e. for "religiously neutral" subjects—such as languages and physics—the child goes to the former; for the social sciences to the latter.)

(2) Those provisions under which public school teachers and public school equipment will be sent into parochial schools under the bill's program of "supplementary educational centers." (Under Title III $100 million was allocated for remedial instruction, teaching machines, and laboratory equipment, teachers, and other services to public *and* non-profit private schools.)

(3) The aforementioned provisions, in Title II of the Act, under which textbooks purchased with $100 million of federal funds will be made available to Catholic, Protestant, and Jewish parochial schools—the vast majority to the first—as well as to public schools.

As of early 1967, the federal judicial branch had not as yet become directly involved in what will surely become a fascinating and far-reaching denouement.[2] It would be folly to predict what the courts,

[1] As quoted in *The Christian Science Monitor*, April 13, 1965.

[2] It is important to recognize here, however, how difficult it is to obtain the necessary "standing" in this type of proposed legal test. In the famous and never overruled 1923 case of *Frothingham v. Mellon*, 262 U.S. 447, the Supreme Court held unanimously that a *federal* taxpayer lacked "standing" to sue and had not presented a *bona fide* "case or controversy" under the Constitution for federal court review of a challenge to appropriations under the federal Maternity Act of

and ultimately the Supreme Court of the United States, will do. Based on precedent and the provisions' clever language, however, item (3) should surely weather the final test. No one, however, could be so bold as to venture even an educated guess regarding items (1) and (2).[1] Unquestionably they modify, if they do not in fact invade, traditional standards of separation of Church and State. The ultimate answer to be sought, however, is whether in the eyes of the Supreme Court they so violate those standards that they must be struck down; or, whether they can be categorized as "auxiliary," and thus the kind of constitutionally permissible services that have been held *not* to breach the "wall" or violate "neutrality," but rather to represent acceptable aspects of "accommodation"—such as: subsidized school-

---

1921. This holding did not then, nor has it since, applied to *state* "taxpayer suits" acting under *state* laws, but it is *res judicata* for federal cases. In order to remedy the latter, a situation that in effect renders it all but impossible to get the federal courts to determine whether, in fact, the First Amendment had been violated by such federal legislation as the 1965 Act, legislation was quickly introduced in Congress. Most promising was S.2097, entitled "An Act to Enforce the First Amendment to the Constitution," co-sponsored by Senator Wayne Morse (D.-Ore.), the floor manager of the 1965 Act, and Senator Sam J. Ervin, Jr. (D.-N.C.), Chairman of the Subcommittee on Constitutional Rights of the Senate Committee on the Judiciary. Their bill, which passed the Senate by voice vote in July 1966, but was not acted upon in the House prior to adjournment, provided specifically for judicial review to determine the constitutionality of grants or loans under nine Acts of Congress. If properly challenged, the constitutionality of seven education and health programs enacted prior to the 89th Congress *in addition* to all other legislation enacted after January 1, 1965, and administered by the Department of Health, Education, and Welfare, would have thus become duly reviewable in the federal courts. Senator Ervin, publicly backed by 207 college and university presidents, announced that he would promptly re-introduce the bill "on the first day of the 90th Congress"—especially in view of the Supreme Court's refusal to upset Maryland's ban on public grants to "essentially secular" colleges. (See p. 233, *supra*.) He did: S-3. For a detailed explanation of "standing" and "case or controversy," see Henry J. Abraham, *The Judicial Process: An Introductory Analysis of the Courts of the United States, England, and France* (New York: Oxford University Press, 1962), pp. 310ff. For a good analysis of the Morse-Ervin bill, see *The Christian Science Monitor*, April 27, 1966, and August 1, 1966, and subsequent reports entitled "Judicial Review and the First Amendment," by the Subcommittee on Constitutional Rights of the Committee on the Judiciary of the United States Senate.

1 On Dec. 1, 1966 a group representing public school parents and teachers filed a federal court action in the form of a motion for an injunction against the Act's allocation of funds to parochial schools by U.S. Education Commissioner Harold Howe and Health, Education and Welfare Secretary John W. Gardner. By February 1967, thirty-two cases were pending—e.g. in New York, Ohio, Pennsylvania, Michigan, Hawaii, New Jersey, Rhode Island, Illinois, Missouri, Oregon.

bussing, attendance-supervised "released time," and the numerous others which we have discussed.

Coda. And, of course, there is a further consideration. Would the Court be willing to strike down provisions that form the very heart of a legislative enactment passed by an almost two-thirds majority of the people's representatives in Congress, who had evidently been converted to the proposition that a price, even perhaps a constitutional one, had to be paid to get the much-needed and much sought aid to our schools as a matter of public policy? It must never be forgotten that, if not in the short run, certainly in the *long* one, the Court reflects even as it reveals the nature of American society; that although it is an educator and teacher there are limits to which it can go in the face of determined, overwhelming opposition by the body-politic—a body-politic wedded to those pluralistic concepts of which diverse schools form such an important part. The intriguing policy question raised by the legislation's opponents, what the expected proliferation of private schools would do to what many regard as the core of America's democratic melting pot, the public school itself, the Court as such can not consider. What the Supreme Court of the United States says and holds indeed "reflects not only the competing interests and values at stake, but also its own role in accommodating constitutional interpretation to the demands of a pluralistic society." [1]

This is not to say that there are no limits: The Court, as we have seen time and again, does ultimately reach and determine lines, and, as the *Bible Reading and Prayer* cases [2] have demonstrated well, no amount of popular reaction and vilification will stop the Court from calling its shots on its often lonely pinnacle of responsibility when, convinced of its rightful duty under our Constitution, it knows it must say "no" to Government and the society which it serves. Another time for decision is already on the horizon.

[1] Kauper, *op. cit.*, p. 79.
[2] *Engel v. Vitale*, 370 U.S. 421 (1962); *Abington School District v. Schempp* and *Murray v. Curlett*, 374 U.S. 203 (1963).

VII

Race: The American Dilemma

IN THEORY the subject of this last chapter in our study should not present the sort of difficult line-drawing that has pervaded considerations of the topics already discussed. Surely, in the third quarter of the twentieth century *race* could hardly, in enlightened democratic society, determine the outcome of an individual's quest for equality before the law and equality of opportunity. Yet theory does not necessarily govern practice, and although we have seen long strides taken toward the egalitarian goals of Negroes, both under law and in the mores of society, racial discrimination is still America's Achilles heel. Great progress has accompanied the decades following World War II, especially since the late 1950's, both in the extra-legal, private sector of our life, and in the legal sector. The sentiments and prejudices of large sections of the people in the North as well as in the South, die hard—if indeed they die at all. And government, under the Constitution the great line-drawer in the absence of voluntary action, must always be cautious lest it move too far in advance of those sentiments and prejudices. For full enforcement of the civil rights of all, there must be mutual trust and respect—and although government can accomplish much to promote trust and respect, it cannot ultimately be a substitute for the slow, hard process of education. Still, as the race problem has shown so well, leadership by responsible public officials is not only desirable but crucial at all stages. When the race controversy reached its zenith in the mid-1950's, it was once again the judicial branch of the government, with the Supreme Court at its apex, which led. While it did not lead eargerly or joyously, a people's rightful claims could no longer be ignored merely because the political, in particular the legislative, branches refused to become involved beyond the most cursory of levels, and in fact passed the proverbial buck to the Court. It is an intriguing question how much strife might have been spared and how much understanding might have been engendered, had the elective branches of the government provided the leadership with which they are charged and, as subsequent events proved, of which they are capable when pressed.

By the start of 1967 there were some 22 million Negroes in the United States—roughly 11 per cent of a total population of close to 200 million. On paper, at least, these Negroes had won their battle for equality. Segregation barriers were indeed tumbling everywhere; all three branches of the federal government, and many state governments, had made resolutely clear that race would no longer be permitted to stand as a valid factor of classification in any public or quasi-public sphere. The tough Civil Rights Act of 1964 and the equally tough Voting Rights Act of 1965 had become the law of the land and were being enforced with considerable vigor; desegregation of public educational facilities in all parts of the country, including the deepest South,[1] had begun; and the Civil Rights Act of 1966 had been submitted to Congress—although it failed to pass (of which more later). High-ranking Negro public officials were in evidence at all levels of government.

The voters of Massachusetts, a state with but 2 per cent Negroes in its population, sent Edward W. Brooke to the U.S. Senate to replace their retiring Brahmin Leverett Saltonstall. For the first time since Reconstruction was a Negro thus chosen to enter "the world's most exclusive club"—and by a whopping majority over a distinguished Massachusetts Yankee of unquestioned civil libertarian persuasion, Endicott Peabody. The catalogue of accomplishments was indeed "proud and impressive." Between the Civil War and the Korean War the Negro rate of illiteracy had dropped from 90 to less than 5 per cent. In a survey of 68 cities the National Urban League, an old and responsible Negro interest group, found that Negro home owners were improving their properties rapidly and that 70 per cent were being rated as "sound" by the government. It was clear that

[1] Generally speaking, five Southern states are usually classified as the Deep South: South Carolina, Georgia, Louisiana, Alabama, and Mississippi. The six other members of the Confederacy are commonly simply called Southern: Virginia, North Carolina, Florida, Arkansas, Tennessee, and Texas. Six are normally classified as Border states: Delaware, Maryland, West Virginia, Kentucky, Oklahoma, and Missouri.

there was now a rising Negro middle class in the United States. In fifteen years the number of Negroes in institutions of higher learning had doubled, and in ten years the number of non-white professional workers had also doubled. The median income of female Negro college graduates exceeded that of white women.[1] As already indicated, Negroes were no longer rarities in the professions or in high government positions.

Yet the demonstrable psychological toll inflicted on the Negro race in America over almost three centuries was clearly in evidence and often characterized by an impatience that, however understandable, threatened to play havoc with the newly established line of equality of opportunity. Moreover, the fires of serious personal prejudice were not only still burning but, because of assertive civil rights clamor, were threatening to engulf areas they had not hitherto reached —especially in Northern urban and suburban areas. The frightful August 1965 riots in the Watts section of Los Angeles—which re-erupted on a minor scale in March and May 1966—lasted six days, resulted in 34 deaths, 1032 injuries, the arrest of 3952 persons, and in $40 million in property damage (more than 600 buildings were damaged, 200 totally destroyed). They—and the serious, often even bloody, riots of 1966 that engulfed the Northern urban centers of Cleveland, Chicago, St. Louis, San Francisco, and many others—served as a shocking and costly reminder that the mere removal of legal barriers to equality was not enough; that the principle of equality included economic, if not social equality; that fear and lack of communication were still rampant; and that frustration could readily lead to anger and thence to blind unreasoned violence. Prejudice and poverty, poverty of both means and demand, still stood in the way. Despite "proud and impressive achievements," President Johnson had said in a commencement address at Harvard University in June 1965, "despite the court orders and the laws, despite the legislative victories and the speeches, ... the walls are rising and the gulf is widening ... for the great majority of Negro Americans—the poor, the unemployed, the uprooted and the dispossessed. ..." [2]

As the President spoke, there was ample evidence of what he called our "American failure." Three times as many Negroes as whites were unemployed. Of Negro women who married 13.7 per cent were

[1] *The Philadelphia Inquirer*, October 21, 1965, p. 13.
[2] *Ibid.*

separated or divorced (compared to 4.3 per cent of white women), and one Negro family in four was fatherless. Infant mortality, which had been 70 per cent greater for non-whites in 1940, was 90 per cent greater in 1960. Of all Negroes 25 years of age or older, 74.4 per cent had not finished high school, compared to 49.8 per cent of whites; the rate of failure on the mental ability examination for the draft was 67.5 per cent, compared to 18.8 per cent among non-Negroes; and 40.9 per cent of Negro male workers had incomes of less than $2000 a year, compared to 24.2 per cent of white male workers. Median income for Negro males was approximately one-half that of whites.[1]

The gulf was not only present, but for a good many Negroes it was widening. Of an extra-legal nature and outside the evident sphere of government, it gave rise to insistent and greater demands, not infrequently backed by what became known as "action in the streets" rather than in the courts or in legislative halls. This action, in turn, prompted considerable feeling on the part of the white community that what had hitherto been regarded as legitimate grievances based on legitimate demands had now become unreasonable and unjustifiable demands for "special" or "privileged" treatment. Public authorities thus found themselves face to face with the problem of drawing lines, particularly in the difficult and uncomfortable sphere of line-drawing between *public* and *private* action, and the attendant legal and governmental responsibilities. Just how, where, and by whom could or should such a line be established? A summary glance into the history of racial discrimination in the United States serves as a prolegomenon to some attempted answers, if indeed we can even speak of answers. There may well be none in practice even if they should be apparent in theory.

A GLANCE AT HISTORY

Although the Declaration of Independence had stipulated, as a self-evident truth, that "all men are created equal," it soon became obvious that, in the pithy comment of George Orwell, "some men are created more equal than others." The second section of the first article of the Constitution clearly recognized the existence of slavery in the United States by directing the inclusion of "three-fifths of all

[1] *Ibid.*, and *The New York Times*, October 9, 1966.

other persons," i.e. the *slaves*, in the enumeration which was to form
the basis for representative apportionment and taxation. True, Section 9 of Article I did make it possible to stop the "migration or
importation" of slaves after 1808, provided Congress chose to do so
then, and the Thirteenth Amendment was designed to settle the matter by outlawing slavery in 1865. But it was not really until the
ratification of the Fourteenth Amendment in 1868, five years after
Lincoln's Emancipation Proclamation, that the white-supremacy concept inherent in Article I was removed from the Constitution. In
the language of the Amendment's second section:

> Representatives shall be apportioned among the several States accord-
> ing to their respective numbers, *counting the whole number of persons
> in each State*, excluding Indians not taxed. . . .[1]

Yet despite these enactments, and despite the ringing exhortation
of Section 1 of Amendment XIV (quoted below), and despite the
language of the Fifteenth Amendment of 1870 that on its face seemed
to assure to the Negro the privilege of the ballot, neither the myth
of white supremacy nor the fact of color prejudice was wiped out.
Section 1 of the Fourteenth Amendment, now so significant but then
so ineffective, would have to wait more than eight decades for its
triumphs on behalf of the Negro:

> *All persons born or naturalized in the United States, and subject to
> the jurisdiction thereof, are citizens of the United States and of the
> State wherein they reside.* No state shall make or enforce any law which
> shall abridge the privileges or immunities of citizens of the United
> States; *nor shall any State deprive* any person of life, liberty, or prop-
> erty, without due process of law; *nor deny to any person within its
> jurisdiction the equal protection of the laws.*[2]

The Emancipation Proclamation and these three Civil War amendments intended, above all, to ameliorate the lot of the Negro by
attacking the constitutional silence on federal protection of civil
rights, a protection which had, until then, been left wholly to the
several states. They proved to be but paper tigers. True, Reconstruction briefly shot the Negro's star skyward; 22 Southern Negroes went
to Congress and two of them became United States senators from
Mississippi. True also that in the decade following the passage of

---

1 Opening sentence. (Italics supplied.)
2 Entire section quoted. (Italics supplied.)

the Thirteenth Amendment Congress enacted five major civil-rights statutes, spelling out the rights of the new Negro freedmen and providing penalties for their denial.[1] But the South proved itself equal to the challenge of restoring the *status quo ante* through a host of ingenious and ingenuous devices. By 1910 every former Confederate state, for example, had succeeded in disfranchising the Negro either by state statute—e.g. the "white primary" and the "grandfather clause"; by state constitutional amendment; or with the aid of such United States Supreme Court decisions as those in the *Slaughterhouse Cases* [2] and the *Civil Rights Cases*.[3] The Court's position, as we noted earlier,[4] was that the Fourteenth Amendment did not place under federal protection "the entire domain of civil rights heretofore belonging exclusively to the states," and that the protection offered by the Fourteenth and Fifteenth Amendments was *against state action only*, not against private action. And in 1896 the Court upheld the convenient discriminatory concept of "separate but equal" in the famous case of *Plessy v. Ferguson*.[5] To all intents and purposes the Negro's lot was at the mercy of the states. Until World War II the federal government assumed at most a limited role in the protection of civil rights on the state level.

In 1900 almost 90 per cent of America's Negroes lived in the South (a figure that had declined to 53 per cent by 1967), and the heart of racial discrimination naturally beat there. Racial discrimination occurred on both the public and the private level. Thus, *public* authorities at the state and local levels, usually under the guise of the Court-upheld "separate but equal" concept, enacted measures (sometimes taking the form of a constitutional provision) *permitting* or even *requiring* segregation of busses, streetcars, taxicabs, railroads, waiting rooms, comfort stations, drinking fountains, state and local schools, state colleges and universities, hospitals, jails, sports, beaches, bath houses, swimming pools, parks, golf-courses, courthouse cafeterias, libraries, housing, theaters, hotels, restaurants, and other similar facilities—be these public, quasi-public, or private in nature. Private individuals and groups, on their own initiative, and not in-

[1] Among them were the "Anti-K.K.K." Act of 1871 and the Public Accommodation Act of 1875.
[2] 16 Wallace 36 (1873).
[3] 109 U.S. 3 (1883).
[4] See Chapter III, *supra*.
[5] 163 U.S. 537.

frequently encouraged by state authorities, acted to deny Negroes, and often other non-Caucasians as well, access to social clubs, fraternities and sororities, private schools, colleges, and universities, churches, hospitals, hotels, housing, restaurants, movies, bowling alleys, swimming pools, bath houses, sporting events, comfort stations, drinking fountains, barber and beauty shops, employment agencies, and employment itself. There was nothing particularly secretive about either public or private discrimination; it was simply an accepted way of life—accepted by many Negroes as well as by almost all whites.

Yet the onset of the Second World War prompted the federal government to take notice of the problem. Although his Administration recommended no civil rights legislation *per se* to Congress, which, needless to say, did not act on its own, President Franklin D. Roosevelt did take two far-reaching executive actions. In 1939, at the prompting of Attorney-General Frank Murphy (who would soon be an Associate Justice of the Supreme Court), he created a Civil Liberties Unit [1] in the Criminal Division of the Department of Justice. Then, since Congress would not have passed such legislation, he established by executive order [2] the first Committee on Fair Employment Practices, or as it was later to be known widely and briefly, the F.E.P.C. The President created it largely at the behest of Negro leaders, other civil rights advocates, and, significantly, Mrs. Eleanor Roosevelt—whose entire life was dedicated to the eradication of injustice. Although its enforcement powers were severely circumscribed, and its domain was exclusively in the federal sphere, the F.E.P.C. did make some progress toward the elimination of discriminatory employment practices in those companies and labor unions that had government contracts or were engaged in activities connected with the Second World War. Yet Congress managed to abolish the Committee in 1946.

The end of the war brought increasing pressure on the federal government to combat the various manifestations of racial discrimination. But the political power of the Southern forces, both in Congress and out and often combined with Northern conservative elements, was able to prevent, or at least to delay, any meaningful legislative aid. The House of Representatives, quite naturally more sensitive to the currents and tides of change, did pass such potentially remedial meas-

---

[1] Subsequently to be called the Civil Rights Section.
[2] Exec. Order 8802, *Federal Register*, Vol. VI (1941), p. 3109.

ures as a permanent, either voluntary or compulsory, F.E.P.C. in 1946 and 1950, but both bills were rejected by the more tradition-bound Senate, where the Southern influence was still decisive in such matters. Again, the House passed legislation designed to outlaw the poll tax in 1945, 1947, and 1949, yet in no instance would the Senate accept it. (It would take another 13 years before Congress legislated against the poll tax in *federal* elections. When it did so, it was by way of the Twenty-Fourth Amendment in 1964.) No action at all was taken on a host of anti-lynching legislative proposals that were introduced at every session of Congress.

Winds of Change: President Truman. With Congress unwilling or unable to make progress on the race problem, President Harry S. Truman—a son of Missouri with Confederate ancestors—determined to take matters into his own hand. In a sense, the catalyst for his initial step was Congress's deliberate failure to include a widely backed anti-discrimination provision in the important Selective Service Act of 1948. Angry and frustrated, the President issued a no-nonsense executive order [1] that specifically banned "separate but equal" recruiting, training, and service in the armed forces. While this did not affect the National Guard and Reserve units under the aegis of certain states, it was an important step in the right direction —in an area of public activity where discrimination based on race was particularly heinous: military service for one's native land. Actually, President Truman was convinced that he had to move on his own, in so far as that was legal and possible, because of the fate that the report of his President's Committee on Civil Rights had suffered at the hands of Congress. In 1946 he had appointed the 15-member blue-ribbon committee,[2] charging it specifically with the careful investigation of the need for legislative and other procedures designed to further and protect civil rights and liberties. One year later, the Committee reported that although civil rights were indeed better and more broadly protected than ever before, there were still alarmingly widespread violations. In its widely distributed report, *To Secure These Rights,* the Committee made numerous recommendations designed to ensure that every violation of a civil right by private persons could

[1] Exec. Order 9981, *Federal Register*, Vol. XIII (1948), p. 4313.
[2] Exec. Order 9808, *Federal Register*, Vol. XI (1946), p. 14153. The Committee was headed by Charles E. Wilson ("Electric Charlie"), president of General Electric.

be treated as a criminal offense. Were these recommendations to be followed, the enforcement of civil rights would become a new and vigorous government activity on a very much extended scale. Specifically, the Committee's proposals included federal laws to forbid lynching and discrimination in voting requirements; to create a permanent Fair Employment Practices Commission and a permanent Commission on Civil Rights; and to expand into a Civil Rights Division the small, undermanned Civil Rights Section in the Department of Justice that had been set up under Attorney General Murphy eight years earlier.

Alas, like all proposals for the extension of government activities, these became quickly a political issue. Still, President Truman courageously committed himself to the implementation of the report as far as federal action could do so and in the face of very considerable risks to his party position and his campaign for re-election in 1948. Indeed, the 1948 campaign started off the "Dixiecrat" revolt in the Democratic Party. Nonetheless, the President made To Secure These Rights an issue throughout his campaign. He won re-election, but he did not obtain—as we have already noted—congressional acquiescence. In fact, the national legislature took no action whatsoever during the remaining four years of the Truman Administration, a hiatus that extended through the first four and a half years of the Eisenhower Presidency. But Truman attempted to salvage what he could by executive order. Shortly before his 1948 order banning segregation in the armed forces, he had issued an executive order [1] establishing a Fair Employment Board to oversee announced policy namely, that henceforth all federal jobs were to be distributed without any regard to "race, color, religion, or national origin." Three years later the President created the Committee on Government Contract Compliance, requiring any business holding a contract with the federal government not only to pledge but to provide bona fide fair employment policies and practices.[2] The general tenor of these several executive moves gradually began to pervade much of the vast executive establishment.

President Eisenhower, on attaining office in 1953, continued President Truman's civil rights policies. Resorting himself to the device

---

[1] Exec. Order 9980, Federal Register, Vol. XIII (1948), p. 4311.
[2] Exec. Order 10308, Federal Register, Vol. XVI (1951), p. 12303.

of the executive order,[1] the new Chief Executive created the President's Committee on Government Contracts, which he asked Vice-President Nixon to head. The Committee was empowered to receive complaints alleging discrimination by government contractors, and to cancel contracts if necessary. Various cabinet departments and agencies continued the policy of earlier administrations against sundry types of obvious internal discrimination.

The Watershed. These activities were of course not lost on the several states. A good many Northern states turned to F.E.P.C. and similar devices to combat discrimination, and the air was filled with the beginnings of change. Yet the South was determined not to budge. And in Congress it had a seemingly eternal ally. President Eisenhower did not recommend any new civil rights legislation until his Administration's Civil Rights Act of 1956. That measure failed of enactment then, but the ice was broken for Congress to pass a modified version in the Civil Rights Act of 1957, the first major piece of civil rights legislation since Reconstruction. It is fair to say, however, that it would never have become law had not the leader of the third branch of the United States Government, the Supreme Court, swung into the fray with its monumentally significant decision in the *Public School Segregation Cases*[2] on May 17, 1954.

That landmark decision was one of the most far-reaching in our history in terms of its social impact, and could quite possibly become the single most important Supreme Court decision in the current century. The *Public School Segregation Cases* became bellwether and catalyst in the issue of racial discrimination; in focusing responsibility for remedial action on government officials everywhere; and especially in pointing an accusing finger at that branch of government presumably responsible for social action: the legislature. The controversy engendered by the 1954 *Public School Segregation Cases* will not soon die, even though it may well gradually subside concerning *some*, but certainly not all, of its implications. Once again the Court had to lead, standing at the pinnacle of the judiciary, and conscious of its position as a national moral goad as well as a teacher in a continuing national constitutional seminar. Against the here necessarily

[1] Exec. Order 10479, *Federal Register*, Vol. XVIII (1953), p. 4899.
[2] *Brown v. Board of Education of Topeka*, 347 U.S. 483 (1954), and *Bolling v. Sharpe*, 347 U.S. 497 (1954).

limited action of the executive branch and the utter inaction of the legislative, the Court decided unanimously that it had to create a line. After two and a half years of deliberation, it chose to attack the concept of "separate but equal" in the field of public school education on the grounds that separate facilities are "inherently unequal" and that the very concept of "separate but equal" in matters of race violates the "equal protection of the laws" clause of the Fourteenth Amendment [1] and (on the federal level) the "due process of law" clause of the Fifth.[2] The fat was in the fire; the die had been cast. The background of these cases is a story at once exciting and controversial.

"Separate but Equal": Rise and Demise

We know that the intent of the three Civil War amendments was to abolish the institution of Negro slavery, to bestow the full benefit of American citizenship upon the Negro, and to enable him to exercise the franchise. And for a brief period of roughly two decades, give or take a few years depending upon the individual state involved, the Negro was indeed in a position to exercise his newly confirmed civil rights relatively effectively—backed, to be sure, by federal Reconstruction forces. But, as we also know—and as C. Vann Woodward, among others, has told us so well [3]—the dominant white elements in the old Confederacy were not about to grant the Negro anything like genuine, lasting freedom and equality; indeed, they utilized every conceivable covert and overt device to bar the one-time slaves from attaining even the semblance of first-class citizenship. As the evangelism and fervor of Northern abolitionists began to subside, especially after the Hayes Compromise of 1877 which resulted in the withdrawal of the troops from the South, Southern leadership all but restored the *status quo ante*, with the overwhelming support of the Southern constituency. By 1900, the Southern Negro had been pushed back into second-class citizenship. Jim Crow, with certain refinements, reigned supreme again.

[1] *Brown v. Board, loc. cit.*—which involved four different states: Kansas, Virginia, Delaware, and South Carolina.
[2] *Bolling v. Sharpe, loc. cit.*—which concerned the District of Columbia.
[3] See his *The Strange Career of Jim Crow*, rev. ed. (New York: Oxford University Press, 1966).

THE RISE OF "SEPARATE BUT EQUAL"

Negro leaders endeavored to battle this trend. Unable to expect any aid in their efforts from either the executive or legislative branches, they turned to the state judiciary. It, too, quickly proved itself generally in sympathy with the point of view of the region's population and its leadership. The Negro's only hope thus hinged on the United States Supreme Court. And *it* proved to be a vain hope for a long time.[1]

An Ill Omen. When the famous *Slaughterhouse Cases*[2] were handed down by the Court in 1873, things began to look bad for the Negro cause. Ironically, Negroes were *not* involved in that litigation, and the Court's language seemed to give distinct comfort to the Negro cause. There were ringing phrases regarding the purposes of the Civil War amendments: the achievement of "freedom for the slave race," the "security and firm establishment of that freedom," and the protection of the "newly-made freeman and citizen from the oppressions of those who had formerly exercised unlimited dominion over him."[3] But, as we saw in our earlier discussion[4] of these cases, the Court's *real* point was that there must be a careful distinction between the "privileges and immunities" of *United States* citizens and *state* (here Louisiana) citizens; that the only privileges attaching to national citizenship are those that "owe their existence to the Federal Government, its National character, its Constitution, or its laws";[5] that, in fine, a citizen of a state derived his "privileges and immunities" from *state* citizenship, a thing quite "distinct" from federal citizenship rights, which "depend upon different characteristics or circumstances in the individual."[6] In other words, if the Negroes had hoped to rely on the "privileges and immunities" clause of that Amendment as a source of salvation in their struggle for equal rights, the Supreme Court's narrow construction of the clause—one never

---

[1] For an engaging account of the story of the Supreme Court of the United States and the Negro, written by the son of a Negro slave and his white wife, see Loren Miller's *The Petitioners* (New York: Pantheon Books, 1966).

[2] 16 Wallace 36.

[3] *Ibid.*, at 71.

[4] See Chapter III, *supra.*

[5] *The Slaughterhouse Cases, loc. cit.,* at 79.

[6] *Ibid.*, majority opinion by Mr. Justice Miller, at 74.

really altered to this day (1967)—rendered it of preciously little value
as a restraint upon state regulation. But what about the "due process
of law" and "equal protection of the laws" clauses of the Fourteenth?

Another Hope Shattered. Things seemed to look up when Congress,
in an effort to aid the Negro, passed the Civil Rights Act of 1875,
which made it a *federal* crime for any owner or operator of, *inter alia*,
a hotel, public conveyance, or theater, to "deny the full enjoyments
of the accommodations thereof" because of race or color. Various
Negroes were nonetheless denied access and brought suit in a series
of cases, ultimately consolidated by the Supreme Court as *The Civil
Rights Cases of 1883.*[1] The story of the cases is well known and well
told.[2] The Court, in an 8:1 decision written by Mr. Justice P. Bradley,
with only Mr. Justice John Marshall Harlan in dissent, declared the
Act of 1875 unconstitutional. The Court did so on the grounds that
the Fourteenth Amendment applies to *state* action only and did not
give Congress authority to forbid discrimination by *private* individuals; that if the state did not assist the discrimination of an individual against another individual, the matter is purely between the
two as private persons. Thus not only had the Supreme Court sharply
limited the "privileges and immunities" that had hopefully come with
national citizenship, it now read the phrase "no state shall" in the
Fourteenth and Fifteenth Amendments to mean solely and literally
the actions of state government *officials*. The decisive Court majority
refused to accept the contention that it was in fact state action when
individuals and corporations *licensed by a state* to "serve all without
discrimination" used race as a criterion. It also rejected the view that
inaction by a state in dealing with mob violence and intimidation
of its citizens required *federal* protection. Indeed, Bradley commented
in an oft-quoted dictum that the Negro should cease endeavoring to
obtain "special treatment"; that there had to be a time when the
Negro stopped being "the special favorite of the law," and adopted
"the rank of a mere citizen."[3] Harlan, however, not only flayed Bradley for these comments, but firmly voted to uphold the Civil Rights
Act of 1875. His most important reasons for doing so were his expressed convictions that it was well settled that "railroad corporations,

[1] 109 U.S. 3.
[2] E.g. Alan F. Westin, "The Case of the Prejudiced Doorkeeper," in John A.
Garraty, ed., *Quarrels That Have Shaped the Constitution* (New York: Harper
& Row, 1904), pp. 128-44.
[3] *The Civil Rights Cases, loc. cit.,* at 25.

keepers of inns, and managers of places of public amusement are *agents or instrumentalities of the State*" [1] and that the Act regardless could and should have been upheld under the congressional power over interstate commerce—foreshadowing the Civil Rights Act of 1964 and its unanimous upholding by the Supreme Court later that year.

Gradually taking their cue from the *Slaughterhouse, Civil Rights*, and related Court decisions, most of the states of the old Confederacy not only closed their eyes to the steadily spreading segregation practices that either sprung up or were revived within their borders; in the four-year period between 1887 and 1891 alone, eight of them enacted legislation *requiring* railroads, for example, to maintain *separate* facilities for whites and Negroes.

Enter Plessy v. Ferguson. There had been earlier legal skirmishes at the state level; indeed, the "separate but equal" concept had been initially propounded by Charles Sumner and formulated by that distinguished Massachusetts jurist, Mr. Justice Lemuel Shaw, almost half a century earlier in 1849, in the Boston public school segregation case of *Roberts v. the City of Boston* [2]—but the issue was first joined at the highest federal level in the enormously important case of *Plessy v. Ferguson*,[3] which was destined to remain the law of the land for 58 years. At the bar of the Court was the constitutionality of Louisiana's "Jim Crow Car Act of 1890," euphemistically entitled "An Act to Promote the Comfort of Passengers." It required railroads "to provide equal but separate accommodations for the white and colored races." Here, then, it was: "EQUAL but SEPARATE." With the exception of an 1892 decision in which the State of Louisiana Supreme Court had held the new law to be inapplicable to an *interstate* passenger—a decision the state did not appeal—all prior tests of the 1890 Act at the level of the state had ended in victory for the new doctrine. Now at last the highest tribunal in the land would hear and adjudicate the problem of "separate but equal," a problem which had been brought to it through the efforts of a group of 18 Negroes who had formed a "Citizens Committee to Test the Constitutionality of the Separate Car Law." As their attorney they selected Albion Winegar Tourgee of Mayville, New York, a leading carpetbagger

---

[1] *Ibid.*, at 58. (Italics supplied.)
[2] 5 Cush. (59 Mass.) 198.
[3] 163 U.S. 537 (1896).

during Reconstruction, who, an Ohioan by birth, had served in the Union Army and then moved to Greensboro, North Carolina, to practice law. There he soon became a leader of the Radical Republican Party, took an active part in the creation of the State's Radical Constitution, and served as a judge of the Superior Court of his adopted state for six years. Tourgee had been chosen by the Citizens' Committee even prior to the 1892 Louisiana "victory," which he obtained. That case had not met the needs and aims of the Jim Crow Act's challengers. Homer Adolph Plessy's case, however, did fit the bill.[1]

Plessy was seven-eighths white; his one-eighth "African blood" was not apparent. The Citizens' Committee had seen to it that the East Louisiana Railroad knew of his background: Duly selected by the Committee to test the statute, Plessy boarded in New Orleans, having purchased a ticket to Covington, Louisiana, and took a seat in the "Whites Only" coach; the conductor requested that he move to the "Colored Only" section, which Plessy refused to do, whereupon he was promptly arrested by Detective Christopher C. Cain, and charged with violating the "Jim Crow Car Act of 1890." Tourgee's defense contended that the Louisiana statute under which Plessy had been arrested and charged was null and void because it was a violation of both the Thirteenth and Fourteenth Amendments. The argument turned on the latter's proscription of the denial of the "equal protection of the laws." Partly because of the fundamental requirement inherent in the judicial process that all remedies "below" must be exhausted before the federal Supreme Court will consider an otherwise properly qualified case, and partly because of its own work load, the high tribunal did not hand down its famed decision until four years later. These intervening years saw a further attrition of the Negro's post-Civil War gains; unless the Supreme Court were to strike down the "separate but equal" doctrine, Jim Crow would reign supreme, indeed.

The opinion of the Court—with Mr. Justice David Brewer not participating—supported the statute 7:1. Once again, the lone dissenter was the same Kentucky ex-slaveholder, who had similarly been alone

---

[1] For a lively and illuminating description of the case and its setting, plus an engaging sketch of the principals, see C. Vann Woodward's "The Case of the Louisiana Traveler," in Garraty, *op. cit.*, pp. 145-58.

on that side of the opinion thirteen years earlier in the *Civil Rights Cases*[1]: John Marshall Harlan, whose grandson and namesake was destined to help preside over Jim Crow's judicial demise in the Court six decades later.[2] Oddly, the majority opinion in *Plessy* was written by Mr. Justice Henry B. Brown, a Yale graduate from Michigan, and one of the seven Northerners then on the Court.[3] Brown's opinion frankly acknowledged Louisiana's action to have been "state action," thus falling under Fourteenth Amendment consideration, *but*, he held for the Court, the action was *not discriminatory* against Negroes since the whites were separated just as much from the Negroes as the Negroes were separated from the whites! As for the charge that the basis for the separation was race, Brown ruled that was not in and of itself a violation of the Constitution at all, for a state had every right under that document to "classify" as long as that classification [4] was not capricious, arbitrary, or unreasonable, and hence a denial of equal protection. "Separate but equal" did not run afoul of these considerations, said Brown, since the Negro belief that the concept intended to "stamp the colored race with a badge of inferiority" (a phrase that would be quoted and construed quite differently by Mr. Chief Justice Earl Warren 58 years later) was "not by reason of anything found in the act, but *solely because the colored race chooses to put that construction upon it.*" And Brown could not forbear to add: "If one race be inferior to another socially, the Constitution of the United States cannot put them upon the same plane...." [5] He admitted that the Fourteenth Amendment was "undoubtedly designed to enforce the absolute equality of the two races before the law," but that "it could not have been intended in the nature of things ... [to] abolish distinction based upon color or to enforce social, as distinct from political equality...." [6]

[1] 109 U.S. 3 (1883).

[2] He joined the Supreme Court approximately one year after the 1954 *Public School Segregation Cases, op. cit.*, and was on the bench when the Court handed down its implementation decision in the second *Public Segregation Cases* (*Brown v. Board of Education of Topeka, et al.*, 349 U.S. 294 [1955]).

[3] The other Southerner was Mr. Justice Edward D. White of Louisiana.

[4] For a discussion of "classification" see Jewell Cass Phillips, Henry J. Abraham, and Cortez A. M. Ewing, *Essentials of American National Government*, 2d ed. (New York: American Book Co., 1966), Ch. VI, pp. 104-12.

[5] *Plessy v. Ferguson*, 163 U.S. 537 (1896), at 551.

[6] *Ibid.*, at 544.

In eloquent anger, Mr. Justice Harlan sternly rejected what he viewed as the majority's social Darwinism. To him, as to many others who would follow, the line drawn here by his colleagues reflected "a compound of bad logic, bad history, bad sociology, and bad constitutional law," in the words of one modern Southern commentator.[1] "The thin disguise of 'equal' accommodations for passengers in railroad coaches will not mislead anyone, nor atone for the wrong this day done," [2] Harlan warned the majority. He attacked the decision as one redolent with sociological speculation:

> The arbitrary separation of citizens on the basis of race, while they are on a public highway, is a badge of servitude wholly inconsistent with the civil freedom and the equality of the law established by the Constitution. It cannot be justified upon any legal grounds.[3]

And in memorable language he went on to note that

> ... in view of the Constitution, in the eye of the law, there is in this country no superior, dominant, ruling class of citizens. There is no caste here. *Our constitution is color-blind, and neither knows nor tolerates classes among citizens.* . . . The law regards man as man, and takes no account of his surroundings or of his color when his civil rights as guaranteed by the supreme law of the land are involved.[4]

Yet, after all, this was but a dissenting opinion; Harlan was not to see its vindication. Meanwhile, the separate but equal concept had not only been adopted; it had been judicially sanctioned. It proved to be most detrimental to the Negro cause in education, public accommodations, the franchise, the administration of justice, housing, employment (including the armed forces), and, needless to add, social relationships. White supremacy seemed to have triumphed; assuredly this was true in the vast majority of the states below the Mason-Dixon line. For that matter, when Brown spoke in *Plessy*, not only the Southern and Border states, but a total of thirty states of the Union, including most of those in the West as well as Indiana, Kansas, and New York, had separate but equal public school statutes—in a very real sense the legally sanctioned children of Massachusetts Supreme Judicial Court Justice Shaw's decision of 1849.

1 Robert J. Harris, *The Quest for Equality: The Constitution, Congress, and the Supreme Court* (Baton Rouge: Louisiana State University Press, 1960), p. 101.
2 163 U.S. 537, at 562.
3 *Ibid.*
4 *Ibid.*, at 559. (Italics supplied.)

CHIPPING AT THE DOCTRINE

Yet, however slowly and imperceptibly, the legal chisels were being readied, and they began to go to work in earnest during Roosevelt's second term of office. They broke through in the post-World War II years. This chipping away at the "separate but equal" line probably had its genesis in the crucial case of *Missouri ex rel Gaines v. Canada* [1] in 1938; actually, the *first* court-enforced admission of a Negro to a heretofore segregated higher institution of learning had come two years earlier, when the Maryland Court of Appeals—that state's highest tribunal—ordered Donald Murray admitted to the University of Maryland Law School.[2] But it was *Gaines* that initially gave notice to the nation that the winds of change had begun to brush the heretofore placid reserve of racial discrimination based on "separate but equal" facilities. The change had its practical roots in certain attitudes, both legal and social, that had begun to crystallize, partly as a result of what might be called a growing egalitarian national conscience and partly because of the imminence of war. In any event, it manifested itself chiefly in the gradual but unquestionably progressive shift in rulings of the United States Supreme Court from acceptance of the separate but equal doctrine to a close examination of the alleged equality to, ultimately, the utter rejection of the constitutionality of the doctrine. It took almost two decades to proceed from stage one to stage three, but the Court finally got there! Although the Supreme Court clearly led—and it did so despite an avalanche of vilification and abuse—it did have an ally, however tenuous, in what might be called the national conscience of white members of the body politic, a conscience that was beginning to evince at least some understanding of the Negro's ever rising claims to justice and equality.

The Gaines Case. Lloyd Gaines was a Missouri Negro who sought, but was denied, admission to the School of Law of the state University of Missouri. He had been graduated from Lincoln University, an all-Negro Missouri institution. There was no claim of lack of qualifications—Canada, the University's registrar, simply pointed to a Missouri statute under which the two races were to be educated "separately

[1] 305 U.S. 337.
[2] *Pearson v. Murray*, 169 Md. 478 (1936). He was admitted and ultimately graduated.

but equally." Canada told Gaines that he could, of course, avail himself of another feature of Missouri law applying specifically to Negro law school applicants: funds made available by the state to qualified Negroes for their legal education in schools of adjacent states that offered unsegregated facilities—e.g. Kansas, Nebraska, Iowa, Illinois. But, encouraged in his stand by the now increasingly active and influential National Association for the Advancement of Colored People, Gaines declined. What he wanted, he said, was what was entitled to him as a full-fledged citizen and taxpayer of his home state of Missouri: the right to attend the state law school and to practice law in Missouri. Canada again refused. The NAACP then financed Gaines's appeal through the courts and ultimately to the Supreme Court of the United States. Mr. Chief Justice Charles Evans Hughes wrote the opinion himself, speaking also for Justices Brandeis, Stone, Cardozo, Roberts, Black, and Reed; only Justices McReynolds and Butler —the two surviving members of the so-called Arch-Conservative Quads [1]—dissented, pleading for a continuation of a practice that, they agreed, was in the "best interests" of Missouri's people.[2]

The Chief Justice praised the state of Missouri for the financial arrangements outlined, but said that since there was no law school for Negroes in the entire state—Lincoln University had none—the equal protection guarantee of the Fourteenth Amendment was in fact denied Lloyd Gaines. Hughes, continuing to give comfort to the partisans of the "separate but equal" doctrine, explicitly stated that Missouri could have fulfilled its obligation to provide legal instruction to its Negro citizens "by furnishing equal facilities in separate schools, a method the validity of which has been sustained by our decisions." [3] In other words, he held that while the Constitution did not guarantee Gaines's admission to the School of Law of the University of Missouri, it did guarantee a legal education in Missouri substantially equal to that afforded by the state to members of the white race. That Gaines happened to be the only Negro wishing such an education was beside the point. The state subsequently decided to set up a separate law school for Negroes at Lincoln University, but Lloyd Gaines, perhaps overcome by notoriety and pressure, disap-

---

[1] The other two were Justices Van Devanter and Sutherland, replaced by Black and Reed, in 1937 and 1938, respectively. Yet it is entirely plausible, indeed probable, that—based on their records in the civil rights and liberties realm— the two departed justices would have joined the majority opinion.

[2] *Missouri ex rel Gaines v. Canada*, 305 U.S. 337, dissenting opinion, at 353.

[3] Majority opinion, *loc. cit.*, at 344.

peared shortly before the Court's decision was handed down. While it remained for someone else then to test the "separate but equal" doctrine *per se*, the *Gaines* case had laid the foundations based on the "equal protection of the laws" clause of Amendment Fourteen. It was this clause that was to bring ultimate victory to the Negroes' strivings; it was this clause that cast the Negro into the role of becoming the Supreme Court's "unwilling ward," its "constant petitioner." [1]

Post-Gaines. Almost ten years elapsed before the Court dealt with the doctrine again. Inconclusively but nonetheless pointedly, it ordered in 1948 the state of Oklahoma to provide a duly qualified, NAACP-backed Negro woman applicant with an equal legal education by a state institution.[2] The results were less than satisfactory in terms of the ultimate goal, but there was no longer any question that, at the very least, *equal* facilities would have to be state-provided—and no nonsense, please!

Two years later, however, the Court handed down two decisions which made painfully clear to the South that while "separate but equal" might still not be unconstitutional, it was on its last legs. The two 1950 cases were announced on the same Opinion Monday, and both were decided unanimously in opinions written by Mr. Chief Justice Vinson. Although neither outlawed the "separate but equal" doctrine *per se*, the conditions posited by the Court for its continued constitutionality were in fact unattainable. Both cases had once again been stimulated and backed by the NAACP's capable legal team. One of them, *Sweatt v. Painter*,[3] concerned the University of Texas's statutorily sanctioned denial of Herman Sweatt's request for admission to its law school solely because he was a Negro. Sweatt, a Houston mail carrier aspiring to be a lawyer, had refused to attend the separate law school for Negroes established by Texas as a result of the *Gaines* case. He argued that because it was inferior, it would deprive him of the equal protection of the laws. The second case, *McLaurin v. Oklahoma State Regents*,[4] dealt with an ingenious requirement by the Oklahoma legislature, which enabled qualified

[1] Terms used repeatedly, and appropriately, by Judge Loren Miller in his *The Petitioners, op. cit.*
[2] *Sipuel v. Oklahoma*, 322 U.S. 631 (1948), and *Fisher v. Hurst*, 333 U.S. 147 (1948), both decided *per curiam*. Miss Sipuel had become Mrs. Fisher in the intervening period.
[3] 339 U.S. 629 (1950).
[4] 339 U.S. 637 (1950).

Negroes, such as Professor G. W. McLaurin, to do graduate study (here toward a doctorate in Education) at the state University of Oklahoma if the University's authorities admitted them as candidates on a "segregated basis." The "segregated basis" was defined as "classroom instruction given in separate classrooms, or at separate times."

Sweatt's argument that the Texas State University for Negroes was simply "inferior" and hence *unequal* found willing ears in the nine justices. The Chief Justice's brief but lucid opinion pointed not only to the obvious physical differences between the two schools—which alone would have made them sufficiently unequal—but, far more significantly, to those "qualities which are incapable of objective measurement but which makes for greatness in a law school." [1] Among these qualities he noted

> ... reputation of the faculty, experience of the administration, position and influence of the alumni, standing in the community, tradition and prestige.[2]

Tongue in cheek, Vinson commented that it was indeed difficult to believe that one who had a free choice between the two law schools involved would "consider the question close." [3] And he went on to point out some of the intensely practical considerations that rendered the new Negro law school so decidedly inferior:

> The law school to which Texas is willing to admit [Sweatt] excludes from its student body members of the racial groups which number 85 per cent of the population of the State and include most of the lawyers, witnesses, jurors, judges, and other officials with whom [Sweatt] will inevitably be dealing when he becomes a member of the Texas Bar. With such a substantial and significant segment of society excluded, we cannot conclude that the education offered [Sweatt] is substantially equal to that which he would receive if admitted to the University of Texas Law School.[4]

While the Court thus held that there was simply no way to make the two schools equal and yet separate, it still had stopped short of declaring the doctrine null and void.[5]

The circumstances surrounding McLaurin's case were just as un-

[1] *Sweatt v. Painter, loc. cit.,* at 634.
[2] *Ibid.*
[3] *Ibid.*
[4] *Ibid.,* at 634.
[5] Sweatt was duly admitted, but flunked out.

propitious for the future of the "separate but equal" concept. After McLaurin had been ordered admitted to the University of Oklahoma's School of Education to work for his Ed.D., and since he was the only Negro so admitted at the time, the University administration endeavored to comply with the state-mandated provisions for "segregated admission" by resorting to the following degrading devices: Rather than arranging for separate classes for him, the University required him to sit apart at a designated desk in what was variously described as a "hallway" or an "anteroom adjoining the classroom," where he could see and hear the instructor, and vice versa, but from which vantage point he would presumably not contaminate the superior race of his fellow students. In the library he was assigned a special desk on the mezzanine floor, but told that he could not use the desks in the regular reading room. In the school cafeteria he was directed to eat at a specifically designated table and to do so at a different time than his white fellow-students. And, as the Chief Justice described it in his opinion:

> For some time, the section of the classroom in which [McLaurin] sat was surrounded by a rail on which there was a sign stating, "Reserved for Colored," but these have been removed. He is now [at the time of the litigation] assigned to a seat in the classroom in a row specified for colored students. . . .[1]

This hocus-pocus, declared the unanimous tribunal, was neither equal nor constitutional—and McLaurin was promptly admitted to full student citizenship and the equal protection of the laws. After the 1950 triumphs of Messrs. Sweatt and McLaurin, the barriers prevalent in the Border states and the South in higher education began to give way, however gradually. But it would take the death of the "separate but equal" doctrine and the employment of federal troops in Tuscaloosa, Alabama, and Oxford, Mississippi, thirteen years later, before *every* state in the heretofore segregated area would admit at least one Negro to at least one of its graduate or professional institutions of higher learning.

Although the effective catalyst was to be the *Public School Segregation Cases* of 1954 and 1955, of course, collateral developments [2] also assisted in chipping away at the "separate but equal" doc-

---

[1] *McLaurin v. Oklahoma State Regents, loc. cit.*, at 640.
[2] See pp. 248ff., *supra*.

trine. Transportation was one of these. As early as 1946, a Virginia segregation statute, as applied to interstate busses, was declared unconstitutional by the Supreme Court.[1] Four years later, compulsory segregation on interstate trains was outlawed—first by another Supreme Court decision,[2] then by the Interstate Commerce Commission, which particularly referred to sleeping and dining cars. Ultimately, the I.C.C. ordered the cessation of all racial segregation on interstate busses and trains and their public waiting rooms in stations and terminals. To the advocates of segregation, if there was such a thing as a last stand at all, it would have to come in *intra*-state matters—of which, hopefully from their point of view, public schools would be one of the most important. Then, on what to the arch-segregationists was to be known as Black Monday, May 17, 1954, came *Brown v. Board of Education of Topeka, et al.*[3] Powerful rearguard actions continued to be fought, and some are still being fought today more than a dozen years later, but the "separate but equal" doctrine was lost as a legal force. When the colorful Mississippi politician and rabid segregationist James K. Vardaman cautioned at the turn of the century that "[t]his education is ruining our Negroes. They're demanding equality," [4] he did not realize how prophetic his words would prove to be some five or six decades later.

THE DEATH OF THE "SEPARATE BUT EQUAL" DOCTRINE

The *Public School Segregation Cases* of 1954, and their implementation decision one year later, transferred, in the words of one commentator, "the legal sanction and moral authority of the nation's basic law from the segregationist forces to the civil rights advocates." [5] It marked the end of an era and the beginning of a new one. Most of the considerable progress the Negro has been able to achieve in his political, economic, and social status stems quite demonstrably from *Brown v. Board* and its offspring—and much of the still raging criticism of the authority of the Supreme Court of the United States is

[1] *Morgan v. Virginia*, 328 U.S. 373 (1946).
[2] *Henderson v. United States*, 333 U.S. 816 (1950).
[3] 347 U.S. 483.
[4] As quoted in Walter Lord, *The Past That Would Not Die* (New York: Harper & Row, 1965), p. 43.
[5] Alan F. Westin, in Redford, Truman, Hacker, Westin, and Wood, *Politics and Government in the United States* (New York: Harcourt, Brace & World, 1965), pp. 619-20.

traceable to that decision and its results. A relatively brief explanation and analysis of the monumental ruling are necessary to its understanding.

Some Groundwork. Following the *Sweatt* and *McLaurin* decisions, the NAACP's now highly encouraged lawyers, headed by Thurgood Marshall, bided their time in the hope that the South might—just might—show some signs, some disposition, to comply with the spirit of those two decisions and embark upon some "gradualist" program of desegregation. It is idle to speculate whether more courageous leadership by Southern and non-Southern leaders, in and out of government, might have brought about the desired change. The fact is that none of any consequence was forthcoming. The evolving Southern strategy now seemed to follow the candid public statement of Governor James F. Byrnes of South Carolina that, indeed, the South had failed properly to facilitate the education of its Negroes and that "to remedy a hundred years of neglect" a crash building program of fine new schools for Negroes must be begun instantly. Byrnes readily admitted that the South would have to act, and act at once, to preserve the "separate but equal" concept, lest the Supreme Court, as he— once (1941-42) a member of that tribunal himself—put it, "take matters out of the state's hands." When all overt and covert entreaties for even a gradualist approach were rejected, particularly by Virginia and South Carolina, the South's two leaders at this juncture of the battle, Marshall and his battery of attorneys determined that the time had come to wage an all-out battle in the courts against "separate but equal." They had no difficulty in finding appropriate vehicles for the desired litigation. Five separate desegregation suits were instituted in carefully selected parts of the country. Four were begun in the states of Delaware, Kansas (Topeka), South Carolina (Clarendon County), and Virginia (Prince Edward County), and one at the federal level in the District of Columbia. Each of the suits, painstakingly presented by NAACP attorneys under Thurgood Marshall's leadership, charged not only that the several local Negro schools involved were *inferior* to their white counterparts, but that the "separate but equal" rule itself violated the "equal protection of the laws" clause of Amendment Fourteen.

To no one's great astonishment the Negro claims lost in each instance except the Delaware suit, which achieved a limited victory. However, the fact that the Supreme Court heard the five cases was a major accomplishment—and the Court did grant *certiorari* during 1952, hearing extensive oral arguments from both sides in December of that year. According to one allegedly authoritative source, the vote to grant review came by the bare minimum of four! [1] Marshall's forces, augmented by other friendly lawyers, and buttressed by a brief *amicus curiae* brought by President Truman's Attorney-General Edward T. McGranahan, were supported in their argument in what was to become a famous appendix to their brief: In that appendix, thirty American social scientists of national and international reputation [2] not only supported the NAACP's fundamental charge of segregation as constituting discrimination but—even more significantly from the standpoint of the Court's ultimate opinion—contended at length that segregation as such was harmful to the psyche of *both* Negro and white children, causing irreparable damage to their development as members of a healthy, heterogeneous community. Arguing on behalf of the segregation status quo, as represented by the five cases, was one of America's foremost constitutional law experts, the well-known trial lawyer John M. Davis, who had not only held numerous high-ranking jobs in government, but had been the unsuccessful Democratic nominee for President in 1924.

Conscious of the great significance of the issue at bar, the Supreme Court bided its time. In fact, six months later, in June 1953, it not only re-scheduled the cases for *re-argument* but submitted a set of fundamental questions to opposing counsel with directions for appropriate responses, questions that dealt chiefly with the meaning and intent of the Fourteenth Amendment vis-à-vis segregation and certain practical aspects of desegregation. However hypothetically they were phrased, the nature of the Court's questions caused the hopes of the NAACP and its supporters to soar. But the battle was not yet won, and Marshall, especially in view of what seemed to be the important historical aspect of the Court's basic *quaere*, once again turned to the academic community—as he had done for the appendix to his brief. Thus, in September 1953 he enlisted the expertise of some 130 noted social scientists and other academicians who specialized in

[1] Fred Rodell, "It is the Earl Warren Court," *The New York Times Magazine*, March 16, 1966, p. 93.
[2] Among them Kenneth Clark, Floyd Allport, Robert M. McIver, Robert Redfield, and Alfred McC. Lee.

various aspects of constitutional history, law, and interpretation.[1] It was a distinguished array of scholars who thus met, chiefly in New York City, and aided Marshall and his immediate lieutenants in the preparation of the new brief.[2] It was filed on November 15, 1953, and argued orally on December 8, 1953, its chief historical contention being that the framers of Amendment Fourteen had *intended* to ban segregation "as a last vestige of slavery." Davis's response was geared to judicial self-restraint as much as to history; neither the Supreme Court nor any other judicial body had the power, he argued, to declare unconstitutional or *ultra vires* on sociological or psychological bases a school system, a way of life, duly enacted by the people's representatives, that "has stood for three-quarters of a century." If change there was in the offing, it would have to come either by evolution or by the legislative process. The now Republican Administration's Attorney-General, Herbert Brownell, although not quite as assertive in his support of desegregation as McGranahan had been, filed a brief *amicus curiae* in favor of desegregation. He did not accept the historical rationale of the main brief but called for a one-year transition period to permit the South to adjust its social and educational problems. Listening intently to these various arguments in the jammed Supreme Court chamber, the full bench of justices peppered counsel with searching and searing questions. The end was not in sight.

May 17, 1954. Five months after oral argument, four years after the *Sweatt* and *McLaurin* decisions, the Supreme Court of the United States gave its historic decision. It did not, however, resort to the historical issue in which it had expressed so much interest. Obviously, and quite wisely, it did not believe it to be either resolvable or, for that matter, necessary to the unanimous conclusion it reached through its new Chief Justice, Earl Warren of California—named by President Eisenhower to replace the Truman-appointed, recently deceased, Mr. Chief Justice Vinson. Evidently the new Chief had labored mightily to get a unanimous opinion; there are indications that three justices were inclined to dissent for some time during the Court's back-stage

[1] Among them: C. Vann Woodward, John Hope Franklin, Alfred H. Kelly, Robert E. Cushman, Robert K. Carr, Milton R. Konvitz, John P. Frank, Walter Gellhorn, Horace Bond, Howard J. Graham.

[2] For an excellent description, see Alfred H. Kelly, "The School Desegregation Case," in Garraty, *op. cit.*, pp. 243-68.

deliberations.[1] Notwithstanding the complex background and the emotional impact, the Warren opinion was amazingly brief, simple, and direct—although certainly controversial! "We must look to the effect that segregation itself has on public education," he noted in nearing the heart of his Court's decision:

> In approaching this problem, we cannot turn the clock back to 1868 when the [Fourteenth] Amendment was adopted, or even to 1896 when *Plessy v. Ferguson* was written. We must consider public education in the light of its full development and its present place in American life throughout the Nation. Only in this way can it be determined if segregation in public schools deprives these [Negroes] of the equal protection of the laws.
>
> Today, education is perhaps the most important function of state and local government. . . . [Education] is the very foundation of good citizenship. Today it is the principal instrument in awakening the child to cultural values, in preparing him for later professional training, and in helping him to adjust normally to his environment. . . .
>
> We come then to the question presented: *Does segregation of children in public schools solely on the basis of race, even though the physical facilities and other "tangible" factors may be equal, deprive the children of the minority group of equal educational opportunity? We believe that it does.*[2]

The Warren opinion then asserted: "Segregation of white and colored children in public schools has a detrimental effect upon the colored children. . . . A *sense of inferiority affects the motivation of a child to learn.*"[3] And, as the Chief Justice had explained a few sentences earlier, to separate children in grade and high schools "from others of similar age and qualifications *solely because of their race generates a feeling of inferiority as to their status in the community that may affect their hearts and minds in a way unlikely ever to be undone.*"[4] Now followed the famous "social science" footnote 11, which cited the writings of those social scientists, chiefly psychologists and sociologists, on whose findings the Court here relied. Among them were the noted Negro psychologist K. B. Clark and, adding insult to injury in the eyes of the South, Gunnar Myrdal, the Swedish

---

[1] See Rodell, n. 1, p. 266, *supra.*

[2] *Brown v. Board of Education of Topeka, et al.*, 347 U.S. 483, at 492. (Italics supplied.)

[3] *Ibid.*, at 494. (Italics supplied.)

[4] *Ibid.* (Italics supplied.)

sociologist whose celebrated *An American Dilemma* [1] had caused such
an uproar in the South and the Border states when it first appeared
ten years before the *Public School Segregation* cases of 1954. Wrote
Warren:

> Whatever may have been the extent of psychological knowledge at
> the time of *Plessy v. Ferguson*, this finding is amply supported by mod-
> ern authority. Any language in *Plessy v. Ferguson* contrary to this find-
> ing is rejected. [2]

Thus out went the ruling of Mr. Justice Brown for his 7:1 Court in
1896—and up went the single dissenting vote of Mr. Justice John
Marshall Harlan. All that now remained for the decision of 1954 was
the dramatic conclusion that

> . . . in the field of public education the doctrine of "separate but equal"
> has no place. Separate educational facilities are inherently unequal.
> . . . the plaintiffs and others similarly situated for whom the actions
> have been brought are, by reason of the segregation complained of,
> deprived of the equal protection of the laws guaranteed by the Four-
> teenth Amendment. . . . [3]

In other words, as the country was to learn, in the mid-twentieth century, the "equal protection of the laws" clause of the Fourteenth
Amendment forbade the racially segregated education of public
school children. Indeed, the strong implication of the *Brown v. Board*
ruling was that *any publicly* authorized or *publicly* permitted racial
segregation would henceforth be unconstitutional. [4] The years ahead
would prove the verity of this assumption, but the chief difficulty
would be lodged in the question of just *what* was public and *when*
it was public?

The Implementation Decision. Meanwhile, the 1954 decision would
have to be implemented—and here the Court bowed to the counsel
of Attorney-General Brownell. Refraining from an immediate desegregation order, given the revolutionary nature of the decision, the

---

[1] *An American Dilemma: The Negro Problem and Modern Democracy* (New
York: Harper & Bros, 1944). Republished in 1946 and in an updated, revised
edition by Harper & Row in 1962.

[2] *Loc. cit.,* at 494. (Italics supplied.)

[3] *Ibid.,* at 495. (Italics supplied.)

[4] The District of Columbia litigation had to be decided on the "due process
of law" clause of Amendment Five, of course (*Bolling v. Sharpe,* 347 U.S. 497).

Court stayed any enforcement mandate, and ordered re-argument in all five cases for April 1955—almost a year later. For that purpose, the Court invited all interested parties, specifically including counsel, the *amici curiae*, the Solicitor-General of the United States, and all state attorneys-general, to file briefs and, if they so chose, participate in oral argument. Most of the Southern states refused to do so, but a few, like Arkansas and Virginia, did argue, dramatically and at length.[1] One month later, another unanimous Warren opinion (for the same Court personnel as its predecessor decision, save that John Marshall Harlan had replaced the deceased Mr. Justice Jackson) announced the implementation or "mandate" decision.[2] Invoking an old principle of equity law,[3] and thereby avoiding any immediate over-all problem of enforcement, it mandated the *local federal courts* to direct and oversee the transition to a racially non-discriminatory system of public school primary and secondary education "with all deliberate speed." It directed these courts to order a "prompt and reasonable start," but clearly left the door ajar for consideration of the manifold peculiar local problems involved. In fact, "wide open door" may be a more appropriate description of the *initial* judicial attitude, compared to what would be a much stiffer attitude as the fifties turned into the sixties. Inevitably the "child of its time," the Court had carefully separated the principle of integration—a word that appears nowhere in the decisions involved—from its actual implementation. Just as the Supreme Court reflected the socio-political realities of a new day and age in Brown I, so did it reflect the judicial-limitation realities in Brown II. As the ensuing months and years would prove only too well, the Court can be a leader and the conscience of its land, but in the political process of which, after all, it is a part, it has only "the power to persuade: purse and sword are in other hands," as Alexander Hamilton truly stated.

Thus, no matter how "deliberate" the "speed" (and there was more deliberation than speed in compliance!), the Court would need immediate help from the executive branch. Overt or covert defiance

[1] The Court allowed 14 hours of argument; the usual allotment is one to two hours.

[2] *Brown v. Board of Education v. Topeka, et al.*, 349 U.S. 294 (1955), and *Bolling v. Sharpe, ibid.*

[3] For a capsule explanation of equity see the author's *The Judicial Process: An Introductory Analysis of the Courts of the United States, England, and France* (New York: Oxford University Press, 1962), pp. 15-18.

became the rule rather than the exception in a good many sectors of the land, predictably chiefly in the Deep South. While the District of Columbia, under direct federal control, did integrate its public schools immediately, the response in the affected states ran the gamut from bowing to the inevitable in more or less good faith, through reasonably delayed action, to absolute refusal to obey. There was occasionally even avowed, outright defiance, accompanied by flurries of violence, in Arkansas, Virginia, South Carolina, Georgia, Florida, Louisiana, Alabama, and Mississippi. Many subterfuges were adopted by these states and others, as, for example, the closing of all public schools in Prince Edward County, Virginia—whence came one of the five 1954 *Public School Segregation Cases*.[1] Public feeling ran high, indeed, over what the majority of the white population in the affected sectors regarded as a threat to their way of life and the right of the states to govern themselves, the latter more often than not being a camouflage for the former. Some two hundred state segregation statutes would be enacted in the decade following the implementation decision! Customs that have stood for generations do not easily die.

Even Force. Still, a start, however halting and sullen, had been made; and it continued to spread through a lengthy process of litigation, a host of patient efforts by many groups and individuals, courageous stances by the fifty-odd Southern federal jurists who in many ways must be recognized as the heroes of the desegregation battles of the decade between 1955 and 1965,[2] the repeated affirmations of the basic decisions by the United States Supreme Court,[3] and, alas, a show of federal military force when deemed necessary as a last resort. President Eisenhower, for the three years since *Brown,* had done his careful best to stay out of the segregation battle and, indeed, had done nothing either to support the Supreme Court so heavily under fire or to explain, let alone defend, its decisions to the country.

[1] *Davis v. County School Board of Prince Edward County, Virginia,* 347 U.S. 483.

[2] *Fifty-Eight Lonely Men: Southern Judges and School Desegregation* (New York: Harcourt, Brace & World, 1961), by Jack W. Peltason, tells their story enlighteningly and engagingly.

[3] Thus, Mr. Justice Hugo Black for a unanimous Supreme Court in 1964 in ultimately striking down the Prince Edward County school closing and related subterfuges: "There has been entirely too much deliberation and not enough speed in enforcing the constitutional rights which we held had been denied.... (*Griffin v. Prince Edward School Board,* 377 U.S. 218).

In the judgment of many an observer, the enormously popular and influential national hero could have achieved something here if *anyone* could. But in the fall of 1957, he found his hand forced by Governor Orville Faubus of Arkansas. Faubus, following a lengthy desegregation battle with federal and state authorities,[1] called out the National Guard to prevent duly scheduled federal court-ordered public school desegregation in Little Rock, an order which involved only nine Negro children! When he was enjoined by the appropriate United States District Court from continued interference, he removed the Guard, thereby encouraging the lawless. Riots and disorders promptly ensued in the face of this well-publicized and deliberate flouting of a federal court's directive. After a dramatic face-to-face confrontation with Governor Faubus at Newport, Rhode Island, failed, an angry and reluctant President Eisenhower felt compelled to federalize the Arkansas National Guard and dispatch federal troops to re-establish law and order and allow desegregation to proceed as directed. Five years later, in the fall of 1962, another President had to use force. John F. Kennedy deployed 25,000 federal troops to overcome the opposition of Mississippi, led by its governor, Ross R. Barnett, to the federal court-ordered admission of Negro James Meredith[2] to the University of Mississippi at Oxford. A bloody all-night battle was fought on and near the campus of "Ole Miss," with many wounded and two lives lost.[3] Eight months later, President Kennedy again had to use troops, this time mobilizing the Alabama National Guard in order to overcome Governor George C. Wallace's defiance of the federal court-ordered admission of Negroes Vivian Malone and James Hood to the University of Alabama at Tuscaloosa.

Although even token integration was often resisted, especially in the "black belt" sections of the Deep South, mixed classes eventually became a reality on all levels of the public school system. "Mixed," of course, sometimes meant the presence of only one colored student in an otherwise all-white classroom, but the principle was being es-

[1] Well told by, among others, Wilson Record and Jane Cassels Record, *Little Rock U.S.A.* (San Francisco: Chandler Publishing Co., 1960).

[2] Four years later, while on a march from Memphis to Jackson to dramatize the Negro registration drive in Mississippi, Meredith was shot and wounded in an ambush.

[3] See University of Mississippi Professor James W. Silver's important book *Mississippi: The Closed Society* (New York: Harcourt, Brace & World, 1964) and his colleague Russell H. Barrett's *Integration at Ole Miss* (Chicago: Quadrangle Books, 1965).

tablished, and the tough financial penalties provided by Title VI of the Civil Rights Act of 1964 could be confidently expected to do the necessary "nudging" in all but the most adamant situations. These last would be left to the judicial process—although it was clear even as late as the start of 1967 that such states as Wallace-led Alabama would continue to pursue a course of "legal defiance" including a rejection of federal funds. In any event, on August 14, 1964, Mississippi became the *last* state to desegregate at least one school district when the Biloxi District bowed to the inevitability of a federal court order decreeing the desegregation of its first-grade classes. Less than six months later, in January 1965, the Greenville, Mississippi, School Board, facing the loss of $272,000 in federal aid-to-education funds if it failed to comply with the provisions of the Civil Rights Act of 1964 affecting such federal aid, voted unanimously to prepare a desegregation plan. Providing the first instance of *non-court-ordered* compliance by that state's authorities, Greenville's Mayor Pat Dunne endorsed the Board's action, pointing out that there was no alternative: "Repugnant as the law is to all of us, it's a Federal law and it's either a case of comply or close the schools." [1]

"Separate but equal" died *legally* on May 17, 1954; it died *practically* only after many a ground-giving battle as the years rolled by. The decision in *Brown v. Board* was but a beginning, of course. It triggered an evolving socio-political conflict reflecting new realities of power, of which the end is not yet in sight. What *is* gone is the concept of "separate but equal."

SOME POST-BROWN DEVELOPMENTS

Implementing the *Public School Segregation Cases* became the foremost concern and task of a host of public and private groups, agencies, and individuals. And, as we have seen, it was initially in the private sector that most changes were affected, with the all-important and now predictable public exception of the judiciary, in general, and the Supreme Court, in particular. Even at the national level, legislature and executive would wait, for all intents and purposes, until 1957, although President Eisenhower did move on the employee-

[1] *The New York Times*, January 16, 1965. (At the level of higher public education, the last bastions, Alabama and South Carolina, had already fallen two years earlier, of course.)

hiring front in 1955 by issuing an Executive Order [1] to create the Committee on Government Employment Policy. This Committee was charged with hearing individual complaints of alleged racial or religious discrimination in hiring or promotion by federal agencies. The Committee became quite active and, on President Kennedy's assumption of office, merged with the Committee on Government Contracts, which had been created by President Truman in 1951, to become the Committee on Equal Employment Opportunities. [2] Now, with Vice-President Johnson as its first chairman, it proved to be a far more significant and powerful body.

Some Major Statutes Reach the Books. By far the most important *legislative* action of the Eisenhower Administration in civil rights, however, was the passage of the *Civil Rights Act of 1957*, the first major enactment of its kind since the Reconstruction. It was enacted largely due to the bipartisan co-operation of the Democratic leaders of Congress, House Speaker Sam Rayburn and Senate Majority Leader Lyndon B. Johnson. Although the final version was much watered-down from initial intentions, it did contain three or four significant provisions. One of these created the United States Commission on Civil Rights which became a busy and assertive unit in the governmental struggle against racial discrimination; a second enlarged the small and weak Civil Rights Section in the Department of Justice into the more promising and more effective Civil Rights Division, to be headed by an Assistant Attorney-General; third and fourth, the 1957 Act not only authorized the federal government to obtain federal civil injunctions against actual or threatened interference with the right to vote (with or without the individual's consent) and pay the costs for the litigation, but it gave the appropriate United States District Courts jurisdiction over such suits without the normal requirement that all state judicial and administrative remedies be first "exhausted below."

Despite considerable and immediate activity by the new Civil Rights Commission, however, the 1957 statute proved to be of only marginal value in the struggle. Nevertheless, it served to focus and popularize aspects of the problem; and its more obvious weaknesses did prompt the Eisenhower Administration to call for a new statute, which was enacted three years later as the *Civil Rights Act of 1960*. No longer did the Southern members of Congress have the neces-

---

[1] Exec. Order 10590, *Federal Register*, Vol. XX (1955), p. 409.
[2] Exec. Order 10925, *Federal Register*, Vol. XXVI (1961), p. 1977.

sary number of votes and allies to block such legislation. The Act of 1960 promised to be a far-reaching piece of legislation chiefly because, in an elaborate provision for appointment of federal "voting referees," it promised to safeguard the Negro's right to vote freely and without arbitrary discrimination. The measure authorized federal district courts, through appointment of these references, to enroll qualified voters for *all* state as well as federal elections in areas where local officials systematically denied them the right to register or to vote. And it enabled the federal Department of Justice to file suit to bring about this desired result. More than fifteen times as many suits were subsequently brought during its first three years of life than had been brought during any similar span of time under the previous statute.

Still, Negro leaders and other civil rights spokesmen regarded the Act of 1960 as too slow, too costly to administer, and too cumbersome. Negro restlessness and impatience—assuredly understandable if not inevitably justifiable in all instances—was intensified; the year 1963 saw the peak of visible public protest movements. Repeating over and over their "loss of faith in the white power structure," Negroes took to the streets in ever increasing numbers throughout the United States. The summer of 1963 became known as the "long, hot summer," culminating late in August in a massive, peaceful, interracial march by some 200,000 in Washington, D.C., billed as the "March on Washington for Jobs and Freedom." Other demonstrations were not as peaceful and orderly, especially some of those that took place in scattered cities in the Deep South where feelings ran high and hostility was rampant. Although not necessarily directly connected with the demonstrations, reprisals by white extremists resulted in 44 violent deaths during 1963, 1964, and 1965.[1] The Negro riots in Northern cities in the summer of 1966 led to a score more. Against this background of mounting anger, threats, and sporadic violence, President Kennedy asked Congress in February and again in June of 1963 for new, strong, and expanded civil rights legislation.

[1] *The Southern Regional Council Report*, released on January 30, 1966. Among these murders were those of Mississippi NAACP leader Medgar Evers near his Jackson home; a pro-civil rights white Baltimore postman, William L. Moore in northeast Alabama; the bomb-murder of four 11- to 14-year-old Negro girls in a Birmingham Baptist church; and, almost on the day of the passage of the 1964 Act, the murder of three young civil rights workers, two white and one Negro, near Philadelphia, Mississippi. According to the S.R.C.'s report, eighty civil rights murders were committed between 1956 and 1966.

President Johnson again asked for it when he first addressed Congress as the nation's new Chief Executive following the tragic assassination of President Kennedy on November 22. Late in June of the following year the *Civil Rights Act of 1964* passed Congress.

1964. The statute was certainly the most comprehensive piece of legislation to be enacted by the federal legislature since the unsuccessful and ill-fated measures of the 1870's. It cleared the House with relative ease, 290:130. But its success in the Senate, by a bipartisan vote of 73:27, was the result of breaking a 75-day Southern filibuster by the application of the Senate's debate-limiting cloture rule on the 83rd day of debate by a vote of 71:29.[1] It was the first time that cloture had been successfully attained on a civil rights filibuster since the adoption of the cloture rule in 1917. The Act consisted of eleven parts or titles; its principal provisions:

> extended the heretofore sharply-limited life of the Civil Rights Commission for four years, to 1968, and broadened both its duties and powers;

> established a Community Relations Service to aid in the conciliation of racial disputes;

> forbade discrimination because of race, color, sex, religion, or national origin either by employers or by labor unions in business concerns with 100 employees or more, this number to drop by stages to 25 by 1968; and created a Federal Fair Employment Practices Commission (F.E.P.C.) to administer that aspect of the Act;

> prohibited voting registrars from applying different standards to white and Negro applicants; required all literacy tests to be in writing; and rendered a sixth-grade education a "rebuttable assumption" of literacy;

> permitted the Attorney-General to bring suit, upon written complaint by aggrieved individuals, to secure desegregation of facilities owned, operated, or managed by state and local governments;

[1] On the final roll call, 46 Democrats and 27 Republicans voted in favor; against it were 21 Democrats and 6 Republicans. Voting to invoke cloture were 44 Democrats and 27 Republicans; opposed were 23 Democrats and 6 Republicans.

authorized, in its tough Title VI, the Executive to halt any federal aid funds to either public or private programs in which racial discrimination is allowed to continue (a provision used since with considerable success by the United States Office of Education, for one);

outlawed, in its controversial Public Accommodations Title II, discrimination because of race, religion, color, or national origin in hotels, restaurants, theaters, gas stations, and all other public accommodations that affect interstate commerce, as well as in all public facilities (Title II was specifically declared to be constitutional in December 1964, the first test of any provision of the Act of 1964 to reach the United States Supreme Court);[1] and

empowered the Attorney-General to file enforcement suits against any owners of public accommodations who discriminate, and on behalf of any persons whose constitutional rights are deemed violated in school segregation or other instances.[2]

Understandably, the two most controversial provisions of the Civil Rights Act of 1964, both prior to and during the national debate that attended its conception and birth, were the two most obviously concerned with delicate "line-drawing": those dealing with Fair Employment Practices and with Public Accommodations. For here the basic issue of individual rights and of societal obligations were patently joined. No other sections of the statute, not even its voting and educational segments received as much controversy and debate or as many negative votes—although Title VI was to be bitterly attacked by Southern congressmen and its application questioned even by Senate Majority Leader Mike Mansfield (D.-Mont.) late in 1966.[3]

[1] *Heart of Atlanta Motel v. United States*, 379 U.S. 241, and *Katzenbach v. McClung*, 379 U.S. 294.

[2] For a table excerpting, comparing, and contrasting the Acts of 1957, 1960, and 1964, see John H. Ferguson and Dean E. McHenry, *The American System of Government*, 8th ed. (New York: McGraw-Hill Book Co., 1965), pp. 163-4.

[3] See John Herber's article in *The New York Times*, September 29, 1966. Senator Mansfield's main contention was that he thought the Department of Health, Education, and Welfare was going "too far" and/or "too fast" in enforcing Title VI. He later amended the statement to confine it to the "too fast" charge. But the Administration, encouraged by favorable federal court decisions in December 1966, made clear early in 1967 that it was determined to stand by its controversial desegregation guidelines for at least another full school year.

One of their steadfast, bitter-end opponents was the future Republican Presidential nominee, Senator Barry M. Goldwater of Arizona, whose recorded "no" votes, both on cloture and on passage of the bill, probably cost him what little Negro support he might have had. Not only did Senator Goldwater oppose the bill in general, and the fair employment and public accommodations sections in particular, but he denounced the entire measure as "unconstitutional" and declared that it would lead to a "police state." Those charges brought on a full-scale attack on Goldwater by Senator Everett McKinley Dirksen, the Republican leader in the Senate, notwithstanding the fact that Dirksen would nominate Goldwater as his party's candidate for the presidency just a few months later. The colorful Illinois Senator ridiculed Goldwater's constitutional argument and self-proclaimed "moral position" on the Senate floor on June 19, 1964, in what proved to be the bill's closing speech. Turning often to Senator Goldwater, and waving his lanky arms, Senator Dirksen, sternly delivered a lecture to the future candidate: "Utter all the extreme opinion that you will," he called out, "[the bill] will carry forward. You can go and talk about conscience! It is man's conscience that speaks in every generation." [1]

Then, in what ultimately would become a part of the Government's case before the Supreme Court when the public accommodations title was challenged—an argument essentially accepted by the Court when it handed down its unanimous decision upholding the title's constitutionality at the end of the year [2]—Dirksen tolled a long list of social and economic legislation that had been similarly called unconstitutional when first proposed. "Today they are accepted," he underscored, "because they were a forward thrust in the whole effort of mankind. There is latitude enough in the Constitution to embrace within its four corners these advances." [3] Evidently, country and Court agreed: Yet there remain many, among them people of good will as well as confirmed bigots, who are not at all convinced that a democratic government should have the power to do what it did in

[1] *The New York Times*, June 20, 1964.
[2] *Heart of Atlanta Motel v. United States* and *Katzenbach v. McClung, loc. cit.* The Clark opinion for the Court rested the case for Title II's constitutionality on the congressional power over interstate commerce—although Justices Douglas and Goldberg stated their beliefs that the "equal protection of the laws" clause of Amendment Fourteen also applied.
[3] *The New York Times*, June 20, 1964.

those two provisos. It had been a hard line to draw between competing values.

Yet still more legislation was to come, legislation replete with provisions that promised to cause lively debate in and out of Congress. While conceding that the fruits of the 1964 Act—and the Voting Rights Act of 1965—were already "impressively apparent," President Johnson sent Congress his third civil rights bill in three years in the spring of 1966, declaring that discriminatory practices "still exist in many American communities." [1] Going beyond its predecessors, the 1966 Civil Rights Act would have rendered the murder of a civil rights worker, or the slaying of anyone else exercising certain fundamental rights, such as voting or seeking to attend school, a federal crime with a maximum penalty of life imprisonment. It would also have instituted procedures for eliminating racial discrimination in federal juries, and would have empowered *federal* as well as state courts to halt trial in state courts when evidence of juror discrimination is present; and the bill would have enabled the U.S. Attorney-General to take independent legal action to compel desegregation of schools and other public facilities without having to wait to receive a formal complaint. But the 1966 bill's most contentious provision would have outlawed discrimination on either racial or religious grounds in the "purchase, rental, lease, financing, use and occupancy" of *all housing*. Chiefly because of the so-called open housing provision, the bill, although it had passed the House in a watered-down version by a vote of 259:157, died on the floor of the Senate in September 1966—against a backdrop of Negro riots and demonstrations in cities throughout the land, particularly in the North, and the rise of resentment to the new "black power" slogan that began to characterize much of the civil rights activity of that year.[2]

The Quest for Suffrage

A good many sincere as well as fair-weather friends of the Negro's striving for a modicum of egalitarianism prior to the decision to concentrate on education, had insisted that it might be wiser to direct the thrust of the movement toward suffrage. It was felt that suffrage

[1] *Time* magazine, May 6, 1966, p. 24.
[2] Twice the Senate refused to shut off debate on the measure that September; the votes were 54:42 and 52:41.

would almost automatically rectify most, if not all, of Negro's grievances in the public sector, the private sector following ultimately.
This feeling that a fundamental error of judgment was made by the
NAACP strategists and their supporters persists in those circles to this
day. Whatever the merit of the argument, the suffrage problem was
not really tackled until the Civil Rights Acts of 1957, 1960, and 1964
became the laws of the land—and not effectively until the passage of
the Voting Rights Act of 1965 early in August of that year.

ANTECEDENTS TO THE VOTING RIGHTS ACT OF 1965

Our nation's history is replete with systematic disfranchisement of
the Negro, particularly in the South and the Border states. Although
prior to the Civil War, especially in the early decades following the
adoption of the Constitution, other groups, too, had experienced considerable difficulty in their quest for suffrage—e.g. Quakers, Catholics,
and Jews—the Negro more than any other single minority group
suffered second-class political citizenship. And, as we have seen, despite the enactment of the Civil War Amendments—in particular
the Fifteenth, which specifically and expressly provided that the
"right of citizens of the United States to vote shall not be denied or
abridged by the United States or by any State on account of race,
color, or previous condition of servitude"—the Negro continued to
find access to the ballot box difficult, and often impossible, in various
sectors of the former Confederacy. That access had been all but
closed by the turn of the century, if not directly then indirectly by
resort to assorted devices, such as the "grandfather clause," the "white
primary," the poll tax, interpretation clauses, understanding clauses,
and sundry other registration requirements—a seemingly inexhausti-
ble array of covert as well as overt tools of discrimination.[1]

Up until the legislative activity in the 1950's on behalf of the
Negro's voting rights, much of this discrimination was made possible
by our federal structure. An important distinction existed, and to
some extent still exists, between the legal right to vote for *federal*
officials and the legal right to vote for *local* and *state* officials. The
latter vote stems from state constitutions and laws and is thus not a

---

[1] For data on Negro registration and the denial of voting rights to the Negro,
see, among others, the 1959 *Report* and the 1961 voting study of the United
States Commission on Civil Rights.

federal right in the same sense and to the same degree as the right to vote for federal officers, such as members of Congress and Presidential electors. Hence, at least until enactment of the three recent Civil Rights Acts and, more pertinently, the Voting Rights Act of 1965, the states were free, indeed, to define their own qualifications for voting, certainly for state and local officials, but at least in part also for their federal representatives. This state power was subject only to the limitations of Amendments Fourteen, Fifteen, Nineteen, and Twenty-Four and that intriguing Article I, Section 4, which, while according the prescription of "times, places, and manner" of holding elections for federal officials to the States, specifically added a clause that was to become an important tool in the judicial arsenal of aid to the Negro:

> but the Congress may at any time by law make or alter such Regulations, except as to the Places of chusing Senators.

When the absence of his proper ballot continued to pinpoint the Negro's inability to exert influence in Southern politics, and Congress was both unwilling and unable to come to his aid legislatively, he turned to the federal judiciary for redress. Initially he found little, because of the then conservative leanings of the judiciary, and because of the absence of much litigation dealing with the problem. When the Court rejected a promising challenge to the Mississippi literacy test in 1898,[1] matters looked bleak, indeed. As recently as 1959, the literacy device was unanimously upheld by the Supreme Court in an Alabama case,[2] in an opinion written by no less firm an exponent of Negro equality than Mr. Justice Douglas.

Light Ahead. However, the hands of the clock were inexorably moving toward those days of the 1950's and 1960's when the Negro was to win equal rights at least on paper and at the bar of the judiciary in all parts of the land. An important judicial tool proved to be the Fifteenth Amendment, although the crucial one, for education, too, became the "equal protection of the laws" clause of Amendment Fourteen. Still, in 1915 the Supreme Court based its decision on the clear-cut language of the Fifteenth Amendment when in a unanimous opinion by Mr. Chief Justice Edward D. White, it struck down the

[1] *Williams v. Mississippi*, 170 U.S. 213 (1898).
[2] *Lassiter v. Northampton Election Board*, 360 U.S. 45.

Oklahoma "grandfather clause." [1] This transparent device, adopted in several Southern and Border states, provided a convenient loophole through which illiterate whites could escape the provisions of literacy tests. It exempted from these tests all "persons and their lineal descendants" who were qualified to vote as of January 1, 1866, or any similarly convenient date prior to Amendments Fourteen and Fifteen which would not apply to Negroes. The word *Negro* did not appear anywhere in the various grandfather clauses, because practically none, if any, voted or were able to vote prior to that date.

After the failure of an attempt to rescuscitate its spirit, if not its letter, in 1939,[2] the "grandfather clause" was indeed gone. But the poll tax, the "white primary" and a number of other devices remained for those state officers bent upon the perpetuation of a pure or almost-pure white suffrage. An important windfall came their way in 1921 when a narrowly divided Supreme Court of the United States ruled —in a rather messy Michigan United States Senatorial primary election case, involving Henry Ford and Truman H. Newberry [3]—that Congress had no power, or at best highly dubious power, to regulate *primary* elections in the states, be they federal or state or local office. Although the litigation itself dealt with fraud rather than racial discrimination, the decision was tailor-made for the devotees of the white primary. Hence Texas went to work at once and passed the now unbelievably blatant Texas White Primary Law of 1924, which read:

> In no event shall a negro be eligible to participate in a Democratic primary election in the State of Texas, and should a negro vote in a Democratic primary election, such ballot shall be void and election officials shall not count the same.

But a Negro physician from El Paso, Dr. L. A. Nixon, was to prove a thorn in the side of the advocates of racial exclusion in Texas and elsewhere. Denied participation in the Democratic Party's primary under the terms of the Texas law, Dr. Nixon challenged its constitutionality. In a 9:0 opinion, written by Mr. Justice Holmes in 1927, the Supreme Court agreed. Without passing on the matter of primaries *versus* general elections, so importantly present in the *New-*

---

[1] *Guinn v. United States*, 238 U.S. 347.
[2] *Lane v. Wilson*, 307 U.S. 268.
[3] *Newberry v. United States*, 256 U.S. 232.

berry decision,[1] the Court declared the Texas White Primary Law unconstitutional as a "direct and obvious infringement" of the "equal protection of the laws" clause of the Fourteenth Amendment. Here, then, that important clause entered the fray in the voting field—fully a decade prior to its first meaningful utilization in the area of educational segregation.[2]

Texas was not so easily discouraged, however: it repealed the 1924 statute and substituted a measure authorizing the State Executive Committee of every political party to "prescribe the qualifications of its own members." The State's Democratic Party then promptly swung into action and "prescribed" that "only whites" shall be eligible in *its* primaries. When Dr. Nixon thus again was denied participation in the electoral affairs of the party of his choice, he returned to court with a constitutional challenge to Texas's enabling statute. The Supreme Court promptly struck down this latest Texas device (albeit this time by the narrowest of margins, 5:4) on the grounds that by setting qualifications the Democratic Party was usurping state law and that, consequently, the State of Texas had in fact *acted through* the Party as its agent, thereby violating once again the "equal protection of the laws" clause of the Fourteenth Amendment.[3] Not to be outdone, Texas now (1932) *repealed* the authorizing clause of the above legislation. Its Democratic Party, in turn, acting through the *Democratic State Convention,* on its own authority and without any statutory sanction, adopted a resolution to make itself a "private group," permitting as members of this *private group* only persons who were white. When this arrangement also was challenged at the bar of the Supreme Court, the high tribunal unanimously accepted the constitutionality of this new loophole on the grounds that the *State of Texas was not involved,* that the private group referred to was not a "creature of the state" but a *voluntary association* that had acted on its own. This appeared to settle the matter at issue, for "private persons or groups cannot violate the Fourteenth Amendment," since there was no state action per se.[4]

But this seemingly absolute triumph of the disfranchisers was short-

---

[1] *Newberry v. United States, loc. cit.*
[2] *Nixon v. Herndon,* 273 U.S. 536.
[3] *Nixon v. Condon,* 286 U.S. 73.
[4] *Grovey v. Townsend,* 295 U.S. 45 (1935), at 52.

lived. In 1941, just six years after the "private group" decision, the
Supreme Court was confronted with a case of fraud that had occurred
in a Louisiana *federal* primary. A Louisiana election official, one
Patrick B. Classic, had crudely transferred 97 votes cast validly for two
candidates in that primary to a third candidate—his own choice! In
its 5:3 holding the Court ruled that the above-mentioned Section 4
of the Constitution's Article I in fact authorized Congress to regulate
primaries as well as *elections* because "primaries" in the words of the
Constitution were tantamount to "elections" and, being "an integral
part of the election machinery," were subject to Congressional regulations.[1] This decision did not, to be sure, settle the question whether
whites were legally at liberty to exclude Negroes from primaries for
state and local officials; indeed, the race question was not involved
at all. What the *Classic* decision did do—and it was a most significant
accomplishment in constitutional interpretation—was to overrule the
Newberry holding, which had separated the concept of federal "primaries" from "elections," [2] thus paving the way for federal regulation.
The *Grovey v. Townsend "Private Group"* case [3] still stood, however.

The White Primary Falls. Yet three years later, in the sin-
gularly important case of *Smith v. Allwright*,[4] the Supreme Court,
in an 8:1 opinion authored by Mr. Justice Reed—a Border state
Democrat from Kentucky [5]—declared the Texas white primary unconstitutional as a violation of the Fifteenth Amendment. Smith, a
Negro, had been denied participation by a Texas election judge, Allwright, who relied on the "voluntary association" concept developed
by the Court in the *Grovey* decision. But now the Court ruled that,
in effect, the Democratic Party of the State of Texas was acting as an
agent of the state because of the character of its duties—such as
providing election machinery—and was thus subject to the pertinent
provisions of Amendments Fourteen and Fifteen, here the latter. In
the *Classic* case,[6] the Court had set up two alternate or complemen-
tary "tests" to determine whether or not a primary was validly affected,

[1] *United States v. Classic*, 313 U.S. 299, at 318.
[2] *Newberry v. United States*, 256 U.S. 232 (1921).
[3] *Loc. cit.*
[4] 321 U.S. 649 (1944).
[5] For a fascinating account, demonstrating that the case had originally been
assigned to Mr. Justice Frankfurter but then re-assigned for "strategic" reasons
to Mr. Justice Reed, see Alpheus T. Mason, *Harlan Fiske Stone: Pillar of the
Law* (New York: The Viking Press, 1956), p. 615.
[6] *United States v. Classic*, 313 U.S. 299 (1941).

and thus regulatable, by the provisions of federal authority under the Constitution:

> (A) had the state law made the primary an integral part of the election machinery; and/or
> (B) did the primary "effectively control the choice." [1]

Now in *Allwright* *both* tests applied! In hortatory as well as prophetic language the Court admonished Texas and the nation that the constitutional right to be free from racial discrimination in voting

> is not to be nullified by a state through casting its electoral process in a form which permits a private organization to practice racial discrimination in the election. . . . It may be taken as a postulate that the right to vote in . . . a primary . . . without discrimination by the State . . . is a right secured by the Constitution.[2]

As had been true of the *Grovey* "*Private Group*" case,[3] the controlling issue had to be the answer to the basic question: had the Negro involved thereby been barred from the primary by *state* action? The Supreme Court ruled that he had—and *Grovey* was thus overruled, nine years after it had become law. Only Mr. Justice Roberts dissented from the *Allwright* decision— and he did so as much on grounds of judicial "self-restraint" as on the merits of the controversy, grumbling that "Supreme Court decisions are becoming in the same class as a restricted railroad ticket, good for this day and train only." [4]

The *Smith v. Allwright* decision did a good deal to stimulate Negro participation in primary elections in the South and the Border states, but the forces of exclusion were far from ineffective, and ingenuity was certainly not lacking. For example, in an attempt to perpetuate white hegemony at the polls and, concurrently, to test the *Allwright* ruling further, South Carolina promptly *repealed* all of its 147 laws and one constitutional provision relating to the conduct of primaries. But a courageous United States District Court jurist, J. Waties Waring—a tenth-generation member of South Carolina aristocracy— held in 1947 in *Rice v. Elmore* [5] that the South Carolina primaries, though denuded of state authorization *per se*, "effectively control the

---

[1] *Ibid.*, at 318.
[2] *Smith v. Allwright*, 321 U.S. 649 (1944), at 661, 664.
[3] *Grovey v. Townsend*, 295 U.S. 45 (1935).
[4] *Smith v. Allwright*, loc. cit., at 669.
[5] 72 F. Supp. 516 (1947).

choice" of candidates for public office. This finding satisfied test B
of the *Classic* case,[1] and Waring held, consequently, that the denial
to Negroes of their right to vote in primaries was *prima facie* evidence
of a violation of both the Fourteenth and Fifteenth Amendments.
On appeal, the United States Court of Appeals for the Fourth Circuit
sitting in Richmond, Virginia, sustained Judge Waring.[2] The opinion
was authored by Chief Judge John J. Parker—the same man who
had been rejected as President Hoover's nominee to the United States
Supreme Court in part because of his alleged anti-Negro bias.[3] And
the highest tribunal of all refused to review the case,[4] thus letting
Waring's holding stand as the law of the land. As a result 35,000
Negroes came to the polls in South Carolina's Democratic primary
in 1948. Judge Waring, now harassed, pilloried, and isolated, found
it necessary within five years to leave his old home and his beloved
bench to move with his family to New York. "My ostracism was
total," he recalled wistfully in a 1963 interview. "After my racial cases
it got very lonely." [5]

Yet, undeterred by the decision in *Rice v. Elmore*, South Carolina
sought to evade it now by vesting control of primaries in private
clubs to which Negroes were not admitted. These clubs required as
a prerequisite to voting in primaries the taking of an oath that was
particularly odious to Negroes. Among other things, it was necessary
to swear to a belief in the social and educational separation of the
races. Predictably, this effort to continue disfranchisement of non-
whites also ran afoul of effective judicial vetoes in 1948 and 1949.[6]
And in 1953 a much more elaborate and less obvious device used to
keep Negroes from voting in Ford Bend County, Texas, fell, the
quaint "preprimary primary," [7] conducted by a group known as the
"Jaybird Democratic Association." [8] Few could continue to doubt

1 *United States v. Classic*, 313 U.S. 299 (1941).

2 *Ibid.*, 165 F. 2d. 387 (1947).

3 See Henry J. Abraham, *The Judicial Process: An Introductory Analysis of the
Courts of the United States, England, and France* (New York: Oxford University
Press, 1962), pp. 78-9.

4 *Ibid.*, 333 U.S. 875 (1948), *certiorari* denied.

5 *The Greenwich* (Conn.) *Times*, Aug. 30, 1963—interviewed by Charles L.
West.

6 *Brown v. Baskin*, 78 F. Supp. 933 (1948) and 174 F.2d 391 (1949).

7 *Terry v. Adams*, 345 U.S. 461 (1953).

8 For an explanatory article see Luther A. Huston, "High Court Upsets a
Limited Primary," *The New York Times*, May 5, 1953.

that the federal authorities really meant business in the voting field. Still, while there was life there was hope, and the shenanigans continued on sundry levels and in various forms, often taking the form of "understanding" and "interpreting" clauses, which were destined to fall, too, sooner or later.[1] Then, of course, there was the poll tax —a device more difficult to indict—which had been specifically *upheld* by the Supreme Court both in 1937[2] and in 1951.[3] While it was perhaps the best known of the several devices, it was the least important. When it was outlawed for *federal* elections by the Twenty-Fourth or Holland Amendment,[4] ratified in January 1964, its Southern presence was confined to Alabama, Arkansas, Mississippi, Texas, and Virginia. But even for state elections its days were numbered: when the question of the constitutionality of the Virginia state poll tax, as applied to state elections, reached the Supreme Court in March 1966, the tax was given a prompt judicial burial.[5] Appropriately, it was Mr. Justice Douglas, the sole dissenter when the Court had upheld the Virginia tax fifteen years before,[6] who spoke for the six-man majority. He leaned heavily on the Court's "one man, one vote" doctrine for his authority that Virginia's $1.50 tax as a prerequisite for voting in state elections violated the "equal protection of the laws" guarantee of the Fourteenth Amendment. Interestingly, although the plaintiffs in the two cases before the Court were Negroes, the majority's holding was based on *economic* discrimination and *not* on racial discrimination. "To introduce wealth or payment of a fee as a measure of a voter's qualifications," wrote Douglas, "is to introduce a capricious or irrelevant factor. The degree of the discrimination is irrelevant."[7] Justices Black, Harlan, and Stewart, on the other hand, dissented on varying grounds; but they were agreed that payment of a poll tax *could* be a reasonable basis for determining the right to vote.[8] Their protest was in a losing cause, however.

The problem with the literacy test, in itself neither unreasonable

---

[1] E.g. *Schnell v. Davis*, 336 U.S. 933 (1949).

[2] *Breedlove v. Suttler*, 302 U.S. 277.

[3] *Butler v. Thompson*, 341 U.S. 937.

[4] Named after U.S. Senator Spessard Holland (D.-Fla.), who "fathered" it.

[5] *Harper v. Virginia State Board of Elections*, 383 U.S. 663 (decided March 25, 1966).

[6] *Butler v. Thompson, loc. cit.*

[7] *Harper v. Virginia State Board of Elections, op. cit.* at 668.

[8] See the separate dissenting opinions by Justices Black and Harlan, *ibid.*, at 670 and 680.

nor discriminatory (something that could be said, at least in theory, of several of the devices used to disfranchise), was its *application*; it was frequently used for gross and rank discrimination against Negroes. Its "non-discriminatory" principle was upheld by the United States Supreme Court as late as 1959,[1] and, as we shall see, when the Voting Rights Act of 1965 launched a selective assault upon the literacy test, almost one-half of the states of the Union were using such a test of one type or another. Although it is perhaps easier to attack the concept of the literacy test as a necessary and desirable suffrage requirement, than it is to attack the more or less essential requirements of residence and registration, it would certainly be unfair to condemn it on its face. There are other causes for non-voting than racial discrimination; apathy, for example, is the chief cause of what has been historically a shamefully low participation by the American electorate—averaging barely 50 per cent of those eligible to vote even in the presumably most popular and significant election of them all, that for the presidency. However, the privilege of voting also contains the privilege of abstinence—regrettable as that may be within the framework and the spirit of representative democracy. But that is a matter lying beyond our scope in these pages.[2]

That the federal government would ultimately be called upon to act, not only through its judicial arm but by legislative action, was a foregone conclusion, given the forces and causes articulated by *Brown v. Board of Education* in 1954 and 1955.[3]

The Voting Rights Act of 1965. Regardless of the weight one might assign to any one of the various factors that have caused the demonstrably low Negro suffrage, mid-twentieth-century statistics serve well as an indictment of a state of affairs that cried out for government action above and beyond the three Civil Rights Acts of 1957, 1960, and 1964. The presidential election year of 1948 saw barely 600,000 Negroes registered in the eleven states of the South, a mere 12 per cent of those of voting age; 1952 saw close to 1,000,000, some 20 per cent; and 1956 roughly 1,250,000, or 25 per cent. Sixty per cent of the eligible whites were registered in the same region. Although the percentage of Negroes *registered* continued to climb—reaching 27

[1] *Lassiter v. Northampton County*, 360 U.S. 45.

[2] For a discussion of the problem of participation, including the matter of compulsory voting, see Henry J. Abraham, *Compulsory Voting* (Washington, D.C.: Public Affairs Press, 1955).

[3] 347 U.S. 483 (1954) and 349 U.S. 294 (1955).

per cent by 1961 and 40 per cent just prior to the enactment of the Voting Rights Act of 1965—two cardinal facts continued to rankle civil rights leaders: one was that even the 50 per cent registration of Negroes in the South, which would become a reality by the end of 1965, would still be considerably less than the 75 per cent of whites registered; the other was the die-hard resistance to any registration in widespread and important areas of the South, particularly in most of Mississippi, much of Alabama, and a good many counties of Louisiana. As late as the summer of 1965, a mere 6.8 per cent of eligible Negroes had been registered in Mississippi, an increase of scarcely 2 per cent after more than four years of activity and three federal statutes! [1]

Counsels of patience were now clearly falling on deaf ears; a century of discrimination would no longer wait; the civil rights movement had begun to take to the streets in 1960; and then, in early 1965, the town of Selma, Alabama, became the catalyst for the new voting law. Civil rights leaders, headed by Dr. Martin Luther King, organized a well-advertised 50-mile march from Selma to Montgomery in support of the Negroes' efforts to obtain greater voter registration in the face of continued difficulty, defiance, and procrastination. The march began on March 7, 1965, only to be brutally broken up by Alabama state troopers, under orders of Governor George C. Wallace, while it was still close to Selma. Employing whips, night sticks, cattle-prods, and tear gas, the troopers injured at least forty of the marchers. The scene flashed on the television screens of homes throughout the nation and the world. Widespread revulsion set in at once and hundreds of additional civil rights supporters, many of them white clergy of all faiths, poured into the Selma area. Tragedy was not long in coming: on March 9, a white Unitarian minister from Boston, the Reverend James J. Reeb, was clubbed down on a Selma street by irate white natives, and died of skull injuries two days later. Civil rights leaders then re-scheduled the march for March 21, and President Johnson ordered the Alabama National Guard into federal service to protect the marchers. Again led by Dr. King, the march was completed peacefully on the 25th, with a crowd of 30,000 gathering on the steps of the Alabama capitol in Montgomery. But on the same

---

[1] Statistics are obtainable from numerous sources, among them the Southern Regional Council, the *Race Relations Reporter*, various almanacs, *The New York Times*, the *Statistical Abstract of the United States*, and annual compendia by the United States Commission on Civil Rights, the American Civil Liberties Union, the American Jewish Congress, and numerous other groups.

night a white woman from Detroit, Mrs. Viola Liuzzo, who was shuttling Negroes back to Selma from Montgomery in her car, was shot and killed by a trio of white ambushers.

Ten days earlier, acting on the wings of public clamor for action following the Selma outrages, President Johnson addressed Congress in an extraordinary Joint Session, calling for the enactment of the strongest voting rights legislation proposed in nine decades. "The time for waiting is gone," the President told his hushed audience, "... outside this chamber is the outraged conscience of a nation—the grave concern of many nations—and the harsh judgment of history on our acts." [1] Against this background the Administration submitted the Voting Rights Bill of 1965, based on the Fifteenth Amendment's exhortation that no person shall be denied the right to vote because of "race, color, or previous condition of servitude," and giving Congress the power to enforce its provisions "by appropriate legislation."

The bill that emerged, ultimately to become law early in August 1965, was a tough one, containing provisions that were almost certain to be challenged at the bar of the Supreme Court. The Court heard argument on a case as early as January 1966. (While it had that case under scrutiny, a lower federal tribunal in Louisiana declared some sections of the statute unconstitutional, tossing out the nation's first voter intimidation suit under the new law.[2])

The legislation which had passed the Senate by a vote of 79:18 and the House of Representatives by 328:74—an even more decisive margin than in the enactment of the Civil Rights Act of 1964—contained these key elements:

> It barred literacy and other tests for voting deemed to be discriminatory, based on a rather complicated formula that affected six states in the Deep South, Alabama, Georgia, Mississippi, Louisiana, South Carolina, and Virginia; 34 counties in North Carolina; all of Alaska; and single counties in Maine, Arizona, and Idaho. (The formula concerning literacy tests extended only to those areas where such tests were in force November 1, 1964, *and* where less than 50 per cent of the voting age population participated in the 1964 presidential election.)

[1] *The New York Times*, March 16, 1965.
[2] *United States v. Harvey*, 34 LW 2424 (February 15, 1966).

It set up new criminal penalties for attempts to keep qualified persons from voting or to threaten or harm civil rights workers assisting potential voters.

It directed the U.S. Department of Justice to begin court suits challenging the constitutionality of poll taxes still used in *state and local* elections. (Arkansas having by then abandoned the poll tax, this provision was directed at Alabama, Mississippi, Texas and Virginia.)

Clearly, the fundamental purpose of the Voting Rights Act of 1965, the passage of which President Johnson termed a "proud moment for this nation," was to facilitate Negro registration and voting by the elimination in those states where discrimination had been proved to be both most rampant and most persistent of all requirements but the basic ones of age, residence, mental competence, and absence of a criminal record. As already noted, these states were ingeniously designated as any state where literacy tests and other devices were employed when less than 50 per cent of the voting-age population either was registered or actually voted in November 1964. Needless to say, this and some other provisions [1] of the Act raised serious problems of constitutionality—given the somewhat murky division of responsibility for suffrage between the federal and state governments. The nation awaited the Supreme Court's impending decision with considerable interest; though it seemed hardly likely that the tribunal would strike down legislation that, however marginal in constitutional interpretation in some of its aspects, was still clearly based upon the letter and spirit of the Fifteenth Amendment—adopted some 95 years before. The Court's answer came rapidly and, as

[1] One of the most contentious was the so-called Kennedy amendment to the statute, which specifically granted the right to vote to Puerto Ricans, of whom 750,000 then lived in New York City, provided they had a sixth-grade education from a Puerto Rican school—in which Spanish is the principal language, of course. In effect, the amendment circumvented the otherwise legal New York literacy test. A three-judge federal district court, one judge dissenting, declared that section of the Voting Rights Act unconstitutional in November 1965 (247 F. Supp. 196). However, in a 7:2 opinion, written by Mr. Justice Brennan, with Justices Harlan and Stewart dissenting, the Supreme Court reversed the lower tribunal, concluding that Congress in passing the special Spanish literacy amendment to the bill had acted legally because it was "appropriate legislation . . . plainly adapted" to the enforcement of the equal protection of the laws clause of the Fourteenth Amendment and otherwise consistent with the letter and spirit of the Constitution.

anticipated, approvingly: Mr. Justice Black dissenting in part and concurring in part, the Court upheld the seven major provisions of the Act in a 31-page opinion written by Mr. Chief Justice Warren.[1] He based his ruling squarely on the Act's constitutionality and, predictably, on the power of Congress to act under the provisions of the Fifteenth Amendment. The Chief Justice wrote that two points "emerge vividly" from the voluminous legislative history of the Act. First, he declared that Congress felt itself "confronted by an insidious and pervasive evil which had been perpetuated in certain parts of our country by unremitting and ingenious defiance of the Constitution"; and, second, he declared that Congress demonstrably concluded that the unsuccessful remedies which it had prescribed in the past would have to be replaced by "sterner and more elaborate measures." [2] Over and over again, he used the phrase "Congress knew...." Indeed, it did—and so did the country and the world. "We may finally look forward to the day," concluded the Chief Justice of the United States, quoting verbatim the commands of Amendment Fifteen, "when truly the right of citizens of the United States to vote shall not be denied or abridged by the United States or by any state on account of race, color, or previous condition of servitude." [3]

The Voting Rights Act of 1965 had hardly become law when the Johnson Administration commenced its enforcement with two steps. First, literacy tests were suspended as a prerequisite to voting in seven states (Alabama, Alaska,[4] Georgia, Louisiana, Mississippi, South Carolina, and Virginia), 26 counties of North Carolina, and one in Arizona; second, the Department of Justice, true to its mandate under the Act, filed suits to abolish the poll tax in the four states that still had one: Alabama, Mississippi, Texas, and Virginia. Moreover, under the provisions of the law, some 45 *federal voting examiners,* all employees of the United States Civil Service Commission, were standing by in the Deep South, waiting to move into 15 to 20 counties that had a history of resistance to Negro voting. The examiners, working in teams, began to register eligible Negroes within a matter of days that August. Results were almost immediately apparent: on the first supervised registration day under the new statute, Negro voter lists

[1] *South Carolina v. Katzenbach,* 383 U.S. 301 (1965).
[2] *Ibid.,* at 309.
[3] *Ibid.,* at 337.
[4] On May 24, 1966, Alaska became the first state to be exempted from the Act's literacy test suspension provisions.

in nine counties with a history of rampant discrimination in Alabama, Louisiana, and Mississippi increased by 65 per cent! A total of 1,144 Negroes added their names to the scrolls that, at least in theory, are the vehicle of a democracy's expression of popular wishes. Extending their work to four other counties, the federal voting examiners had registered almost 20,000 Negroes within ten days. In the first two months after the enactment of the new voting law, about 110,000 Negroes were registered voluntarily by *local officials* and more than 56,000 had been registered by the federal examiners sent to areas designed by Attorney-General Nicholas de B. Katzenbach. For the first time, Negroes voted in large numbers in the Deep South in the May 1966 primaries—and they elected their candidate to office. Thus 150,000 voted in Alabama alone!

But, although the federal government continued to apply pressure, the above pace could hardly be expected to be maintained, and civil rights leaders as well as government officials began to reduce by as much as 50 per cent their original estimate of some one million new Negro registrants during the first year of the 1965 Act. Despite the increase of federal examiners in additional Southern hard-core counties, the number of applications had perceptibly decreased by the end of 1965 both in the voluntarily registering areas and in those that would not register Negroes without the federal hand. By early March 1966, under pressure of the new law, federal examiners had enrolled 101,370 Negroes; local registrars another 201,000.[1] By November 1966, the percentage of eligible Negroes registered to vote in the South ranged from 27.8 per cent in Mississippi to 48.9 per cent in Alabama to 71.7 per cent in Tennessee, averaging 50.1 per cent. Although the Negro apathy and fear about voting that had been so firmly established by decades of white exclusionary rule could not be eradicated overnight, the Southern Negro registration had now reached 2,671,514, fully 1,200,000 more than as of July 1960.[2] Tools for change were now at hand against a background of new and novel tactics of protest, and for some time now there had been movement, coupled with difficulties, on other fronts of the race issue as well.

[1] *The New York Herald Tribune*, March 7, 1966.
[2] *The New York Times*, July 27, 1966, and November 27, 1966. As of September 1, 1966, a total of 1,147,236 Negroes had registered in the five "black belt" states of Mississippi, Alabama, Georgia, Louisiana, and South Carolina, compared with 687,000 when the Voting Rights Act of 1965 became law one year earlier. (*Ibid.*, October 21, 1966.)

New Tactics for Old Problems and New

The evolving desegregation process, described in the preceding pages of this chapter, underwent a major change following that Opinion Monday on May 17, 1954, when Mr. Chief Justice Warren announced the Court's decision in *Brown v. Board of Education*.[1] The change in tactics, if not in strategy did not really begin until the Montgomery Bus Boycott in December 1955, and perhaps it was not dramatically evident until the Greensboro "sit-ins" early in 1960. But whatever its genesis, the protest movement was now clearly tired of delays, frustrated by creeping gradualness, angered by physical outrages. Generally feeling his socio-political oats, the Negro became militant.

This growing militancy on the parts of thousands of Negroes—and a good many white supporters—has not abated and is not likely to do so for some time, despite some serious excesses and despite some questionable tactics. The initiative for change has demonstrably shifted from a relatively few professional desegregationists, in such traditional organizations as the NAACP and the Urban League, to large numbers of average citizens who concluded somewhere along the line that they had no choice but to do battle against "The System" by direct action "in the streets." This development both stemmed from and gave rise to a coterie of new and formally organized protest groups, particularly the Southern Christian Leadership Conference (SCLC), created under the leadership of Dr. Martin Luther King, Jr., in 1956-57; the Congress of Racial Equality (CORE), established in 1943 but not really coming to the fore until the 1950's; and the Student Non-Violent Co-ordinating Committee (SNCC), the youngest "action" group, founded in 1960.[2] While SCLC under Dr. King's guidance steadfastly maintained its dedication to non-violence, CORE and especially SNCC—despite "Non-Violent" in its name—proved to be not averse to violent action, as demonstrated in 1965 and 1966 under the direction of such fiery, young, and new leaders as CORE's Floyd McKissick and SNCC's Stokely Carmichael.

[1] 347 U.S. 483.
[2] See the illuminating article by James H. Laue, "The Changing Character of Negro Protest," in 357 *The Annals of the American Academy of Political and Social Science* 119 (January 1965).

The "sit-in" movement of 1960 first illustrated the belief that only *action* would obtain results, a belief which became a religious conviction of these groups and their followers—action as a supplement or complement to the educational and legal means heretofore employed predominantly. For Dr. King and other protest movement leaders and the vast number of Negroes, while the educational and especially the legal tools had produced significant results since World War II, they were nevertheless too slow in producing change. In certain communities, not even a gradualist approach was acceptable to the white "power structure." Turning then to "action," the Negro leadership rapidly discovered that the development of community "crisis situations," such as economic boycotts, by the Negro protest movements, was usually at least partly successful simply because the crises demanded a speedy resolution by the community decision-makers. Yet "activism" was certain to raise serious problems in and for society —problems of the limits of civil disobedience—problems, once again, of where to draw the line.

Illustrations of New Tactics. Of course, some "action" had accompanied the movement even prior to the days of Greensboro; there were sporadic rallies, marches, boycotts, and picket lines. Almost none really attained major significance.

But the Montgomery, Alabama, bus boycott, a year and a half after *Brown*, did. It was a stubborn, year-long boycott of the city's busses in protest against Montgomery's continued segregated seating practices. The action began when a Negro seamstress, Mrs. Rosa Parks, refused to give up her seat to a white rider and was fined $10.00. Led by Dr. King, Montgomery's entire Negro community participated in the boycott. No longer willing to sit in the "Jim Crow"[1] section, something they had done all their lives, they were ready to walk miles or wait hours for car pools. As one 72-year-old Negro woman said, "my feets is tired but my soul is rested."[2] The boycott did not end until, one entire year later, segregation was outlawed by a federal court injunction. It is not astonishing that the so successful Montgomery boycott set a precedent for similar boycotts and demonstrations in

[1] For a superb analysis of "Jim Crow," see C. Vann Woodward's *The Strange Career of Jim Crow, op. cit.*

[2] As quoted by Alan F. Westin in Emmette S. Redford, *et al.*, *Politics and Government in the United States* (New York: Harcourt, Brace & World, 1965), p. 632.

cities throughout the South, extending to retail stores, produce markets, and a host of other sales and service facilities.

Yet a boycott destined to be far more militant and far more controversial began on February 1, 1960, when four Negro boys, all freshmen at North Carolina Agricultural and Technical College, began what at first was a spontaneous "sit-in" demonstration at the lunch counter of Woolworth's dime store in Greensboro. They had asked for cups of coffee, and had done so politely, but were refused service. They then simply continued to sit at the counter in protest—notwithstanding cursing, pushing, spitting, and catsup-throwing by their white neighbors. Ultimately, the four filed out, formed a tight circle on the sidewalk, and recited the Lord's Prayer. Then another group took over for them inside.

This example of non-violent protest spread to six other North Carolina cities and seven other Southern states within four weeks. Not only did the Greensboro sit-in set a precedent, it led directly to the organization of the Student Non-Violent Co-ordinating Committee. SNCC quickly began to serve both in the South and in the North as an organizer and backer for "sit-ins" and a large variety of other "ins," such as "stand-ins," "read-ins," "pray-ins," "wade-ins," "sleep-ins," and "lie-ins." [1] Thousands who had never before taken an active part in the protest movement now joined. The new movement was variously successful, but it also gave rise to an intricate set of legal problems stemming from the action of the protesters themselves or the local authorities who, either by request or on their own initiative, would often arrest the "ins" for such common law offenses as "breach of the peace" or "trespassing." When statutes compelling, permitting, or

[1] Sit-in demonstrations in Southern cities during the 14 months from Feb. 1, 1960, to March 1961 were as follows (adapted from the special report of the Southern Regional Council, *The Freedom Ride*, published in Atlanta in May 1961):

				Demonstrators	Arrests
Feb.	1, 1960	North Carolina	Greensboro	4,200	268
Feb.	11	Virginia	Hampton	11,000	235
Feb.	12	South Carolina	Rock Hill	4,000	947
Feb.	12	Florida	Deland	2,500	243
Feb.	13	Tennessee	Nashville	16,000	692
Feb.	25	Alabama	Montgomery	5,500	86
Feb.	27	Kentucky	Lexington	6,000	374
March	5	Texas	Houston	6,500	317
March	10	Arkansas	Little Rock	50	20
March	15	Georgia	Atlanta	7,000	292
March	28	Louisiana	Baton Rouge	10,000	71
March	27, 1961	Mississippi	Jackson	1,600	40
		Totals		74,350	3,585

forbidding segregation were present, the legal setting was relatively tailor-made for litigation, of course; but a legal controversy did arise over the actions of the "ins" and their *private* inhospitable hosts acting in their *private* capacity. Here line-drawing would naturally be far more difficult; here, indeed, the Supreme Court's usually unanimous opinion on race discrimination issues would be bitterly split.

Other participants in "ins" movements, mounted largely by CORE, were so-called freedom riders. The chief target of these riders was transportation, supposedly desegregated for some time. The "rides" not only pin-pointed but actually tested, often at the cost of imprisonment and violence, the still prevalent segregation practices in almost all interstate travel and terminal facilities in the Deep South. In general, these rides accomplished their purpose: the exposure of continued, rampant violation of what was now the law of the land. Yet it was the racial cauldron of Birmingham, Alabama, that was destined to become the center of the militant Negro activism of 1963 and the years to follow.

The Birmingham Trigger, April 1963. Having failed to make any meaningful headway in the quest for desegregation in Alabama's largest and most highly industrialized city, Dr. King and his associates staged mass demonstrations there. Led by Dr. King, his faithful ally, the Reverend Ralph D. Abernathy, and another well-known leader, the Reverend Fred L. Shuttlesworth,[1] thousands of Negroes, including school children, began street demonstrations in Birmingham during the first week of April 1963. Some 150 demonstrators were arrested on the first day, but the protests continued with a march and a "kneel-in" in the face of a court injunction. When the three leaders were also arrested, the street demonstrations grew larger daily. So did the prison populace. A month later, on May 2 alone, police arrested 500, a figure that reached 2500 in a matter of days. Failing to obtain any concessions in their "quest for justice" and thus continuing to demonstrate, the Negroes now met high-pressure water hoses, police dogs, and cattle-prods. The entire nation was outraged, and the Birmingham authorities, under pressure from both the Kennedy Administration and local business leaders, agreed to a "truce," and promised alleviation of the Negroes' grievances in such areas as public ac-

[1] Shuttleworth's belligerence had taken him to the U.S. Supreme Court fully eight times by the Spring of 1966, thus making him the most litigious individual in the Court's 177-year history.

commodation, employment opportunities, and inter-racial commit-
tees. But Governor Wallace promptly denounced the agreement, and
after a series of bomb blasts directed against, among others, Dr. King
and his brother, thousands of irate Negroes resumed demonstrations
on May 11. Within hours the streets were filled with uncontrollable
rioters battling with the police. At this juncture President Kennedy,
having experienced nothing but defiance from Governor Wallace,
dispatched 3000 federal troops to the area—but not to Birmingham
itself. This seemed to achieve results; racial tensions gradually sub-
sided. And although they were revived by Governor Wallace's infamous "schoolhouse door stand," which unsuccessfully tried to prevent the court-ordered admission of two Negroes to the University
of Alabama at Tuscaloosa, an important corner had been turned.
After his interference with court-ordered desegregation of certain public schools that September was blocked by the federalization of the
Alabama National Guard, a tenuous peace finally came to Birmingham. Tragically it came only after four little Negro girls had died in
the wreckage of the bombed Sixteenth Street Baptist Church and two
Negro teenagers had been gunned down by white terrorists.

The 1963 Birmingham events set off chain reactions throughout
the country. In the seventy days following the Birmingham "truce,"
almost 800 racial demonstrations took place in the nation. They culminated in the mammoth, orderly Washington march of August
1963, in which, as we have noted, more than 200,000 Negroes and
whites participated. Racial demonstrations continued during the sum-
mers of 1963, 1964, 1965, and 1966 in such Northern cities as New
York, Philadelphia, Chicago, Newark, Rochester, St. Louis, Cleveland, San Francisco, Los Angeles (the bloody Watts riots already
described), and Jersey City. Not even the new federal civil rights and
voting statutes would lessen the now determined, often militant and
impatient drive for Negro equality. It had obtained results! For most
Southerners, adaptation to change had become a fact of daily life for
state and local governments; racial incidents had to be avoided; and
resistance to federal authority was, in the long run, futile. Still, the
Southern leadership was allowed to move slowly and, with some exceptions, to do nothing more than the bare minimum. "Tokenism"
was the word of the day.

This attitude, however understandable it might be in terms of the
practices and traditions of generations, continued to incite militancy

on the part of the increasingly restive Negroes—and now particularly those in the ghettos of the Northern cities. They were tired of waiting, tired of gradualism, tired of tokenism. In effect, they demanded what was patently impossible: full equality "here and now"—and if that meant "favored treatment," so be it! But Negro poverty, both of means and of opportunity, and prejudice—always prejudice—could not so quickly be eradicated. The resultant frustration frequently generated an excessive belligerency, often referred to by the participants as "direct action," which did more harm than good to the Negro cause, and, as we have indicated, provoked a serious split in the Supreme Court,[1] which had been supporting civil rights causes with unanimity.

Questionable and Tragic Tactics. The continuing actions were less "demonstrations" than they were "community harassment," and they usually occurred in the large urban Northern centers. Thus, for example, the prostrate bodies of Negroes and white supporters halted traffic during rush hours on such vital arteries as the Brooklyn Bridge; there was deliberate stalling of automobiles on the highways to the World's Fair and to baseball games; in Cleveland demonstrators lay down in the path of bulldozers on construction projects, resulting in the tragic death of a white minister who was run over; in Philadelphia a private school was picketed and harassed daily for months, necessitating the employment of a large additional police detail at great expense to the city; there were sit-ins in the offices of governors (e.g. Rockefeller and Scranton) and of mayors (e.g. Wagner and Tate). These and similar disruptive tactics raised serious questions of both their legality and regard for the rights of others.

Worse, of course, was the wave of wanton riots that swept many Northern cities in 1965 and 1966. There could be no excuse for the looting, the burning, the destruction, the loss of lives—the reckless dedication to licentious manifestations of hate. As a result, at the end of 1966 there was mounting fear among civil rights leaders and supporters that the days of wide national support for civil rights had come to an end, at least temporarily. Indeed there were those who felt that the now mounting Northern white disaffection could lead to such a setback that it would be years before the movement, and

[1] See, among others, *Bell v. Maryland*, 378 U.S. 226 (1964); *Hamm v. City of Rock Hill*, 370 U.S. 306; *Elton v. Cox*, 379 U.S. 536 (1965); *Brown v. Louisiana*, 383 U.S. 131 (1966); and *Adderley v. Florida*, 385 U.S. 39 (1966).

the Negro masses, would recover. The failure of Congress to pass the 1966 Civil Rights bill was a case in point. As President Johnson told a group of visiting bishops from the all-Negro African Methodist Episcopal Church in October of that year:

> We have entered a new phase. . . . What if the cry for freedom becomes the sound of a brick cracking through a store window, turning over an automobile in the street, or the sound of the mob? If that sound should drown out the voices of reason, frustration will replace progress and all of our best work will be undone.[1]

In any event, it was now crystal clear that even in the non-violent sector of the Negro protest lines were becoming increasingly blurred: had not the limits of civil disobedience in a free representative democracy now been reached, and sometimes execeded? It became clear that there was a difference between the exercise of constitutional rights that are inherent in the freedoms of speech, press, assembly, and petition and the kind of militant, often lawless, activities that were becoming frequent. The basic issues of racial discrimination, of the injustices of generations, were clear to all now and there could no longer be any doubt regarding the need for the acknowledgment, both legally and morally, of full egalitarianism. Yet, it was obvious that it would take a long time to achieve it in the public sphere—and still much longer in the private sector.

Since the means of amelioration of injustice in a representative democracy are patently lodged in the public sector, one of the great issues of the day became: Just what constitutes that "public" sphere, and is hence reachable by the authority of government under law? Just when does an action became "state action"—an action subject to the commands and sanctions of the Constitution, in general, and Amendment Fourteen, in particular?

STATE ACTION AND BEYOND: A TRUE DILEMMA

The words of the famed second sentence of Section 1 of the Fourteenth Amendment concerning "state action" would seem to be quite clear:

> No *State shall make or enforce any law* which shall abridge the privileges or immunities of citizens of the United States; *nor shall any State*

[1] *Time*, October 7, 1966.

deprive any person of life, liberty, or property without due process of law; *nor deny to any person within its jurisdiction the equal protection of the laws.*[1]

What is proscribed here is *discriminatory state action* only; it does not extend to *private action*. And this is the interpretation the judiciary has quite naturally and appropriately given to the Amendment. But at what point has a State, or its "agent," deprived an individual of life, liberty, or property without due process of law; or, more appropriately since Negro litigants have relied predominantly upon the "equal protection of the laws" clause, when has a State, or its "agent," denied an individual that equal protection?

THE DILEMMA

Technically, state action is any action taken by legislative, executive, or judicial instrumentalities of the state. Private is any act or action engaged in or perpetrated by any individual in his private capacity and associations.[2] But six Supreme Court justices in a highly significant set of racial violence cases in 1966,[3] warned that they would feel bound to uphold any appropriate law aimed at punishing *private* individuals who use violence to deny persons their Fourteenth Amendment rights. Of course, *state* activity causing or abetting racial discrimination would, under present-day interpretations by the courts, clearly and obviously be regarded as violating the Fourteenth Amendment injunctions against discriminatory state action. It is thus that the "separate but equal" clause met its doom, along with the manifold instances of state-authored or state-enforced racial discrimination in education, transportation, housing, employment, voting, and a number of other areas. But *private* discrimination, or so it might be

---

[1] Italics added.

[2] One expert, Professor Louis Henkin, suggests three bases for holding the state legally responsible *when private discrimination is involved:* 1) "The state is responsible for what it could prevent, and should prevent, and fails to prevent." 2) "The state is responsible for discrimination which it encourages or sanctions." 3) "The state is responsible when its courts act to render discrimination effective." "*Shelley v. Kraemer:* Notes for a Revised Opinion," 110 *University of Pennsylvania Law Review* 481-87 (February 1962). Yet some of his arguments in this important and scholarly article would seem to cast doubt on his own tests.

[3] *United States v. Price*, 383 U.S. 688 (1966), and *United States v. Guest*, 383 U.S. 746 (1966). Expressed in two concurring opinions, severally joined by the Chief Justice and Associate Justices Black, Douglas, Clark, Brennan, and Fortas.

assumed, would be entirely legal, even though not democratic or just. Hence, until the passage of the federal Civil Rights Act of 1964, it was not considered illegal to refuse to serve or admit Negroes in privately owned establishments, such as restaurants, hotels, motels, or theaters, as long as the owner was *really* a *private* person, acting in his *private* capacity, and, of course, provided that *state* law did not forbid such discrimination.

Even before the Civil Rights Act of 1964 extended the reach of governmental proscription of discrimination on racial, religious, nationality and other related grounds to such contentious areas as "public accommodations" and "'employment," the distinction between "public" and "private" under certain conditions had been legally questioned, but never really effectively challenged. Perhaps the first such instance to raise and at the same time to befuddle the basic issue at the bar of the judiciary was the now so well-known *Restrictive Covenant* decision, *Shelley v. Kraemer.*[1] Briefly, in the lead case, J. D. and Ethel Lee Shelley, Negroes from St. Louis, Missouri, had "for valuable consideration" received in 1945 from one Josephine Fitzgerald a warranty deed to a parcel of land situated in an area restricted by common agreement of some thirty resident-owners to persons of "the Caucasian race." The restrictive covenant, originally scheduled to run from 1911 to 1961, specifically barred "people of the Negro or Mongolian race." Louis and Fern E. Kraemer, for the restrictive covenanters, attempted to block the Fitzgerald-to-Shelley sale in the appropriate Missouri State Circuit Court, but they lost—more or less on an interpretative technicality. The Supreme Court of Missouri reversed the lower court's ruling and directed it to order the Shelleys to vacate their newly occupied property.

With Justices Reed, Jackson, and Rutledge taking no part in either the consideration or the decision of the case, the Supreme Court of the United States unanimously *reversed* the highest Missouri court. Speaking through Mr. Chief Justice Vinson, the Court affirmed that orders by state courts *enforcing* restrictive covenants based on race and color are violative of the "equal protection of the laws" clause of the Fourteenth Amendment. Restrictive covenants drawn up by private individuals, reasoned the Court, are not in themselves a violation of the Amendment's commands as long as they are completely

[1] 334 U.S. 1 (1948). A similar question was raised by a Detroit group and was decided concurrently.

private and voluntary (and, of course, do not breach some state law or state ordinance, which restrictive covenants would have done in some twenty-odd states in 1967).[1] "Here, however," the Chief Justice pointed out, "there was more," because the State of Missouri, through its judicial branch, not only *aided in the enforcement* of the restrictive covenant—which would in itself have constituted forbidden state action—but, in effect, rendered the agreements workable.[2] "We have no doubt," concluded America's highest judicial official, "that there has been *state action* in the full and complete sense of the phrase." [3]

In other words, *Shelley* presented the intriguing dichotomy of permissible private discrimination so long as no state aid in its implementation or enforcement was sought—and the judicial aid desired by Kraemer and his supporters was regarded as such state aid. The implications of the *Shelley* case for allied areas became quickly apparent, and the decision evoked a flood of favorable, unfavorable, and tentative commentary by laymen and professionals alike.[4] But whatever one's feelings regarding either the equity of the decision or the viability of the dichotomy which it enunciated at so crucial a time—although it did of course not really originate it [5]—the decision brought the state action problem to the fore with a vengeance. In brief, the problem comes down to the crucial question of a free democratic society: how to reconcile the competing rights and claims of *equality and liberty*—a question as old as the ages. Where does the Constitution draw the line between the right to legal equality and to equality of opportunity, and the rights of liberty, property, privacy, and voluntary association? Where do we draw it? Where should we draw it? Where can we draw it? It is, of course, a balancing problem. Yet "balancing" is a delicate matter, often regarded as a "nasty," even unconstitutional one in some quarters, particularly when applied to

[1] Also to be kept in mind, of course, are the now applicable *federal* anti-discrimination rules and regulations in the housing field.

[2] *Loc. cit.*, at 13.

[3] *Ibid.*, at 19.

[4] See, for example, Herbert Wechsler, "Toward Neutral Principles of Constitutional Law," 73 *Harvard Law Review* 1 (1959); Louis Henkin, "Some Reflections on Current Constitutional Controversy," 109 *University of Pennsylvania Law Review* 637 (1961); Louis Henkin, "*Shelley v. Kraemer*: Notes for a Revised Opinion," *op. cit.*; and Louis Pollak, "Racial Discrimination and Judicial Integrity: A Reply to Professor Wechsler," 108 *University of Pennsylvania Law Review* 1 (1959).

[5] The problem had been raised early and notably in the *Civil Rights Cases*, 109 U.S. 3 (1883).

the Bill of Rights. We have seen Mr. Justice Black's avowedly absolutist position on the First Amendment,[1] but we now see him deeply
disturbed over the implications of the broad interpretation of "state
action" under the Fourteenth Amendment; he has come in fact, to
"balance" *here*—most notably in some of the sit-in and demonstration race cases [2]—although he did *not* in the cases concerning the
First Amendment. A few additional illustrations of the problem of
private and state action and rights may be helpful (although it ought
to be noted that the problem is assuredly not confined to matters of
race).

Three years prior to the enactment of the public accommodations
provisions of the Civil Rights Act of 1964, for example, the Court
faced the dilemma of private versus state (or "governmental," as some
prefer to call it) in a case involving a private restaurant in Wilmington, Delaware, that had leased its space in a parking garage from a
municipal authority, an agency of the State of Delaware.[3] In a five-
man majority opinion, authored by Mr. Justice Clark, with Mr. Justice Stewart concurring in the decision on separate grounds, the Court
ruled that the Eagle Coffee Shoppe, Inc., in refusing to serve Negroes,
had violated the equal protection clause because the services furnished
by the parking authority to the lessee constituted the kind of "state
action" which falls under the Fourteenth Amendment's purvey. In
Clark's concluding words:

> . . . what we hold today is that when a State leases public property in
> the manner and for the purpose shown to have been the case here, the
> proscriptions of the Fourteenth Amendment must be complied with by
> lessee as certainly as though they were binding covenants written into
> the agreement itself.[4]

But Justices Frankfurter, Harlan, and Whitaker dissented in separate opinions written by the first two. They held variously that the
majority had reached the constitutional issue prematurely and un-
necessarily, thus giving a definitive judgment to a matter so complicated that it ought to have been permitted the benefit of the doubt,
at least for the time being, and in the absence of legislative action.[5]

1 See his "The Bill of Rights," 35 *New York University Law Review* 866
(1960).
2 See footnote 1, p. 299, *supra*.
3 *Burton v. Wilmington Parking Authority*, 365 U.S. 715 (1961).
4 *Ibid.*, at 726.
5 *Ibid.*, at 727-30.

What of "private" versus "public" action inherent in the spate of "sit-in" demonstration cases that reach the Court prior to the Civil Rights Act of 1964? [1] The Act settled the matter in terms of the constitutionality of the pertinent section, based on congressional power over interstate commerce, *provided* the establishment concerned came under the provisions of the statute governing "public accommodations"; but did it really settle the problem of liberty versus equality in philosophical terms? Mr. Justice Black had joined in the unanimous opinion in the two late 1964 cases upholding [2] the law's public accommodations section; yet obviously he did so only because he believed Congress to have had the power to legislate as it had, precisely *because* it *expressly* invoked its authority over interstate commerce. But, as he had noted orally from the bench in conjunction with his dissenting opinion in one of the sit-in cases a few months earlier in 1964, "this Court has never said, in the school segregation decisions or any before or since, that the prejudice of individuals could be laid to the state." [2] And again, from the bench on the very last day of the Court's 1963-64 term, this great champion of the individual said sarcastically that the idea that the Fourteenth Amendment *itself* prohibited segregation in public accommodations made "the last six months' struggle in Congress a work of supererogation" [4]—a reference to the prolonged debate that preceded passage of the legislation. As his long-time jurisprudential "adversary," the retired Mr. Justice Frankfurter, had done so often, Hugo Lafayette Black then again admonished his country that:

> The worst citizen no less than the best is entitled to equal protection of the laws of his state and of his nation.[5]

And it was Black again, this time joined by his colleagues Harlan, Stewart, and White, who, having all voted to uphold the constitutionality of the contentious provision of the Civil Rights Act of 1964,

[1] For example, *Edwards v. South Carolina*, 372 U.S. 229 (1963), *Peterson v. Greenville*, 373 U.S. 244 (1963); *Lombard v. Louisiana*, 373 U.S. 267 (1963); *Griffin v. Maryland*, 378 U.S. 130 (1964); *Robinson v. Florida*, 378 U.S. 153 (1964); *Barr v. City of Columbia*, 378 U.S. 146 (1964); and *Bell v. Maryland*, 378 U.S. 226 (1964).

[2] *Heart of Atlanta Motel v. United States*, 379 U.S. 241 (1964), and *Katzenbach v. McClung*, 379 U.S. 294 (1964).

[3] *Barr v. City of Columbia*, loc. cit., June 23, 1964.

[4] As quoted in *The New York Times*, June 23, 1964.

[5] *Bell v. Maryland*, 378 U.S. 226 (1964), dissenting opinion, at 328.

took pains to emphasize on the very same Opinion Monday what should be obvious to all believers in law and order and the dignity of liberty: that the passage of the Act did *not* authorize persons

> who are unlawfully refused service a "right" to take the law into their own hands by sitting down and occupying the premises for as long as they choose to stay. . . .[1]

Black's deep concern continued to make itself known, albeit in the minority. Yet he carried three other justices with him when, in a public library "stand-in" case in 1966, he asked impassionedly:

> Can any provision of the United States Constitution tell any citizens —white or colored—they can march with impunity into a public library and demonstrate against some public policy? . . . It has become automatic for people to be turned loose as long as whatever they do has something to do with race. That is not the way I read the Constitution.[2]

That spring the Court summarily *upheld* the conviction of 25 New York City racial demonstrators on a housing project [3] and the conviction of a CORE "stand-in" at the office of the police chief of Syracuse.[4] And on the last day of the 1965-66 term, Mr. Justice Clark formally provided the fifth vote for that point of view, and thus a Court majority: He joined his colleagues Black, Harlan, Stewart, and White in holding that 29 persons arrested on various local charges arising from civil rights movements in 1964 in Leflore County, Mississippi, could not have their trials transferred from state to federal courts, merely upon their contention that their rights of free speech may be infringed by prejudicial treatment in state courts.[5]

Lest that decision be regarded as a procedural "fluke" or one based on a wavering majority, the same five justices were together late in 1966 in a case of particular significance in the fundamental freedom-versus-order clash because the civil rights demonstrations involved were directed against *public* rather than *private* property. Speaking through Mr. Justice Black, the new five-man majority upheld the "willful trespass" conviction of Harriet Adderley and 31 other Florida A & M University Negro students who had demonstrated outside the

1 *Hamm v. City of Rock Hill*, 379 U.S. 306, dissenting opinion, at 318.
2 *Brown v. Louisiana*, 383 U.S. 131 (1966), at 168, dissenting opinion.
3 *Penn v. New York*, 383 U.S. 969 (1966).
4 *Baer v. New York*, 384 U.S. 154 (1966).
5 *Greenwood v. Peacock*, 384 U.S. 808 (1966).

Leon County jail in Tallahassee, Florida.[1] The earlier decisions had involved prosecutions for *breach of the peace* rather than trespass. "[N]othing in the Constitution of the United States, wrote Black, attempting to draw the line between speech and conduct,

> prevents Florida from even-handed enforcement of its general trespassing statute against those refusing to obey the sheriff's order to remove themselves. . . . *The state, no less than a private owner of property has power to preserve the property under its control for* the use to which it is lawfully dedicated.[2]

But to Mr. Justice Douglas, dissenting in a vigorously-worded opinion, in which he was joined by Warren, Brennan, and Fortas, the Black view represented "a great break with the traditions of the Court." Now, he said, trespass laws could be used as a "blunderbuss" to suppress civil rights, and he concluded that the Court has "now set into the record a great and wonderful police-state doctrine." [3]

State Action or Routine Service. What of such services rendered by the state as licensing or the probation of wills that do involve the state, but which had heretofore been regarded as *routine services* rather than as state action? If these services were to be construed as "state action," would not almost *everything* then be state action? Would anything remain in the private sphere at all?

Girard College. The matter of the probation of discriminatory wills (of which there are innumerable examples) underwent its first important post-*Brown* litigation in the *Girard College* cases.[4] These cases involved Philadelphia's famed Girard College, actually a private elementary and high school for "male, white orphans," as provided in the generous will of Stephen S. Girard, a Philadelphia merchant in the early nineteenth century. The trust established by Girard's will was being administered by the Board of Directors of the City of Philadelphia when the Supreme Court of the United States, citing the precedent of the *Public School Segregation Cases*,[5] ruled unconsti-

---

[1] *Adderley v. Florida*, 385 U.S. 39 (1966). The Florida statute reads: "Every trespass on the property of another, committed with a malicious and mischievous intent . . . shall be punished."

[2] *Ibid*, at 47. (Italics supplied.)

[3] *Ibid.*, extemporaneous remark from the bench, November 14, 1967.

[4] *Pennsylvania v. Board of Directors of City Trusts of the City of Philadelphia*, 353 U.S. 230 (1957) and 357 U.S. 570 (1958), *certiorari* denied.

[5] *Brown v. Board of Education of Topeka*, 347 U.S. 483 (1954).

tutional as a violation of the "equal protection of the laws" clause of
Amendment Fourteen the municipality's described participation in
the Girard Trust's administration. It was deemed "state action." But
then an interesting turn of events took place: the City asked the
Orphans Court, the appropriate tribunal of jurisdiction, to *remove
the municipal trustees* and to *substitute private trustees*. This the
Orphans Court did promptly, and the Supreme Court of the Commonwealth of Pennsylvania upheld the action as not being violative
of the equal protection clause's "state action" concept. In other words,
the state judiciary did not regard either the administration of the
trust by private individuals or the role of the two courts in facilitating
it to be constitutionally proscribed. On Pennsylvania Attorney-General's petition for a writ of *certiorari*, the United States Supreme
Court denied review. Such denial, as we have noted, does not necessarily mean approval of the action below, but it assuredly ends the
matter in so far as the unsuccessful petitioner is concerned. Nonetheless, the Girard problem continued to simmer and became acute again
late in 1966.[1]

Bacon's Park. But the Supreme Court's action did not indubitably
signify "the end of every day's evening." In a noteworthy 1966 decision, the Court dealt with the pertinent question of whether a pri-
vately-owned park in Macon, Georgia, could discriminate because of
the terms of the original donor's will. In 1914, the 100-acre park at
issue had been left in trust to the City of Macon by the will of a
former Confederate general, Senator Augustus Octavius Bacon. The
will stipulated that the park's use be reserved for "white women and
children." As did parts of the Girard will, Bacon's bequest contained
a number of features that were ultimately branded as "state action"
by civil rights leaders. The will had been drawn up under a Georgia
law that, unlike Pennsylvania, specifically permitted segregation in
charitable trusts. But like Philadelphia, Macon appointed the trustees,
and, like Girard College, Bacon's Park was considered an eleemosynary institution and therefore tax exempt. Similar to the Philadelphia
activities involving Girard, Macon withdrew as trustee in 1963 and
transferred the fiduciary authority to private trustees after lower federal courts had ruled unmistakably that a municipality could not constitutionally operate a segregated park.

[1] See n. 2, p. 310, *infra*.

Six Negroes succeeded in getting the trustee transfer question to the Supreme Court, contending that Macon had become so intimately involved in the operations of Bacon's Park that to permit private individuals to take over and continue to discriminate racially would be tantamount to "unconstitutional state action." In a 6:3 decision, with Mr. Justice Douglas delivering the Court's opinion, the Supreme Court agreed with the six petitioners.[1] It held that Macon had become so "entwined" in the park's operation that the mere change of trustees could not constitutionally remove the command to desegregate. Park services, Douglas held for himself, the Chief Justice, and Associate Justices Brennan, Clark, and Fortas, are "municipal in nature" and in the "public domain." Under the circumstances, he ruled, "we cannot but conclude that the public character of this park requires that it be treated as a public institution" and therefore subject to the commands of the "equal protection of the laws" clause of the Fourteenth Amendment. As opposed to golf clubs, social centers, *schools*, and other similar organizations, a park, Douglas explained, "is more like a fire department or police department that traditionally serves the community. Mass recreation through the use of parks is plainly in the public domain." [2]

Justices Harlan and Stewart dissented, as did Black, but the latter did so on separate and largely jurisdictional grounds. To Harlan and Stewart, the Douglas theme was at best dubious. Noting that Douglas had specifically excepted private schools, Harlan was nonetheless alarmed, contending that the Douglas theory could

> be spun out to reach *privately owned* orphanages, libraries, garbage collection companies, detective agencies, and a host of other functions *commonly regarded as nongovernmental though paralleling fields of governmental activity.*[3]

As for private schools, Harlan argued cogently that the "public function" of privately established schools and privately established parks is assuredly similar. If, Harlan continued, the majority really believed that its ruling left "unaffected the traditional view that the Fourteenth Amendment does *not* compel private schools to adapt their

[1] *Evans v. Newton*, 382 U.S. 296 (1966).
[2] *Ibid.*, at 302.
[3] *Ibid.*, at 322. (Italics added.)

admission policies to its requirements," he certainly could not agree with their interpretation in the light of the *Bacon's Park* case. He regarded it as indeed difficult

> to avoid the conclusion that this decision opens the door to reversal of these basic constitutional concepts. . . . The example of schools is, I think, sufficient to indicate the pervasive potentialities of this "public function" theory . . . a catch phrase as vague and amorphous as it is far-reaching.[1]

"Pervasive potentialities," indeed! It will be interesting to see what effect, if any, the *Bacon's Park* case will have upon the Girard College situation. Three months prior to the Macon holding, Pennsylvania's Republican governor, William W. Scranton, instituted a suit in federal court to require the desegregation of Girard College, will or no will. Would the decision in *Bacon's Park* case strengthen his chance of success? A good many civil rights attorneys were convinced that it would, yet one must indeed be wary of predicting Court actions—despite the claims of our contemporary methodological prognosticators. Moreover, Mr. Justice Douglas almost seemed to establish an out for himself and his doctrine by specifically *exempting* private schools. Still, private schools—including Girard College—are universally the beneficiaries of tax exemptions, and often of other governmental services.[2]

CODA

Thus we return to the basic question of establishing a viable line between "private" and "state" action. Does the line *really* serve the desired purpose when it is applied to such utterly routine governmental services as business registration, licensing, contract enforcement, or

[1] *Ibid.*, at 322.
[2] The *Girard* case did begin to boil up again: In September 1966, following lengthy sparring between the NAACP and the school's board of trustees, U.S. District Court Judge Joseph S. Lord, III, ruled that Negroes cannot be excluded from Girard College *under Pennsylvania law*. Specifically *refusing to pass on the probate problem*, Judge Lord simply held that the Pennsylvania Public Accommodations Act of 1939—which threw open all *public* institutions and accommodations—applied to Girard College, for he classified it as a "public institution." Shortly thereafter, he ordered the admission of seven Negro orphans if they were otherwise found to qualify. The trustees appealed his decision to the U.S. Third Circuit Court of Appeals which stayed Judge Lord's order pending its own disposition of the case scheduled for early 1967. Few doubted that it would eventually reach the U.S. Supreme Court once again.

probation of wills? One may question the choice of the adjective "utterly" in conjunction with "routine services," yet we must still acknowledge that when services such as those indicated are categorized as "state action" the private sector becomes an anomaly. Perhaps this has happened, but it is doubtful that a majority of the American polity would subscribe to such a conclusion. As Professor Joseph Tussman, a dedicated partisan of the cause of civil rights and liberties, put the matter of the private-public distinction:

> ...Do we really want, in the end, to make impossible an Armenian or Jewish Home for the Aged? Do we really wish to deny to the harassed ethnocentric commuter to the polyglot city the solace of spending the evenings of his life in the bosom of a monochromatic suburb? Must the Black Muslims admit White Christians? Must the Far Eastern Cafe hire blond waiters? Cannot the Cosmos Club be silly without losing its liquor license? Is there not some point of saying that much must wait on the slow process of education and maturation? [1]

One can wholly support, encourage, fight for, and even die for, the eradication of the fundamental injustices in the realm of racial discrimination. Equality before the law and of economic, educational, and cultural opportunity; the suffrage; access to the rewards and responsibilities of public office; the end of state-supported or state-enforced segregation—these are the aspects of the problem that should, and do matter! Pale, in contrast, are those marginal areas of wills and clubs and societies! There *is* something to be said for privacy of association, no matter how silly, undemocratic, or puerile. While, generally, the "equal protection" clause does preclude state enforcement of private discrimination, there may thus well be, in the words of Professor Louis Henkin, one of the foremost students of the field —and a devoted libertarian—"a small area of liberty favored by the Constitution even over claims to equality. Rights of liberty and property, of privacy and voluntary association, must be balanced, in close cases, against the right not to have the state enforce discrimination against the victim. In the few instances in which the right to discriminate is protected or preferred by the Constitution, the state may enforce it." [2] Unquestionably, this stance raises as many problems as it professes to solve, but a dogmatic approach is no answer either. In

---

[1] (Ed.), *The Supreme Court on Racial Discrimination* (New York: Oxford University Press, 1963), p. 5. Reprinted by permission.
[2] *"Shelley v. Kraemer,* Notes for a Revised Opinion," *op. cit.,* p. 496.

part, of course, such legislation as the public accommodations title of the Civil Rights Act of 1964, duly enacted by an overwhelming vote of the nation's legislative representatives, and subsequently upheld by the Supreme Court, settles the matter in an orderly and legal fashion.

Yet not all aspects of the vexatious public versus private problem can be conclusively settled by legislative action; nor should they be. There will always be gray areas that should be treated with common sense—a common sense cognizant of our responsibilities as well as our ideals, a common sense that is conscious both of constitutional commands and of the need to strike a balance between liberty and equality. When all other avenues fail, the last word will have to be given by the judiciary, that branch of our government that has proved itself more capable than any other of guarding our basic civil rights and liberties.

To the Supreme Court of the United States we have thus turned again and again to help us in our unending need to draw lines. Despite the storms of controversy that have engulfed it, it has remained true to its acquired role as our national conscience and our institutional common sense. In the long run, if not always in the short, the Court has served us well in maintaining that blend of change and continuity which is so necessary to the stability of the governmental process of a democracy. It has seemed to adhere to the basic American value so beautifully phrased by Thomas Jefferson and inscribed around the ceiling of the rotunda of the Jefferson Memorial—an admonition that ought to be like a beacon for all of us who cherish our traditions and responsibilities as free citizens in free democratic society: "I have sworn upon the altar of God eternal hostility against every form of tyranny over the mind of man." That commitment represents *the* basic value and line!

Appendix

Statistical Data on Supreme Court Justices

Appointing President	President's Political Party	Dates of President's Service	Name of Justice	Dates of Birth & Death	Justice's Nominal Party Allegiance on Appointment	Justice's Home State	Dates of Service on Supreme Court
Washington	Federalist	1789-1797	1. Jay, John *	1745-1829	Federalist	N.Y.	1789-1795
"	"	"	2. Rutledge, John	1739-1800	"	S.C.	1789-1791 †
"	"	"	3. Cushing, William	1732-1810	"	Mass.	1789-1810
"	"	"	4. Wilson, James	1724-1798	"	Pa.	1789-1798
"	"	"	5. Blair, John	1732-1800	"	Va.	1789-1796
"	"	"	6. Iredell, James	1750-1799	"	N.C.	1790-1799
"	"	"	7. Johnson, Thomas	1732-1819	"	Md.	1791-1793
"	"	"	8. Paterson, Wm.	1745-1806	"	N.J.	1793-1806
"	"	"	9. Rutledge, John *	1739-1800	"	S.C.	1795 ‡
"	"	"	10. Chase, Samuel	1741-1811	"	Md.	1796-1811
Adams	"	1797-1801	11. Ellsworth, Oliver *	1745-1807	"	Conn.	1796-1800
"	"	"	12. Washington, Bushrod	1762-1829	"	Pa.	1798-1829
"	"	"	13. Moore, Alfred	1755-1810	"	N.C.	1799-1804
"	"	"	14. Marshall, John *	1755-1835	"	Va.	1801-1835
Jefferson	Republican	1801-1809	15. Johnson, Wm.	1771-1834	Republican	S.C.	1804-1834
"	"	"	16. Livingston, Brockholst	1757-1823	"	N.Y.	1806-1823
"	"	"	17. Todd, Thomas	1765-1826	"	Ky.	1807-1826
Madison	"	1809-1817	18. Duval, Gabriel	1752-1844	"	Md.	1811-1835
"	"	"	19. Story, Joseph	1779-1845	"	Mass.	1811-1845
Monroe	"	1817-1825	20. Thompson, Smith	1768-1843	"	N.Y.	1823-1843
Adams	"	1825-1829	21. Trimble, Robert	1777-1828	"	Ky.	1826-1828
Jackson	Democrat	1829-1837	22. McLean, John	1785-1861	Democrat	Ohio	1829-1861
"	"	"	23. Baldwin, Henry	1780-1844	"	Pa.	1830-1844
"	"	"	24. Wayne, James M.	1790-1867	"	Ga.	1835-1867
"	"	"	25. Taney, Roger B. *	1777-1864	"	Md.	1836-1864
"	"	"	26. Barbour, Philip P.	1783-1841	"	Va.	1836-1841
"	"	"	27. Catron, John	1778-1865	"	Tenn.	1837-1865
Van Buren	"	1837-1841	28. McKinley, John	1780-1852	"	Ky.	1837-1852
"	"	"	29. Daniel, Peter V.	1784-1860	"	Va.	1841-1860
Tyler	Whig	1841-1845	30. Nelson, Samuel	1792-1873	"	N.Y.	1845-1872

* Chief Justice. † Resigned without sitting. ‡ Unconfirmed recess appointment, rejected by Senate, Dec. 1795.

Statistical Data on Supreme Court Justices—Continued

Appointing President	President's Political Party	Dates of President's Service	Name of Justice	Dates of Birth & Death	Justice's Nominal Party Allegiance on Appointment	Justice's Home State	Dates of Service on Supreme Court
Polk	Democrat	1845-1849	31. Woodbury, Levi	1789-1851	"	N.H.	1845-1851
"	"	"	32. Grier, Robert C.	1794-1870	"	Pa.	1846-1870
Fillmore	Whig	1850-1853	33. Curtis, Benjamin R.	1809-1874	Whig	Mass.	1851-1857
Pierce	Democrat	1853-1857	34. Campbell, John A.	1811-1889	Democrat	Ala.	1853-1861
Buchanan	"	1857-1861	35. Clifford, Nathan	1803-1881	"	Me.	1858-1881
Lincoln	Republican	1861-1865	36. Swayne, Noah H.	1804-1884	Republican	Ohio	1862-1881
"	"	"	37. Miller, Samuel F.	1816-1890	"	Iowa	1862-1890
"	"	"	38. Davis, David	1815-1886	"	Ill.	1862-1877
"	"	"	39. Field, Stephen J.	1816-1899	Democrat	Cal.	1863-1897
"	"	"	40. Chase, Salmon P.*	1808-1873	Republican	Ohio	1864-1873
Grant	"	1869-1877	41. Strong, William	1808-1895	"	Pa.	1870-1880
"	"	"	42. Bradley, Joseph P.	1803-1892	"	N.J.	1870-1892
"	"	"	43. Hunt, Ward	1810-1886	"	N.Y.	1872-1882
"	"	"	44. Waite, Morrison R.*	1816-1888	"	Ohio	1874-1888
Hayes	"	1877-1881	45. Harlan, John M.	1833-1911	"	Ky.	1877-1911
"	"	"	46. Woods, William B.	1824-1887	"	Ga.	1880-1887
Garfield	"	Mar.-Sept.	47. Matthews, Stanley	1824-1889	"	Ohio	1881-1889
Arthur	"	1881-1885	48. Gray, Horace	1828-1902	"	Mass.	1881-1902
"	"	"	49. Blatchford, Samuel	1820-1893	"	N.Y.	1882-1893
Cleveland	Democrat	1885-1889	50. Lamar, Lucius Q. C.	1825-1893	Democrat	Miss.	1888-1893
"	"	"	51. Fuller, Melville*	1833-1910	"	Ill.	1888-1910
Harrison	Republican	1889-1893	52. Brewer, David J.	1837-1910	Republican	Kans.	1889-1910
"	"	"	53. Brown, Henry B.	1836-1913	"	Mich.	1890-1906
"	"	"	54. Shiras, George, Jr.	1832-1924	"	Pa.	1892-1903
"	"	"	55. Jackson, Howell E.	1832-1895	Democrat	Tenn.	1893-1895
Cleveland	Democrat	1893-1897	56. White, Edward D.	1854-1921	"	La.	1894-1910
"	"	"	57. Peckham, Rufus W.	1838-1909	"	N.Y.	1895-1909
McKinley	Republican	1897-1901	58. McKenna, Joseph	1843-1926	Republican	Cal.	1898-1925
Roosevelt	"	1901-1909	59. Holmes, Oliver W., Jr.	1841-1935	"	Mass.	1902-1932
"	"	"	60. Day, William R.	1849-1923	"	Ohio	1903-1922
"	"	"	61. Moody, William H.	1853-1917	"	Mass.	1906-1910

President	Party	Term	No.	Justice	Dates	Party	State	Service
"	"		63.	Hughes, Charles E.	1862-1948	Republican	N.Y.	1910-1916
"	"		64.	White, Edward D.†*	1845-1921	Democrat	La.	1910-1921
"	"		65.	Van Devanter, Willis	1859-1941	Republican	Wyo.	1910-1937
"	"		66.	Lamar, Joseph R.	1857-1916	Democrat	Ga.	1910-1916
Wilson	Democrat	1913-1921	67.	Pitney, Mahlon	1858-1924	Republican	N.J.	1912-1922
"	"		68.	McReynolds, J. C.	1862-1946	Democrat	Tenn.	1914-1941
"	"		69.	Brandeis, Louis D.	1856-1941	Republican ‡	Mass.	1916-1939
Harding	Republican	1921-1923	70.	Clarke, John H.	1857-1945	Democrat	Ohio	1916-1922
"	"		71.	Taft, William H.*	1857-1930	Republican	Conn.	1921-1930
"	"		72.	Sutherland, George	1862-1942	Republican	Utah	1922-1938
"	"		73.	Butler, Pierce	1866-1939	Democrat	Minn.	1922-1939
Coolidge	"	1923-1929	74.	Sanford, Edward T.	1865-1930	Republican	Tenn.	1923-1930
Hoover	"	1929-1933	75.	Stone, Harlan F.	1872-1946	"	N.Y.	1925-1941
"	"		76.	Hughes, Charles E.*	1862-1948	"	N.Y.	1930-1941
"	"		77.	Roberts, Owen J.	1875-1955	"	Pa.	1930-1945
Roosevelt	Democrat	1933-1945	78.	Cardozo, Benjamin	1870-1938	Democrat	N.Y.	1932-1938
"	"		79.	Black, Hugo L.	1886-	"	Ala.	1937-
"	"		80.	Reed, Stanley F.	1884-	"	Ky.	1938-1957
"	"		81.	Frankfurter, Felix	1882-1965	Independent	Mass.	1939-1962
"	"		82.	Douglas, William	1898-	Democrat	Conn.	1939-
"	"		83.	Murphy, Frank	1893-1949	"	Mich.	1940-1949
"	"		84.	Byrnes, James F.	1879-	"	S.C.	1941-1942
"	"		85.	Stone, Harlan F.†*	1872-1946	Republican	N.Y.	1941-1946
"	"		86.	Jackson, Robert H.	1892-1954	Democrat	N.Y.	1941-1954
"	"		87.	Rutledge, Wiley B.	1894-1949	"	Iowa	1943-1949
Truman	Democrat	1945-1953	88.	Burton, Harold H.	1888-1965	Republican	Ohio	1945-1958
"	"		89.	Vinson, Fred M.*	1890-1953	Democrat	Ky.	1946-1953
"	"		90.	Clark, Tom C.	1899-	"	Tex.	1949-
"	"		91.	Minton, Sherman	1890-	"	Ind.	1949-1956
Eisenhower	Republican	1953-1961	92.	Warren, Earl*	1891-	Republican	Cal.	1953-
"	"		93.	Harlan, John M. Jr.	1899-	"	N.Y.	1955-
"	"		94.	Brennan, Wm. J.	1906-	Democrat	N.J.	1956-
"	"		95.	Whitaker, Charles	1900-	Republican	Mo.	1957-1962
"	"		96.	Stewart, Potter	1915-	"	Ohio	1958-
Kennedy	Democrat	1961-1963	97.	Goldberg, Arthur	1908-	Democrat	Ill.	1961-1965
"	"		98.	White, Byron R.	1917-	"	Colo.	1962-1965
Johnson	"	1963-	99.	Fortas, Abe	1910-	"	Tenn.	1965-

* Chief Justice. † Promoted from Associate Justice. ‡ Many—and with some justice—consider Brandeis a Democrat; however, he was in fact a registered Republican when nominated.

Bibliographical Note

THE NATURE of the relationship of the judicial process to civil rights and liberties has been the subject of a profusion of pertinent writings. In the first edition of my *The Judicial Process: An Introductory Analysis of the Courts of the United States, England, and France* (Oxford University Press, 1962), I compiled four separate bibliographies of constitutional law totaling some twelve hundred books. And the second edition (due late in 1967) will have an even longer list, much of it separated into appropriate categories for each major segment of the field. Not all of these apply here, but a good many apply at least tangentially. Yet specific works on the problem of "line-drawing" itself are scarce, indeed; most of the published material treats the problem implicitly, rather than explicitly, and within the context of the particular publication's general theme. On the other hand there are some trenchant and stimulating works, generally relatively brief and topical, that do address themselves to line-drawing in a few selected fields. Among these are Sidney Hook's thoughtful *The Paradoxes of Freedom* (University of California Press, 1962), which deals with "intelligence and human rights," "democracy and judicial review," and "intelligence, conscience, and the right to revolution"; David Fellman's *The Limits of Freedom* (Rutgers University Press, 1959), an incisive and clearly written consideration of religious freedom, "the right to communicate," and "the right to talk politics"; Alan P. Grimes's intriguing study, *Equality in America: Religion, Race, and the Urban Majority* (Oxford University Press, 1964), in which he analyzes aspects of religious and racial equality with insight and perception; and John P. Roche's *Courts and Rights: The American Judiciary in Action*, 2nd ed. (Random House, 1966), which deals briefly but engagingly with the rule of law, the judicial process, and certain rights of the citizen in democratic society.

The "double standard," discussed at length in my second chapter, has absorbed and troubled many students of the judicial process: Paul A. Freund outlines its difficulties in his *The Supreme Court of the United States: Its Business and Purposes* (Meridian Press, 1961); Judge Learned Hand opposes it in—among other works—*The Bill of Rights* (Harvard University Press, 1958); Mr. Justice Hugo L. Black upholds it in many of his opinions and most dramatically perhaps in his famous essay "The Bill of Rights," 35 *New York University Law Review* 866 (April 1960); Loren P. Beth favors it in "The Case for Judicial Protection of Civil

Liberties," 17 *The Journal of Politics* 112 (February 1955); and Robert G. McCloskey is critical of it in "Economic Due Process and the Supreme Court: An Exhumation and Reburial," in Philip B. Kurland, ed., *The Supreme Court Review 1962* (University of Chicago Press, 1962), pp. 34-62.

Further reading on "The Bill of Rights and Its Applicability to the States," the topic of Chapter III, may be done in a number of works. Robert A. Rutland's *The Birth of the Bill of Rights, 1776-1791* (Collier Books, 1962), provides valuable background to the document's purpose and framing. The elusive intentions of the framers of the Fourteenth Amendment, which have been interpreted and re-interpreted from all points of view and often with diametrically opposed conclusions, should not be considered without some reference to the records of the actual debates in the Thirty-ninth Congress during 1866. *The Globe* will help. The major protagonists of the two sides in the controversy over "incorporation" of the Bill of Rights are identified and evaluated both in the text and in the footnotes in Chapter III, especially between pages 31 and 46, so that there is no need to cite them here. While there is very little material available on the evolution of "incorporation" or "absorption" and the position of the justices, a host of writings, chiefly journal articles, exist on specific clauses of the Bill of Rights and on the attitudes of the justices collectively as well as singly. A perusal of the *Index to Legal Periodicals*, the *Public Affairs Information Service*, and the *Reader's Guide to Periodical Literature* will provide a good many of the necessary citations. The leading Supreme Court decisions themselves are rich natural fare for analysis and debate: *Palko v. Connecticut*, 302 U.S. 319; *Adamson v. California*, 332 U.S. 46 (1947); *Ker v. California*, 374 U.S. 23 (1963); and *Griswold v. Connecticut*, 381 U.S. 479 (1965), to name just four, feature numerous opinions on the question of applying the Bill of Rights to several states of the Union. A good summary of its evolution is available in Arthur A. North, S.J., *The Supreme Court: Judicial Process and Judicial Politics* (Appleton-Century-Crofts, 1966). Mr. Justice Black's essay, "The Bill of Rights," is again pertinent here; and a sophisticated, up-to-date analysis of the Black position is presented by Norman G. Rudman in "Incorporation Under the Fourteenth Amendment—The Other Side of the Coin," in 3 *Law in Transition Quarterly* 3 (Spring 1966).

"Due process" and questions of criminal justice are ever timely and are treated in many media. The Supreme Court's "liberalizing" decisions in this field, beginning about 1961, have given rise to a stream of commentaries in the daily press, the weeklies, and sundry journals. The stream became a flood after the Court's opinions in the landmark cases of *Escobedo v. Illinois*, 378 U.S. 478 (1964), and *Miranda v. Arizona*, 384 U.S. 436 (1966); and the end is hardly in sight. Some fine books on procedural due process generally are David Fellman's *The Defendant's Rights* (Rinehart, 1958) which, although somewhat dated now, is still a superb reference work; Roscoe Pound's still pertinent *Criminal Justice in America* (Holt, 1945); and an excellent, fairly recent volume by an active participant in the pursuit of criminal justice, Arnold S. Trebach, *The Rationing of Justice: Constitutional Rights and the Criminal Process* (Rutgers University Press, 1964). To cite just a few of the many important books available in specific areas of due process: for two opposite views on the meaning and application of the Fifth Amendment's self-incrimination clause, we have Erwin N. Griswold's *The Fifth Amendment Today* (Harvard University Press, 1955) and Sidney Hook's *Common Sense and the Fifth Amendment* (Criterion Books, 1957). The United States Commission on Civil Rights has some interesting things to say about confessions in its 1961 publication *Justice* (U.S. Government Printing Office). Joseph A. Varon writes knowledgeably about *Searches, Seizures, and Immunities* (Bobbs-Merrill, 1961). Walter F. Murphy's case study on the judicial process and wire-tapping, *Wiretapping on Trial* (Random House, 1965) deals lucidly and engagingly with an as yet unresolved matter. There is no better book extant on the right to counsel than Anthony Lewis's justly praised study of the travail of Clarence Earl Gideon, *Gideon's Trumpet* (Random House, 1964). And the much neglected problem of bail is persuasively criticized by Ronald Goldfarb in *Ransom* (Harper and Row, 1965).

There is probably more material available in the area of freedom of expression than in any of the others that I have treated in the book. A fair number of these are mentioned in Chapter V. The classic study is still Zechariah Chafee, Jr., *Free Speech in the United States* (Harvard University Press, 1954); his contributions to the comprehension and appreciation of freedom of expression are towering. The writings, both on and off the bench, of such steadfast supporters of free speech as Justices Holmes, Brandeis, Hughes, Stone, Cardozo, Black, and Douglas deserve the same respect. Another important work is *Free Speech and Its Relation to Self-Government* (Harper, 1948) by Alexander Meiklejohn, who taught Chafee but outlived him. Meiklejohn's book goes beyond Chafee's limits, but remains a fine testament to the freedom to speak and to write. Chafee's review of this book in 62 *Harvard Law Review* 891 (1949) is necessary reading for anyone interested in line-drawing and in the two men who did so much to analyze it in terms of the freedom of expression. A timely, if wistful, evaluation of the Meiklejohn position is presented by Mr. Justice William J. Brennan, Jr., in his "The Supreme Court and the Meiklejohn Interpretation of the First Amendment," 79 *Harvard Law Review* 1 (November 1965). A working champion of the free press, James R. Wiggins, has given us a fine treatment of it in his *Freedom or Secrecy?* (Oxford University Press, 1956), and Charles E. Rice does equally well for association and assembly in *Freedom of Association* (New York University Press, 1962). Two representative works on the issues of obscenity, morals, and censorship, so closely related to freedom of expression, are Morris L. Ernst and Alan U. Schwartz, *Censorship: The Search for the*

Obscene (Macmillan, 1964), and a superb study by Alexander Meiklejohn's son, Donald, *Freedom and the Public: Public and Private Morality in America* (Syracuse University Press, 1965).

There is no dearth of works in the area of religion and there is a particularly heavy output on the question of the separation of Church and State. Here Leo Pfeffer's excellent and welcome one-volume condensation of Anson Phelps Stokes's monumental *Church and State in the United States* (Harper, 1950), published by Harper and Row in 1964 under the same title, is the key work for both its historical account and its sound analysis—although the author and editor hold points of view which are not necessarily universally accepted in the United States. Representative Roman Catholic stances on the matter of separation of Church and State may be found in Robert F. Drinan, *Religion, the Courts, and Public Policy* (McGraw-Hill, 1963); Jerome G. Kerwin, *Catholic Viewpoint on Church and State* (Hanover House, 1960); and Neil G. McCluskey, *Catholic Viewpoint on Education* (Hanover House, 1959). The other side is ardently presented in, for example, Paul Blanshard's *American Freedom and Catholic Power*, rev. ed. (Beacon Press, 1958), and in his *Religion and the Schools: The Great Controversy* (Beacon Press, 1963). An excellent collection of assorted viewpoints is *The Wall Between Church and State* edited by Dallin H. Oaks (University of Chicago, 1963). A nicely done volume by a political scientist and prominent church-layman is Murray S. Stedman's *Religion and Politics in America* (Harcourt, Brace, and World, 1964). Among other scholarly works which evaluate the establishment problem are Paul G. Kauper, *Religion and the Constitution* (Louisiana State University Press, 1964); Robert Gordis, *Religion and the Schools* (Fund for the Republic, 1959); Wilbur G. Katz, *Religion and American Constitutions* (Northwestern University Press, 1964); Philip B. Kurland, *Religion and the Law: Of Church and State and the Supreme Court* (Aldine Publishing Co., 1962); and Charles E. Rice, *The Supreme Court and Public Prayer: The Need for Restraint* (Fordham University Press, 1964). Two interesting case studies are Theodore Powell, *The School Bus Law: A Case Study in Education, Religion, and Politics* (Wesleyan University Press, 1960), and Orville H. Zabel, *God and Caesar in Nebraska: A Study of the Legal Relationship of Church and State, 1854-1954* (University of Nebraska, 1955). The best work extant on the controversial problem of the free exercise of religion and conscientious objection is still Mulford Q. Sibley and Philip E. Jacob, *Conscription of Conscience: The American State and the Conscientious Objector, 1940-1947* (Cornell University Press, 1952), though it should be supplemented with readings of recent significant Supreme Court decisions, such as *United States v. Seeger*, 380 U.S. 163 (1965). Gordon W. Allport's *The Individual and His Religion* (Macmillan, 1950) blends philosophical with pragmatic considerations; William H. Marnell's *The First Amendment: The History of Religious Freedom in America* (Doubleday, 1964) is a valuable account; and Davis R. Manwaring's *Render Unto Caesar: The Flag-Salute Controversy* (University of Chicago Press, 1962) gives us the

exciting, engagingly written story of the *Flag Salute* cases of the early
1940's—cases that tell us much about line-drawing and the judicial
process.

Lastly, some suggested further readings on the problem of race. Gunnar
Myrdahl's epic *An American Dilemma: The Negro Problem and Modern
Democracy*, rev. ed. (Harper, 1962), is still an essential introduction to
the problem. C. Vann Woodward's informative and purposeful work,
The Strange Career of Jim Crow, 2nd ed. (Oxford University Press, 1966),
better than any other book explains the origin and development of "Jim
Crow." Loren Miller, son of a Negro slave and his white wife, has written
a highly useful work on the story of the Court and the Negro, *The Petitioners* (Pantheon Books, 1966). Paul Lewinson's *Race, Class, and Party:
A History of Negro Suffrage and White Politics in the South* (Russell and
Russell, 1963) illustrates well the rocky road that led to the Voting
Rights Act of 1965. To understand that other road, which—at least on
paper—reached its destination faster by a decade, the road to the desegregated schoolhouse, one could do no better than to read some of the
pertinent key Supreme Court decisions: *The Civil Rights Cases*, 109 U.S.
3 (1883); *Plessy v. Ferguson*, 163 U.S. 537 (1896), which made "separate but equal" king for almost six decades; *Missouri ex rel Gaines v.
Canada*, 305 U.S. 337 (1938); *Sweatt v. Painter*, 339 U.S. 629 (1950);
and, of course, the *Public School Desegregation Cases* of 1954 and 1955
(see Chapter VII), which heralded the death of "separate but equal"—
not only in education but elsewhere. A handy and factual description of
these vital decisions is Daniel M. Berman's *It Is So Ordered: The Supreme
Court Rules on School Segregation* (Norton, 1966). Literally hundreds
of books have appeared on the subject of race; among those that stand out
are Walter Lord's *The Past That Would Not Die* (Harper and Row,
1965); Robert J. Harris's eloquent activist plea, *The Quest for Equality:
The Constitution, Congress, and the Supreme Court* (Louisiana State
University Press, 1960); and Charles E. Silberman's *Crisis in Black and
White* (Random House, 1964), an important analysis of fundamentals.
Also outstanding are Lerone Bennett, Jr., *Confrontation: Black and White*
(Penguin Books, 1966), and James W. Silver's courageous analysis of
Mississippi's determined posture, *Mississippi: The Closed Society* (Har-
court, Brace and World, 1966), which has become a classic example of
the basic problem in certain areas of the Deep South.

For works on the newer and emerging techniques of the Negro civil
rights movement, which have led to serious line-confrontations both in a
physical and a legal sense, important treatises are Estelle Fuchs, *Pickets
at the Gates* (Free Press, 1966), which deals with difficulties inherent in
the metropolis of New York City; W. Haywood Burns, *The Voices of
Negro Protest in America* (Oxford University Press, 1963), an excellent
historical and analytical study of Negro pressure groups, especially the
Muslims; Everett C. Ladd, Jr., *Negro Political Leadership in the South*
(Cornell University, 1966), an important analysis of an all too neglected
aspect of the problem; Howard Zinn's description and evaluation of the

"energetic young radicals" of our day in *SNCC: The New Abolitionists* (Beacon Press, 1964); Arthur I. Waskow's overview, *From Race Riot to Sit-In: 1919 and the 1960's* (Doubleday, 1966); and the intelligent political analysis of the rising influence of the Negro voter by Donald R. Matthews and James W. Prothro, *Negroes and the New Southern Politics* (Harcourt, Brace and World, 1966).

Finally in this brief bibliography, the vexatious "state action" problem, which has dominated so many facets of the race issue, is discussed in several excellent works. Among them are Paul G. Kauper's penetrating chapter "Private and Governmental Actions: Fluid Concepts," in his *Civil Liberties and the Constitution* (University of Michigan Press, 1962); Jerre Williams's "Twilight of State Action," 4 *Texas Law Review* 347 (February 1963); and the already listed book by Robert J. Harris. Two distinguished scholars have raised several basic issues of the state action problem that will probably always be with us in some form even though the legislative and judicial processes have to some extent passed them by: Herbert Wechsler, "Toward Neutral Principles of Constitutional Law," 73 *Harvard Law Review* 1, which appeared in November 1959 and is still widely discussed; and Louis Henkin, "*Shelley v. Krammer:* Notes for a Revised Opinion," 110 *University of Pennsylvania Law Review* 473 (February 1962), a searching, troubled, and honest essay.

It would be easy to continue—but here, too, lines must be drawn.

General Index

Cross references to cases will be found in the Index to Court Cases.

Index to Court Cases

DATE DUE

AG 16 '68			
MR 5 - '69			
OC 29 '70			
NO 12 '70			
NO 25 '70			
DE 9 - '70			
MY 31 '72			
MY 31 '72			
NO 13 '72			
FE 24 '74			
APR 18 '78			
AUG 2 2 1984			
121803			
			PRINTED IN U.S.A.